# CHILD CARE ISSUES
FOR PARENTS
AND SOCIETY

# SOCIAL ISSUES AND SOCIAL PROBLEMS INFORMATION GUIDE SERIES

Series Editors: Kenneth D. Sell, Chairman, Department of Sociology, Catawba College, Salisbury, North Carolina and Betty Sell, Director, Catawba College Library, Salisbury, North Carolina

*Also in this series:*

DIVORCE—*Edited by Kenneth Sell**

RIGHT OF PRIVACY—*Edited by Stephen Harter and Ann F. Harter**

SOCIAL INSURANCE—*Edited by Robert J. Myers**

SUICIDE—*Edited by David Lester**

*in preparation

---

The above series is part of the
# GALE INFORMATION GUIDE LIBRARY

The Library consists of a number of separate series of guides covering major areas in the social sciences, humanities, and current affairs.

General Editor: Paul Wasserman, Professor and former Dean, School of Library and Information Services, University of Maryland

Managing Editor: Dedria Bryfonski, Gale Research Company

# CHILD CARE ISSUES FOR PARENTS AND SOCIETY

## A GUIDE TO INFORMATION SOURCES

*Volume 2 in the Social Issues and Social Problems Information Guide Series*

**Andrew Garoogian**

*Reference Librarian, Brooklyn College Library,
City University of New York, New York*

**Rhoda Garoogian**

*Assistant Dean, Graduate School of
Library and Information Science, Pratt Institute
Brooklyn, New York*

**Preface by Gloria Weinberger**

*Supervisor, Developmental Education Programs
United Cerebral Palsy Treatment and Rehabilitation Center
Nassau County, Roosevelt, Long Island, New York*

*Gale Research Company*
Book Tower, Detroit, Michigan 48226

**Library of Congress Cataloging in Publication Data**

Garoogian, Andrew.
  Child care issues for parents and society.

  (Social issues and social problems information guide series ; v. 2)
(Gale information guide library)
  Includes indexes.
  1. Child development--Bibliography. 2. Children--Care and hygiene--Bibliography. I. Garoogian, Rhoda, joint author. II. Title. III. Series.
Z7164.C5G37 [HQ767.9]     016.1554      77-82800
ISBN 0-8103-1314-6

Copyright © 1977 by
Andrew Garoogian and

No part of this book may
writing from the publish
passages or entries in connection with a review written for inclusion in a magazine or newspaper. Manufactured in the United States of America.

## VITAE

Andrew Garoogian is presently a social science reference librarian at Brooklyn College. He received his B.A. and M.A. degrees in political science from Brooklyn College and his M.L.S. degree from Pratt Institute. He has contributed to THE NEW FUNK AND WAGNALLS ENCYCLOPEDIA and written for THE UNABASHED LIBRARIAN and the LACUNY journal.

Rhoda Garoogian is currently assistant dean of the Graduate School of Library and Information Science, Pratt Institute. She received her B.A. and M.A. degrees in English from Brooklyn College and her M.L.S. degree and Advanced Certificate in Library and Information Studies from Pratt Institute. In addition to writing THE LIBRARY TECHNICAL ASSISTANT, she has contributed to REFERENCE QUARTERLY and the DICTIONARY OF AMERICAN LIBRARY BIOGRAPHY.

# CONTENTS

Foreword ................................................. ix
Preface .................................................. xi
Introduction ............................................. xiii

Adolescence .............................................. 1
Adoption, Child Welfare, and Foster Care ................. 11
Behavior Modification .................................... 19
Child Abuse .............................................. 23
Child Development--General ............................... 29
Child Development--Infancy to Five Years ................. 41
Child Development--Six to Twelve Years ................... 51
Child Development--Black Experience ...................... 55
Child Development--Sex Roles ............................. 59
Children's Rights ........................................ 61
Day Care ................................................. 69
Death, Divorce, and Separation ........................... 75
Discipline ............................................... 79
Drugs, Alcohol, and Their Abuse .......................... 83
Emotionally Disturbed .................................... 95
Exceptional Child--General ............................... 101
Exceptional Child--Autism ................................ 113
Exceptional Child--Cerebral Palsy ........................ 117
Exceptional Child--Down's Syndrome ....................... 119
Exceptional Child--Mental Retardation .................... 121
Exceptional Child--Spina Bifida .......................... 129
Exceptional Child--Visual and Hearing Impairment ......... 131
Food, Clothing, and Furniture ............................ 137
Genetic Diseases ......................................... 147
Gifted Child ............................................. 151
Health--General .......................................... 155
Health--Allergies and Respiratory Illnesses .............. 163
Health--Diabetes ......................................... 167
Health--Epilepsy ......................................... 169
Health--Eye and Dental Care .............................. 171
Health--Heart Condition .................................. 175
Health--Leukemia ......................................... 177

# Contents

| | |
|---|---|
| Health--Sudden Infant Death Syndrome | 179 |
| Health--Miscellaneous | 181 |
| Hyperactive Child | 183 |
| Learning and Creativity | 187 |
| Learning Disabilities | 199 |
| Multiple Births | 207 |
| Parenthood | 209 |
| Play | 223 |
| Safety | 231 |
| Sex Education | 241 |
| Sports and Recreation | 249 |
| Television | 253 |
| Working Mother | 257 |
| Appendix A - Indexes of General Interest | 261 |
| Appendix B - Children's Magazines | 263 |
| Appendix C - Directory of Poison Control Centers | 267 |
| Appendix D - Directory of Book Publishers | 311 |
| Author Index | 321 |
| Title Index | 331 |
| Index of Organizations and Sources of Information | 347 |
| Subject Index | 351 |

# FOREWORD

The purpose of this series is to provide authoritative and systematic guides to significant sources of information on selected current social issues and social problems. The guides are planned to be useful to students, educators, researchers, librarians and information scientists, agencies, clinicians, practitioners, and others in need of locating reliable information for their specific needs and purposes, as efficiently as possible. This second volume of the series, CHILD CARE ISSUES FOR PARENTS AND SOCIETY, by Andrew and Rhoda Garoogian, is also of special interest to parents.

Information on social issues and social problems is scattered throughout the literature of many disciplines, in an ever increasing variety of formats. This makes it very difficult for the interested or concerned person to find the specific kind of information he or she needs. Compounding this situation is the fact that the quantity of information on social issues and social problems has been expanding very rapidly in recent years. It appears that in many cases information guides, such as those in this series, are fast becoming a necessity. It is the expectation of the series editors that this series will be very useful in providing efficient and systematic access to the literature and information sources on the topics represented.

One of the basic concerns and issues in any society is that of care of its children. Publication on child care concerns and issues today exhibits the same characteristics of scattering and increasing expansion as described above. In order to facilitate quick access to reliable information, the authors of this present guide have selected sources, both print and nonprint, which they consider most relevant, important, and helpful, and have organized their material effectively by topics within the broad area of child care. This information guide therefore should prove to be a valuable resource.

> Kenneth D. Sell, Series Editor
> Betty H. Sell, Associate Series Editor
> Catawba College, Salisbury, N.C.

# PREFACE

When a child is born--everyone learns. The learning ability of newborn infants between the first few days and early weeks has finally been documented after many years of research. Infants, we are told, begin to learn immediately--they are able to see from the very moment of birth and instinctively turn their heads toward sounds. Shortly they will begin to associate what they see with what they hear. We've been told, for example, that newborn babies can learn how to change their rate of sucking and how to move a mobile with their toes when pleasurably stimulated by sound and light. I am continually fascinated, and almost overwhelmed, at the vast new landscapes of knowledge in the area of cognitive and mental development in a child's first five years of life. Some researchers believe that the most important learning occurs between ten and eighteen months of life, and that once these optimal learning timetables are missed children may not learn the same--or as well--or at least what they are capable of learning. In this brief and decisive period, it is believed that a parent can do more to determine his or her child's future competence than at any time before or after. Yet there is no one to warn the parent of the promises and the pitfalls of this period of development. How are most parents learning? What are they learning and who is translating the implications of this research to the parent?

In most cases, grandma is still teaching her daughter or son that natural instincts will suffice. Parents tend to rear their child in the manner that they themselves were reared. How many in our culture are actually prepared to be parents? Unfortunately, very little emphasis is placed in our educational system on the preparation of young people for the role they will play some day as parents; on developing just those skills which will some day enable them to function effectively as parents. The preparation for the parent of a child who will be a handicapped learner is virtually nonexistent. Yet it is just these parents who are not only the earliest, but the most influential educators of their children. They heavily influence how the child develops and who he or she becomes.

Somehow professionals in the field of child rearing must begin to transfer this information to parents and make them aware of their importance in the development of their children. It is the informed parent who can truly capture the

# Preface

essence of his or her child and of his or her child's emerging competencies. The needs and developmental stages are pretty much the same for all children; each stage being dependent on the outcome of the stage before it. The role and progress, of course, will vary with each individual child. Parents must learn that children need to develop a self-concept, a body image, a feeling of being loved, needed, and accepted--and finally, a feeling of achievement. For the child who is "different" or handicapped, this can be an extremely difficult and prolonged process, requiring special skills on the part of his or her parents.

Parents need to be guided and taught skills along with each step. In efforts to help the child, often a parent must first be helped. Professionals are now learning the implications of taking this step.

When a child is born, professionals learn that they are not totally responsible for the development of that child. In the past they have provided direct care for children and have assumed total responsibility for the education of children. Professions and institutions have been developed to supplement family care and to provide substitute or special care. They are now learning that without special emphasis on how parents learn and what they must know, the child's prime teacher, his or her parent, cannot be effective.

In an effort to strengthen and support family care this bibliography is now available. Finally, in one book, we have a resource of books, pamphlets, journals, organizations, non-print materials, and government documents compiled for all those interested in the functional application of the latest research in child care from infancy to the adolescent. This resource for information can be easily read and understood on any educational level, and is written primarily as a resource guide for all concerned with children; the educator, the health professional, the volunteer worker, the parent-to-be, and most importantly, the parent.

What have we all learned? We've come to the realization that our goals must be directed primarily to help all children see themselves and to feel themselves as youngsters who are loved, who are worthwhile, who are capable of tasting success, who can communicate and relate to their peers and adults, who can grow, experience, and learn. The development of a positive self-image, then, is a major goal. The child who has learned to like himself or herself will be motivated to learn and will feel confident in his or her ability to grow. It is the enlightened parent who can give or withhold this gift. It is the informed parent who can help children to gain independence, to understand their unique importance, to form judgments, to cope with their problems, to improve their skills, to learn from play--basically to live a fuller life!

> Gloria Weinberger
> Supervisor--Developmental Education Programs
> United Cerebral Palsy Treatment and Rehabilitation Center
> Nassau County, Roosevelt, Long Island, New York

# INTRODUCTION

Despite widespread interest in the care and development of children from birth through adolescence, current information on the subject is often not conveniently accessible to those who most need it. Our intention, therefore, is to bring together in one publication the most current and relevant sources of information that meet the needs of parents, parents-to-be, and those who work with parents.

We strongly feel that a volume of this type should be a guide not only to books and periodicals of a nontechnical nature, but also to audiovisual aids, sources of free and inexpensive materials, and organizations to which parents can turn in time of need. The government, as well as the private sector, publishes much material in the area of child care. We have selectively included the most useful documents and pamphlets. These publications are free except those where price information is given. Prices quoted in the annotations represent 1975 levels and are subject to change.

In keeping with our purpose of providing only current sources, we have not included any materials published prior to 1970 except in the following sections:

1. "Dated but still Relevant"--contains those books published prior to 1970 that are still considered most helpful.

2. "Historical Perspective"--lists works no longer of practical value to modern parents but which do provide a historical viewpoint.

3. "Audiovisual Materials"--in this case, a 1970 cutoff date would have eliminated many titles in subjects of greatest concern to parents.

It is highly unlikely that every pertinent resource has been included. In general, however, we have attempted to present the sources and resources that have emerged in the field of child care during the past five years.* Any material

---

*June 1975 was the cutoff for inclusion of materials.

# Introduction

which we thought had little or no value to parents was excluded from the guide.

We have elected to organize the volume by subject. The various resources, i.e., books, pamphlets, periodicals, audiovisual materials, organizations, and sources of free and inexpensive materials are listed by form under each subject.

It is our hope that public, school, and college libraries, information and referral agencies, and social and health agencies involved in child care, as well as individual parents, will find this guide useful for their collections.

We would like to thank our sons, David and Neill, who have been most patient while we have been preparing this guide. We sincerely hope that it proves useful to the reader.

# ADOLESCENCE

(See also Behavior Modification; Child Development—Six to Twelve Years;
Discipline; Drugs, Alcohol, and Their Abuse)

## BOOKS

### Historical Perspective

Hall, Granville Stanley. ADOLESCENCE: ITS PSYCHOLOGY AND ITS RE-
LATIONS TO PHYSIOLOGY, ANTHROPOLOGY, SOCIOLOGY, SEX, CRIME,
RELIGION AND EDUCATION. 2 vols. 1904. Reprint. New York: Arno
Press, 1969. 1,373 p. Biblio., index.

    Grand work of America's first famous developmental psychologist.

_____. YOUTH: ITS EDUCATION, REGIMEN, AND HYGIENE. 1906.
Reprint. New York: Arno Press, 1972. 379 p. Biblio.

    Hall popularized his two-volume work, ADOLESCENCE, for parents
and teachers.

White House Conference on Child Health and Protection. THE ADOLESCENT
IN THE FAMILY: A STUDY OF PERSONALITY DEVELOPMENT IN THE HOME
ENVIRONMENT. 1934. Reprint. New York: Arno Press, 1972. 491 p.
Diags.

    Results of a study of questionnaires completed by 13,000 public
schoolchildren and several hundred schoolteachers regarding the
home environment and its importance in the development of the
child. Should be of interest in the light of the changes taking
place in families today.

### Dated but Still Relevant

Gesell, Arnold, et al. YOUTH: THE YEARS FROM TEN TO SIXTEEN. New
York: Harper & Bros., 1956. 542 p. Biblio., index.

    Completes the trilogy (INFANT AND CHILD IN THE CULTURE OF

# Adolescence

TODAY, THE CHILD FROM FIVE TO TEN) describing the first sixteen years of mental life and growth.

Ginott, Haim [G.]. BETWEEN PARENT AND TEENAGER. New York: Macmillan, 1965. 223 p. Biblio., index.

> For the most part, when not superficial, the author offers constructive advice on the peaceful coexistence of parents and teenagers. Specific problems such as authority conflicts, drugs, teenage sex, and homosexuality are covered.

## Reference

Beitler, Ken. NATIONAL DIRECTORY OF HOTLINES, SWITCHBOARDS, AND RELATED SERVICES. Minneapolis, Minn.: The Exchange, 1972. 50 p.

> Comprehensive directory, arranged geographically, of crisis intervention centers in the United States and Canada. Includes phone numbers, hours, clientele, facilities, and type of service provided.

## Current Sources

Albrecht, Margaret. PARENTS AND TEEN-AGERS: GETTING THROUGH TO EACH OTHER. New York: Parents' Magazine Press, 1972. 288 p. Biblio., illus., index.

> Helpful and sympathetic discussion of problems which concern parents of children in the late teens and early twenties. Covers subjects such as money, marriage, sex, venereal disease, and drugs.

Ambrosino, Lillian. RUNAWAYS. Boston: Beacon Press, 1971. 150 p. Photos.

> A guide for the runaway and his parents. Includes thorough lists of Traveler's Aid societies, halfway houses, hotlines, and other services. An important work considering approximately one million persons under age twenty-two ran away from home in 1969.

Arnstein, Helene S. GETTING ALONG WITH YOUR GROWN-UP CHILDREN. New York: M. Evans & Co., 1970. 207 p.

> For middle-class parents, this is a sensitive approach to dealing with such problems as prolonged financial dependency, disenchantment with traditional life-styles and values, changing sexual mores, etc.

Blaine, Graham B. ARE PARENTS BAD FOR CHILDREN? New York: Coward, McCann & Geoghegan, 1973. 160 p. Biblio.

# Adolescence

As a medical doctor and psychiatrist, the author is concerned with the alienation of adolescents from their parents and society. He faults the nuclear family, calls for additional adult help from the community in the child-rearing process, and offers suggestions for alternative forms of outside involvement.

Blum, Jeffrey D., and Smith, Judith E. NOTHING LEFT TO LOSE: STUDIES OF STREET PEOPLE. Boston: Beacon Press, 1972. 142 p.

Presenting thirty-three case studies of runaway boys and girls from broken homes, the authors discuss the encounters between the youths and the street workers of a storefront counseling service in Cambridge, Massachusetts.

Bock, Richard, and English, Abigail. GOT ME ON THE RUN: A STUDY OF RUNAWAYS. Boston: Beacon Press, 1973. 237 p.

This study of Boston-area runaways and their experiences with parents, counselors, teachers, and legal officials shows why many of these social institutions are ineffective and fail the young. Case studies illuminate the need for changes in child welfare policies.

Elbert, Edmund J. YOUTH: THE HOPE OF THE HARVEST. New York: Sheed & Ward, 1972. 244 p.

Practical guidebook which offers suggestions for understanding and dealing with the generation gap, adolescence, drug abuse, sexual revolution, and maturity.

Finch, Stuart McIntyre, and Poznanski, Elva O. ADOLESCENT SUICIDE. Springfield, Ill.: Charles C. Thomas, Publisher, 1971. 66 p. Tables.

Very brief discussion of adolescent suicides and the environmental and personality factors related to suicidal behavior. Case studies describe the different clinical types.

Gersh, Marvin J., M.D., and Litt, Iris F., M.D. THE HANDBOOK OF ADOLESCENCE: A MEDICAL GUIDE FOR PARENTS AND TEEN-AGERS. New York: Stein & Day Publishers, 1971. 225 p.

Covers physical development, heredity, skin, weight problems, glandular diseases, smoking, drugs, and so forth.

Gold, Don. LETTERS TO TRACY. New York: David McKay Co., 1972. 142 p.

A loving divorced father advises his teenage daughter in areas of love and sex, alcohol, politics, art, sports, and travel, in an attempt to bridge the generation gap.

# Adolescence

Josselyn, Irene M., M.D. ADOLESCENCE. New York: Harper & Row Publishers, 1971. 213 p. Biblio., index.

    A report written for the Joint Commission on the Mental Health of Children, this informative study examines the complications of climbing from childhood to adulthood.

Minton, Lynn. GROWING INTO ADOLESCENCE. New York: Parents' Magazine Press, 1972. 288 p. Biblio., illus., index.

    Readable text to help parents better understand their children during the ages of eleven to fourteen. Covers problem areas such as drugs, dating, sexuality, health, and school with suggestions for dealing with each. An understanding and compassionate treatment of the subject.

Needleman, Jacob. THE NEW RELIGIONS. Rev. ed. New York: Pocket Books, 1972. 240 p. Paperbound.

    For parents interested In knowing why the "Eastern" religions appeal to American youth.

Self, William L. BRIDGING THE GENERATION GAP. Nashville, Tenn.: Broadman Press, 1971. 95 p. Paperbound.

    A Baptist minister's advice to parents and young people.

Sorenson, Robert C. ADOLESCENT SEXUALITY IN CONTEMPORARY AMERICA; PERSONAL VALUES AND SEXUAL BEHAVIOR AGES THIRTEEN TO NINETEEN. Mountainview, Calif.: World Publications, 1973. 549 p. Tables.

    A social psychologist has compiled a massive amount of data on current sexual attitudes and behavior patterns of adolescents.

U.S. President's Science Advisory Committee. Panel on Youth. YOUTH: TRANSITION TO ADULTHOOD. Report of the Panel on Youth. Chicago: University of Chicago Press, 1974. 193 p. Biblio., index.

    The biological, psychological, social, and cultural aspects of the transition from childhood to adulthood are examined by a panel of educators and social scientists in a concise and readable way.

Winship, Elizabeth C. ASK BETH: YOU CAN'T ASK YOUR MOTHER. New York: Houghton Mifflin Co., 1972. 244 p.

    Collection of letters from junior high and high school students written to the column, "Ask Beth," in the BOSTON GLOBE. The advice given in response will interest both youngsters and parents.

Wood, Abigail. THE SEVENTEEN BOOK OF ANSWERS TO WHAT YOUR

# Adolescence

PARENTS DON'T TALK ABOUT AND YOUR BEST FRIENDS CAN'T TELL YOU . . . New York: David McKay Co., 1972. 266 p. Illus.

    Answers to questions submitted by teenage girls to the "Young Living" column of SEVENTEEN. Questions revolve around identity, dating, sex and sexuality, parents, friendships, love, and so forth.

## PERIODICALS

ADOLESCENCE. Roslyn Heights, N.Y.: Libra Publishers, 1966-- . Quarterly.

    This journal covers the education and problems of adolescents. While primarily directed to the experienced psychologist, psychiatrist, and sociologist, it can be useful to the better educated parent.

JOURNAL OF YOUTH AND ADOLESCENCE. New York: Plenum Publishing Corp., 1972-- . Quarterly.

    Covers the psychological, sociological, biological, and educational aspects of the youth culture and what makes the teenager function; also includes articles on youth and the law. For the better educated layman.

YOUTH AND SOCIETY. Beverly Hills, Calif.: Sage Publications, 1969-- . Quarterly.

    Concerned with the social and political implications of youth culture and development.

## PAMPHLETS AND/OR GOVERNMENT DOCUMENTS

Unless otherwise noted, the materials are available free of charge. Where prices are quoted please be advised they are subject to change. Payment should accompany order.

AN ADOLESCENT IN YOUR HOME. 1975. 27 p. Publication no. (OHD) 75-41. Available from: Office of Human Development, Publications Distribution Unit, Switzer Building, Department of Health, Education and Welfare, Washington, D.C. 20201.

    Intended to help parents understand the physical, emotional, and mental changes that teenagers go through during adolescence.

PARENTS AND TEENAGERS. By Margaret Hill. 1973. 24 p. Pamphlet no. 490. 35 cents. Available from: Public Affairs Committee, 381 Park Avenue S., New York, N.Y. 10016.

# Adolescence

Sensible advice on why teenagers act, dress, and behave as they do.

THE POCKET GUIDE TO BABYSITTING. Children's Bureau. 1974. 48 p. Publication no. (OHD) 74-45. Available from: Office of Human Development, Publications Distribution Unit, Switzer Building, Department of Health, Education and Welfare, Washington, D.C. 20201.

Advice and guidelines for both beginning and seasoned babysitters.

## ORGANIZATIONS AND/OR SOURCES OF MATERIALS, FREE OR AT LOW COST

National Commission on Resources for Youth
36 West Forty-fourth Street
New York, N.Y. 10036

A nonprofit organization whose primary goals are to collect and distribute information and to develop models for programs that allow youth to assume responsible social roles. Issues RESOURCES FOR YOUTH, a free quarterly publication describing programs that young people themselves have initiated. The organization also provides do-it-yourself materials.

National Runaway Switchboard
Chicago, Ill.
Toll-free number: (800) 621-4000

Runaway youths anywhere in the United States can call the toll-free number and request that a message be delivered to their families. They may also obtain information on the various services available to them. This particular hot line is operated by Metro-Help, of Chicago with a grant from the Office of Youth Development, Department of Health, Education and Welfare.

National Youth Alternatives Project
1830 Connecticut Avenue
Washington, D.C. 20009    (202) 785-0764

Nonprofit organization concerned with the rights and needs of youth; operates a "national clearinghouse for alternative youth programs and training programs for youth workers in alternative social service fields." Publishes YOUTH ALTERNATIVES a monthly newsletter and the NATIONAL DIRECTORY OF RUNAWAY CENTERS.

Operation Peace of Mind
Houston, Tex.
Toll-free out-of-state number:   (800) 231-6946
Toll-free Texas number:   (800) 392-3352

# Adolescence

A hot line telephone service whose function is to relay messages between runaway children and their parents. The organization maintains an extensive list of agencies nationwide that will provide shelter, health care, food, legal assistance, and other services for runaways. Service is available to runaways anywhere in the contiguous forty-eight states.

## AUDIOVISUAL MATERIALS

### Films

A TO B. 1973. 16mm, 35 min., sound, color. Producer: Nell Cox.

Documentary exploration of a middle-class white girl and her relationships with family and friends. Good for initiating discussion.

Available from: Time Life Films, 43 West Sixteenth Street, New York, N.Y. 10011.

BEYOND LSD. 1969. 16mm, 25 min., sound, color. Producer: Max Millee-Avanti Films.

A medical doctor discusses preconceived notions that parents have regarding the long hair, dress, music, and LSD involvement of teenagers. He emphasizes bridging the communications gap. Film should be viewed by both teenagers and parents together.

Available from: BFA Educational Media, 2211 Michigan Avenue, Santa Monica, Calif. 90404

BRIAN AT SEVENTEEN. 1971. 16mm, 30 min., sound, black and white.

Realistic portrayal of a fatherless high school senior in search of identity. A really fine depiction of adolescence and the parent-child relationship.

Available from: National Institute of Mental Health, Abuse Film Collection, National Audiovisual Center, General Services Administration, Washington, D.C. 20409.

DISCIPLINE DURING ADOLESCENCE. 1958. 17 min., sound, black and white.

Depicts parents who are concerned about discipline and the ways in which they deal with it. For parents as well as teachers.

Available from: McGraw-Hill Films, 330 West Forty-second Street, New York, N.Y. 10036.

THE DROP OUT. 1962. 27 min., sound, black and white. Producer: Af-

# Adolescence

filiated Film Producers for the Mental Health Film Board and the National Education Association.

This film examines the pressures that force a child to leave school and suggests some possible remedies.

Available from: International Film Bureau, 332 South Michigan Avenue, Chicago, Ill. 60604.

GRADUATION DAY. 1972. 16mm, 28 1/2 min., sound, color, also black and white.

Dramatic probe into the process of growing up as experienced by a troubled teenager.

Available from: Paulist Productions, 17575 Pacific Coast Highway, Pacific Palisades, Calif. 90272.

GUIDANCE FOR THE 70'S: KIDS, PARENTS, PRESSURES. 1971. 16mm, 16 1/4 min., sound, color. Producer: Robert Sande Productions.

Teenagers describe their tensions, pressures, and conflicts as well as their negative relationships with parents and teachers. Be a bit wary of the film's optimism, otherwise it is a fine presentation.

Available from: BFA Educational Media, 2211 Michigan Avenue, Santa Monica, Calif. 90404.

I JUST DON'T DIG HIM. 1969. 16mm, 11 min., sound, color. Producer: Mental Health Film Board.

Dramatizes the problem of communication between father and son. Focuses on the generation gap and the search for identity and independence. Parents' and teenagers' views are objectively shown.

Available from: International Film Bureau, 332 South Michigan Avenue, Chicago, Ill. 60604.

THE INVISIBLE CHILD. 197?. 16mm, 27 min., sound, color.

Documentary on the causes, treatment, and prevention of juvenile delinquency.

Available from: Association-Sterling Films, Executive Office, 866 Third Avenue, New York, N.Y. 10022.

KINSHIPS. 1973. 16mm, 12 min., sound, color.

Exploration of the dynamics of the adolescent-parent relationship.

Available from: Paulist Productions, 17575 Pacific Coast Highway, Pacific Palisades, Calif. 90272.

# Adolescence

MOM, WHY WON'T YOU LISTEN? 1970. 16mm, 13 min., sound, color.

> Problems encountered by young people when they try to communicate with their parents.
>
> Available from: Churchill Films, 662 North Robertson Boulevard, Los Angeles, Calif. 90069. Phone (213) 657-5110.

SATURDAY MORNING. 16mm and 35mm, 8 min., sound, color.

> Excellent, albeit controversial, exploration of the vital issues of adolescence--family, sex, dating, marriage, values, etc.
>
> Available from: Churchill Films, 662 North Robertson Boulevard, Los Angeles, Calif. 90069. Phone (213) 657-5110.

WALK IN THEIR SHOES. 1968. 24 min., sound.

> Teenager given an opportunity to be in an authority position relative to his sister--begins to act like his parents.
>
> Available from: Brigham Young University Educational Media Services, 290 Herald R. Clark Building, Provo, Ut. 84601.

WALLS AND WINDOWS. 1973. 16mm, 12 min., sound, color.

> Four sequences wherein a father and a teenager explore the problems of communication between adolescents and parents.
>
> Available from: Paulist Productions, 17575 Pacific Coast Highway, Pacific Palisades, Calif. 90272.

## Filmstrips

GETTING ALONG WITH THE OPPOSITE SEX. 1966. 40 frames, sound, color.

> Discusses various situations and problems that children of high school age face including dating, going steady, sensitivity in human relationships, and communication with parents.
>
> Available from: Popular Science Publishing Co., 355 Lexington Avenue, New York, N.Y. 10017.

TEENAGE REBELLION: CHALLENGE TO AUTHORITY. 1971. 18 min., sound, color.

> Young people and parents discuss social and personal rebellion.
>
> Available from: Guidance Association, 41 Washington Avenue, Pleasantville, N.Y. 10570.

THE TUNED-OUT GENERATION. 1966. 2 filmstrips (82 frames, 76 frames), 30 min., sound.

# Adolescence

Positive view of the generation gap that shows the similarities between teens and parents.

Available from: Guidance Association, 41 Washington Avenue, Pleasantville, N.Y. 10570.

YOU AND THE OTHER GENERATION. 1967. 41 frames, sound, color.

This filmstrip analyzes some typical causes of parent-teenager conflict and indicates possible solutions.

Available from: Popular Science Publishing Co., 355 Lexington Avenue, New York, N.Y. 10017.

# ADOPTION, CHILD WELFARE, AND FOSTER CARE

(See also Child Development—Black Experience)

## BOOKS

### Historical Perspective

Folks, Homer. THE CARE OF DESTITUTE, NEGLECTED AND DELINQUENT CHILDREN. 1900. Reprint. New York: Arno Press, 1971. 142 p. Biblio.

    A detailed study of child care organizations from colonial America to the Progressive era by a pioneer leader in social welfare.

Thurston, Henry W. THE DEPENDENT CHILD: A STORY OF CHANGING AIMS AND METHODS IN THE CARE OF DEPENDENT CHILDREN. 1930. Reprint. New York: Arno Press, 1974. 337 p. Biblio., index.

    A specialist in child welfare reports on the placement and care of neglected children in both foster homes and institutions during the period from 1850 to the 1920s.

### Dated but Still Relevant

Rondell, Florence, and Michaels, Ruth. THE ADOPTED FAMILY. Rev. ed. 2 vols. New York: Crown Publishers, 1965. 198 p.

    Contains two books in one. Volume 1, YOU AND YOUR CHILD, is a guide for adoptive parents which gives excellent advice. Volume 2, THE FAMILY THAT GREW, is a picture book to be read to the adopted child.

### Reference

Croner, Helga B., comp. NATIONAL DIRECTORY OF PRIVATE SOCIAL AGENCIES. New York: Croner Publications, 1964-- . Looseleaf. Annual, with monthly supplements.

    This annual is classified by services offered and listed by states

# Adoption, Child Welfare, Foster Care

and cities in the United States.

Karraker, David, ed. 1973 PUBLIC WELFARE DIRECTORY. Chicago: American Public Welfare Association, 1973. 216 p. Appendix, tables.

This annual publication includes information on the basic programs, practices, and staff of all public welfare and related public agencies in the United States and Canada.

## Current Sources

Anderson, David C. CHILDREN OF SPECIAL VALUE: INTERRACIAL ADOPTION IN AMERICA. New York: St. Martin's Press, 1971. 184 p.

The author, a journalist and adoptive father, has written a perceptive and sensitive book on the adoption of nonwhite children by white parents. Covers the experiences of families who have adopted nonwhite children, theories of adoption, and the role of the agency with regard to transracial adoption.

Ansfield, Joseph G., M.D. THE ADOPTED CHILD. Springfield, Ill.: Charles C. Thomas, Publisher, 1971. 56 p.

Written for parents and prospective parents, this book airs the fears and resentments that adoptive parents harbor but are afraid to acknowledge.

Berman, Claire. WE TAKE THIS CHILD: A CANDID LOOK AT MODERN ADOPTION. Garden City, N.Y.: Doubleday & Co., 1974. 203 p. Biblio.

Candid opinions and experiences of parents who adopted white, multiracial, and handicapped children. Includes an appendix of citizens organizations concerned with adoption.

Dwyasuk, Colette T. ADOPTION--IS IT FOR YOU? New York: Harper & Row Publishers, 1973. 175 p. Biblio., index.

A mother of three natural children and one adopted child discusses the aspects of adopting older and handicapped children. For both single people and couples contemplating adoption. Includes a directory of adoptive parent organizations.

Fanshel, David. FAR FROM THE RESERVATION: THE TRANSRACIAL ADOPTION OF AMERICAN INDIAN CHILDREN. Metuchen, N.J.: Scarecrow Press, 1972. 338 p.

This study, a cooperative project of the Bureau of Indian Affairs and the Child Welfare League of America, describes the experiences of ninety-seven American Indian children adopted by white families. Provides insight into adoption across ethnic and racial lines.

## Adoption, Child Welfare, Foster Care

Felker, Evelyn H. FOSTER PARENTING YOUNG CHILDREN. New York: Child Welfare League of America, 1974. 85 p. Photos. Paperbound.

    Felker shares her own experiences as a foster parent regarding such aspects as the daily caring for foster children, preparing for foster parenthood, as well as working with the biological parents, caseworker, and the agency.

Festinger, Trudy Bradley. WHY SOME CHOOSE NOT TO ADOPT THROUGH AGENCIES. New York: Metropolitan Applied Research Center, 1972. 61 p. Paperbound.

    Critical study of the failures of adoption agencies in relation to prospective black parents.

Goldstein, Joseph, et al. BEYOND THE BEST INTERESTS OF THE CHILD. New York: Free Press, 1973. 170 p. Index.

    Written by a noted lawyer, a psychologist, and a pediatrician, this book stresses that a child's psychological and emotional needs are of paramount importance when his placement is decided. Recommends that the child be given the right to counsel.

Grow, Lucille J., and Shapiro, Deborah. BLACK CHILDREN--WHITE PARENTS. New York: Child Welfare League of America, 1974. 239 p. Paperbound.

    This three-year research study focuses on the behavior and adjustment of black children six years of age and older who are adopted by white parents. It provides valuable information to both parents and professionals considering transracial adoption as an alternate means of placing black children.

_____. TRANSRACIAL ADOPTION TODAY: VIEWS OF ADOPTIVE PARENTS AND SOCIAL WORKERS. New York: Child Welfare League of America, 1975. 91 p.

    This study shows that transracial adoption, seen by social workers as a "better alternative for black children than indeterminate long-term foster care," is a risky option which needs more thought and makes heavy demands on adoptive parents.

Jenkins, Shirley, and Norman, Elaine. FILIAL DEPRIVATION AND FOSTER CARE. New York: Columbia University Press, 1972. 296 p.

    This research study of 390 families in foster care in New York City is the first volume in a projected three-part series. It focuses upon the feelings and responses of parents whose children are receiving foster care.

Kadushin, Alfred. ADOPTING OLDER CHILDREN. New York: Columbia University Press, 1970. 245 p.

# Adoption, Child Welfare, Foster Care

A study of the positive and negative experiences of a group of parents who adopted children from five to twelve years of age. Good for prospective adoptive parents.

_____. CHILD WELFARE SERVICES: A SOURCEBOOK. New York: Macmillan, 1970. 554 p. Biblio., charts, tables.

Comprehensive overview covering such areas as foster care, day care, adoption services, child-caring institutions, and protection services.

Klibanoff, Susan, and Klibanoff, Elton. LET'S TALK ABOUT ADOPTION. Boston: Little, Brown and Co., 1973. 263 p. Appendices.

A clear and practical handbook for the prospective adoptive applicant. Writing from experience, the Klibanoffs discuss two-parent, single-parent, transracial, and older child adoptions, as well as the legal questions involved.

McNamara, Joan. THE ADOPTION ADVISER. New York: Hawthorn Books, 1975. 233 p. Biblio., index.

Comprehensive, current, and informative manual for both prospective adoptive parents and professionals. Covers single-parent and transracial adoption, adoption and the law, and finding a child. Includes a very useful directory of adoption resources.

Meredith, Judith C. AND NOW WE ARE A FAMILY. Boston: Beacon Press, 1971. 32 p. Illus.

A book for adoptive parents to read aloud to their young children. Explains the meaning of and reasons for adoption.

Raymond, Louise. ADOPTION AND AFTER. Revised by Colette T. Dywasuk. New York: Harper & Row Publishers, 1974. 254 p. Biblio., index.

Informative book that focuses on day-to-day realities and problems in an effort to help families adjust to adoption.

Rondell, Florence, and Murray, Anne-Marie. NEW DIMENSIONS IN ADOPTION. New York: Crown Publishers, 1974. 120 p.

Basic description of adoption, especially the emotional needs of children; also discusses the special needs of children formerly considered unsuitable for adoption--handicapped, older, emotionally disturbed, or of another racial group or culture.

## PAMPHLETS AND/OR GOVERNMENT DOCUMENTS

Unless otherwise noted the materials are available free of charge. Prices

# Adoption, Child Welfare, Foster Care

quoted are subject to change. Payment should accompany order.

ADOPTION: THE MEDICAL ASPECTS. 1974. 6 p. Publication no. 298C. Available from: Consumer Information, Public Documents, Distribution Center, Pueblo, Colo. 81009.

> For prospective adoptive parents.

GUIDELINES FOR ADOPTION SERVICE. 1971. 22 p. 75 cents. Available from: Child Welfare League of America, 67 Irving Place, New York, N.Y. 10003.

> Designed for parents and volunteer workers, this publication discusses the "Standards for Adoption Service" issued by the Child Welfare League and presents some current thinking on adoption.

HOW PARENTS TELL THEIR CHILDREN THEY ARE ADOPTED. 1970. 21 p. Available from: Children's Home Society of California, 3100 West Adams, Los Angeles, Calif. 90018. Phone (213) 733-1141.

> Sensitive treatment with humor.

STATEMENTS REGARDING INSURANCE POLICIES AND WILLS DIRECTED TO ADOPTIVE PARENTS. 1972. 4 p. Publication no. (OCD) 72-39. Available from: Office of Human Development, Box 1182, Washington, D.C. 20013.

> Advises parents to ensure that their adopted children are adequately protected in insurance policies and wills. Suggestions on appropriate drafting and wording of wills.

## ORGANIZATIONS AND/OR SOURCES OF MATERIALS, FREE OR AT LOW COST

Adoption Resource Exchange of North America
67 Irving Place
New York, N.Y. 10003    Phone (212) 254-7410

> This organization will help any licensed U.S. adoption agency to place children of minority or mixed racial background, older children, family groups, or children with emotional or physical handicaps. Its aims are to break down agency and state barriers to adoption, and to aid in matching homes available to children awaiting placement.

Aid to Adoption of Special Kids
P.O. Box 11212
Oakland, Calif. 94611    Phone (415) 451-1748

> Seeks to educate the public to the needs of special children and

# Adoption, Child Welfare, Foster Care

to encourage their removal from foster homes into adoptive homes. Maintains programs to aid potential adoptive parents of difficult-to-place children.

Child Welfare League of America
67 Irving Place
New York, N.Y. 10003          Phone (212) 254-7410

A national, nonsectarian, privately-supported organization devoted to improving care and services for the nation's deprived, neglected, and dependent children. Serves as a national clearinghouse and forum for professionals in the field, develops standards for child welfare services, and publishes CHILD WELFARE (monthly), as well as a newsletter and other books and monographs. A publications list is available on request.

Council on Adoptable Children
302 Leslie Street
Lansing, Mich. 48912          Phone (517) 484-7376

Organization of persons who have already adopted or are considering adoption, child welfare workers, and others interested in children available for adoption. Focuses on those children who are difficult to place in adoptive homes, for example, the physically or emotionally handicapped, the older child, or the child of mixed race. Assists agencies in finding adoptive homes for children; is affiliated with the National Council of Adoptive Parents Organizations. Publishes a list of adoptive parent organizations.

Foreign Adoption Center
P.O. Box 2158
Boulder, Colo. 80302          Phone (303) 443-3659

A licensed adoption agency that provides information and counseling to parents wishing to adopt foreign children.

National Council of Adoptive Parents Organizations
P.O. Box 543
Teaneck, N.J. 07666

Liaison organization for regional, state, and local groups interested in the problems of adoptive, foster, and institutionalized children. Attempts to broaden adoption agency policies toward children of mixed race. Works for the release of foster children into adoptive homes.

## Adoption, Child Welfare, Foster Care

## AUDIOVISUAL MATERIALS

### Films

EVERY FAMILY IS SPECIAL. 1972. 3 1/2 min., sound.

    Story of a small boy who runs away from home after learning that he is adopted.

    Available from: Sutherland Learning Associates, 8425 West Third Street, Los Angeles, Calif. 90048.

I'LL NEVER GET HER BACK. 1968. 16mm, 25 min., sound, color.

    Feelings of an unwed mother who has given up her baby for adoption.

    Available from: NBC Educational Enterprises, 30 Rockefeller Plaza, New York, N.Y. 10020.

TO LOVE A CHILD. 1966. 16mm, 30 min., sound, color.

    Dramatic story of a young couple as they undertake adoption.

    Available from: 3M Company, Film Lending Service, 220-6W, 2501 Hudson Road, St. Paul, Minn. 55119.

A WAY OUT. 1971. 22 1/2 min., sound.

    Depicts the emotional problems of adopting older, multiracial, or physically handicapped children.

    Available from: Westminster Films, 259 Gerard Street, East, Toronto 225, Canada.

# BEHAVIOR MODIFICATION

(See also Discipline; Hyperactive Child)

## BOOKS

Current Sources

Bannatyne, Alexander, and Bannatyne, Maryl. HOW YOUR CHILDREN CAN LEARN TO LIVE A REWARDING LIFE: BEHAVIOR MODIFICATION FOR PARENTS AND TEACHERS. Springfield, Ill.: Charles C. Thomas, Publisher, 1973. 119 p. Biblio., index.

    Guide to changing undesirable behavior in such areas as tantrums and toilet training and to teaching sharing, kindness, honesty, and independence. The vocabulary is well defined.

Becker, Wesley C. PARENTS ARE TEACHERS: A CHILD MANAGEMENT PROGRAM. Champaign, Ill.: Research Press, 1971. 194 p. Paperbound.

    Manual and programmed instruction guide to help parents understand and use behavior modification techniques with their own children. Highly readable.

Beltz, Stephen E. HOW TO MAKE JOHNNY WANT TO OBEY. Englewood Cliffs, N.J.: Prentice-Hall, 1971. 255 p. Index.

    A behavioral psychologist shows parents how to increase the child's motivation to obey through a system of incentives.

Hergenhahn, Baldwin Ross. SHAPING YOUR CHILD'S PERSONALITY. Englewood Cliffs, N.J.: Prentice-Hall, 1972. 179 p. Illus., index.

    Explores the many ways that parents and teachers can use the newly discovered techniques of behavior modification to direct children's development.

Krumboltz, John D., and Krumboltz, Helen B. CHANGING CHILDREN'S BEHAVIOR. Englewood Cliffs, N.J.: Prentice-Hall, 1972. 268 p. Biblio., illus., index.

# Behavior Modification

Based on recent psychological research, the volume describes basic behavior modification principles and their application. Examples drawn from the experiences of parents, counselors, and the authors themselves illustrate practical ways to change such behavior as temper tantrums, sulking, and sibling rivalry.

McIntire, Roger W. FOR LOVE OF CHILDREN: BEHAVIORAL PSYCHOLOGY FOR PARENTS. Del Mar, Calif.: CRM Books, 1970. 208 p. Illus.

For parents of children up to and including adolescents interested in applying behavior modification to elicit change in such areas as fears, compulsions, tantrums, toilet training, sociability, and so forth.

Madsen, Clifford K., and Madsen, Charles H. PARENTS/CHILDREN/DISCIPLINE: A POSITIVE APPROACH. Boston: Allyn & Bacon, 1972. 213 p. Paperbound.

Behaviorist principles are used to develop parental confidence in dealing with children.

Moore, Dewey J. PREVENTING MISBEHAVIOR IN CHILDREN. Springfield, Ill.: Charles C. Thomas, Publisher, 1972. 171 p. Paperbound.

Practical advice for parents and teachers on preventing behavior problems in children. Specific problems are examined; reasons for misbehavior and parental mistakes are discussed.

Watson, Luke S., Jr. CHILD BEHAVIOR MODIFICATION: A MANUAL FOR TEACHERS, NURSES, AND PARENTS. Elmsford, N.Y.: Pergamon Press, 1973. 147 p. Biblio., illus.

Written in layman's language, this handbook is designed to convey basic and fundamental information to people who work with emotionally disturbed and mentally retarded children at home, in school, and in institutions.

Wiener, Daniel E., and Phillips, Lakin E. TRAINING CHILDREN IN SELF-DISCIPLINE AND SELF-CONTROL. Englewood Cliffs, N.J.: Prentice-Hall, 1971. 257 p.

Both psychologists espouse behavior modification techniques in the training of children, stressing freedom of choice through self-discipline and self-control. Geared towards the college-educated parent.

Zifferblatt, Steven Michael. YOU CAN HELP YOUR CHILD IMPROVE STUDY AND HOMEWORK BEHAVIOR. Champaign, Ill.: Research Press, 1970. 96 p. Illus. Paperbound.

Written in a completely nontechnical manner, this manual is designed to help parents learn to manage their children, partic-

# Behavior Modification

ularly in areas of school work and learning.

## PAMPHLETS AND/OR GOVERNMENT DOCUMENTS

Unless otherwise noted the materials are available free of charge. Prices quoted are subject to change. Payment should accompany order.

BEHAVIOR MODIFICATION IN CHILD AND SCHOOL MENTAL HEALTH: AN ANNOTATED BIBLIOGRAPHY ON APPLICATIONS WITH PARENTS AND TEACHERS. By Daniel G. Brown. 1971. 56 p. Publication no. (HSM) 71-9043. 30 cents. Available from: Superintendent of Documents, Government Printing Office, Washington, D.C. 20402.

    Lists materials from which parents can learn behavior modification techniques for dealing with both normal and exceptional children.

## AUDIOVISUAL MATERIALS

### Films

CHILD BEHAVIOR--YOU. 1973. 16mm, 8mm, and Super 8mm, 15 min., sound, color.

    Shows methods of modifying child behavior to help children grow into well-adjusted adults.

    Available from: Benchmark Films, 145 Scarborough Road, Briar Cliff Manor, N.Y. 10510.

HELP FOR MARK. 1971. 17 min., sound, color.

    An introduction to behavior modification for parents and teachers of trainable retarded children.

    Available from: Appleton-Century-Crofts, 440 Park Avenue, South, New York, N.Y. 10016.

# CHILD ABUSE

## BOOKS

### Current Sources

Bakan, David. SLAUGHTER OF THE INNOCENTS. San Francisco: Jossey-Bass, Publishers, 1971. 128 p. Index.

>Battered child syndrome from cultural, psychological, and biological perspectives--beautifully and perceptually written.

Chase, Naomi F. A CHILD IS BEING BEATEN. New York: Holt, Rinehart and Winston, 1975. 225 p. Biblio.

>The author examines violence against children in the United States as a serious social problem that results from increasing family disorganization and from inadequacies in our federal and local social service systems.

D'Ambrosio, Richard Anthony. NO LANGUAGE BUT A CRY. Garden City, N.Y.: Doubleday & Co., 1970. 252 p.

>True story of a physically deformed, brutally abused, 12-year-old girl who retreated into silence and was finally rescued by a dedicated therapist.

De Courcy, Peter, and De Courcy, Judith. A SILENT TRAGEDY: CHILD ABUSE IN THE COMMUNITY. Princeton, N.J.: Alfred Publishing Co., 1973. 231 p. Biblio.

>A clearly-written plea for improved legal protection for child victims of physical, sexual, and mental abuse. Twelve case histories (from middle-class communities) are cited which indicate the court's failure to protect the abused child. Includes a list of child, family, and social welfare agencies.

Fontana, Vincent James, M.D. THE MALTREATED CHILD. 2d ed. Springfield,

# Child Abuse

Ill.: Charles C. Thomas, Publisher, 1971.  96 p.  Illus.

Simple, basic, and easily read discussion of the problem of maltreated children. Written by the former chairman of the New York City Task Force on Child Abuse.

_____. SOMEWHERE A CHILD IS CRYING.  New York: Macmillan, 1973. 268 p.  Index.

After detailing case studies of child abuse and discussing the reasons for the increasing number of such cases, the author calls for a national program to detect and combat child maltreatment in the early stages. He is concerned for both child and parent.

Gil, David G.  VIOLENCE AGAINST CHILDREN:  PHYSICAL CHILD ABUSE IN THE UNITED STATES.  Cambridge, Mass.:  Harvard University Press, 1970. 204 p.  Index.

A survey of 13,000 cases of child abuse with conclusions regarding prevalence, causes, and so forth.

Helfer, Ray E., and Kempe, C. Henry, eds.  THE BATTERED CHILD.  2d ed. Chicago:  University of Chicago Press, 1974.  262 p.  Appendix, illus., index.

Updated and expanded revision of the challenging 1968 edition, which gave the nation its first real glimpse into the tragic problem of child abuse. Covers the medical, social, and legal aspects of the subject, along with recent developments in treatment programs for abused children and for the parents who maltreat them.

_____. HELPING THE BATTERED CHILD AND HIS FAMILY.  Philadelphia: J.B. Lippincott Co., 1972.  313 p.

This timely book by professionals from many disciplines offers a practical and positive approach to help both the abused child and his family.

Leavitt, Jerome E., ed.  THE BATTERED CHILD: SELECTED READINGS. Morristown, N.J.:  General Learning Press, 1974.  268 p.  Biblio.

Comprehensive compilation of material from other sources on child abuse. Covers perspectives ranging from the social-psychological to the legal. Includes an extensive bibliography.

Steinmetz, Suzanne K., and Straus, Murray A., eds.  VIOLENCE IN THE FAMILY.  New York:  Dodd, Mead & Co., 1974.  337 p.  Paperbound.

Thirty-eight articles of research and theory that examine the connection between marital violence and child abuse by focusing on the family as a training ground for social violence.

# Child Abuse

## PAMPHLETS AND/OR GOVERNMENT DOCUMENTS

Unless otherwise noted the materials are available free of charge. Prices quoted are subject to change. Payment should accompany order.

### Bibliographies

SELECTED REFERENCES ON THE ABUSED AND BATTERED CHILD. 1973. 19 p. Available from: National Institute of Mental Health, 5600 Fishers Lane, Rockville, Md. 20852.

> This bibliography lists books and periodicals published from 1968 through 1973. Of use to research investigators, medical personnel, and the general public.

### Current Sources

CHILDREN TODAY. Vol. 4, May-June 1975. $1.00. Available from: Superintendent of Documents, Government Printing Office, Washington, D.C. 20402.

> Special issue devoted to the problem of child abuse and neglect. Includes articles on working with abusive parents, prevention and treatment programs, foster placement of abused children, and the reasons doctors are reluctant to become involved in child abuse cases.

PLAIN TALK ABOUT CHILD ABUSE. By Herb Stoenner. 24 p. 35 cents. Available from: American Humane Association, Children's Division, P.O. Box 1266, Denver, Colo. 80201.

> Six articles from the DENVER POST which expose the myths popularly accepted about parents who abuse children. Interprets for the general public the nature, causes, and treatment of neglect and abuse.

TO COMBAT CHILD ABUSE AND NEGLECT. By Theodore Irwin. 1974. 28 p. 35 cents. Available from: Public Affairs Pamphlets, 381 Park Avenue, South, New York, N.Y. 10016.

> Brief, informative, and readable survey of a major cause of death among children today; covers theories on the causes of child abuse and describes treatment programs.

WHY DO THEY BEAT THEIR CHILD. 1973. Publication no. 73-02027. Available from: SRS (Social & Rehabilitation Service) Publication Distribution Unit, Room G-115B, 330 C Street, S.W., Washington, D.C. 20201.

# Child Abuse

Simple explanations as to why parents abuse children.

## ORGANIZATIONS AND/OR SOURCES OF MATERIALS, FREE OR AT LOW COST

American Humane Association
Children's Division
5351 Roslyn
Denver, Colo. 80201

    This nationwide organization works to prevent neglect, abuse, and exploitation of children. They prepare and publish materials that interpret to lay people the problems and solutions to child neglect and abuse.

End Violence Against the Next Generation
977 Keeler Avenue
Berkeley, Calif. 94708    Phone (415) 527-0454

    A national organization of psychologists, educators, lawyers, social workers, parents, and others who hope to eliminate corporal punishment from schools and institutions. Provides speakers, consulting services, counseling, and a slide lecture on Violence Against Children.

National Center for the Prevention and Treatment
  of Child Abuse and Neglect
1001 Jasmine Street
Denver, Colo. 80220

    A good source of materials on child abuse.

National Center on Child Abuse and Neglect
Office of Child Development
Children's Bureau
Washington, D.C. 20201

    Established by the 1974 Child Abuse Act, the center is responsible for nationwide studies, information, technical assistance, and grants that are designed to prevent, identify, and treat child abuse.

National Clearinghouse on Child Neglect and Abuse
P.O. Box 1266
Denver, Colo. 80202

    Established in 1973 by the Children's Division of the American Humane Association, the clearinghouse acts as a national resource of information. It issues periodic reports on the nature, incidence, and characteristics of child neglect and abuse.

# Child Abuse

National Committee for Prevention of Child Abuse
111 East Wacker Drive
Chicago, Ill. 60601    Phone (312) 565-1100

>This organization aims to prevent child abuse by developing tests to screen parents and identify potential child abusers. Publishes NATIONAL DIRECTORY OF CHILD ABUSE SERVICES AND INFORMATION (annual), BIBLIOGRAPHY OF CHILD ABUSE LITERATURE, and various reports.

New York State Child Abuse and Maltreatment Register
1450 Western Avenue
Albany, N.Y. 12203    Phone toll-free 1-800-342-3720

>Source of information on child abuse and maltreatment.

Parents Anonymous
2810 Artesia Blvd., Suite F
Redondo Beach, Calif. 90278    Phone (213) 371-3501

>Organization of adults who have abused their children as well as other people who are concerned about child abuse. Its aims are to rehabilitate child abusers and to ensure the physical and emotional well-being of their children. Programs include voluntary group and intra-group participation. Provides speakers for different groups. Has over 200 chapters across the United States and Canada and over 5,000 members. Operates two toll-free numbers for information concerning the nearest chapter: (800) 352-0386 for California residents; (800) 421-0353 for all others.

## AUDIOVISUAL MATERIALS

### Films

THE BATTERED CHILD. 1969. 16mm, 58 min., sound, black and white.

>Documentary of child abuse based upon the book by Helfer and Kempe (see above). Argues for psychiatric care rather than penal action for child abusers.

>Available from: Indiana University, Audio-Visual Center, Bloomington, Ind. 47401.

# CHILD DEVELOPMENT—GENERAL

(See also Discipline; Chapters on Health; Parenthood)

## BOOKS

### Historical Perspective

Buhler, Charlotte M. THE CHILD AND HIS FAMILY. 1939. Reprint. Westport, Conn.: Greenwood Press, 1972. 187 p. Charts, index.

>Studies the influence of the environment on a child's development.

Child, Lydia Maria. THE MOTHER'S BOOK. 1831. Reprint. New York: Arno Press, 1972. 169 p.

>One of the more popular guides to child rearing and adolescent discipline in Jacksonian America.

THE CHILD REARING LITERATURE OF TWENTIETH CENTURY AMERICA. New York: Arno Press, 1972. Var. pag. Biblio., illus.

>A compilation of six Children's Bureau publications on child care. Illustrates the changes in child management from 1914 to 1963.

Gesell, Arnold, et al. BIOGRAPHIES OF CHILD DEVELOPMENT: THE MENTAL GROWTH CAREERS OF EIGHTY-FOUR INFANTS AND CHILDREN; A TEN YEAR STUDY FROM THE CLINIC OF CHILD DEVELOPMENT AT YALE UNIVERSITY. 1939. Reprint. New York: Arno Press, 1975. 328 p. Diags., tables, index.

>For those parents interested in Arnold Gesell and the ten-year study that formed the basis of his school of developmental diagnosis.

Hogan, Louise E. A STUDY OF A CHILD. 1898. Reprint. New York: Arno Press, 1975. 219 p. Illus.

>Portrays a young child's development in an American home in the late nineteenth century.

# Child Development—General

Isaacs, Susan [Sutherland]. SOCIAL DEVELOPMENT IN YOUNG CHILDREN: A STUDY OF BEGINNINGS. 1933. Reprint. New York: Schocken Books, 1972. 480 p. Biblio., index.

> Observations of the spontaneous behavior of children during the years 1924-27. Geared towards the scientific community but could be of interest to parents.

THE PHYSICIAN AND CHILD-REARING: TWO GUIDES, 1809-1894. Reprint. New York: Arno Press, 1972. 191 p.

> Contains two guides, William Buchanan's ADVICE TO MOTHERS (1809) and Emmett Luther Holt's THE CARE AND FEEDING OF CHILDREN (1894). Shows the changes in child-rearing advice and therefore in the viewpoints on maternal health and child development between the beginning and the end of the nineteenth century.

White House Conference on Child Health and Protection. THE YOUNG CHILD IN THE HOME: A SURVEY OF THREE THOUSAND AMERICAN FAMILIES. 1936. Reprint. New York: Arno Press, 1972. 415 p.

> Based on interviews with 3,000 mothers, this is but one of three thorough studies emerging from the Hoover conference. Details all facets of child rearing in the city and on the farm during the 1930s.

## Dated but Still Relevant

Abrahamsen, David, M.D. THE EMOTIONAL CARE OF YOUR CHILD. New York: Trident Press, 1969. 287 p. Biblio.

> Excellent guide to the emotional development of children from birth to adolescence.

Fahs, Sophia L. TODAY'S CHILDREN AND YESTERDAY'S HERITAGE: A PHILOSOPHY OF CREATIVE RELIGIOUS DEVELOPMENT. Boston: Beacon Press, 1952. 224 p.

> Useful book, nonsectarian in view, about the child s religious development and the role of parents and teachers in the development of faith.

Jones, Eve. THE INTELLIGENT PARENTS' GUIDE TO RAISING CHILDREN. New York: Free Press, 1959. 288 p.

> The original title of this book was NATURAL CHILD REARING. Covers emotional development from birth to adolescence, including an invaluable chapter on the unreasonable expectations parents can have of babies and young children. Little, however,

## Child Development—General

is mentioned of the child's intellectual development.

Lee, Ray S. YOUR CHILD GROWING AND RELIGION: A PSYCHOLOGICAL ACCOUNT. New York: Macmillan, 1963. 224 p.

>An English chaplain who is also a psychologist developed the thesis that a "mature moral sense and view of God stem from the enlightened handling of children during their early years, rather than from formal religious instruction."

Spock, Benjamin, M.D. BABY AND CHILD CARE. Rev. ed. New York: Pocket Books, 1968. 620 p. Illus., index. Paperbound.

>Revised and enlarged edition of the original classic. Describes in lay language the most common developments and problems to help the parent understand children, their troubles, and their needs. Covers all aspects of child care. Newly revised edition forthcoming.

Stone, Lawrence Joseph, and Church, Joseph. CHILDHOOD AND ADOLESCENCE. New York: Random House, 1968. 616 p. Biblio., illus., index.

>Highly readable college text covering birth through adolescence. The single most complete book on the subject.

## Reference

Bremner, Robert H., ed. CHILDREN AND YOUTH IN AMERICA: A DOCUMENTARY HISTORY. 3 vols. Cambridge, Mass.: Harvard University Press, 1970-74. Biblio., chronology, illus., tables, index.

>A comprehensive record of the social and health history of children in America. Reproduces original sources with editorial comment. The three volumes cover from 1600 to 1973.

Gruenberg, Sidonie M. THE NEW ENCYCLOPEDIA OF CHILD CARE AND GUIDANCE. Rev. ed. Garden City, N.Y.: Doubleday & Co., 1968. 1,016 p. Illus.

>More than a thousand entries clearly and simply written on all phases of child development. Includes thirty chapters by such specialists as Dr. Benjamin Spock, Margaret Mead, and Dr. Mary Calderone.

Levine, Milton I., M.D., and Seligmann, Jean H. THE PARENTS' ENCYCLOPEDIA OF INFANCY, CHILDHOOD AND ADOLESCENCE. Foreword by Lee Salk. New York: Thomas Y. Crowell Co., 1973. 619 p. Appendices, biblio., illus.

>Useful alphabetized, up-to-date, and simply written guide to child raising and guidance. Handy appendices on poison control

# Child Development—General

centers, community mental health clinics, genetic counseling services, and an immunization chart.

Smith, Lendon H., M.D.  THE ENCYCLOPEDIA OF BABY AND CHILD CARE. Englewood Cliffs, N.J.: Prentice-Hall, 1972.  500 p.  Biblio., charts, index.

> Comprehensive, authoritative guide to the health, treatment, and behavior of children from birth through adolescence. Sixteen specialized sections cover such topics as drugs and medicines; poisonings and first aid; fevers; diet and feeding; ears, eyes, nose, throat; allergies; nervous system; and bones. Offers definitions, diagnoses, and rules.

Weiss, Mark.  FREE FOR BABY AND MOTHER: AN ENCYCLOPEDIA OF THINGS AVAILABLE TO PARENT AND CHILD AT NO COST.  Cranbury, N.J.: A.S. Barnes & Co., 1972.  121 p.

> Lists by subject free and inexpensive pamphlets for mothers and expectant mothers concerning prenatal care for mother, the nursery, breastfeeding, adoption, childhood illnesses, day care, and so forth. The pamphlets are published by the federal government, organizations such as the National Safety Council, and manufacturers of baby products.

## Current Sources

Adler, Manfred.  A PARENT'S MANUAL: ANSWERS TO QUESTIONS ON CHILD DEVELOPMENT AND CHILD REARING.  Springfield, Ill.: Charles C. Thomas, Publisher, 1971.  111 p.

> Based on the author's weekly column in the CLEVELAND PRESS. A nontechnical and at times humorous guide designed as a beginning source for concerned parents on such aspects as behavior and discipline; the preschool years; psychological, intellectual, and physical development.

Ames, Louise B[ates].  CHILD CARE AND DEVELOPMENT.  Philadelphia:  J.B. Lippincott Co., 1970.  426 p.  Biblio., glossary, illus., tables, index.

> Though written as a textbook, the detailed coverage of the physical, mental, and emotional growth of children from birth through ten years is useful information for parents.

Briggs, Dorothy Corkille.  YOUR CHILD'S SELF-ESTEEM: THE KEY TO HIS LIFE.  Garden City, N.Y.: Doubleday & Co., 1970.  341 p.  Biblio., index.

> Advice on helping a child develop the very important sense of self.

## Child Development—General

Cable, Mary. THE LITTLE DARLINGS: A HISTORY OF CHILD REARING IN AMERICA. New York: Charles Scribner's Sons, 1975. 214 p. Biblio., illus., index.

In a comprehensive and readable manner, the author traces child-rearing from the strictness of colonial times to Dr. Spock and beyond. She also examines changes in attitudes toward sex education, clothing, toilet training, girls' liberation, and discipline.

Cava, Esther Laden. THE COMPLETE QUESTION-AND-ANSWER BOOK OF CHILD TRAINING. New York: Hawthorn Books, 1972. 376 p.

This is an informative and easy-to-read guidebook by an experienced psychologist who answers very specific questions on baby care and child raising. Covers such commonly encountered problems as anger, bedtime, discipline, death, feeding, siblings, and temper tantrums.

Della-Piana, Gabriel. HOW TO TALK WITH CHILDREN, (AND OTHER PEOPLE). New York: John Wiley & Sons, 1973. 171 p. Illus.

A well-organized guide to help parents and professionals improve their relations with children at home, in school, and in child care settings. Stresses positive communication skills in talking to children, offering explanations, directing children, and punishing them. Provides adults with additional insights into the reasons for a child's behavior.

de Mause, Lloyd. THE HISTORY OF CHILDHOOD. New York: Psychohistory Press, 1974. 450 p. Biblio.

Psychohistorian's view of the evolution of child care from the time of Christ to the twentieth century.

Ferguson, Lucy Rau. PERSONALITY DEVELOPMENT. Monterey, Calif.: Brooks/Cole Publishing Co., 1970. 213 p. Paperbound.

Concentrates on the development of the child's interpersonal relations from birth to adolescence.

Gardner, George E., M.D., et al. THE EMERGING PERSONALITY: INFANCY THROUGH ADOLESCENCE. New York: Delacorte Press, 1970. 292 p.

A child psychiatrist delineates personality development from infancy through adolescence. He also advises parents on aiding their children's development and urges them to talk and play a great deal with their babies.

Homan, William E., M.D. CHILD SENSE: A PEDIATRICIAN'S GUIDE FOR TODAY'S FAMILIES. New York: Basic Books, Publishers, 1970. 308 p. Index.

# Child Development—General

A clear and straightforward handbook based on Dr. Homan's vast experience with parents and children. Covers such areas as discipline, independence; discusses the problems of younger and older children ranging from toilet training and temper tantrums to school problems and sex education. Includes a chapter on problems in family relationships such as sibling rivalry, the handicapped child, and divorce.

Hopper, Robert, and Naremore, Rita C. CHILDREN'S SPEECH: A PRACTICAL INTRODUCTION TO COMMUNICATION DEVELOPMENT. New York: Harper & Row Publishers, 1973. 140 p. Biblio., tables, index. Paperbound.

A well-written introductory book on how children learn to talk for use by parents and prospective teachers. Describes language acquisition and offers suggestions for oral and written exercises. Contains references for further reading.

Isaacs, Susan Sutherland. TROUBLES OF CHILDREN AND PARENTS. New York: Schocken Books, 1973. 238 p. Paperbound.

Advice for mothers in question-and-answer format. Training in politeness, obedience, discipline, tantrums, shyness, sibling rivalry, phobias, and head-rocking are among the many areas covered.

Kappelman, Murray. WHAT YOUR CHILD IS ALL ABOUT. New York: Reader's Digest Press, 1975. 223 p.

With a sense of understanding and optimism, the author guides parents through the everyday situations that comprise normal behavior. Also details the emotional and physical problems of young children.

Krogman, W.M. CHILD GROWTH. Ann Arbor: University of Michigan Press, 1972. 231 p. Biblio.

Covers the biological and behavioral growth patterns of the child.

Lesowitz, Robert I. RULES FOR RAISING KIDS. Springfield, Ill.: Charles C. Thomas, Publisher, 1974. 186 p. Illus.

Specific suggestions to help parents, teachers, and physicians deal with children's problems.

Peairs, Lillian, and Peairs, Richard. WHAT EVERY CHILD NEEDS. New York: Harper & Row Publishers, 1974. 396 p. Biblio., index.

Combining a knowledge of the relevant literature in child psychology with their own understanding of parenthood, the authors guide

# Child Development—General

both parents and professionals in handling crucial aspects of a child's life: anger, jealousy, toilet training, bedtime. The authors offer a most sympathetic approach.

Post, Elizabeth. PLEASE SAY PLEASE: A COMMON SENSE GUIDE TO BRINGING UP YOUR CHILD. Boston: Little, Brown and Co., 1972. 300 p.

Offers practical information and instruction for infancy through preteen years on such subjects as trusting a child's motives and keeping promises. For those parents concerned with eliciting good manners from their children.

Richmond, Peter Graham. AN INTRODUCTION TO PIAGET. Boston: Routledge & Kegan Paul, 1970. 120 p. Illus.

A comprehensive study of Piaget's massive contribution to child psychology.

Robinson, Halbert B., et al. EARLY CHILD CARE IN THE UNITED STATES OF AMERICA. New York: Gordon and Breach, Science Publishers, 1973. 224 p. Appendix, biblio., illus.

Comprehensive overview of historical developments and current attitudes about the upbringing of infants and children; covers health, nutrition, recreation, day care, social welfare. Should be of interest to professionals, students, and the general public.

Rowan, Robert L., M.D. BED-WETTING: A GUIDE FOR PARENTS. New York: St. Martin's Press, 1974. 112 p. Appendix, biblio.

A slim but detailed analysis of the psychological causes of bedwetting with a discussion of the best method of handling individual problems, and a guide to proper toilet training.

Sime, Mary. A CHILD'S EYE VIEW: PIAGET FOR YOUNG PARENTS AND TEACHERS. New York: Harper & Row Publishers, 1974. 144 p. Biblio., illus., index.

A well-presented summary of Piaget's theories coupled with an examination of the process whereby children learn to think, understand, and reason logically.

Weiner, Irving B., and Elkind, David. CHILD DEVELOPMENT: A CORE APPROACH. New York: John Wiley & Sons, 1972. 247 p.

General introduction to child development, covering the basic stages of infancy, preschool, middle years, and adolescence. Covers physical and mental growth, social development, individual differences, and personality development.

# Child Development—General

Yamamoto, Kaoru, ed. THE CHILD AND HIS IMAGE: SELF-CONCEPT IN THE EARLY YEARS. New York: Houghton Mifflin Co., 1972. 235 p. Illus. Paperbound.

> In nontextbook style, specialists in early childhood education and child psychology stress that forming a positive self-concept is an important aspect of child development. A useful resource for teachers of young children and for parents because it discusses the parental role in the development of self-concept.

## PERIODICALS

CHILDHOOD EDUCATION. Washington, D.C.: Association for Childhood Education International, 1924-- . Monthly.

> Written in a language understandable to both parents and teachers, this journal covers child development in the home and classroom from infancy through early adolescence.

CHILDREN TODAY. Washington, D.C.: Office of Child Development, United States Department of Health, Education and Welfare, 1954-- . Bimonthly.

> Major articles on health and welfare needs of children (infancy through high school) by pediatricians, parents, teachers, psychologists, social workers, civic leaders, scientists, and volunteers. Section on government publications--either free or at low cost.

INTERNATIONAL JOURNAL OF EARLY CHILDHOOD. Oslo, Norway: Universitetsforlaget, Blindern, 1969-- . Biannual.

> Covers every aspect of preschool and elementary school children. Somewhat technical, but should be of interest to parents.

JOURNAL OF CLINICAL CHILD PSYCHOLOGY. St. Louis, Mo.: American Psychological Association, 1971-- . Three issues a year.

> Each issue is devoted to a single subject such as child abuse, new directions for the retarded, etc., with contributions from psychologists, educators, and other professionals. Articles are authoritative, readable, and useful for both parents and professionals.

PARENTS' MAGAZINE. New York: Parents' Magazine Enterprises, 1926-- . Monthly.

> This magazine covers health, education, personality, and child development in an intelligent fashion.

# Child Development—General

## PAMPHLETS AND/OR GOVERNMENT DOCUMENTS

Unless otherwise noted the materials are available free of charge. Prices quoted are subject to change. Payment should accompany order.

## Bibliographies

CHILDREN'S BUREAU PUBLICATIONS FOR PARENTS. 1973. Available from: Office of Child Development, Department of Health, Education and Welfare, Washington, D.C. 20201

    List of selected publications for parents including some that are available in Spanish.

PUBLICATIONS OF THE OFFICE OF HUMAN DEVELOPMENT. 1975. 52 p. Available from: Office of Human Development, Department of Health, Education and Welfare, Washington, D.C. 20201.

    Describes publications of various agencies including the Office of Child Development.

## Current Sources

ADULTS LOOK AT CHILDREN'S VALUES. 1973. Available from: Hogg Foundation for Mental Health, Publications Division, University of Texas, Austin, Tex. 78712.

    A look at children's values and role of parents in their development.

FACTS ABOUT THE MENTAL HEALTH OF CHILDREN. 1973. 13 p. Publication no. 73-9130. Available from: National Institute of Mental Health, 5600 Fishers Lane, Rockville, Md. 20852.

    Discusses the basic factors that play an important part in helping children grow well.

GROWING PAINS. [n.d.] 28 p. Publication no. (12-A)2. Available from: Connecticut Mutual Life Insurance Co., Human Relations Program, 140 Garden Street, Hartford, Conn. 06115.

    Advice for parents presented in cartoon format.

PLAYMATES: THE IMPORTANCE OF CHILDHOOD FRIENDSHIPS. 1975. 24 p. 35 cents. Publication no. 525. Available from: Public Affairs Committee, 381 Park Avenue S., New York, N.Y. 10016.

    Informative discussion on how friendships develop, how they meet children's needs, why they change, and how parents can help

# Child Development—General

children to cope with the problems in friendships.

## ORGANIZATIONS AND/OR SOURCES OF MATERIALS, FREE OR AT LOW COST

Child Study Association of America
50 Madison Avenue
New York, N.Y. 10010     Phone (212) 369-6300

> A voluntary, nonprofit organization which provides services for children, teenagers, and adults including counseling and family life education. Publishes books, pamphlets, and annotated booklists for parents, students, and those who work with students.

Public Affairs Committee
381 Park Avenue S.
New York, N.Y. 10016

> Issues a variety of pamphlets on child guidance, family well-being, marriage, and special family concerns. Write for their list of publications.

## AUDIOVISUAL MATERIALS

### Films

CHILDHOOD: THE ENCHANTED YEARS. 1971. 16mm, 60 min., sound, color.

> A study of prominent child development specialists, their research, and its implications for parents.

> Available from: NBC-TV, 30 Rockefeller Plaza, New York, N.Y. 10020.

CHILDREN GROWING UP SERIES. 9 films. 16mm, 25 min. each, sound, color.

> Shows child growth and development.

> Available from: Time-Life Films, 43 West Sixteenth Street, New York, N.Y. 10011.

DEVELOPMENT. 16mm, 26 min., sound, color.

> Nine experts discuss the stages of psychological development from birth through adolescence. One of a series of PSYCHOLOGY TODAY films.

## Child Development—General

Available from: CRM Productions, 9263 Third Street, Beverly Hills, Calif. 90210.

THE DEVELOPMENT OF FEELINGS IN CHILDREN. 1974. 16mm, sound, color.

Depicts how feelings develop in children and suggests ways parents can help a child express his/her feelings.

Available from: Parents' Magazine Films, 52 Vanderbilt Avenue, New York, N.Y. 10017.

EVAN'S CORNER. 1970. 23 min., sound, color.

Evan, one of six children, gets help from his mother in selecting a place where he can be alone.

Available from: Bailey Film Associates, 11559 Santa Monica Boulevard, Los Angeles, Calif. 90025.

GUIDANCE--BIG SISTER. 1971. 16mm, 10 1/2 min., sound.

Sibling rivalry is discussed.

Available from: AIMS Instructional Media, Box 1010, Hollywood, Calif. 90028.

SANDCASTLES. 1971. 6 min., sound.

Some promises are broken because of circumstances--children don't understand.

Available from: AIMS Instructional Media, Box 1010, Hollywood, Calif. 90028.

## Filmstrips and Slides

CHILD CARE AND DEVELOPMENT. 1971. 2 sets (4 filmstrips each, 60 frames each), sound, color.

Set 1 includes "Food Needs of Children," "Clothing Needs of Children," "Children's Play," "Caring for Children: An Important Job." Set 2 includes "Discipline and Punishment," "Intellectual Development of Children," "Anxieties of Children," and "Influences on Children." The set covers the spectrum of physical and psychological needs of children.

Available from: McGraw-Hill Films, 330 West Forty-second Street, New York, N.Y. 10036.

## Child Development—General

DEVELOPING BASIC VALUES. 4 filmstrips (with records or cassettes), sound, color.

Each strip stresses the moral and ethical values that are essential to an individual's social growth and development: respect for property, consideration of others, acceptance of differences, recognition of responsibilities.

Available from: Singer/SVE, 1345 Diversey Parkway, Chicago, Ill. 60614.

# CHILD DEVELOPMENT—INFANCY TO FIVE YEARS

## BOOKS

### Historical Perspective

Dewey, Evelyn. BEHAVIOR DEVELOPMENT IN INFANTS: A SURVEY OF THE LITERATURE ON PRENATAL AND POSTNATAL ACTIVITY 1920-1934. 1935. Reprint. New York: Arno Press, 1973. 334 p. Biblio., index.

   Reviews research by Gesell, Buhler, McGraw, and others on infant behavior and motor patterns.

Isaacs, Susan [Sutherland]. THE NURSERY YEARS: THE MIND OF THE CHILD FROM BIRTH TO SIX YEARS. 1932. Reprint. New York: Schocken Books, 1968. 140 p. Biblio., illus. Paperbound.

   English classic with much relevance for American parents.

THE MATERNAL PHYSICIAN: A TREATISE OF THE NURTURE AND MANAGEMENT OF INFANTS, FROM THE BIRTH UNTIL TWO YEARS OLD, BEING THE RESULT OF SIXTEEN YEARS' EXPERIENCE IN THE NURSERY. ILLUSTRATED BY EXTRACTS FROM THE MOST APPROVED MEDICAL AUTHORS. BY AN AMERICAN MATRON. 2d ed. 1818. Reprint. New York: Arno Press, 1972. 288 p.

   First American guide to child care.

Watson, John B. PSYCHOLOGICAL CARE OF INFANT AND CHILD. 1928. Reprint. New York: Arno Press, 1972. 195 p.

   Watson, a psychologist, reversed many earlier concepts by insisting on a comparatively rigid and fixed schedule for the infant and opposing the coddling of children. His work was most influential.

# Infancy to Five Years

## Dated but Still Relevant

BETTER HOMES AND GARDENS BABY BOOK. New York: Bantam Books, 1969. 383 p. Illus., index.

>Authoritative day-by-day, month-by-month, year-by-year guide to child care through the first six years. Covers first aid, common diseases, and complaints. Photographs illustrate how to feed, bathe, dress, and care for the baby.

Brazelton, T. Berry, M.D. INFANTS AND MOTHERS: DIFFERENCES IN DEVELOPMENT. New York: Delacorte Press, 1969. 296 p. Biblio., illus., index.

>Excellent discussion of child development during the first year of life and of the personality differences in babies and parents which affect the child's behavior.

Burnett, Dorothy. YOUR PRESCHOOL CHILD: MAKING THE MOST OF THE YEARS FROM 2 TO 7. New York: Holt, Rinehart and Winston, 1961. 272 p. Biblio.

>Practical suggestions for mothers of preschoolers.

Chess, Stella, M.D., et al. YOUR CHILD IS A PERSON: A PSYCHOLOGICAL APPROACH TO PARENTHOOD WITHOUT GUILT. New York: Viking Press, 1965. 213 p. Paperbound.

>Emphasizes the individuality of the child (birth to six) and the reactions of parents. Certain professionals contradict some of the book's advice, particularly in regard to toilet training.

Fraiberg, Selma H. THE MAGIC YEARS. 1959. Reprint. New York: Charles Scribner's Sons, 1968. 305 p.

>Well-written and intelligent approach by a psychotherapist to questions such as sibling rivalry, toilet training and discipline, development of masculinity and femininity, and the growth of conscience.

Gesell, Arnold. THE FIRST FIVE YEARS OF LIFE: A GUIDE TO THE STUDY OF THE PRESCHOOL CHILD. New York: Harper & Row Publishers, 1940. 393 p. Illus.

>Classic in-depth study of normal child development covering the various periods of growth and development and their related traits.

Glover, Leland. HOW TO GIVE YOUR CHILD A GOOD START IN LIFE. New York: Collier, 1962. 223 p. Biblio. Paperbound.

# Infancy to Five Years

Assuming that the first five years of life are the most formative, the author advises parents on enhancing this period for their child.

Hymes, James. THE CHILD UNDER SIX. Englewood Cliffs, N.J.: Prentice-Hall, 1963. 342 p. Biblio.

Development of the child during the first five years--well covered.

Liley, Helen Margaret Irwin, M.D., and Day, Beth. MODERN MOTHERHOOD: PREGNANCY, CHILDBIRTH AND THE NEW BORN BABY. Rev. ed. New York: Random House, 1969. 239 p. Illus.

Common-sense information on the newborn's characteristics and on baby care through the early months. The emphasis is on the behavior of the infant.

## Current Sources

Akmakjian, Haig. THE NATURAL WAY TO RAISE HEALTHY CHILDREN. New York: Praeger Publishers, 1975. 320 p. Biblio.

Modern approach to child development based on the psychological and physical needs of the child. Also includes a section on the women's movement and parenting.

Azrin, Nathan H., M.D., and Foxx, Richard M., M.D. TOILET TRAINING IN LESS THAN A DAY. New York: Simon & Schuster, 1974. 160 p. Index.

Step-by-step instructions to be followed after the child passes an all-important readiness test. Includes a list of things to remember or obtain before, during, and after the actual training.

Bax, Martin, and Bernal, Judy. YOUR CHILD'S FIRST FIVE YEARS. New York: St. Martin's Press, 1974. 141 p. Illus.

Here the emphasis is on the development and handling of the two- to five-year-old. Most clearly delineated are the complicated and fascinating changes in the child.

Boston Children's Medical Center. PREGNANCY, BIRTH AND THE NEWBORN BABY. New York: Delacorte Press, 1972. 474 p. Illus.

Pregnancy, birth, and newborn care are discussed by pediatricians, obstetricians, psychiatrists, psychologists, a social worker, and an anthropologist. Gives more in-depth information than the generally simpler manuals. Well written.

Brazelton, T. Berry, M.D. TODDLERS AND PARENTS: A DECLARATION OF INDEPENDENCE. New York: Delacorte Press, 1974. 250 p. Biblio., index.

# Infancy to Five Years

Clear and readable discussion of child growth and development between the ages of one and three. The author deals with the problems of working parents and single parents; examines such issues as sibling rivalry, the withdrawn child, the aggressive child, and the hyperactive child; offers practical advice using real cases.

Brenner, Erma. A NEW BABY! A NEW LIFE! New York: McGraw-Hill Book Co., 1973. 128 p. Illus.

This book with its simply written text and fine drawings should be helpful to new parents. It discusses the baby's development in the first year of life and the role parents play in this development.

Cattell, Psyche. RAISING CHILDREN WITH LOVE AND LIMITS. Chicago: Nelson-Hall Co., 1972. 240 p.

Many years experience in child psychology back the author's non-technical discussion and concise observations on raising children under eight years of age; stresses the importance of rules and routines to strengthen parent-child relationships in such areas as eating, sleeping, dressing, and toilet training.

Church, Joseph. UNDERSTANDING YOUR CHILD FROM BIRTH TO THREE: A GUIDE TO YOUR CHILD'S PSYCHOLOGICAL DEVELOPMENT. New York: Random House, 1973. 207 p. Index.

A specialist in infant behavior and development offers advice, information, and reassurance to help young parents deal with their child naturally and lovingly. Topics covered include sleep, feeding, children's fears, sexuality, language development, discipline, and working mothers. The author interweaves common sense with modern science.

Gesell, Arnold. INFANT AND CHILD IN THE CULTURE OF TODAY. Rev. ed. New York: Harper & Row Publishers, 1974. 420 p. Appendix, illus.

Basic and authoritative guide to child rearing from birth to five years by a noted specialist. Covers behavior patterns at different developmental stages and practical techniques for parents and professionals in effectively guiding the child's development. Also includes lists of suggested toys and books for children.

Gilbert, Sara D. THREE YEARS TO GROW: GUIDANCE FOR YOUR CHILD'S FIRST THREE YEARS. New York: Parents' Magazine Press, 1972. 256 p. Biblio., illus., index.

Reflecting current thinking on the care of infants, the author offers new parents a practical approach to the baby's physical, mental, and emotional growth through the third year. Such topics as feeding, discipline, toilet training, accidents, babysitters, and intelligent management of the routine are covered.

Lowndes, Marion. A MANUAL FOR BABY-SITTERS. Boston: Little, Brown and Co., 1975. 184 p.

   Informative guide for baby-sitters and parents on caring for children from infancy through age seven.

Neisser, Edith G. PRIMER FOR PARENTS OF PRESCHOOLERS. New York: Parents' Magazine Press, 1972. 320 p. Biblio.

   Overview of the physical, mental, and emotional development of children between three and six, tenderly presented in a question-and-answer format.

Pomeranz, Virginia E., M.D., and Schultz, Dodi. THE FIRST FIVE YEARS: A RELAXED APPROACH TO CHILD CARE. Garden City, N.Y.: Doubleday & Co., 1973. 248 p. Biblio., index.

   The authors reassure new parents that there is more than one right way to raise children. They focus on the practical concerns in raising one- to five-year-olds.

Princeton Center for Infancy and Early Childhood. THE FIRST TWELVE MONTHS OF LIFE: YOUR BABY'S GROWTH MONTH BY MONTH. Edited by Frank Caplan. New York: Grosset & Dunlap, 1973. 255 p. Biblio., charts, photos., index.

   The director of the Princeton Center for Infancy and Early Childhood describes month-by-month growth and development in a baby's first year. Some of the subjects which are sympathetically and skillfully handled include feeding, sleeping, language, physical skills, and parental emotions. Individual growth charts are most illuminating.

Robertson, Elizabeth Chant, and Wood, Margaret I. TODAY'S CHILD: A MODERN GUIDE TO BABY CARE AND CHILD TRAINING. New York: Charles Scribner's Sons, 1972. 338 p. Appendix, biblio., index.

   Two Canadian pediatricians offer the new parent an informative and practical handbook in nontechnical language on many aspects of prenatal and infant care and training including feeding and food preparation, toilet training, first aid, play, and travel care. The appendix listing common diseases and suggestions for home care is well worth examining.

Rutherford, Frederick W. YOU AND YOUR BABY: A GUIDE TO PREGNANCY, BIRTH, AND THE FIRST YEAR. New York: New American Library, 1971. 480 p. Biblio., illus. Paperbound.

## Infancy to Five Years

Guide to care of baby and mother from conception through the child's first year.

YOUR CHILD FROM ONE TO TWELVE. Foreword by Lee Salk. New York: New American Library, 1970. 303 p.

Several classic government pamphlets on child care plus an appendix on diseases, emergencies, and other physical and emotional problems of children are incorporated into a single, most useful volume.

### PERIODICALS

American Baby. New York: American Baby, 1960--. Monthly.

Formerly MOTHERS-TO-BE. Contains helpful suggestions on baby care, fashions, and other special features for both new and seasoned parents. Copies are mailed to mothers free of charge.

BABY TALK. New York: Leam Corp., 1935-- . Monthly.

Includes informative, accurate, and well-written articles for parents of babies and children up to three years of age. Only baby magazine with a paid circulation.

### PAMPHLETS AND/OR GOVERNMENT DOCUMENTS

Unless otherwise noted the materials are available free of charge. Prices quoted are subject to change. Payment should accompany order.

AS YOUR CHILD GROWS: FIRST 18 MONTHS. $1.00. Available from: Child Study Association of America/Wel-Met, 50 Madison Avenue, New York, N.Y. 10010.

For parents and professionals who work with children.

CHILD DEVELOPMENT IN THE HOME. 1974. 20 p. Publication no. (OHD) 74-42. Available from: Office of Human Development, U.S. Department of Health, Education and Welfare, Washington, D.C. 20201.

Guidelines to help parents develop happy, self-confident and self-disciplined children. Emphasizes first five years.

INFANT CARE. 1973. 72 p. Illus., index. Publication no. (OHD) 75-15. Available from: Office of Human Development, Publications Distribution Unit, Department of Health, Education and Welfare, Washington, D.C. 20201.

## Infancy to Five Years

One of the government's most popular publications. The sixth revision covers all aspects of infant care including feeding, discipline, first aid and emergency treatment, and care of a sick child. A Spanish version is also available.

THE PREMATURE BABY. 1971. 9 p. 20 cents. Publication no. S/N 1791-0155. Available from: Superintendent of Documents, Government Printing Office, Washington, D.C. 20402.

Explains the differences and difficulties of premature babies.

PRENATAL CARE. 1973. 70 p. Publication no. (OCD) 73-17. Available from: Office of Human Development, Publications Distribution Unit, Department of Health, Education and Welfare, Washington, D.C. 20201.

New edition of the best-seller first issued in 1913. Provides advice for women who are pregnant or planning pregnancy. Attempts to answer the questions most frequently asked about pregnancy and the care of the baby in early life. A Spanish version is also available.

WHEN YOUR CHILD FIRST GOES OFF TO SCHOOL. 1973. Publication no. (HS) 73-9045. Available from: National Institute of Mental Health, 5600 Fishers Lane, Rockville, Md. 20852.

Suggestions for parents at this highly important time in a young child's life.

YOUR BABY'S FIRST YEAR. 1972. 15 p. Available from: Channing L. Bete Co., 45 Federal Street, Greenfield, Mass. 01301.

Basics of infant care.

YOUR CHILD FROM 1 TO 6. 1962. Reprint. 1973. 98 p. Illus., index. Publication no. (OCD) 74-26. Available from: Office of Human Development, Publications Distribution Unit, Department of Health, Education and Welfare, Washington, D.C. 20201.

Describes the world and needs of children from ages one to six including food habits, nutrition, illness, psychological and physical development.

YOUR FIRST FIVE MONTHS WITH YOUR FIRST BABY. 1972. 24 p. 35 cents. Publication no. 478. Available from: Public Affairs Committee, 381 Park Avenue, S., New York, N.Y. 10016.

Intended for new parents. Describes the physical development and psychological needs of infants during the first year of life. Discusses the parental adjustments required to meet these needs.

## Infancy to Five Years

### ORGANIZATIONS AND/OR SOURCES OF MATERIALS, FREE OR AT LOW COST

Beech-Nut
460 Park Avenue
New York, N.Y. 10022

 Various pamphlets on infants.

John Hancock Mutual Life Insurance Co.
Community Relations
200 Berkely Street
Boston, Mass. 02117

 Booklet for new mothers on infant care.

Johnson & Johnson
Consumer Services
501 George Street
New Brunswick, N.Y. 08903

 Pamphlets, folder, and chart on child development from birth to two years.

Mead Johnson & Co.
2404 West Pennsylvania Street
Evansville, Ind. 47712

 Booklets for future mothers on baby care.

Medical Marketing Department
Carnation Co.
5045 Wilshire Boulevard
Los Angeles, Calif. 90036

 Pamphlets on prenatal and postnatal care.

### AUDIOVISUAL MATERIALS

### Films

BATHS AND BABIES. 1965. 16mm, 17 1/2 min., sound, color.

 A professional nurse shows the steps in bathing a baby. Also shows new mothers' first attempts.

 Available from: Association-Sterling Films, Johnson & Johnson, Executive Offices, 866 Third Avenue, New York, N.Y. 10022.

# Infancy to Five Years

THE FIRST YEARS TOGETHER . . . TO BEGIN A CHILD. 16mm, 28 min., sound, color.

> Child's behavior from birth through age five and the importance of love and understanding.
>
> Available from: Modern Talking Pictures Service, 1145 North McCadden Place, Los Angeles, Calif. 90038. Phone (213) 469-8282.

INFANCY. 1972. 16mm, 19 min., sound, color.

> Discusses behavior and learning patterns as well as individual differences exhibited by infants.
>
> Available from: CRM Productions, 9263 Third Street, Beverly Hills, Calif. 90210.

NEWBORN. 1973. 16mm, 28 min., sound, color.

> Focuses on the first three months of life. Depicts the joys and problems of parenthood through the experiences of a first-time mother and father.
>
> Available from: Johnson & Johnson Baby Products, Consumer & Professional Services, New Brunswick, N.J. 08903.

PREFACE TO A LIFE. 29 min., sound.

> A preschool child's feelings about the addition of a new baby into his family and how his parents helped him adjust.
>
> Available from: Sun Dial Films, 341 East Forty-third Street, New York, N.Y. 10017.

## Filmstrips and Slides

HOW AN AVERAGE CHILD BEHAVES--FROM BIRTH TO AGE FIVE. 1968. Rev. ed. 5 filmstrips (50 frames each), color. LP record or 3 cassettes.

> Includes segments on infants, toddlers, and preschoolers. Comes with audio script booklets and discussion guides.
>
> Available from: Parents' Magazine Films, 52 Vanderbilt Avenue, New York, N.Y. 10017.

INFANT CARE AND DEVELOPMENT. 2 sets (4 filmstrips each) 7-8 min. each, sound, color.

> Set 1: "Prenatal Care and Planning," "The Family and the New Baby," "Parental Responsibility," "A Baby's Day." Set 2: "Infants and Learning," "Growth in the First Year," "Infants' Food Needs," "Breast Feeding and Bottle Feeding." Stresses parental

# Infancy to Five Years

responsibility before and after birth.

Available from: McGraw-Hill Films, 330 West Forty-second Street, New York, N.Y. 10036.

UNDERSTANDING EARLY CHILDHOOD--AGES 1 THROUGH 6. 5 filmstrips (50 frames each), color. 12 inch LP record or 3 cassettes.

Includes: "The Child's Relationship with the Family," "Preparing the Child for Learning," "The Child's Point of View," and "The Development of Feelings in Children."

Available from: Parents' Magazine Films, 52 Vanderbilt Avenue, New York, N.Y. 10017.

# CHILD DEVELOPMENT—SIX TO TWELVE YEARS

(See also Child Development—Infancy to Five Years)

## BOOKS

### Dated but Still Relevant

Gesell, Arnold, and Ilg, Frances L. THE CHILD FROM FIVE TO TEN. New York: Harper, 1946. 475 p. Biblio., diags., illus.

>Continuation of the summary begun in INFANT AND CHILD IN THE CULTURE OF TODAY (see "Child Development--Infancy to Five Years") of the behavior at each stage of development; in this case, ages five to ten.

Glover, Leland. HOW TO GUIDE YOUR SCHOOL-AGE CHILD. New York: Collier, 1965. 285 p. Biblio., index. Paperbound.

>Based on careful research, this book deals with the child between six and thirteen.

Ilg, Frances L., and Ames, Louise Bates. CHILD BEHAVIOR. New York: Harper & Bros., 1955. 364 p. Index.

>Condensation of material from INFANT AND CHILD IN THE CULTURE OF TODAY and THE CHILD FROM FIVE TO TEN-- very handy.

### Current Sources

Elkind, David. A SYMPATHETIC UNDERSTANDING OF THE CHILD SIX TO SIXTEEN. Boston: Allyn & Bacon, 1971. 154 p. Paperbound.

>The social and mental development of children in this age group.

Gardner, Richard A., M.D. UNDERSTANDING CHILDREN. New York: Jason Aronson, 1973. 258 p. Index.

# Six to Twelve Years

This well-written and highly organized study introduces parents to the psychological behavior of grade school children and to the common difficulties which confront them. The author's aim is to help parents understand unhealthy traits in children, thus lessening their extent and intensity. This book should be welcome to interested parents.

Mogal, Doris P. CHARACTER IN THE MAKING: THE MANY WAYS PARENTS CAN HELP THE SCHOOL-AGE CHILD. New York: Parents' Magazine Press, 1972. 224 p. Biblio., index.

Concise and readable guide designed to aid parents in understanding and enhancing the mental, emotional, and physical development of their children ages six to ten. Topics covered include drugs, sex education, problem of self-image, influence of TV and leisure, health concerns, and the meaning of friends.

Tough, Joan. TALKING, THINKING, GROWING: LANGUAGE WITH THE YOUNG CHILD. New York: Schocken Books, 1974. 144 p. Biblio.

A specialist in linguistics discusses the development and use of language by children from birth to ages six to eight. For parents and teachers.

## PERIODICALS

CENTER FOR CHILDREN'S BOOKS. BULLETIN. Chicago: University of Chicago Press, 1945-- . Monthly.

Excellent source for reviews of books geared to elementary and junior high school levels.

## PAMPHLETS AND/OR GOVERNMENT DOCUMENTS

Unless otherwise noted the materials are available free of charge. Prices quoted are subject to change. Payment should accompany order.

PRE-ADOLESCENTS--WHAT MAKES THEM TICK? By Fritz Redl. Rev. ed. 1972. 17 p. 75 cents. Available from: Child Study Association of America/Wel-Met, 50 Madison Avenue, New York, N.Y. 10010.

Some very helpful hints on handling this particularly difficult age group.

YOUR CHILD FROM 6 TO 12. 1966. Reprint. 1973. 80 cents. Publication no. (OCD) 73-40. Available from: Superintendent of Documents, Government Printing Office, Washington, D.C. 20402.

# Six to Twelve Years

Readable, practical guide to the development and behavior of this age group. Also gives advice on handling special situations such as preparation for school, emergencies, and illnesses.

## AUDIOVISUAL MATERIALS

### Films

AFRAID OF SCHOOL. 1966. 30 min., sound, black and white. Producer: Robert Anderson Associates.

Interviews between Tommy (six years old) who refuses to stay in school, his parents, and the psychiatrist. Some techniques for handling "school phobia" are shown.

Available from: McGraw-Hill Films, 330 West Forty-second Street, New York, N.Y. 10001.

# CHILD DEVELOPMENT—BLACK EXPERIENCE

(See also Child Development—Sex Roles)

## BOOKS

Current Sources

Comer, James P., M.D., and Poussaint, Alvin F., M.D. BLACK CHILD CARE. New York: Simon & Schuster, 1975. 408 p. Biblio., index.

    An important and unique study in question-and-answer format of the black child's development from infancy and preschool years through puberty and adolescence. The authors' primary concern is to show black parents how to help their children develop with self-confidence and emotional security.

Harrison-Ross, Phyllis, M.D., and Wyden, Barbara. THE BLACK CHILD: A PARENTS' GUIDE. New York: Peter H. Wyden/Publisher, 1973. 360 p.

    Forthright and nontechnical text by a black pediatric psychiatrist and a white magazine writer on overcoming the problems encountered in raising a black child in a white society. The authors touch upon aspects of black history, black psychology, and child psychology but are most helpful when they describe how even the most well-intentioned parents can unknowingly plant the seeds of bigotry in their children.

Porter, Judith D.R. BLACK CHILD, WHITE CHILD: THE DEVELOPMENT OF RACIAL ATTITUDES. Cambridge, Mass.: Harvard University Press, 1971. 278 p. Biblio., illus., tables.

    Study of three- to five-year-olds offering evidence that children of both races seem to have negative attitudes about blacks. A word of caution--the research was conducted before the "Black is Beautiful" concept and may therefore need some updating.

Willie, Charles V., et al. RACISM AND MENTAL HEALTH. Foreword by Justice Thurgood Marshall, U.S. Supreme Court. Pittsburgh: University of

# Black Experience

Pittsburgh Press, 1973. 604 p. Illus. Paperbound.

An anthology of fifteen essays by black and white authors from the fields of educational and social psychology, psychiatry, social work, and sociology. Essay topics range from the development of a national minority mental program, to the self-concept of black and white children, to guilt feelings in white children as a consequence of racism.

## PERIODICALS

INTERRACIAL BOOKS FOR CHILDREN. New York: Council on Interracial Books for Children, 1966-- . 8 issues per year.

Confronts the problem of racism and sexism in children's literature by analyzing textbooks and juvenile trade titles. Additional pertinent information is included.

## PAMPHLETS AND/OR GOVERNMENT DOCUMENTS

Unless otherwise noted the materials are available free of charge. Prices quoted are subject to change. Payment should accompany order.

### Bibliographies

THE BLACK EXPERIENCE IN CHILDREN'S BOOKS. 50 cents. Available from: Office of Branch Libraries, New York Public Library, 8 East Fortieth Street, New York, N.Y. 10016.

Compiled by Augusta Baker, Coordinator of Children's Services at the New York Public Library. Recommends books for children through the age of twelve that help black and white children understand each other; also books that help black children find their own identity.

## ORGANIZATIONS AND/OR SOURCES OF MATERIALS, FREE OR AT LOW COST

Black Child Development Institute
1028 Connecticut Avenue, N.W.
Washington, D.C. 20036    Phone (202) 659-4010

"Seeks to provide educational, racial, and cultural awareness for black youngsters by developing quality child-centered programs buttressed by community and economic development." Maintains Black Child Advocacy Adoption Project to find homes for black children. Publishes newsletter and research reports. Disseminates

## Black Experience

information on federal and state programs.

The Council on Interracial Books for Children
1841 Broadway
New York, N.Y. 10023

Nonprofit organization founded in 1965 to promote antiracist and antisexist literature and instructional materials for children. Publishes the INTERRACIAL BOOKS FOR CHILDREN BULLETIN.

# CHILD DEVELOPMENT—SEX ROLES

(See also Children's Rights)

## BOOKS

### Current Sources

Biller, Henry B. FATHER, CHILD, AND SEX ROLES: PATERNAL DETERMINANTS OF PERSONALITY DEVELOPMENT. Lexington, Mass.: D.C. Heath & Co., 1971. 193 p.

> Review of the literature involving the formation of sex identity and sex roles.

Gersoni-Stavn, Diane. SEXISM AND YOUTH. New York: R.R. Bowker Co., 1974. 468 p. Index.

> Comprehensive anthology of journal articles, essays, studies, government reports, and resource lists that deal with sexism in education and the schools, socialization, children's literature, films, toys, and games.

Women on Words and Images. CHANNELING CHILDREN: SEX STEREOTYPING ON PRIME TIME TV. Princeton, N.J.: 1975. 84 p. Appendix, biblio.

> Examines the roles of women in prime-time programs of 1973 and 1974. Discusses the effect of such portrayals on the child viewer.

## PAMPHLETS AND/OR GOVERNMENT DOCUMENTS

Unless otherwise noted the materials are available free of charge. Prices quoted are subject to change. Payment should accompany order.

### Bibliographies

HELPING BOYS AND GIRLS UNDERSTAND SEX ROLES. By Milton I. Levine, M.D. and Jean H. Seligman. 1971. 54 p. 75 cents. Available from: Science Research Associates, 259 East Erie Street, Chicago, Ill. 60611.

# Sex Roles

There are differences, but neither sex is superior. A very brief but helpful examination of these differences and how parents, school, and peer group contribute to the child's picture of male and female sex roles.

LITTLE MISS MUFFET FIGHTS BACK. Rev. ed. 1974. 62 p. $1.00. Available from: Feminist Book Mart, 162-11 Ninth Avenue, Whitestone, N.Y. 11357.

A bibliography of children's books that counteracts the stereotyping of sex roles.

A NEW LIST OF BOOKS FOR FREE CHILDREN. 1975. 4 p. 25 cents. Available from: Books for Free Children, Ms. Magazine, 370 Lexington Avenue, New York, N.Y. 10017.

List of books that tend to overcome sex role stereotyping. Include self-addressed stamped envelope.

THIS LIST IS NOT FOR GIRLS ONLY! 1974. 21 p. 25 cents. Available from: Child's Play, 226 Atlantic Avenue, Brooklyn, N.Y. 11201.

Selected list of current titles of nonsexist children's books.

## ORGANIZATIONS AND/OR SOURCES OF MATERIALS, FREE OR AT LOW COST

Change for Children
2588 Mission Street, Room 226
San Francisco, Calif. 94110      Phone (415) 282-3142

This organization works with parents, teachers, and administrators to overcome the limitations sex role and racial stereotyping impose on children. They maintain a library of multi-ethnic, non-sexist childrens books and pamphlets.

## AUDIOVISUAL MATERIALS

### Films

SEX ROLE DEVELOPMENT. 1974. 16mm, 23 min., sound, color.

Examines male/female sex roles and discusses ways to avoid transmitting the traditional stereotypes to children.

Available from: CRM Educational Films, 9263 West Third Street, Beverly Hills, Calif. 90210.

# CHILDREN'S RIGHTS

## BOOKS

### Historical Perspective

Hart, Hastings H. PREVENTIVE TREATMENT OF NEGLECTED CHILDREN. 1910. Reprint. New York: Arno Press, 1971. 419 p. Illus.

An expert in the field of child care describes and analyzes the viewpoints and programs in the organization of reformatories, juvenile courts, settlement houses, and big brother clubs.

Key, Ellen. THE CENTURY OF THE CHILD. 1909. Reprint. New York: Arno Press, 1972. 339 p. Illus.

This book written by a noted Swedish feminist was a best-seller in the United States and Europe. The author argued for greater independence for women and children.

THE LEGAL RIGHTS OF CHILDREN. Introduction by Sanford N. Katz. New York: Arno Press, 1974. Var. pag. Biblio.

Compilation of articles, reprinted from periodical and government sources, that depict the changing legal status of the child from the 1880s to the 1970s.

Lou, Herbert H. JUVENILE COURTS IN THE UNITED STATES. 1927. Reprint. New York: Arno Press, 1972. 277 p. Biblio., index.

An account of the major changes in the treatment of youthful offenders and their families. Also traces the development of the juvenile courts in the early part of the twentieth century, describing the underlying philosophy and modus vivendi.

Polier, Justine Wise. EVERYONE'S CHILDREN, NOBODY'S CHILD: A JUDGE LOOKS AT UNDERPRIVILEGED CHILDREN IN THE UNITED STATES. 1941.

# Children's Rights

Reprint. New York: Arno Press, 1974. 331 p. Biblio., illus., index.

> A thorough study by a Children's Court judge on the care and treatment of neglected and delinquent children. Emphasizes the circumstances that will produce "persons in need of supervision."

Riis, Jacob A. THE CHILDREN OF THE POOR. 1892. Reprint. New York: Arno Press, 1971. 300 p. Illus.

> A noted social reformer details the hardships of the lower-class tenement dwellers and appraises new efforts at improving the condition of poverty.

White House Conference on Child Health and Protection. Section IV. The Handicapped Committee on Socially Handicapped. DEPENDENT AND NE-GLECTED CHILDREN: REPORT OF THE COMMITTEE ON SOCIALLY HANDI-CAPPED; DEPENDENCY AND NEGLECT. 1933. Reprint. New York: Arno Press, 1974. 439 p. Biblio., index.

> This report stems from the 1930 White House Conference chaired by the pioneer child welfare leader, Homer Folks. Recommends new approaches for protecting dependent and neglected children. Also evaluates the general condition of children's needs at the beginning of the New Deal.

White House Conference on Children in a Democracy. FINAL REPORT OF THE WHITE HOUSE CONFERENCE ON CHILDREN IN A DEMOCRACY. 1942. Reprint. New York: Arno Press, 1974. 372 p. Biblio.

> Contains much historical background on child life in America and calls for new efforts in promoting the rights and welfare of American children.

## Reference

Institute of Judicial Administration. JUVENILE JUSTICE STANDARDS PROJ-ECT: JUVENILE LAW LITIGATION DIRECTORY. New York: New York University School of Law, 1973. Unpaged, index.

> Nationwide directory of law offices and national organizations that are engaged in juvenile litigation. Alphabetized by state and city with phone numbers and names of individual lawyers in each office.

## Current Sources

Cole, Larry. OUR CHILDREN'S KEEPERS: INSIDE AMERICA'S KID PRISONS. New York: Grossman Publishers, 1972. 140 p.

# Children's Rights

First-hand accounts of the misery heaped upon the children in reform schools and detention centers in New York City, Denver, San Francisco, and Baton Rouge. Analyzes remedies for the situation. Names the guilty institutions.

Davis, Samuel M. RIGHTS OF JUVENILES: THE JUVENILE JUSTICE SYSTEM. New York: Clark Boardman Co., 1974. 300 p. Biblio., appendices, table of cases, index.

The author, an associate professor of law at the University of Georgia School of Law, presents a current view of the historic 1967 Supreme Court decision In re Gault, which introduced constitutional due process standards in juvenile proceedings. Written for a general audience, the book examines the role of the attorney in the juvenile justice process and discusses the future direction of the juvenile court.

Denzin, Norman K., ed. CHILDREN AND THEIR CARETAKERS. New Brunswick, N.J.: Transaction Books, 1973. 333 p.

Collection of essays charging that parents, schools, and juvenile courts are failing in their responsibilities to children. The evils of both day care centers and the Department of Defense military summer programs for ghetto youth are particularly singled out. The battered child and the juvenile court system are also discussed.

Farson, Richard. BIRTHRIGHTS: A BILL OF RIGHTS FOR CHILDREN. New York: Macmillan, 1974. 248 p.

The author expresses his concern that the basic rights and needs of children are ignored by society. He cites inadequately designed classrooms and playgrounds, a failing child health care system, a lack of inexpensive day care facilities and harmful toys and play equipment to support his case. He pleads for adults to respond to child suffering in a more positive way.

Foster, Henry H. A "BILL OF RIGHTS" FOR CHILDREN. Foreword by Justine Wise Polier. Springfield, Ill.: Charles C. Thomas, Publisher, 1974. 88 p. Biblio., index.

Legal rights of children as people: current problems and remedies.

Gottlieb, David, ed. CHILDREN'S LIBERATION. Englewood Cliffs, N.J.: Prentice-Hall, 1973. 192 p.

A collection of essays which speak to adults on behalf of children. Children as victims, industrialization and urbanization, parent-child relationships, the inadequacies of the educational system, and the effects of environment and pollution on the child are all discussed.

# Children's Rights

Harvard Educational Review. THE RIGHTS OF CHILDREN. Cambridge, Mass.: November 1973 and February 1974.

A special two-part section of the HARVARD EDUCATIONAL REVIEW comprising thirteen thorough articles on such topics as hyperactive children, abused and neglected children, foster care, and so forth.

Holt, John Caldwell. ESCAPE FROM CHILDHOOD. New York: E.P. Dutton & Co., 1974. 286 p.

A plea that children be granted the rights, privileges, and responsibilities that adults are accorded.

James, Howard. CHILDREN IN TROUBLE. New York: David McKay Co., 1970. 340 p.

A journalist depicts the grim conditions of facilities for youthful delinquents and orphaned children. Suggests ways to help.

Katz, Sanford N. WHEN PARENTS FAIL: THE LAW'S RESPONSE TO FAMILY BREAKDOWN. Boston: Beacon Press, 1971. 251 p. Appendix.

Basic information supporting the current argument that a child's rights and emotional well-being should be the primary considerations when social agencies and the courts intervene in family life. The author contends that when parents fail, the laws, the courts, and the agencies also fail.

\_\_\_\_\_, ed. THE YOUNGEST MINORITY: LAWYERS IN DEFENSE OF CHILDREN. Chicago: American Bar Association, 1974. 350 p.

A collection of nontechnical articles from the FAMILY LAW QUARTERLY covering the legal rights of children in areas such as child custody, foster care, child abuse, and right to treatment. Presents a bill of rights for children.

National Council on Crime and Delinquency. JUVENILE JUSTICE CONFOUNDED: PRETENSIONS AND REALITIES OF TREATMENT SERVICES. Hackensack, N.J.: 1972. 124 p. Appendix, tables.

Highly critical study of the services available to children being placed by the Family Court in New York City. Discusses the children appearing before the court; the policies and practices of voluntary child-care agencies; and the environment of state institutions for delinquent, mentally ill, and mentally retarded children.

Norman, Sherwood. THE YOUTH SERVICE BUREAU: A KEY TO DELINQUENCY PREVENTION. Hackensack, N.J.: National Council on Crime and Delinquency, 1973. 256 p.

# Children's Rights

The Youth Service Bureau is a new type of voluntary, noncoercive, neighborhood-controlled community agency whose purpose is to divert youngsters from the juvenile justice system. This book, based on two years of research, describes the establishment, funding, operation, and achievements of such agencies.

Rioux, J. William, and Sandow, Stuart A. CHILDREN, PARENTS AND SCHOOL RECORDS. Columbia, Md.: National Committee for Citizen Education, 1974.

The authors discuss the reasons why parents should have access to their children's school records and provide a step-by-step procedure for gaining such access.

Schorr, Alvin L., ed. CHILDREN AND DECENT PEOPLE. New York: Basic Books, Publishers, 1974. 222 p. Biblio., index.

Eleven essays that provide insight into the needs of children by examining the failures of child care and child welfare programs. Presents different viewpoints on the status of day care, children's institutions, child health programs, foster care, and the juvenile justice system. Offers proposals to overcome the inherent weaknesses.

Soman, Shirley Camper. LET'S STOP DESTROYING OUR CHILDREN. New York: Hawthorn Books, 1974. 274 p. Illus., index.

A social worker points out the mental and physical mistreatment of children by parents, the courts, industry (clothing and toy), news media, and even the social welfare structure. She appeals for a fifteen-point program, backed by federal and private funds, to protect the rights of children.

Strouse, Jean. UP AGAINST THE LAW: THE LEGAL RIGHTS OF PEOPLE UNDER TWENTY-ONE. New York: New American Library, 1970. 269 p. Biblio., illus. Paperbound.

For young people as well as parents, this useful book answers some questions and lists sources of legal help and advice.

Wilkerson, Albert E., ed. THE RIGHTS OF CHILDREN: EMERGENT CONCEPTS IN LAW AND SOCIETY. Philadelphia: Temple University Press, 1973. 313 p.

Twenty essays encompassing the opinions of noted lawyers, judges, and social workers on the legal and social rights of children. Covers the advancements in children's rights, as well as the problems awaiting solution.

# Children's Rights

## PERIODICALS

CHILD WELFARE. New York: Child Welfare League of America, 1920-- . Monthly.

    Contains articles on child welfare services written by social workers, psychiatrists, and social scientists.

## PAMPHLETS AND/OR GOVERNMENT DOCUMENTS

Unless otherwise noted the materials are available free of charge. Prices quoted are subject to change. Payment should accompany order.

THE JUVENILE COURT COMES OF AGE. By Junius L. Allison, 1973. 35 cents. Publication no. 419. Available from: Public Affairs Pamphlets, 381 Park Avenue, South, New York, N.Y.

    Discusses the reform of court proceedings and the fundamental rights of juveniles under its jurisdiction.

WHITE HOUSE CONFERENCE ON CHILDREN, 1970. Report to the President. 1971. 451 p. Appendix. $4.75. Available from: Superintendent of Documents, Government Printing Office, Washington, D.C. 20402.

    Major report calls for reforms that make children and families first priority. Urges creation of a national center for child advocacy and a "National Children's Media Foundation."

## ORGANIZATIONS AND/OR SOURCES OF MATERIALS, FREE OR AT LOW COST

Children's Defense Fund
1520 New Hampshire Ave., N.W.
Washington, D.C. 20036

    Formed in 1973 as a nonprofit organization of "lawyers, federal policy monitors, researchers and community liaison people" who seek to "improve the conditions of American children through public information, research, administrative agency monitoring, litigation and through technical backup to local groups working with children." Has issued two reports, CHILDREN OUT OF SCHOOL IN AMERICA, and SCHOOL SUSPENSION--ARE THEY HELPING CHILDREN? 1976 reports will focus on children's rights to privacy, children in adult jails, improvements in health services for children, and banished children.

# Children's Rights

Children's Rights
3443 Seventeenth Street, N.W.
Washington, D.C. 20010        Phone (202) 462-7573

    An organization of individuals interested in legislation concerning children's welfare, particularly federal legislation concerning child snatching. Conducts public education programs.

Citizen's Committee for Children of
   New York City
2 Park Avenue
New York, N.Y. 10016        Phone (212) 725-7940

    Organization of professional and lay persons that acts as an advocate for the children of New York. Supports research, investigation, and reports on the fields of mental health, education, health, child welfare, and children's rights.

National Association for the Education
   of Young Children
1834 Connecticut Avenue, N.W.
Washington, D.C. 20009        Phone (202) 232-8777

    Develops standards to ensure high quality programs for young children. Serves as national information resource: issues the journal YOUNG CHILDREN, as well as books, pamphlets, and educational materials on the education and development of young children.

National Council on Crime and Delinquency
Continental Plaza
411 Hackensack Avenue
Hackensack, N.J. 07601        Phone (201) 488-0400

    "National organization of social workers, prison officials, judges and others interested in probation, parole, juvenile and family courts, detention services, and the prevention, control, and treatment of crime and delinquency." Furnishes legal advisory service. Publishes numerous books, pamphlets, and training materials. Publications list is available on request.

## AUDIOVISUAL MATERIALS

### Films

THIS CHILD IS RATED "X." 1971. 16mm, 53 min., sound, color.

    Describes abuses at juvenile correctional facilities throughout the United States.

    Available from: NBC Educational Enterprises, 30 Rockefeller Plaza, New York, N.Y. 10020.

# DAY CARE

(See also Adoption, Child Welfare, and Foster Care; Food, Clothing, and Furniture)

## BOOKS

### Current Sources

Breitbart, Vicki. THE DAY CARE BOOK: THE WHY, WHAT AND HOW OF COMMUNITY DAY CARE. New York: Alfred A. Knopf, 1974. 211 p. Illus. Paperbound.

> A practical handbook of articles and ideas that guides the reader through the steps in setting up and running a day-care collective. Incorporates information on acquiring funds, licences, space, staff, equipment, and curriculum assistance.

Child Welfare League of America. THE CHANGING DIMENSIONS OF DAY CARE. New York: 1970. 62 p. Biblio.

> Eleven articles on the many facets of day care.

Day Care and Child Development Council of America. ALTERNATIVES IN QUALITY CHILD CARE: A GUIDE FOR THINKING AND PLANNING. New York: Behavioral Publications, 1972. 80 p.

> Types of day care, styles of day-care programs, degrees of parental involvement, and community and family impact. A readable, basic resource for making decisions on day-care programming.

Evans, E. Belle, et al. DAY CARE: HOW TO PLAN, DEVELOP, AND OPERATE A DAY CARE CENTER. Boston: Beacon Press, 1971. 337 p. Biblio., illus., index.

> First-hand information on choosing and equipping a site, securing funding and licensing, and training staff. Excellent for anyone interested in starting a day-care center.

## Day Care

Evans, E. Belle, and Saia, George E. DAY CARE FOR INFANTS. Boston: Beacon Press, 1972. 216 p. Biblio., appendices, illus., index.

    Informative and practical guide to starting and operating a quality day-care program for infants under the age of three. The authors also offer a rationale for placing infants in group day-care centers.

Fein, Greta G., and Clarke-Stewart, Alison, with the support of the Foundation for Child Development. DAY CARE IN CONTEXT. New York: John Wiley & Sons, 1973. 359 p.

    Traces the history of the day-care movement and discusses the participants and the programs therein. The total day-care program as it affects the growth and development of children is evaluated. This is a comprehensive examination of the subject.

Griffin, Al. HOW TO START AND OPERATE A DAY CARE HOME. Chicago: Henry Regnery Co., 1973. 233 p. Biblio., index.

    Fourteen chapters of advice on how to organize, run, and improve a child care center. Covers such topics as licensing requirements, zoning laws, equipment, meals, and parent relationships.

Keyserling, Mary Dublin. WINDOWS ON DAY CARE. New York: National Council of Jewish Women, 1972. 248 p.

    A timely and readable report based on a survey of actual day-care conditions in seventy-seven communities. After analyzing the survey data, the former director of the Women's Bureau, U.S. Department of Labor, concludes that day care is costly and in increasingly short supply. She recommends that a comprehensive, nationwide child care service be made available to all families who wish to use it.

Parker, Ronald K., and Knitzer, Jane. DAY CARE AND PRESCHOOL SERVICES: TRENDS AND ISSUES. Atlanta, Ga.: Avatar Press, 1972. 74 p.

    Originally prepared as a background paper for the 1970 White House Conference on Children and Youth, this clearly written and concise revision surveys past and present day-care service, with trends for the future.

Roby, Pamela, ed. CHILD CARE--WHO CARES?: FOREIGN AND DOMESTIC INFANT AND EARLY CHILDHOOD DEVELOPMENT POLICIES. Foreword by Shirley Chisholm. New York: Basic Books, Publishers, 1973. 456 p. Illus., index.

    Child care experts analyze the need for child care programs, "current" practices in the United States and other countries, and proposals for creating and expanding existing programs.

Practical aspects as well as public policy and national goals are covered. Wealth of information for concerned parents.

Steinfels, Margaret O'Brien. WHO'S MINDING THE CHILDREN: THE HISTORY AND POLITICS OF DAY CARE IN AMERICA. New York: Simon & Schuster, 1973. 281 p. Biblio., index.

>Seeing the great potential for child-centered day-care facilities, the author details the history of day care in America, criticizes the 1971 presidential veto of the Comprehensive Child Development Act, and focuses on day care as a positive response to the changing needs of changing families.

## PERIODICALS

DAY CARE AND CHILD DEVELOPMENT REPORTS. Washington, D.C.: Plus Publications, 1971-- . Biweekly.

>Newsletter on child care legislation and happenings.

DAY CARE AND EARLY EDUCATION. New York: Human Sciences Press, 1973-- . Bimonthly.

>Popular-styled bimonthly that draws together reports and progress from the diverse areas of early childhood, politics, child psychology, business, labor, and community activism. For professionals, paraprofessionals, and concerned parents. Includes book reviews.

YOUNG CHILDREN. Washington, D.C.: National Association for the Education of Young Children, 1964-- . Six times a year.

>Articles of interest to personnel who work with young children (preschool and nursery) and their parents in day-care centers, camps, and nursery schools.

## PAMPHLETS AND/OR GOVERNMENT DOCUMENTS

Unless otherwise noted the materials are available free of charge. Prices quoted are subject to change. Payment should accompany order.

### Bibliographies

A DAY CARE BIBLIOGRAPHY. 1971. 9 p. Available from: New York State Department of Education, Bureau of Child Development and Parent Education, Albany, N.Y. 12224.

>Selected list of sources (books, articles, organizations) relating to day care.

# Day Care

DAY CARE REFERENCE SOURCES: AN ANNOTATED BIBLIOGRAPHY. 1970. 29 p. Available from: Institute for Interdisciplinary Studies, American Rehabilitation Foundation, 123 East Grant Street, Minneapolis, Minn. 55403.

    Lists references on day care and related subjects available from the federal government and national voluntary organizations.

## Current Sources

DAY CARE: SERVING INFANTS. 1972. 87 p. Publication no. (OCD) 73-14. Available from: Office of Human Development, Publications Distribution Unit, Department of Health, Education and Welfare, Washington, D.C. 20201.

    How to organize a day-care center, including daily planning and specific activities for babies of various ages.

DAY CARE: SERVING PRESCHOOL CHILDREN. By Donald J. Cohen, M.D. 1974. 164 p. Biblio., photos. Publication no. (OHD) 75-1057. Available from: Office of Human Development, Publications Distribution Unit, Department of Health, Education and Welfare, Washington, D.C. 20201.

    This basic handbook provides a broad overview of all aspects of day care for children aged three to six years. Covers budgeting, licensing, parent involvement, and curriculum staffing. Describes nine day-care programs. For parents and professionals.

DAY CARE: SERVING SCHOOL AGE CHILDREN. 1971. 71 p. 70 cents. Available from: Superintendent of Documents, Government Printing Office, Washington, D.C. 20402.

    This pamphlet, the fourth in a series on day care from the Office of Child Development, examines the developmental needs of children (aged six to fourteen) in a day-care setting.

DAY CARE FOR AMERICA'S CHILDREN. By E. Robert La Crosse, Jr., M.D. 1971. 24 p. 35 cents. Available from: Public Affairs Committee, 381 Park Avenue, South, New York, N.Y. 10016.

    The various aspects of day-care programs covered briefly and concisely.

DAY CARE FOR YOUR CHILDREN. 1974. 15 p. Publication no. (OHD) 74-47. Available from: Office of Human Development, Publications Distribution Unit, Department of Health, Education and Welfare, Washington, D.C. 20201.

    Advice and guidelines for selecting good day-care services.

EARLY CHILDHOOD PROGRAMS FOR MIGRANTS: ALTERNATIVES FOR THE STATES. 1972. 71 p. $1.00. Available from: Education Commission of the States, 300 Lincoln Tower, 1860 Lincoln Street, Denver, Colo. 80203.

    This carefully prepared and informative pamphlet presents a quick look at the present status of preschool programs for children of migrant families. Also recognizes the need for expanded, alternative programs.

## Day Care

FEDERAL FUNDS FOR DAY CARE PROJECTS. U.S. Department of Labor, Women's Bureau. 1972. 91 p. $1.00. Available from: Superintendent of Documents, Government Printing Office, Washington, D.C. 20201.

    This publication outlines the programs of federal agencies that fund day-care projects.

"THE GOOD LIFE" FOR INFANTS AND TODDLERS. By Mary Elizabeth Keister. 1970. 48 p. Illus. Available from: National Association for the Education of Young Children, 1834 Connecticut Avenue, N.W., Washington, D.C. 20009.

    Report on a federally funded infant care project at the University of North Carolina at Greensboro. Covers aspects of equipment and staff and provides a workable blueprint for future care of preschoolers.

A GUIDE FOR PLANNING FOOD SERVICE IN CHILD CARE CENTERS. 1971. 22 p. Available from: U.S. Department of Agriculture, Food and Nutrition Service, Washington, D.C. 20250.

    This guide describes ways to plan food service for preschoolers in child care centers. Covers food preparation, suggested menus, tips for purchasing, and sanitation.

GUIDES FOR DAY CARE LICENSING. 1973. 59 p. Publication no. (OCD) 73-1053. Available from: Office of Child Development, Day Care Service Division, P.O. Box 1182, Washington, D.C. 20013.

    Compilation of suggested licensing guidelines to insure quality care for all children in day-care programs.

A MODEL FOR QUALITY DAY CARE. 1973. 11 p. 25 cents. Available from: Business and Professional Women's Foundation, 2012 Massachusetts Avenue, N.W., Washington, D.C. 20036.

    Dr. Joan Bergstrom, consultant on child care and day-care services, gives useful statistics about the need for child care services and provides guidelines for the operation of such services.

NUTRITION AND FEEDING OF INFANTS AND CHILDREN UNDER THREE IN GROUP DAY CARE. 1973. 32 p. Available from: Maternal and Child Health Service, 5600 Fishers Lane, Rockville, Md. 20852.

    For parents interested in day care, this booklet discusses the nutritional needs of infants and children under three. Gives information on daily food plans, food preparation, and equipment for feeding. Lists of suggested readings on nutrition and food service.

TAX DEDUCTIONS FOR CHILD CARE. 1974. 4 p. Publication no. 254C. Available from: Consumer Information, Public Documents Distribution Center, Pueblo, Colo. 81009.

    Practical tips.

# Day Care

## ORGANIZATIONS AND/OR SOURCES OF MATERIALS, FREE OR AT LOW COST

The Day Care and Child Development
  Council of America
1012 Fourteenth Street, N.W.
Washington, D.C. 20005     Phone (202) 638-2316

> "Nonprofit advocacy organization committed to increasing the availability of child services and raising the quality of all child care programs" through a program of information dissemination of publications, technical assistance to day-care projects, and public education. Annual publications catalog is available free; also publishes a bimonthly newsletter, RESOURCES FOR CHILD CARE, and a monthly magazine, VOICE FOR CHILDREN.

Education Development Center
55 Chapel Street
Newton, Mass. 02158

> Free pamphlets available on day care and ealy childhood matters.

Women's Action Alliance
370 Lexington Avenue
New York, N.Y. 10017

> Resource and consultation center concerned with day care. Publications include HOW TO ORGANIZE A CHILD CARE CENTER and NON-SEXIST CHILD DEVELOPMENT PROJECT.

## AUDIOVISUAL MATERIALS

### Films

DAY CARE TODAY. N.d. 27 min., color.

> Up-to-date view of three day-care centers and how they respond parents' needs. Good for parents of young children.
>
> Available from: Polymorph Films, 331 Newbury Street, Boston, Mass. 02115.

# DEATH, DIVORCE, AND SEPARATION

## BOOKS

### Dated but Still Relevant

Arnstein, Helene [S.]. WHAT TO TELL YOUR CHILD ABOUT BIRTH, DEATH, ILLNESS, DIVORCE, AND OTHER FAMILY CRISES. New York: Bobbs-Merrill Co., 1962. 202 p. Biblio.

> Most comprehensive and devoid of pat formulas, this book stresses the importance of effective communication between parents and children in the crisis situations that they both face.

Despert, J. Louise, M.D. CHILDREN OF DIVORCE. Garden City, N.Y.: Doubleday & Co., 1953. 298 p.

> Leading child psychiatrist in her classic work describes the impact of divorce on children and offers suggestions for helping the child adjust.

Grollman, Earl A., ed. EXPLAINING DEATH TO CHILDREN. Introduction by Louise Bates Ames. Boston: Beacon Press, 1967. 296 p. Biblio.

> Various authorities focus on the feelings and reactions of a child faced with the loss of a loved one. Helps parents face and answer the child's questions about death and dying.

_____. EXPLAINING DIVORCE TO CHILDREN. Introduction by Louise Bates Ames. Boston: Beacon Press, 1969. 257 p. Biblio.

> Covers counseling before divorce, telling children about the divorce, visiting privileges, remarrying, and adjusting to the stress that accompanies a family breakup.

# Death, Divorce, Separation

Jackson, Edgar N.  TELLING A CHILD ABOUT DEATH.  New York:  Hawthorn Books, 1965.  91 p.

    Reverend Jackson discusses how to talk to children about death and how to include them in the family experience in a reassuring way.

## Current Sources

Abt, Lawrence E., and Stuart, Irving, eds.  CHILDREN OF SEPARATION AND DIVORCE.  New York:  Grossman Publishers, 1972.  313 p.  Biblio., index.

    Various psychologists, lawyers, social workers, and clergymen present a broad view of the problems that divorced and separated parents face in dealing with their children.  Topics include the views of parents, children's perceptions, religious conceptions, deprived children, education, and socialization of the child.  The editors also include a helpful chapter on "Community Resources and Assistance Available for Parents and Children."

Anthony, Sylvia.  THE DISCOVERY OF DEATH IN CHILDHOOD AND AFTER.  New York:  Basic Books, Publishers, 1972.  280 p.

    Helpful for those looking for a way to understand and deal with the child's discovery of death.  Examines children's responses to death.

Easson, William M., M.D.  THE DYING CHILD:  THE MANAGEMENT OF THE CHILD WHO IS DYING.  Springfield, Ill.:  Charles C. Thomas, Publisher, 1970.  103 p.

    Well-written and clear examination of what dying means to children at various stages of development.  The reactions of the family are included.

Gardner, Richard A., M.D.  THE BOYS AND GIRLS BOOK ABOUT DIVORCE, WITH AN INTRODUCTION FOR PARENTS.  New York:  Science House, 1970.  159 p.  Illus.

    Well-illustrated book for children of divorce.  Covers the child's fears and pains.  Good for parents as well.

Grollman, Earl A.  TALKING ABOUT DEATH:  A DIALOGUE BETWEEN PARENT AND CHILD.  Boston:  Beacon Press, 1970.  29 p.  Illus.

    To help parents explain death to children.

Halporn, Roberta, comp. and ed.  CHILDREN AND DYING:  AN EXPLORATION AND A SELECTIVE BIBLIOGRAPHY.  2d rev. and enl. ed.  New York:

## Death, Divorce, Separation

Health Sciences Publishing Corp., 1974. 106 p. Paperbound.

> These essays plead for more research on the psychological aspects of dying children, and offer advice to nurses, physicians, and parents for handling this all-too-painful experience. Useful bibliographies are included.

Noble, June, and Noble, William. THE CUSTODY TRAP. New York: Hawthorn Books, 1975. 163 p. Index.

> Candid examination (through case histories, interviews, and court records) of the custody problems in divorce proceedings. Offers suggestions to ease the plight of both parents and children.

Reed, Elizabeth L. HELPING CHILDREN WITH THE MYSTERY OF DEATH. Nashville, Tenn.: Abingdon Press, 1970. 143 p.

> Guidance, within a religious framework, for parents, teachers, and ministers in helping children face the reality of death. Includes source materials, practical suggestions, poems and prose, and Scripture selections.

Rowland, Peter. CHILDREN APART: HOW PARENTS CAN HELP YOUNG CHILDREN COPE WITH BEING AWAY FROM THE FAMILY. New York: Pantheon Books, 1974. 150 p. Biblio., index.

> Simply written, practical guide to the problems resulting when young children are separated from their parents because of hospital stay, adoption, divorce, and so on.

Ruina, Edith. MOVING: A COMMON-SENSE GUIDE TO RELOCATING YOUR FAMILY. New York: Funk & Wagnalls, 1970. 238 p.

> Practical advice by a social worker on the many aspects of moving, including helping children adjust.

Wolf, Anna W.M. HELPING YOUR CHILD TO UNDERSTAND DEATH. New York: Child Study Press, 1973. 64 p. Paperbound.

> A thoughtful guide for parents, written in a question-and-answer format.

Zeligs, Rose. CHILDREN'S EXPERIENCE WITH DEATH. Springfield, Ill.: Charles C. Thomas, Publisher, 1974. 247 p. Biblio.

> Written for professionals and parents. Covers the child's developmental concepts of death, his or her fears, response to the loss of a parent, the influence of religion, and the dying child himself.

# Death, Divorce, Separation

## PAMPHLETS AND/OR GOVERNMENT DOCUMENTS

Unless otherwise noted the materials are available free of charge. Prices quoted are subject to change. Payment should accompany order.

HELPING YOUR CHILD TO UNDERSTAND DEATH. 1973. 64 p. $1.50. Available from: Child Study Association of America/Wel-Met, 50 Madison Avenue, New York, N.Y. 10010

    Handling a sensitive problem.

WHEN CHILDREN MOVE FROM SCHOOL TO SCHOOL. 1972. 48 p. Available from: Association for Childhood Education International, 3615 Wisconsin Avenue, N.W., Washington, D.C. 20016.

    Revised edition covers the social, emotional, and academic problems of the child who changes schools. Includes a reading list for children.

# DISCIPLINE

(See also Adolescence; Behavior Modification;
Chapters on Child Development)

## BOOKS

### Historical Perspective

Homan, Walter Joseph. CHILDREN AND QUAKERISM. 1939. Reprint. New York: Arno Press, 1972. 162 p. Biblio.

    Training Quaker children to respect family and community traditions by strong parental guidance.

### Dated but Still Relevant

Baruch, Dorothy. NEW WAYS IN DISCIPLINE. New York: McGraw-Hill Book Co., 1949. 280 p. Illus.

    Informed, practical, and highly respected work.

Dreikurs, Rudolf, M.D., and Soltz, Vicki. CHILDREN: THE CHALLENGE. New York: Duell, Sloan & Pearce, 1964. 335 p. o.p.

    This book deals with discipline and provides illustrative examples.

### Current Sources

Corsini, Raymond J., and Painter, Genevieve, M.D. THE PRACTICAL PARENT. New York: Harper & Row Publishers, 1975. 248 p. Biblio., index.

    A clinical psychologist, using the theories of Alfred Adler, counsels parents on common problems of child guidance and discipline such as eating, bedtime, temper tantrums, messy rooms, and fighting at home.

De Camp, Catherine Crook, and U.S. News and World Report Books, eds.

# Discipline

TEACH YOUR CHILD TO MANAGE MONEY: A GUIDE FOR TOTS THROUGH TEENS. New York: U.S. News and World Report, 1975. 285 p. Index, photos.

> Written for parents, although some sections can be read by children. Presents the steps for training children and young people to manage money.

Dobson, James C., Jr. DARE TO DISCIPLINE. Wheaton, Ill.: Tyndale House Publishers, 1972. 228 p.

> A psychologist advises parents and teachers on managing children.

Dreikurs, Rudolf, M.D. THE CHALLENGE OF CHILD TRAINING: A PARENT'S GUIDE. New York: Hawthorn Books, 1972. 160 p. Index. Paperbound.

> Well-known psychiatrist explores the reasons behind children's behavior, discusses some common mistakes in child training, and describes the most effective methods of training.

_____. COPING WITH CHILDREN'S MISBEHAVIOR: A PARENT'S GUIDE. New York: Hawthorn Books, 1972. 162 p. Index.

> Discusses the reasons for misbehavior and gives different methods for dealing with trying situations including temper tantrums and eating difficulties.

Dreikurs, Rudolf, M.D., and Grey, Loren. A PARENT'S GUIDE TO CHILD DISCIPLINE. New York: Hawthorn Books, 1970. 112 p. Index.

> A new approach to child-rearing known as "logical consequences" and its applications in such disciplinary problems as refusing to eat, fighting with siblings, bedwetting, and neglecting household chores. Specific step-by-step instructions are included.

Gordon, Thomas. PARENT EFFECTIVENESS TRAINING: THE "NO-LOSE" PROGRAM FOR RAISING RESPONSIBLE CHILDREN. New York: Peter H. Wyden/Publisher, 1970. 338 p. Biblio., illus.

> Deals most effectively with the problems confronting parents and children. Parents, however, should be a bit wary of the author's supreme confidence in his methods.

Grey, Loren. DISCIPLINE WITHOUT FEAR: CHILD TRAINING DURING THE EARLY SCHOOL YEARS. New York: Hawthorn Books, 1974. 191 p.

> The principles of Adler and Dreikurs applied to the practical problems of raising children. Gives examples of specific situations and follow-up suggestions for correcting children's misbehavior.

# Discipline

_____. DISCIPLINE WITHOUT TYRANNY: CHILD TRAINING DURING THE FIRST FIVE YEARS. New York: Hawthorn Books, 1972. 192 p. Index.

    Using the theories of Alfred Adler, the author discusses the behavior of preschool children and advises parents on coping with and curbing the "tyranny" of their children.

Madsen, Clifford K., and Madsen, Charles H., Jr. PARENTS/CHILDREN/ DISCIPLINE: A POSITIVE APPROACH. Boston: Allyn & Bacon, 1972. 213 p.

    See Madsen, p. 20.

Moore, Dewey J. PREVENTING MISBEHAVIOR IN CHILDREN. Springfield, Ill.: Charles C. Thomas, Publisher, 1972. 171 p. Paperbound.

    See Moore, p. 20.

Schwarz, Berthold Eric, M.D., and Ruggieri, Bartholomew A., M.D. YOU CAN RAISE DECENT CHILDREN. New Rochelle, N.Y.: Arlington House, 1971. 345 p. Index.

    A psychiatrist and a pediatrician join forces to attack the parent's permissiveness in children's antisocial behavior. They show parents how to cope with the problems of drug use, disrespect, sexual misbehavior, stealing, and similar problems.

Sheen, Fulton J. CHILDREN AND PARENTS. New York: Simon & Schuster, 1970. 121 p.

    A series of pastoral essays by the noted Catholic bishop on such subjects as the duties of children and parents, teenage rebellion, the sexual revolution, courtesy, and spanking.

Weinstein, Grace W. CHILDREN AND MONEY. New York: Charterhouse Books, 1975. 214 p. Biblio., index.

    Practical suggestions on teaching children the use of money. Ranges from the piggy bank to the checking account. Covers allowances, payment for chores, shoplifting, and the impact of advertising.

## PAMPHLETS AND/OR GOVERNMENT DOCUMENTS

Unless otherwise noted the materials are available free of charge. Prices quoted are subject to change. Payment should accompany order.

THE WHY AND HOW OF DISCIPLINE. 75 cents. Available from: Child Study Association of America, Wel-Met, 50 Madison Avenue, New York, N.Y. 10010.

    For professionals as well as parents.

# DRUGS, ALCOHOL, AND THEIR ABUSE

(See also Adolescence)

## BOOKS

### Dated but Still Relevant

Land, Herman W. WHAT YOU CAN DO ABOUT DRUGS AND YOUR CHILD. Hertfordshire, Engl.: Hart, 1969. 240 p. Biblio.

> A book for parents concerned about the potential or actual problem of teenage drug abuse.

### Reference

National Coordinating Council on Drug Abuse Education and Information. DRUG EDUCATION DIRECTORY. Washington, D.C.: 1972. 139 p.

> For each organization belonging to the council, the book lists the purpose, executives and representatives, publications, films and services, meetings and conferences.

### Current Sources

Andrews, Matthew. THE PARENT'S GUIDE TO DRUGS. Garden City, N.Y.: Doubleday & Co., 1972. 186 p. Illus. (color).

> Concise handbook that describes the most commonly used drugs, gives a state-by-state directory of sources for emergency aid, and lists educational films and organizations active in drug education.

Association for Childhood Education. CHILDREN AND DRUGS. Washington, D.C.: 1972. 64 p.

> Discusses causes of drug abuse in younger children and presents guidelines for parents who fear that their child is using drugs.

# Drugs, Alcohol, and Their Abuse

Includes an annotated bibliography.

Barnes, Donald E., ed. PREVENTING DRUG ABUSE: IDEAS, INFORMATION, AND LINES OF ACTION FOR PARENTS, YOUNG PEOPLE, SCHOOLS, AND COMMUNITIES. New York: Holt, Rinehart and Winston, 1972. 109 p.

> Information geared to parents and youths concerning the prevention of drug abuse in schools and in the community.

Blum, Richard H., et al. HORATIO ALGER'S CHILDREN. San Francisco: Jossey-Bass, Publishers, 1972. 327 p.

> The author shows that family characteristics such as class, religion, drinking habits, medical practices, and attitudes toward authority are the key influences on drug use by young people.

Brenner, Joseph, M.D., et al. DRUGS AND YOUTH: THE MEDICAL, PSYCHIATRIC AND LEGAL FACTS. New York: Liveright Publishing Corp., 1970. 258 p. Biblio., illus.

> Practical information on drugs including definitions. Summarizes the laws concerning drugs in all the states.

Child Study Association of America. YOUR CHILD AND DRUGS. New York: 1971. 73 p.

> This book clears up some misconceptions. It discusses parental intervention, drug education, and the problem of communicating with children. Suggests that parents explore their own attitudes toward drugs.

Gannon, Frank. DRUGS: WHAT THEY ARE/HOW THEY LOOK/WHAT THEY DO. New York: Third Press, 1971. 182 p. Illus.

> Practical guide to identifying drugs.

Goldhill, Paul M. A PARENT'S GUIDE TO THE PREVENTION AND CONTROL OF DRUG ABUSE. Chicago: Henry Regnery Co., 1971. 185 p. Biblio.

> This book, by a specialist in pediatric psychiatry, underscores the need for healthy family relationships as deterrents to drug abuse. The author also describes the professional help available for drug abusers.

Lieberman, Florence. BEFORE ADDICTION: HOW TO HELP YOUTH. New York: Behavioral Publications, 1973. 131 p. Biblio., index.

> Alerts parents to the circumstances and difficulties which can

## Drugs, Alcohol, and Their Abuse

launch adolescents into drug use; gives advice on coping with such situations.

Louria, Donald Bruce, M.D. OVERCOMING DRUGS. New York: McGraw-Hill Book Co., 1971. 233 p.

> Complete discussion of all aspects of the drug problem, including an excellent chapter on a program for parents.

Love, Harold D. YOUTH AND THE DRUG PROBLEM: A GUIDE FOR PARENTS AND TEACHERS. Springfield, Ill.: Charles C. Thomas, Publisher, 1971. 101 p.

> Defines and explains drug abuse, drug dependence, and the motivations for drug use. Treatment, prevention, and legal controls are covered in depth.

Marin, Peter. UNDERSTANDING DRUG ABUSE: AN ADULT'S GUIDE TO DRUGS AND THE YOUNG. New York: Harper & Row Publishers, 1971. 163 p.

> Covers toxic reactions and side effects of drugs, community programs available to the drug user, and the laws regarding drug abuse. The book's purpose is to give parents information on which to base their decisions.

Meyer, Roger E., M.D. GUIDE TO DRUG REHABILITATION. Boston: Beacon Press, 1972. 171 p.

> A down-to-earth guide containing major approaches to drug rehabilitation.

Rosenthal, Mitchell S. DRUGS, PARENTS AND CHILDREN: THE THREE-WAY CONNECTION. New York: Houghton Mifflin Co., 1972. 182 p.

> A guidebook for parents.

Schepp, Steven, and Rydell, Wendy. POT, PILLS AND POWDERS: THE TRUTH ABOUT DRUGS. New York: Western Publishing Co., 1972. 125 p.

> An excellent overview of all aspects of drug use. Should appeal to both children and parents.

Scott, Edward M. THE ADOLESCENT GAP: RESEARCH FINDINGS ON DRUG USING AND NON-DRUG USING TEENS. Foreword by the Reverend Theodore Hesburgh. Springfield, Ill.: Charles C. Thomas, Publisher, 1972. 143 p. Biblio., illus., tables.

> This well-written and useful volume deals with the social and psychological aspects of drug abuse in youth from the viewpoints

# Drugs, Alcohol, and Their Abuse

of both user and nonuser. Required reading for parents, teachers, and counselors.

Sorenson, Andrew A., ed. CONFRONTING DRUG ABUSE: APPROACHES TO ITS PREVENTION AND TREATMENT. Philadelphia, Pa.: Pilgrim Book Press, 1972. 128 p.

Readable guide for parents, teachers, clergymen, and politicians interested in combating drug abuse at the level of the local community.

Travers, Milton. EACH OTHER'S VICTIMS. New York: Pocket Books, 1971. 141 p. Paperbound.

A father relates his experiences when he learns that his son is hooked on drugs.

## PAMPHLETS AND /OR GOVERNMENT DOCUMENTS

Unless otherwise noted the materials are available free of charge. Prices quoted are subject to change. Payment should accompany order.

### Bibliographies

A GUIDE TO DRUG ABUSE EDUCATION AND INFORMATION MATERIALS. 1972. 45 p. 50 cents. Available from: Superintendent of Documents, Government Printing Office, Washington, D.C. 20402.

Lists films, filmstrips, simulation games, and so forth.

SELECTED REFERENCES FOR DRUG INFORMATION CENTERS. Selected Reference Series 8, no. 1. 1974. 30 p. Available from: Alcohol, Drug Abuse and Mental Health Administration, 5600 Fishers Lane, Rockville, Md. 20852.

Lists books, periodicals, organizations, and information resources on drug education, law and public policy, marijuana treatment, and rehabilitation. Helpful to staff and clients of new drug information centers.

### Current Sources

ADDICTION: WHY DRUGS, ALCOHOL, TOBACCO? 1971. 47 p. 40 cents. Available from: Xerox Education Publications, 245 Long Hill Road, Middletown, Conn. 06457.

Discusses physical and psychological causes for addiction to alcohol, tobacco, and drugs. Describes the available medical treatments.

## Drugs, Alcohol, and Their Abuse

ANSWERS TO THE MOST FREQUENTLY ASKED QUESTIONS ABOUT DRUG ABUSE. 1971. 30 p. Available from: National Clearinghouse for Drug Abuse Information, P.O. Box 1635, Rockville, Md. 20850.

> Nontechnical answers at that.

DRUG ABUSE AND YOUR CHILD. 1970. 28 p. Publication no. 448. 35 cents. Available from: Public Affairs Committee, 381 Park Avenue South, New York, N.Y. 10016.

> The reasons young people turn to drugs, the signs of drug abuse, and some suggestions for combating abuse.

DRUG TAKING IN YOUTH. By Louise G. Richards and John H. Langer. 1972. 48 p. Appendix, biblio. 40 cents. Available from: Superintendent of Documents, Government Printing Office, Washington, D.C. 20402.

> Concise overview of the social and psychological aspects of youthful drug taking plus a discussion of educational programs for preventing drug abuse.

GROWING UP IN AMERICA: A BACKGROUND TO CONTEMPORARY DRUG ABUSE. By Anne MacLeod. 1973. 98 p. $1.25. Available from: Superintendent of Documents, Government Printing Office, Washington, D.C. 20402.

> Pulling together material from numerous publications by educators and psychologists, the author examines the complexities and stresses of modern society. She looks at the effects of boredom and frustration on both city and suburban children and suggests corrective measures that may prevent the alienation and despair that turn many young people to drugs.

MARIJUANA, LSD, NARCOTICS, SEDATIVES, STIMULANTS--FIVE LEAFLETS. 1968, 1969, 1971. 8-10 pages each. Available from: Office of Communications, National Institute of Mental Health, 5454 Wisconsin Avenue, Chevy Chase, Md. 20015.

> Comprehensive, accurate information in answer to the most frequently asked questions.

THE NEW ALCOHOLICS: TEENAGERS. 1973. 20 p. 35 cents. Publication no. 499. Available from: Public Atfairs Committee, 381 Park Avenue South, New York, N.Y. 10016.

> Discusses the increasing use of alcohol among youth and suggests ways to help teenagers overcome or prevent excessive drinking.

PROBLEM DRINKER AT HOME? By Barry Leach. 1973. 32 p. Publication no. CP270. Available from: Claretian Publications, Pamphlet Department, 221 Madison Street, Chicago, Ill. 60606.

# Drugs, Alcohol, and Their Abuse

The author talks about the problems of children of alcoholic parents.

TIPS ON DRUG ABUSE PREVENTION. 1972. 14 p. Available from: National Clearinghouse for Drug Abuse Information, 5600 Fishers Lane, Rockville Md. 20852.

Tells parents what to say when giving medicine to young children.

WHAT EVERY PARENT SHOULD KNOW ABOUT DRUGS AND DRUG ABUSE. 1973. 15 p. Available from: Channing L. Bete Co., 45 Federal Street, Greenfield, Mass. 01301.

Symptoms and dangers of drug abuse.

YOUR CHILD AND DRUGS: A PREVENTIVE APPROACH. 1972. 15 p. Available from: Guidance Awareness Publications, Box 106, Rancocas, N.J. 08073.

Guidelines for both parent and teacher in preparing the elementary school child for the day when he or she must decide not to use drugs.

YOUR HEAD IS YOUR OWN THING BUT . . . DON'T BLOW YOUR KID'S MIND. n.d. 6 p. Available from: National Association for Retarded Children, 2709 Avenue E East, Arlington, Tex. 76011.

Deals with the potential damage to the fetus when the mother uses certain drugs (LSD, amphetamines) during pregnancy.

## ORGANIZATIONS AND/OR SOURCES OF MATERIALS, FREE OR AT LOW COST

Alcohol and Drug Abuse Education
American Council on Alcohol Problems
119 Constitution Avenue, N.E.
Washington, D.C. 20002

Pamphlets on alcohol and drugs.

American Medical Association
535 North Dearborn Street
Chicago, Ill. 60610

Information on drug abuse.

American Pharmaceutical Association
2215 Constitution Avenue, N.W.
Washington, D.C. 20037

List of sources on drug abuse.

## Drugs, Alcohol, and Their Abuse

Bureau of Narcotics & Dangerous Drugs
Region VII
Federal Building
219 South Dearborn
Chicago, Ill. 60604    Phone 353-7875
   or
U.S. Department of Justice
Washington, D.C. 20537

    The Bureau of Narcotics and Dangerous Drugs sends out pamphlets and also has a free loan service for films.

Narcotic Educational Foundation of America
5055 Sunset Boulevard
Los Angeles, Calif. 90027    Phone (213) 663-5171

    Disseminates information in such a way that youth and adults will gain protective warning about the dangers resulting from abusively using any drug. Produces television and radio programs and a wide variety of printed materials.

National Clearinghouse for Alcohol Information
P.O. Box 2345
Rockville, Md. 20852    Phone (301) 948-4450

    Acts as a service of the National Institute on Alcohol Abuse and Alcoholism. Distributes alcohol-related pamphlets, books, posters to professionals and the public. Material is free of charge--send for their publications list.

National Clearinghouse for Drug Abuse Information
National Institute for Mental Health
5600 Fishers Lane
Rockville, Md. 20852    Phone (301) 443-4443

    Acts as a focal point for federal information on drug abuse. It provides consultation, reference, literature searching, and abstracting services. Single copies of selected publications and posters are available to the public. Twenty-four hour telephone information line: (301) 443-4426.

National Coordinating Council on Drug Education
1526 Eighteenth Street, N.W.
Washington, D.C. 20036    Phone (202) 332-1512

    Private, nonprofit organization formed in 1968 to organize effective community action programs, evaluate drug education programs, and disseminate information on drugs and alcohol. They will answer inquiries from the public and provide materials on drug abuse, including a monthly evaluation of drug abuse films and

# Drugs, Alcohol, and Their Abuse

the biweekly newsletter, DRUG EDUCATION REPORT.

National Institute of Drug Abuse
Department of Health, Education
  and Welfare
11400 Rockville Pike
Rockville, Md. 20852

    Source of publications and pamphlets on drug abuse.

New Dimensions Publishing Co.
151 West Twenty-fifth Street
New York, N.Y. 10001

    Publishes a series on narcotics.

Smith, Kline and French Laboratories
1500 Spring Garden Street
Philadelphia, Pa. 19101

    Free materials relating to children and drugs.

Special Action Officer for Drug
  Abuse Prevention
726 Jackson Place, N.W.
Washington, D.C. 20506

    Free materials on prevention of drug abuse.

Student Association for the Study of
  Hallucinogens, (STASH)
118 South Bedford Street
Madison, Wis. 53703

    Free material on hallucinogens.

## AUDIOVISUAL MATERIALS

### Films

ALMOST EVERYONE DOES. 1970. 16mm, 14 min., sound, color.
    Looks at drug dependency through the eyes of young children including daddy's cocktail, mommy's cigarettes and coffee, and the TV commercial aimed at products that help you to "feel good." The film also attempts to offer alternatives to drug use.

## Drugs, Alcohol, and Their Abuse

Available from: Wombat Productions, 77 Tarrytown Road, White Plains, N.Y. 10607. Phone (914) 428-6220.

CRISIS HOUSE. 1970. 16mm, 22 min., sound, color. Study guide included.

Rap session in a halfway house for young people who have been drug addicts. Their concerns are personal identity, self-hatred, peer pressures, and parents.

Available from: Churchill Films, 662 North Robertson Boulevard, Los Angeles, Calif. 90069.

DARKNESS, DARKNESS. 1970. 16mm, 37 min., color.

Heroin addicts and ex-addicts express their feelings about being addicted; their parents describe their emotions about dealing with a child who has become an addict.

Available from: See-Saw Films, P.O. Box 262, Palo Alto, Calif. 94302.

DRUG AGE--WHAT DO YOU THINK OF YOUR FATHER. 1969. 16mm, 30 min., sound, black and white. Producer: National Office of Catholic Radio and TV.

A priest and a counselor moderate a panel discussion in which a mother and daughter and a father and son relate drug abuse to the lack of communication between parents and children. It should be helpful to parents whose children are about to enter a drug rehabilitation program.

Available from: Association Sterling Films, 600 Grand Avenue, Ridgefield, N.J. 07657.

FLIP CITY: THE PSYCHOTROPICS AND YOU. 1971. 16mm, 44 min., sound, color.

Comments from students, faculty, a judge, a doctor, and law enforcement representatives.

Available from: VTR Productions, 1249 Field Street, Ottawa, Canada.

GLASS HOUSES. 1972. 16mm, 22 min., sound, color. Producer: Nolan, Wilton and Wooten.

Personal experiences of thirteen people with barbiturates and drugs.

Available from: See-Saw Films, P.O. Box 262, Palo Alto, Calif. 94302.

# Drugs, Alcohol, and Their Abuse

GROOVING. 1972. 16mm, 31 min., sound, color.

Teenagers discuss their motivations for using drugs.

Available from: Benchmark Films, 145 Scarborough Road, Briarcliff Manor, N.Y. 10510.

I THINK. 1970. 16mm, 19 min., sound, color.

Sympathetic presentation of the influences on children's attitudes in an effort to understand the causes of drug abuse.

Available from: Wombat Productions, 77 Tarrytown Road, White Plains, N.Y. 10607.

MR. SMITH, YOUR KID'S TAKING DRUGS. 1971.

Reactions of an American parent to being told that his child is taking drugs.

Available from: University of Michigan T.V. Center, 46 Fourth Street, Ann Arbor, Mich. 48103.

NINETY-NINE BOTTLES OF BEER. 1973. 23 min., sound, color.

By depicting the actual experiences and feelings of some young people, this film points out the underlying psychological basis for involvement with alcohol and drugs.

Available for purchase from: Hollywood Film Enterprise, 6060 Sunset Boulevard, Hollywood, Calif. 90028. Phone (213) 464-2181. Available for preview from: CAO Motion Picture Unit, County of Los Angeles, 500 West Temple Street, Los Angeles, Calif. 90012. Phone (213) 625-3611, ext. 65528.

SELF-AWARENESS FILM MODULES ON DRUG ABUSE FOR PARENTS. 1971. 16mm, sound, color. 2 parts: 13 min., 11-12 min. Comes with a reader's guide designed to help parents become aware of their feelings and attitudes.

Part 1, "Fear and Anger," depicts drug taking and conversation at a party. Part 2, "Humiliation and Compassion," shows parents reacting to their discovery of children taking drugs. Both should be viewed with well-trained group leaders.

Available from: Film Modules Distribution, 496 Deer Park Avenue, Babylon, N.Y. 11702.

For additional information on available drug films write for the film lists of the National Audiovisual Center, Washington, D.C. 20409.

# Drugs, Alcohol, and Their Abuse

## Filmstrips and Slides

DRUG INFORMATION SERIES--NARCOTICS. 1970. Filmstrip. 101 frames, 35mm, 15 min., color.

> Identifies drugs, terminology, reasons for using, and treatment available.
>
> Available from: Guidance Associates, 41 Washington Avenue, Pleasantville, N.Y. 10570.

DRUG INFORMATION SERIES--PSYCHEDELICS. 1970. Filmstrip. 80 frames, 35mm, 12 min., color.

> Identifies the types of hallucinogens, the experiences they bring about, and their potential for damage after long-term usage.
>
> Available from: Guidance Associates, 41 Washington Avenue, Pleasantville, N.Y. 10570.

DRUG INFORMATION SERIES--SEDATIVES. 1970. Filmstrip. 98 frames, 35mm, 14 min., sound, color.

> Indicates differences between the various sedatives: alcohol, barbiturates, and marijuana.
>
> Available from: Guidance Associates, 41 Washington Avenue, Pleasantville, N.Y. 10570.

DRUG INFORMATION SERIES--STIMULANTS. 1970. Filmstrip. 85 frames, 35mm, 11 min., sound, color.

> Professionals discuss the broad range of drugs from caffeine to speed.
>
> Available from: Guidance Associates, 41 Washington Avenue, Pleasantville, N.Y. 10570.

DRUGS, VALUES AND PERSONAL PROBLEMS. 1971. 6 filmstrips. 63-78 frames each, 10-12 min. each.

> Six dramatic situations, "Lonely Boy," "The Neighborhood," "Honor Students," "Track Star," "Growing Up Fast," and "Caught in the Middle," which present the common problems that often lead young people to drug use.
>
> Available from: Warren Schloat Productions, 115 Tompkins Avenue, Pleasantville, N.Y.

MARIJUANA: WHAT CAN YOU BELIEVE? 1969. 6 filmstrips. 35mm, 32 min., color.

> In part 1, a physician provides the facts; in part 2, teenagers

# Drugs, Alcohol, and Their Abuse

relate their experiences.

Available from: Guidance Associates, 41 Washington Avenue, Pleasantville, N.Y. 10570.

## Records, Tapes, Cassettes

A DOCTOR ANSWERS YOUR QUESTIONS ABOUT DRUGS. 1970. Phonograph record, 33 1/3 rpm., 20 min. Producer: Bernard V. Dryer, M.D.

Dr. Dryer answers questions commonly asked by parents about drug use.

Available from: Media Medica, 555 Fifth Avenue, New York, N.Y. 10017.

THE TRUTH ABOUT DRUGS. Cassette.

For adults and teenagers, this valuable cassette includes information regarding the composition and actions of drugs ranging from legal barbiturates to psychedelics.

Available from: Multimedia Education, 11 West Forty-second Street, New York, N.Y. 10036.

# EMOTIONALLY DISTURBED

(See also Adolescence; Chapters on Exceptional Child; Chapters on Health)

## BOOKS

### Dated but Still Relevant

Axline, Virginia M. DIBS: IN SEARCH OF SELF. New York: Houghton Mifflin Co., 1964. 186 p.

> A classic which describes the psychotherapeutic experience of a little boy. Should give parents a feeling for the world of the child.

_____. PLAY THERAPY: THE INNER DYNAMICS OF CHILDHOOD. New York: Ballantine Books, 1969. 374 p. Illus., index. Paperbound.

> Primarily written for child therapists but equally good for parents, this book describes the "feedback" technique of Dr. Carl Rogers.

Moak, Helen R. THE TROUBLED CHILD. New York: Holt, Rinehart and Winston, 1958. 172 p.

> A classic and helpful book about emotional disturbance in children.

### Current Sources

Burch, Claire. STRANGER IN THE FAMILY: A GUIDE TO LIVING WITH THE EMOTIONALLY DISTURBED. New York: Bobbs-Merrill Co., 1972. 233 p. Biblio., glossary.

> Intended to aid families in coping with the disruptive behavior of children suffering from drug addiction, alcoholism, or mental retardation. Alternatives to home care, such as halfway houses and night and weekend hospitals, are noted. Addresses of relevant organizations are included.

# Emotionally Disturbed

Clinebell, Charlotte H., and Clinebell, Howard J. CRISIS AND GROWTH: HELPING YOUR TROUBLED CHILD. Philadelphia, Pa.: Fortress Press, 1971. 56 p. Biblio. Paperbound.

> How to recognize the troubled child and find professional help for him.

Despert, J. Louise, M.D. THE EMOTIONALLY DISTURBED CHILD: INQUIRY INTO FAMILY PATTERNS. Garden City, N.Y.: Doubleday & Co., 1970. 339 p.

> Study of patterns in families having emotionally disturbed children.

Joint Commission on Mental Health of Children. CRISIS IN CHILD MENTAL HEALTH: CHALLENGE FOR THE 1970'S. New York: Harper & Row Publishers, 1970. 578 p. Biblio., illus., tables.

> Carefully documented final report of the first nationally sponsored commission on the mental health of children. The commission was established in 1965 to assess the care provided for emotionally and mentally disturbed children in the United States. The study pinpoints the deficiencies in past and present child mental health programs, discusses such negative influences as poverty and racism, and recommends improvements and innovations. Of special interest to professionals and knowledgeable parents alike.

Love, Harold D. THE EMOTIONALLY DISTURBED CHILD: A PARENT'S GUIDE FOR PARENTS WHO HAVE PROBLEM CHILDREN. Springfield, Ill.: Charles C. Thomas, Publisher, 1970. 105 p.

> How parents can recognize emotional problems and deal with them. Includes several case histories and a chapter on private and public mental facilities for children.

Mayer, Greta, and Hoover, Mary [B.]. WHEN CHILDREN NEED SPECIAL HELP WITH EMOTIONAL PROBLEMS. Rev. ed. New York: Child Study Press, 1974. 55 p.

> Designed to help parents determine the need for professional help and then find it.

Schiff, Jacqui Lee, and Day, Beth. ALL MY CHILDREN. New York: M. Evans & Co., 1970. 233 p.

> The story of a couple who act as foster parents to schizophrenics and guide them towards emotional health. Contains much that parents of emotionally disturbed children can learn.

Shaw, Charles, M.D. WHEN YOUR CHILD NEEDS HELP. New York: William Morrow & Co., 1972. 309 p. Index.

# Emotionally Disturbed

Written for parents who either have an emotionally disturbed child or suspect that they do. Using case studies, the book describes the major disorders in terms of the child's personality, behavior, and feelings. Also presents the causes, diagnosis, treatment, and future outlook for each disorder. Not intended for parents trying to decide whether to seek help.

## PAMPHLETS AND/OR GOVERNMENT DOCUMENTS

Unless otherwise noted the materials are available free of charge. Prices quoted are subject to change. Payment should accompany order.

### Bibliographies and Directories

FILMS CONCERNING EMOTIONALLY HANDICAPPED CHILDREN. 1973. 19 p. Available from: New York State Department of Education, Division for Handicapped Children, Albany, N.Y.

Select annotated list for the general public, parents, and professionals. Includes purchase and rental prices and names and addresses of film distributors.

U.S. FACILITIES AND PROGRAMS FOR CHILDREN WITH SEVERE MENTAL ILLNESSES. 1974. 448 p. Appendix, index. Available from: National Institute of Mental Health, 5600 Fishers Lane, Rockville, Md. 20852.

Prepared by the National Society for Autistic Children, this comprehensive directory lists more than 400 programs and facilities which serve children suffering from severe mental disorders such as autism and schizophrenia. Facilities are listed by state in alphabetical order, and are described in terms of program, staff, fees, physical plant, and admission restrictions.

### Current Sources

CHILDREN OF THE EVENING. By Bert K. Smith. 1972. 54 p. Available from: Hogg Foundation for Mental Health, P.O. Box 7998, University of Texas, Austin, Tex. 78712.

Discusses the severely disturbed adolescent, reviews the current literature about mentally ill children, and describes patterns for helping such young people.

HELP FOR YOUR TROUBLED CHILD. 1970. 24 p. Publication no. 454. 35 cents. Available from: Public Affairs Committee, 381 Park Avenue South, New York, N.Y. 10016.

Describes the kinds of behavior that require professional help,

# Emotionally Disturbed

as well as sources of such help.

## ORGANIZATIONS AND/OR SOURCES OF MATERIALS, FREE OR AT LOW COST

Clearinghouse for Mental Health Information
National Institute of Mental Health
Health Services and Mental Health
    Administration
5600 Fishers Lane
Rockville, Md. 20852    Phone (301) 443-4573

> Provides information about mental health issues to professionals as well as the public. Wealth of available material.

Hogg Foundation for Mental Health
Publications Division
Box 7998
University of Texas
Austin, Tex. 78712

> Free publications on mental health, maternal and infant welfare, and adolescence.

National Association for Mental Health
1800 North Kent Street
Arlington, Va. 22209    Phone (703) 528-6405

> A national voluntary organization of citizens dedicated to improving services for the mentally ill, preventing mental illness, and promoting mental health. It directs a research program and a public information program. Some local affiliates provide services such as clinics and halfway houses, while others only make referrals to clinics, treatment centers, and hospitals. Good source of pamphlets, books, and films on the subject.

## AUDIOVISUAL MATERIALS

### Films

AGGRESSIVE CHILD. 1966. 30 min., sound, black and white. Producer: Robert Anderson, Associates.

> Film shows that serious emotional problems cause disruptive behavior in children and indicates sources of help for such children.
>
> Available from: McGraw-Hill Films, 330 West Forty-second

# Emotionally Disturbed

Street, New York, N.Y. 10001.

IVAN AND HIS FATHER. 1971. 14 min., sound.

Problems faced by a young man because of the way his father communicated with him as a child.

Available from: Churchill Films, 662 North Robertson Boulevard, Los Angeles, Calif. 90069.

JOHNNY. 1972. 16mm, 32 min., sound, black and white.

Camera-psychiatrist-eye watches Johnny, a "disturbed" nine-year-old, in a therapeutic camp. Reveals the conflict and inner torment, the wistful and troubled moments, and the pain which triggers uncontrollable anger.

Available from: Wediko Films-Documentaries for Learning, 267 West Twenty-fifth Street, New York, N.Y. 10001.

# EXCEPTIONAL CHILD—GENERAL

(See also Food, Clothing, and Furniture; Play; Sex Education)

## BOOKS

### Dated but Still Relevant

Ayrault, Evelyn West. YOU CAN RAISE YOUR HANDICAPPED CHILD. Preface by Margaret Mead. New York: G.P. Putnam's Sons, 1964. 318 p. Appendix.

> Designed to help parents cope with the psychological, social, and emotional problems of the handicapped. Easy-to-read book by an authority in the field. Includes "Directory of Rehabilitation Services for Your Child" and "Digest of State Laws and Regulations Affecting the Handicapped."

Lowman, Edward, M.D., and Klinger, Judith L. AIDS TO INDEPENDENT LIVING: SELF-HELP FOR THE HANDICAPPED. New York: McGraw-Hill Book Co., 1969. 796 p. Biblio., index.

> Two staff members of the Institute of Rehabilitation Medicine, New York University Medical Center, have compiled a comprehensive catalog of devices that help disabled persons perform everyday functions. Includes sources and prices of equipment, emphasizing those available by mail order. Also provides bibliographies of agencies and periodicals. Useful to the handicapped and to professionals who work with them outside the medical center, e.g., occupational and physical therapists, or vocational counselors.

Spock, Benjamin, M.D., and Lerrigo, Marion O. CARING FOR YOUR DISABLED CHILD. New York: Collier, 1965. 373 p. Biblio., index.

> General advice on family living, medical care, education, vocational future, recreation, and home management. A list of community resources is included.

# Exceptional Child—General

Wright, Beatrice A.  PHYSICAL DISABILITY: A PSYCHOLOGICAL APPROACH. New York: Harper & Row Publishers, 1960.  408 p.  Biblio.

> Well-written exploration into the psychological development of the handicapped and the influence of their environments.  The basic premise of the book is that the disabled can be helped to cope and to grow.

## Reference

DIRECTORY FOR EXCEPTIONAL CHILDREN.  7th ed.  Boston: Porter Sargent, 1972.  1,248 p.

> Comprehensive listing of educational and training facilities for handicapped and maladjusted children including deaf-blind, emotionally disturbed, autistic, epileptic, braindamaged, and others.  Also lists national associations, societies, foundations, federal and state agencies concerned with the welfare of the exceptional child.

REGISTRY OF PRIVATE SCHOOLS FOR CHILDREN WITH SPECIAL EDUCATIONAL NEEDS.  Baltimore, Md.: National Educational Consultants, 1971.  Unpaged.

> Over 800 schools for exceptional children in the United States are listed in alphabetical order by state and then by city.  Gives the location and services of each school.  This book was produced using a computerized data bank.

Weiner, Florence.  HELP FOR THE HANDICAPPED CHILD.  New York: McGraw-Hill Book Co., 1973.  221 p.  Index.

> Guide to public and private services available to parents of handicapped children.  Describes each handicap, its diagnosis, and its treatment.  Also explains the meaning of the technical words used by the physicians.

## Current Sources

Apgar, Virginia, M.D., and Beck, Joan.  IS MY BABY ALL RIGHT?  New York: Trident Press, 1973.  492 p.  Illus., index.

> An authoritative and readable description of the biology of prenatal development and the birth defects that can afflict infants.  Contains a most helpful chapter for young marrieds who are concerned about their family history and the possibility of having a disabled child.  Some of the birth defects specifically discussed include spina bifida, clubfoot, cleft

## Exceptional Child—General

palate, hydrocephalus, and minimal brain dysfunction. Dr. Apgar is a well-known clinical professor of pediatrics.

Ayrault, Evelyn W[est]. HELPING THE HANDICAPPED TEENAGER MATURE. New York: Association Press, 1971. 224 p. Appendices.

The author, who has worked with many adolescents, discusses the physical, psychological, social, and sexual problems of growing up including career fulfillment. Offers practical methods for helping handicapped teenagers become psychologically and emotionally mature. Appendices include lists of rehabilitation services, agencies and associations, as well as a directory of camps and colleges (somewhat out of date) providing special facilities for the handicapped.

Biklen, Douglas. LET OUR CHILDREN GO: AN ORGANIZING MANUAL FOR ADVOCATES AND PARENTS. Syracuse, N.Y.: Human Policy Press, 1974. 144 p. Illus.

An easy-to-read and practical handbook for parents who wish to organize in order to secure certain basic rights for their handicapped children.

Brown, Diana L. DEVELOPMENTAL HANDICAPS IN BABIES AND YOUNG CHILDREN: A GUIDE FOR PARENTS. Springfield, Ill.: Charles C. Thomas, Publisher, 1972. 89 p. Biblio.

This is a highly useful nontechnical guide to the symptoms of developmental handicaps (orthopedic, vision and hearing, speech, and minimal brain dysfunction). Offers a course of action for concerned parents. Also includes a dictionary of terms and a list of national agencies providing specialized help.

Doman, Glenn. WHAT TO DO ABOUT YOUR BRAIN-INJURED CHILD. New York: Doubleday & Co., 1974. 291 p. Appendix, biblio., illus., index.

The controversial pioneer documents the successes obtained when his unique method of patterning (Doman-Delacato method) is used to treat brain injury.

Hart, Verna. BEGINNING WITH THE HANDICAPPED. Springfield, Ill.: Charles C. Thomas, Publisher, 1974. 140 p. Charts.

Written for parents, teachers, and paraprofessionals who work with handicapped children at the early stages of their development. Presents activities designed to help such children attain higher levels of functioning. Easy-to-use charts are provided.

# Exceptional Child—General

Heisler, Verda. A HANDICAPPED CHILD IN THE FAMILY: A GUIDE FOR PARENTS. New York: Grune & Stratton, 1972. 160 p.

    A psychotherapist, who is herself handicapped, stresses that parents need to understand their own responses, including the negative ones, to their child's handicap. In this way, they can deal more effectively with the situation. Written with a minimum of jargon.

Hoggman, Ruth B. HOW TO BUILD FURNITURE & EQUIPMENT FOR HANDICAPPED CHILDREN. Springfield, Ill.: Charles C. Thomas, Publisher, 1970. 88 p. Illus., diags., index.

    Step-by-step directions including illustrations and diagrams with exact dimensions.

Kamenetz, Herman L., M.D. THE WHEELCHAIR BOOK: MOBILITY FOR THE DISABLED. Springfield, Ill.: Charles C. Thomas, Publisher, 1970. 267 p. Appendices, biblio., index.

    A practical guide to the types of wheel chairs available to the handicapped. Lists manufacturers and names of wheelchairs, lifts, home elevators, and stair lifts.

Karnes, Merle B. HELPING YOUNG CHILDREN DEVELOP LANGUAGE SKILLS: A BOOK OF ACTIVITIES. Reston, Va.: Council for Exceptional Children, 1973. 168 p.

    Primarily geared for the professional, but the activities can aid the parent who is working with a language therapist.

Love, Harold [D.]. PARENTAL ATTITUDES TOWARD EXCEPTIONAL CHILDREN. Springfield, Ill.: Charles C. Thomas, Publisher, 1970. 167 p.

    Parental influence on the behavior of exceptional children.

Melton, David. WHEN CHILDREN NEED HELP: AN UP-TO-DATE HANDBOOK OF GUIDANCE FOR PARENTS OF CHILDREN WHO HAVE BEEN DIAGNOSED AS BRAIN-INJURED, MENTALLY RETARDED, CEREBRAL PALSIED, LEARNING DISABLED, OR AS SLOW LEARNERS. New York: Thomas Y. Crowell Co., 1972. 257 p. Biblio., index.

    A father of a brain-injured child suggests ways to cope with the problems that surround the handicapped child in a family setting. He also discusses many aspects of the education of special children including classes, teachers' and doctors' attitudes, institutionalization, and new methods of therapy.

Nordoff, Paul, and Robins, Clive. MUSIC THERAPY IN SPECIAL EDUCATION. New York: John Day Co., 1971. 253 p.

## Exceptional Child—General

Not written for parents but should make them aware of the role that music therapy can play in enriching the lives of handicapped children.

Roskies, Ethel. ABNORMALITY AND NORMALITY: THE MOTHERING OF THALIDOMIDE CHILDREN. Ithaca, N.Y.: Cornell University Press, 1972. 347 p. Biblio., illus.

> Parents of thalidomide children reveal their reactions to their severely handicapped children and the effect of these feelings on the behavior and personality of the youngsters. Highly relevant for parents of children with other disabilities as well.

Siegel, Ernest. THE EXCEPTIONAL CHILD GROWS UP: GUIDELINES FOR UNDERSTANDING AND HELPING THE BRAIN-INJURED ADOLESCENT AND YOUNG ADULT. New York: E.P. Dutton & Co., 1974. 227 p. Appendix, biblio., index.

> Practical guidelines for helping the brain-injured child through the difficult years of adolescence. Discusses psychological, social, educational, and vocational goals and their achievement.

Stein, Sara Bonnett. ABOUT HANDICAPS: AN OPEN FAMILY BOOK FOR PARENTS AND CHILDREN TOGETHER. New York: Walker & Co., 1974. 46 p. Illus., some in color.

> This unique resource is designed to help children cope with handicaps, either their own or those of others. Two separate texts are included, one at the child's level and one at the adult's, so that the parent can share the experience with the child and handle his questions.

Wentworth, Elise H. LISTEN TO YOUR HEART: A MESSAGE TO PARENTS OF HANDICAPPED CHILDREN. New York: Houghton Mifflin Co., 1974. 262 p. Biblio.

> This book attempts to help parents deal with the realities of having a handicapped child as part of the family unit. Special attention is paid to the feelings of the various family members.

### PERIODICALS

ACCENT ON LIVING. Bloomington, Ind.: 1956-- . Quarterly.

> Magazine for the disabled and their families. Contains classified advertisements for items of interest to the handicapped.

CLOSER LOOK REPORT. Washington, D.C.: National Information Center for the Handicapped, 1972-- . Three to four times a year.

# Exceptional Child—General

CLOSER LOOK is an information service established by the Bureau of the Education of the Handicapped, U.S. Office of Education. Designed to help parents find services for children with mental, physical, emotional, and learning handicaps. Parents of exceptional children can be placed on the mailing list for the report. Information packets are also available.

EXCEPTIONAL CHILDREN. Arlington, Va.: Council for Exceptional Children, 1934-- . Monthly.

Concerned with the psychologically and/or physiologically handicapped child. Primarily for educators but of value to better-educated parents.

THE EXCEPTIONAL PARENT. Boston: Phy-Ed, 1971-- . Bimonthly.

Offers practical and useful advice to parents of exceptional children on daily problems as well as long-range care and planning.

REHABILITATION LITERATURE. Chicago: National Easter Seal Society for Crippled Children and Adults, 1940-- . Monthly.

Monthly professional articles plus book reviews and abstracts of current literature.

TEACHING EXCEPTIONAL CHILDREN. Washington, D.C.: Council for Exceptional Children, 1968-- . Quarterly.

Although aimed at educators, this periodical is a practical teaching guide of use to parents as well.

## PAMPHLETS AND/OR GOVERNMENT DOCUMENTS

Unless otherwise noted the materials are available free of charge. Prices quoted are subject to change. Payment should accompany order.

## Bibliographies, Directories, Guides

BEST RECORDS AND BOOKS FOR EXCEPTIONAL CHILDREN. Published annually. 40 p. Available from: Children's Music Center, 5373 West Pico Boulevard, Los Angeles, Calif. 90019.

Free to teachers and parents, this pamphlet lists records for both listening and physical activity.

## Exceptional Child—General

DIRECTORIES OF SERVICES AND FACILITIES: A SELECTIVE BIBLIOGRAPHY. 1972. 20 p. Exceptional Child Bibliography, Series no. 638. Available from: Council for Exceptional Children, 1920 Association Drive, Reston, Va. 22091.

> Covers the period 1966-72 and includes seventy-five abstracts of articles relating to services for exceptional children. The source for each abstracted article is also given.

EASTER SEAL DIRECTORY OF RESIDENT CAMPS FOR PERSONS WITH SPECIAL HEALTH NEEDS. 1973. 77 p. $1.00. Available from: National Easter Seal Society, 2023 West Ogden Avenue, Chicago, Ill. 60612.

> Lists and describes 240 camps for children and adults with physical, mental, and/or emotional handicaps. Includes name and location of camp, degree of independence required, age range, length of sessions, fees, capacity, and address of the sponsoring organization.

THE EXCEPTIONAL CHILD. n.d. 8 p. Available from: St. Paul Public Library, Publications Department, 90 West Fourth Street, St. Paul, Minn. 55102.

> Over 130 books are listed and annotated in such categories as speech and hearing defects, blind and partially sighted, brain-damaged child, Mongoloid, etc. A list of directories and pamphlets is also included.

NATIONAL PARK GUIDE FOR THE HANDICAPPED. 1971. 79 p. 40 cents. Available from: Superintendent of Documents, Government Printing Office, Washington, D.C. 20402.

> A handy booklet which describes the provisions that have been made for the blind or the wheelchair-bound visitor to national parks and monuments. Parks are listed by state, and accessible areas are noted.

OPENING DOORS FOR PHYSICALLY HANDICAPPED AND EMOTIONALLY DISTURBED CHILDREN. 1973. 52 p. $1.00. Available from: Colorado State Department of Social Services, Division of Public Welfare, 1575 Sherman Street, Denver, Colo. 80203.

> Bibliography.

SELECTED CAREER EDUCATION PROGRAMS FOR THE HANDICAPPED. 1972. 114 p. $1.25. Available from: Superintendent of Documents, Government Printing Office, Washington, D.C. 20402.

# Exceptional Child—General

Alphabetical list by state of 120 career education programs for handicapped adolescents. Names the state directors of special education and vocational education, and provides the name and address of a state contact. Program descriptions include title, location, local representative, number of students, type of handicap served, and objectives.

SELECTED PUBLICATIONS CONCERNING THE HANDICAPPED. 1974. 45 p. Available from: Office for the Handicapped, U.S. Department of Health, Education and Welfare, Washington, D.C. 20201.

Compilation of publications of the Department of Health, Education and Welfare which relate to handicapped persons (including mentally and physically handicapped children). Many of the items listed are free.

SERVICES FOR CRIPPLED CHILDREN. 1972. 20 p. Available from: Bureau of Community Health Services, 5600 Fishers Lane, Rockville, Md. 20852.

Employing a question-and-answer format, this pamphlet informs parents about services for crippled children and the state agencies which administer them.

TOYS FOR THE HANDICAPPED: SELECTED REFERENCES. 1975. 8 p. Available from: Special Education Instructional Materials Center, 55 Elk Street, Albany, N.Y. 12234.

Lists books, pamphlets, articles, booklets, and instructional guides.

## Current Sources

ACCESS WASHINGTON. 1975-- . Annual. 131 p. Available from: Information Center for the Handicapped, 1413 K Street, N.W., Washington, D.C. 20001.

This valuable annual contains hotels, restaurants, and places of interest to the handicapped. Includes specific information such as width of doorways for wheelchair entry.

AIRLINE TRANSPORTATION FOR THE HANDICAPPED AND DISABLED. By Stanley G. Hogsett. 1971. 45 p. Available from: Easter Seal Society for Crippled Children and Adults, 2023 West Ogden Avenue, Chicago, Ill. 60612.

Provides a chart of twenty-two domestic airlines listing the services

## Exceptional Child—General

available to handicapped travelers and the airline representative responsible for the service. Also gives hints for the traveler who is physically handicapped.

CARRIAGE OF THE PHYSICALLY HANDICAPPED ON DOMESTIC AND INTERNATIONAL AIRLINES: A REPORT ON THE POLICIES, RULES AND REGULATIONS AFFECTING TRAVEL OF THE HANDICAPPED. By Jacob S. Schleichkorn. 1972. 44 p. $1.25. Available from: United Cerebral Palsy Association, 815 Second Avenue, New York, N.Y. 10017.

Practical information on each airline's procedures and recommendations for transportation of the disabled. Lists the physical handicaps which the airlines may refuse to transport as well as those which may require more care than the airlines provide.

A HANDICAPPED CHILD IN YOUR HOME. 1973. 16 p. Publication no. (OHD) 73-29. Available from: Office of Human Development, Department of Health, Education and Welfare, Washington, D.C 20201.

Designed for parents who have to care for their handicapped child at home. Spanish version is also available.

HELPING THE HANDICAPPED TEENAGER MATURE. By Evelyn W[est]. Ayrault. 1974. 28 p. Illus. Publication no. 504. 35 cents. Available from: Public Affairs Committee, 381 Park Avenue South, New York, N.Y. 10016.

Worthwhile pamphlet by an expert.

ON BEING THE PARENT OF A HANDICAPPED CHILD. n.d. 18 p. 25 cents. Available from: National Easter Seal Society for Crippled Children and Adults, 2023 West Ogden Avenue, Chicago, Ill. 60612.

Dr. Spock suggests ways in which parents can help their physically handicapped children.

WHEELCHAIR INTERIORS. 1973. 46 p. $1.50. Publication no. E52. Available from: National Easter Seal Society for Crippled Children and Adults, 2023 West Ogden Avenue, Chicago, Ill. 60612.

Practical suggestions and advice to help wheelchair users live at home independently, comfortably, and safely.

THE WHEELCHAIR TRAVELER. 1973. Unpaged. $3.00. Available from: Douglass R. Annand, Ball Hill Road, Milford, N.H. 03055.

Annual travel guide by a world-traveling paraplegic, Douglass R. Annand. Lists accessible motels, restaurants, and sightseeing

# Exceptional Child—General

areas in the United States, Canada, and Mexico. Offers helpful hints to make travel easier for the disabled.

## ORGANIZATIONS AND/OR SOURCES OF MATERIALS, FREE OR AT LOW COST

Bureau of Education for the Handicapped
U.S. Office of Education
400 Maryland Avenue, S.W.
Washington, D.C. 20202     Phone (201) 245-9661

>   The bureau coordinates and administers all Office of Education programs for the handicapped. Will supply reports of current federal activity on behalf of learning-disabled children. Produces and distributes media and materials for the handicapped including captioned films for the deaf.

Closer Look
Box 1492
Washington, D.C. 20013

>   Administered by the Bureau of Education for the Handicapped in the U.S. Office of Education, Closer Look is a government information service that helps parents find services for children with all forms of handicaps. The service will send a list of all facilities in your state that work with learning-disabled children. However, it does not endorse any of these facilities, meaning that parents must make their own evaluations.

Community Services Administration
Social and Rehabilitation Service
U.S. Department of Health, Education
  and Welfare
Washington, D.C. 20201

>   Pamphlets and leaflets.

Council for Exceptional Children
1920 Association Drive
Reston, Va. 22091     Phone (703) 471-5110

>   This private organization, concerned with both handicapped and intellectually gifted children, provides information in the area of state and federal laws and rulings concerning the education of exceptional children. It also monitors current litigation nationwide involving children who have been excluded from appropriate public education. Conducts research and publishes books and pamphlets. Their list is available on request.

# Exceptional Child—General

Foundation for Child Development
345 East Forty-sixth Street
New York, N.Y. 10017

> Books, pamphlets, and reprints on child care and development.

National Easter Seal Society for
    Crippled Children and Adults
2023 West Ogden Avenue
Chicago, Ill. 60612    Phone (312) 243-8400

> A voluntary organization serving the disabled through a program of care and treatment, education, and research. Issues a free newsletter, EASTER SEAL COMMUNICATOR and a directory, EASTER SEAL GUIDE FOR PROGRAMS FOR THE DEVELOPMENTALLY HANDICAPPED PRESCHOOL CHILD. Branch offices in many U.S. cities have published travel guides for the disabled which include information about accessible motels, restaurants, theaters, and other public places in their area. The Chicago office will provide a list of directories and the addresses of the respective branch offices. Issues many inexpensive pamphlets.

## AUDIOVISUAL MATERIALS

### Films

DIAGNOSIS BEFORE BIRTH. 1971. 16mm, 8 min., sound, color.

> Dr. Kurt Hirschhorn, professor of pediatrics at Mt. Sinai School of Medicine in New York, explains for the layman, recent scientific advances in the prevention of birth defects.

> Available from: The National Foundation--March of Dimes, Division of Public Education, Box 2000, White Plains, N.Y. 10602.

THE EXCEPTIONAL CHILD SERIES. 1959. 15 films, 29 min. each, sound, color.

> Each film discusses different types of exceptional children and how parents can cope with them.

> Available from: Indiana University, Audio-Visual Series, Bloomington, Ind. 47401.

MY SON, KEVIN. 1974. 24 min. with guide. Producer: Allan Segal for Granada Television International.

> Frank, revealing, and unsentimental rendering of the everyday

## Exceptional Child—General

care of a child born without limbs (thalidomide baby). A lesson for all who live or work with handicapped individuals.

Available from: Wombat Productions, 77 Tarrytown Road, White Plains, N.Y. 10607.

THE ONLY KID ON THE BLOCK. 1968. 16mm, 14 1/2 min., sound, color.

This film deals with a couple's suffering when they learn their first child has a serious birth defect. Care and treatment at the March of Dimes Birth Defects Center corrected the defect.

Available from: National Foundation--March of Dimes, Division of Public Education, Box 2000, White Plains, N.Y. 10602.

# EXCEPTIONAL CHILD—AUTISM

## BOOKS

### Dated but Still Relevant

Bettelheim, Bruno. THE EMPTY FORTRESS: INFANTILE AUTISM AND THE BIRTH OF THE SELF. New York: Free Press, 1967. 484 p. Index

> A technical but informative presentation by the noted psychiatrist of the developmental patterns of behavior in autistic children.

Rimland, Bernard. INFANTILE AUTISM: THE SYNDROME AND ITS IMPLICATIONS FOR A NEURAL THEORY OF BEHAVIOR. New York: Appleton-Century-Crofts, 1964. 282 p. Biblio., index.

> Basic, concise discussion of the severe emotional disturbance of childhood.

### Current Sources

Delacato, Carl H. THE ULTIMATE STRANGER: THE AUTISTIC CHILD. Garden City, N.Y.: Doubleday & Co., 1974. 226 p. Index.

> A specialist in the field of brain-injured children describes for parents the world of the autistic child. After years of observation and research, the author has devised a new theory, and offers new techniques to be used by parents of autistic children.

Greenfield, Josh. A CHILD CALLED NOAH: A FAMILY JOURNEY. New York: Holt, Rinehart and Winston, 1972. 224 p.

> Narrative of the Greenfield's experiences with their five-year-old autistic son. Their true emotions are revealed in unsentimental terms. The book ends on an upbeat note--with new treatment techniques developed at UCLA.

# Autism

Grossman, Frances Kaplan. BROTHERS AND SISTERS OF RETARDED CHILDREN: AN EXPLORATORY STUDY. Syracuse, N.Y.: Syracuse University Press, 1972. 249 p. Biblio., index.

> Albeit technical, this is an important and helpful book on the relationships between the retarded child and the normal sibling.

Hundley, Joan M. THE SMALL OUTSIDE: THE STORY OF AN AUTISTIC CHILD. New York: St. Martin's Press, 1972. 150 p. Illus.

> The mother of an autistic child writes for other families who must face this serious form of mental illness.

Strauss, Susan. IS IT WELL WITH THE CHILD? Garden City, N.Y.: Doubleday & Co., 1975. 152 p.

> A mother of an autistic child describes the daily life in her son's school and in his home. She offers practical advice on finding day schools, residential facilities, and diagnostic centers. Contains a section on parents' organizations.

Tustin, Frances. AUTISM AND CHILDHOOD PSYCHOSIS. New York: Jason Aronson, 1973. 200 p. Illus., index.

> A child psychotherapist opens new vistas to the field of childhood behavior problems. Her findings, based on twenty years experience, are presented in layman's language and are effectively illustrated with useful charts. The book is of value to anyone concerned with the psychological care of children.

Wing, Lorna, M.D. AUTISTIC CHILDREN: A GUIDE FOR PARENTS AND PROFESSIONALS. New York: Brunner/Mazel, 1972. 157 p. Biblio., index.

> Through extensive research and experience, the author presents a clear, informative guide to the understanding and education of autistic children. She discusses the roles of parents, doctors, and teachers in assisting these children, and she offers hope.

## PAMPHLETS AND/OR GOVERNMENT DOCUMENTS

Unless otherwise noted the materials are available free of charge. Prices quoted are subject to change. Payment should accompany order.

FACTS ABOUT AUTISM. 1972. 10 p. Publication no. 72-9150. Available from: National Institute of Mental Health, 5600 Fishers Lane, Rockville, Md. 20852.

> Pamphlet on the characteristics and treatment of autistic children.

RECREATION FOR AUTISTIC AND EMOTIONALLY DISTURBED CHILDREN. By Margaret A. Dewey. 1973. 18 p. Biblio., illus. Available from: Alcohol, Drug Abuse and Mental Health Administration, 5600 Fishers Lane, Rockville, Md. 20852.

> Booklet for parents and interested community workers which presents the recreational activities that appeal to autistic children. Provides practical suggestions for activities ranging from arts and crafts, music, dance, and games to sports and outdoor activities.

## ORGANIZATIONS AND/OR SOURCES OF MATERIALS, FREE OR AT LOW COST

National Society for Autistic Children
169 Tampa Avenue
Albany, N.Y. 12208    Phone (518) 489-7375

> An organization of parents, professionals, and interested citizens working to inform the public of the symptoms and problems connected with autistic children. They are also interested in the areas of legislation, education, and research. Their newsletter covers the latest developments in schools, camps, and recreational services.

National Society for Autistic Children
Information and Referral Service
101 Richmond Street
Huntington, W. Va. 25702    Phone (303) 523-1912

> Established in 1970 as a central source of information about infantile autism. Their publications include pamphlets and other materials on autism and related subjects.

## AUDIOVISUAL MATERIALS

### Films

JENNIFER IS A LADY. 1972. Sound, color.

> Depicts the language development of an autistic child.
>
> Available from: New York University Film Library, 26 Washington Place, New York, N.Y. 10003.

# EXCEPTIONAL CHILD—CEREBRAL PALSY

## BOOKS

### Current Sources

Finnie, Nancie R. HANDLING THE YOUNG CEREBRAL PALSIED CHILD AT HOME. Rev. ed. New York: United Cerebral Palsy Association, 1975. 224 p. Biblio., illus.

> This book covers problems of management and development that parents are most likely to encounter in living with the cerebral palsied child. Day-to-day activities are discussed and the importance of parental involvement in the child's development is emphasized. A most valuable book.

Hewett, Sheila. THE FAMILY AND THE HANDICAPPED CHILD: A STUDY OF CEREBRAL PALSIED CHILDREN IN THEIR HOMES. Chicago, Ill.: Aldine Publishing Co., 1970. 240 p. Illus.

> First this book skillfully defines cerebral palsy using descriptions given by parents and therapists, then it discusses aspects of day-to-day living including guilt, overprotection, discipline, internal family relations, and external social relations.

Napear, Peggy. BRAIN CHILD: A MOTHER'S DIARY. New York: Harper & Row Publishers, 1974. 503 p. Biblio., illus., index.

> The mother of a spastic cerebral palsied two-year-old was told that her child would never be able to walk or talk. Undaunted, she adhered to the "patterning" program prescribed by the Institute for the Achievement of Human Potential. Results--at age ten Jane walks.

Ramah [pseud.]. LEAVE THE LIGHT ON FOR KENT: THE TRUE STORY OF A CEREBRAL PALSY CHILD. Jericho, N.Y.: Exposition Press, 1971. 79 p.

# Cerebral Palsy

The mother of a cerebral palsied son tells of her experiences--despair, sacrifice, therapy, and joy.

## PAMPHLETS AND/OR GOVERNMENT DOCUMENTS

CEREBRAL PALSY. 1975. 6 p. Publication no. (NIH) 75-159. Available from: National Institute of Neurological and Communicative Disorders and Stroke, Bethesda, Md. 20014.

Various kinds of cerebral palsy, its causes and treatment.

HOPE THROUGH RESEARCH: CEREBRAL PALSY. 1972. 7 p. Available from: National Institute of Neurological and Communicative Disorders and Stroke, Bethesda, Md. 20014.

Briefly describes the causes, prevention, multiple handicaps, treatment, and research.

TOMORROW IS TODAY. Reprint. 1975. 33 p. Available from: United Cerebral Palsy Association, Medical and Scientific Department, 66 East Thirty-fourth Street, New York, N.Y. 10016.

Guide for parents on planning the future of the cerebral palsied child.

## ORGANIZATIONS AND/OR SOURCES OF MATERIALS, FREE OR AT LOW COST

United Cerebral Palsy Associations
66 East Thirty-fourth Street
New York, N.Y. 10016     Phone (212) 889-6655

A national association of state and local groups which supports research, provides traineeships for medical personnel, and sponsors professional and public education in the interest of preventing and managing cerebral palsy. Local affiliates sponsor special education for children, arrange for home instruction, and maintain recreational facilities for children and adults. They also offer psychological guidance to parents of cerebral palsied children. They publish many pamphlets on the subject.

# EXCEPTIONAL CHILD--DOWN'S SYNDROME

## BOOKS

### Current Sources

Horrobin, J. Margaret, and Rynders, John E., eds. TO GIVE AN EDGE: A GUIDE FOR NEW PARENTS OF DOWN'S SYNDROME (MONGOLOID) CHILDREN. Minneapolis, Minn.: Colwell Press, 1974. 97 p. Paperbound.

> Parents, pediatricians, and educators guide new parents of infants with Down's Syndrome in such activities as toilet training, hygiene, eating habits, and dressing. The authors present these children as individuals who can be helped.

Smith, David W., and Wilson, Ann A. THE CHILD WITH DOWN'S SYNDROME (MONGOLISM). Philadelphia: W.B. Saunders Co., 1973. 106 p. Biblio., illus. Paperbound.

> Examines the causes, characteristics, and acceptance of the mongoloid child. Useful for parents, physicians, educators, and caretakers.

## PAMPHLETS AND/OR GOVERNMENT DOCUMENTS

Unless otherwise noted the materials are available free of charge. Prices quoted are subject to change. Payment should accompany order.

FACTS ABOUT MONGOLISM FOR WOMEN OVER 35. 1973. 16 p. Publication no. 74-536. Available from Public Inquiries Office, National Institute of Child Health and Human Development, National Institutes of Health, Bethesda, Md. 20014.

> Answers questions from women who are planning a pregnancy after age thirty-five and from mothers who have a child with Down's Syndrome.

# Down's Syndrome

MONGOLISM (DOWN'S SYNDROME). 1972. 8 p. Publication no. 72-72. Available from: National Institute of Neurological and Communicative Disorders and Stroke, National Institutes of Health, Bethesda, Md. 20014.

> Story of the research in this area.

WHAT IS MONGOLISM? 1973. 5 p. Publication no. 73-537. Available from: Public Inquiries Office, National Institute of Child Health and Human Development, National Institutes of Health, Bethesda, Md. 20014.

> Answers five of the most basic questions.

YOUR DOWN'S SYNDROME CHILD. n.d. 32 p. Available from: National Association for Retarded Citizens, P.O. Box 6109, Arlington, Tex. 76011.

> Describes the behavior of the mongoloid child at each age level from infancy through adolescence. Suggestions on coping with specific problems are also included.

## ORGANIZATIONS AND/OR SOURCES OF MATERIALS, FREE OR AT LOW COST

Mothers of Children with Down's Syndrome
c/o Northern Virginia Association for
   Retarded Citizens
105 East Annandale Road, Suite 203
Falls Church, Va. 22046      Phone (703) 532-3214

> Organization of mothers of Down's Syndrome children under eleven years of age. Its activities include "parent-to-parent counseling, contacting new mothers of mongoloid children to advise them of reading material, diagnostic tests and clinics, area schools and recreation programs, psychological, genetic and educational counseling." Distributes parent information kits.

National Association for Down's Syndrome
628 Ashland Avenue
River Forest, Ill. 60305

> This association has two aims: to encourage research on mongolism, and to help mongoloid children develop to their fullest and be accepted by the community.

# EXCEPTIONAL CHILD—MENTAL RETARDATION

(See also Behavior Modification)

## BOOKS

### Dated but Still Relevant

Kirk, Samuel A., et al. YOU AND YOUR RETARDED CHILD: A MANUAL FOR PARENTS OF RETARDED CHILDREN. Rev. ed. Palo Alto, Calif.: Pacific Books, 1968. 164 p.

> This helpful and authoritative manual should help parents decide on the degree of residential care needed by a retarded child. It presents methods of caring for a child in the home.

### Current Sources

Baldwin, Victor L., et al. ISN'T IT TIME HE OUTGREW THIS?: OR A TRAINING PROGRAM FOR PARENTS OF RETARDED CHILDREN. Springfield, Ill.: Charles C. Thomas, Publisher, 1973. 272 p. Illus.

> A training program, for parents of retarded children, that explains the basic principles of behavior modification in nontechnical terms. Parents learn to use these principles to teach their child self-help skills and language. The emphasis is on reinforcement.

Blodgett, Harriet E. MENTALLY RETARDED CHILDREN: WHAT PARENTS AND OTHERS SHOULD KNOW. Minneapolis: University of Minnesota Press, 1971. 165 p.

> The aims of this book are to define retardation, to give parents a picture of what to expect from the child at various levels of development, and to help parents adjust. The emphasis is on much needed self-help skills and socialization, rather than academic ability.

# Mental Retardation

Bucker, Beatrice. LIVING WITH A MENTALLY RETARDED CHILD: A PRIMER FOR PARENTS. New York: Hawthorn Books, 1971. 242 p. Appendices, biblio., index.

Focuses on helping mentally retarded children to become useful members of society. Includes practical suggestions for home training, recreation, education, and job training; an excellent bibliography; and a directory of diagnostic centers and residential facilities.

Carver, John N., and Carver, Nellie Enders. THE FAMILY OF THE RETARDED CHILD. Syracuse, N.Y.: Syracuse University Press, 1972. 156 p.

Covers the difficulties encountered in keeping a retarded child at home, the initial reactions at the discovery of retardation, and the effect on family finances and life-style. Based on a study of thirty-seven families with a severely retarded child.

Foxx, Richard M., M.D., and Azrin, Nathan H., M.D. TOILET TRAINING THE RETARDED: A RAPID PROGRAM FOR DAY & NIGHTTIME INDEPENDENT TOILETING. Champaign, Ill.: Research Press, 1973. 120 p.

Contains a complete method of toilet training for the mentally retarded.

Gordon, Michael Lewis, et al. HELPING THE TRAINABLE MENTALLY RETARDED CHILD DEVELOP SPEECH AND LANGUAGE: A GUIDEBOOK FOR PARENTS, TEACHERS AND PARAPROFESSIONALS. Springfield, Ill.: Charles C. Thomas, Publisher, 1972. 80 p.

This easy-to-use guide emphasizes the need for greater home-school coordination in developing speech and language.

Higgins, Jean C. LINDY, MY RETARDED CHILD. Valley Forge, Pa.: Judson Press, 1970. 64 p. Paperbound.

A mother's tribute to a child who taught her so much about living.

Hunter, Marvin H., et al. THE RETARDED CHILD FROM BIRTH TO FIVE: A MULTIDISCIPLINARY PROGRAM FOR THE CHILD AND FAMILY. New York: John Day Co., 1972. 250 p. Biblio.

Discusses the early identification and treatment of the trainable mentally handicapped child, taking into account the various components of the diagnostic process. The author also emphasizes the importance of the family in the development and treatment of the retarded child.

Kirman, Brian H., M.D. THE MENTALLY HANDICAPPED CHILD. New York: Taplinger Publishing Co., 1973. 240 p. Biblio.

Concise nontechnical overview of the medical and historical aspects of mental retardation, along with a clear survey of treatment programs.

Koch, Richard, M.D., and Koch, Kathryn J. UNDERSTANDING THE MENTALLY RETARDED CHILD. New York: Random House, 1974. 301 p. Biblio., glossary, index.

Gives parents current information about the causes, approved treatments, therapies, and proper diets as well as guardianship, legal rights, and job opportunities. Includes a useful list of organizations and publications. Sensitively written.

Lind, Miriam Sieber. NO CRYING HE MAKES. Scottdale, Pa.: Herald Press, 1972. 93 p.

Sensitive record of a family raising a retarded child and learning to love.

Linde, Thomas F., and Kopp, Thusnelda. TRAINING RETARDED BABIES AND PRESCHOOLERS. Springfield, Ill.: Charles C. Thomas, Publisher, 1974. 200 p. Illus.

Designed to be used for children age one day to six years, this book contains specific procedures for shaping basic skills. Each technique is presented in clear and precise language. Useful for both professionals and parents.

Love, Harold D. THE MENTALLY RETARDED CHILD AND HIS FAMILY. Springfield, Ill.: Charles C. Thomas, Publisher, 1973. 203 p. Biblio.

Helps parents become better equipped to handle the problems associated with a retarded child, including their own feelings and those of the sibling's. Mentions services, agencies, and organizations for the retarded and defines the responsibility of local and state governments in this regard.

Mannoni, Maud. THE BACKWARD CHILD AND HIS MOTHER: A PSYCHO-ANALYTIC STUDY. Translated by A.M. Sheridan Smith. New York: Pantheon Books, 1972. 242 p.

The "stigma" of mental retardation and its effects on both the family and the child.

National Association of Coordinators of State Programs for the Mentally Retarded. THE RIGHTS OF THE MENTALLY HANDICAPPED: PROCEEDINGS FROM A BI-REGIONAL CONFERENCE. Arlington, Va.: 1973. 110 p.

The 1972 conference was attended by representatives from mental health and mental retardation agencies and from state attorney

# Mental Retardation

general offices. They focused on the implications of current court cases in protecting the rights of the mentally retarded and the mentally ill.

Nichtern, Sol, M.D. HELPING THE RETARDED CHILD. New York: Grosset & Dunlap, 1974. 289 p. Biblio., index.

    A child psychiatrist and former pediatrician offers a broad realistic perspective on the care and treatment of the retarded. At the same time, he describes the development of normal behavior. Dr. Nichtern feels that families and communities, rather than institutions, best serve the needs of retarded children.

Perske, Robert. NEW DIRECTIONS FOR PARENTS OF PERSONS WHO ARE RETARDED. Nashville, Tenn.: Abingdon Press, 1973. 64 p. Illus. Paperbound.

    Slim straightforward handbook for parents who have recently learned that their child is retarded.

Rivera, Geraldo. WILLOWBROOK: A REPORT ON HOW IT IS AND WHY IT DOESN'T HAVE TO BE THAT WAY. New York: Random House, 1972. 147 p. Photos.

    This well-known television reporter finds that Willowbrook, a state school for the mentally retarded, is horrendously understaffed and medieval in its methods. The pictures really tell the story.

Rothstein, Jerome. MENTAL RETARDATION. 2d ed. New York: Holt, Rinehart and Winston, 1971. 696 p. Appendices, index.

    Comprehensive collection of resources and readings for parents and professionals on modern trends and issues in mental retardation. Includes diagnosis, school programs, institutional care, parent counseling, and research.

White, Robin. BE NOT AFRAID: THE STORY OF A TRAGICALLY AFFLICTED CHILD AND HIS STUBBORNLY COURAGEOUS FAMILY. New York: Dial Press, 1972. 235 p.

    Well-written description of the trials faced by the author's family after the oldest son (eight years old) is diagnosed as an epileptic with progressive mental retardation. Contains many insights for the parents of handicapped children and the professionals who work with them.

# Mental Retardation

## PAMPHLETS AND/OR GOVERNMENT DOCUMENTS

Unless otherwise noted the materials are available free of charge. Prices quoted are subject to change. Payment should accompany order.

### Bibliographies and Directories

CLINICAL PROGRAMS FOR MENTALLY RETARDED CHILDREN. 1974. 36 p. Available from: U.S. Health Services Administration, Bureau of Community Health Services, 5600 Fishers Lane, Rockville, Md. 20852.

> State-by-state listing of special clinical facilities for mentally retarded children. Gives name, address, phone number, director, area served, ages accepted, and clinic hours for each facility.

DIRECTORY OF STATE AND LOCAL RESOURCES FOR THE MENTALLY RETARDED. 1970. 124 p. Available from: President's Committee on Mental Retardation, U.S. Department of Health, Education and Welfare, Washington, D.C. 20201.

> Comprehensive checklist of state and local agencies, state and private residential facilities, clinical programs, and other resources which serve the mentally retarded. Information covers admissions policies, area served, and fees.

SELECTED READING SUGGESTIONS FOR PARENTS OF MENTALLY RETARDED CHILDREN. Edited by Kathryn A. Gorham. 1970. 58 p. Available from: Office of Human Development, Publications Distribution Unit, Department of Health, Education and Welfare, Washington, D.C. 20201.

> Includes suggestions for help from national organizations plus annotated readings on the management, education, and protection of the mentally retarded child.

### Current Sources

MAKE THE MOST OF YOUR BABY. 1974. 26 p. Illus. Available from: National Association for Retarded Children, 2709 Avenue E, East, Arlington, Tex. 76011.

> Booklet shows how parents can provide positive play experiences for mentally retarded infants and preschool children. Written by June Mather, a mother of two mentally retarded children.

THE MENTALLY RETARDED CHILD AT HOME: A MANUAL FOR PARENTS. By Laura L. Kittman. 1971. 99 p. 35 cents. Available from: Superintendent of Documents, U.S. Government Printing Office, Washington, D.C. 20402.

# Mental Retardation

Practical, informative guide which covers the everyday care of retarded children (i.e., play, speech, behavior) from infancy through adolescence.

PHENYLKETONURIA: AN INHERITED METABOLIC DISORDER ASSOCIATED WITH MENTAL RETARDATION. 1972. 28 p. 25 cents. Available from: Superintendent of Documents, Government Printing Office, Washington, D.C. 20402.

An updated edition which summarizes the current knowledge about phenylketonuria (PKU)--its detection and treatment.

PRIMER FOR PARENTS OF A MENTALLY RETARDED CHILD. 1974. 8 p. 50 cents. Available from: National Association for Retarded Children, 2709 Avenue E, East, Arlington, Tex. 76011.

Answers questions frequently asked by parents.

RETARDED CHILDREN OF THE POOR: A CASEBOOK. By Marjorie H. Kirkland. 1971. Reprint. 1973. 66 p. Available from: U.S. Department of Health, Education and Welfare, Social & Rehabilitation Service, Washington, D.C. 20201.

This document deals with mentally retarded children in poverty-stricken families. Useful for family and child welfare service agencies and workers.

WHAT DO YOU KNOW ABOUT PKU? 1971. 4 p. Available from: Office of Information, Maternal & Child Health Services, Parklawn Building, Rockville, Md. 20852.

Briefly explains the causes, detection, incidence, and treatment of PKU. If undetected, PKU causes mental retardation.

## ORGANIZATIONS AND/OR SOURCES OF MATERIALS, FREE OR AT LOW COST

Association for Children with Retarded
　Mental Development
902 Broadway
New York, N.Y. 10010   Phone (212) 677-5800

An organization of doctors, teachers, parents, and other citizens interested in mentally retarded children and young people. Offers programs for the mentally retarded including rehabilitation centers, recreational day centers, and parent-child counseling. Seeks additional educational opportunities within the New York City school system for mentally retarded children and teenagers.

# Mental Retardation

National Association for Retarded Citizens
2709 Avenue E, East
Arlington, Tex. 76011

> This group is interested in fostering research, treatment, referral services, and community facilities for the mentally retarded child. They also provide parent counseling and publish pamphlets for both parents and professionals. A complete publications list is available without charge.

Retarded Infants Services
386 Park Avenue, South
New York, N.Y. 10016     Phone (212) 889-5464

> Nonprofit agency founded in 1954 whose purpose is to help families with the problems involved in the care and treatment of retarded children. Its services include information and referral, family counseling, home aides, and so on. Membership applications can be sent to the above address. Fees for RIS services are based on ability to pay.

Young Adult Institute and Workshop
229 Park Avenue, South
New York, N.Y. 10003     Phone (212) 982-4600

> A pioneer agency established to provide a comprehensive program that enables mentally handicapped young adults with mental retardation, emotional disturbance, or brain damage to progress from a state of isolation and dependency to financial and social independence.

## AUDIOVISUAL MATERIALS

### Films

BECKY. 16mm, 19 min., sound, color.

> This film attempts to illustrate how a young retarded child spends most of her time at home--an area little explored in films.
>
> Available from: Stuart Finley, Falls Church, Va. 22041.

GREENE VALLEY GRANDPARENTS. 1973. 16mm, 10 min., sound, black and white.

> Describes a program in which a variety of people from the community serve as foster grandparents to mentally retarded children.
>
> Available from: Center for Southern Folklore, 3756 Mimosa Avenue, Memphis, Tenn. 38111.

# EXCEPTIONAL CHILD—SPINA BIFIDA

## BOOKS

### Reference

Pilling, Doria. THE CHILD WITH SPINA BIFIDA: SOCIAL, EMOTIONAL AND EDUCATIONAL ADJUSTMENT. Atlantic Highlands, N.J.: Humanities Press, 1973. 46 p.

> A comprehensive annotated bibliography.

## PAMPHLETS AND/OR GOVERNMENT DOCUMENTS

Unless otherwise noted the materials are available free of charge. Prices quoted are subject to change. Payment should accompany order.

CHILD WITH SPINA BIFIDA. By Chester A. Swinyard, M.D. 1974. 29 p. 50 cents. Available from: Institute of Rehabilitation Medicine, New York University Medical Center, Publications Department, 400 East Thirty-fourth Street, New York, N.Y. 10016.

> A specialist explains the condition, and discusses the problems involved in caring for the child afflicted with a "cleft spine."

HOPE THROUGH RESEARCH: SPINA BIFIDA. 1972. 11 p. Available from: National Institute of Neurological and Communicative Disorders and Stroke, Bethesda, Md. 20014.

> Information about spina bifida: symptoms, complications, causes, frequency, treatment, and research.

SPINA BIFIDA--A BIRTH DEFECT. Publication no. (NIH) 72-309. Available from: National Institute of Neurological and Communicative Disorders and Stroke, Bethesda, Md. 20014.

# Spina Bifida

Spina bifida or "cleft spine" is a birth defect in which one or more of the individual bones of the back fail to close completely. This pamphlet offers basic information about this handicap.

## ORGANIZATIONS AND/OR SOURCES OF MATERIALS, FREE OR AT LOW COST

National Easter Seal Society for Crippled
   Children and Adults
2023 West Ogden Avenue
Chicago, Ill. 60612     Phone (312) 243-8400

    Provides pamphlets on spina bifida. State and local chapters have information on services available to children with spina bifida.

Spina Bifida Association of America
209 Shilo Drive
Madison, Wis.

    Offers programs and guidance to benefit those born with spina bifida. Services can be obtained through local chapters.

## AUDIOVISUAL MATERIALS

### Films

WHO WILL LOVE MY CHILD? 1968. 16mm, 14 1/2 min., sound, color.

    Tells the story of a young couple whose first child was born with hydrocephalus and spina bifida. Emphasizes parental and genetic counseling and describes surgical procedures for spina bifida.

    Available from: The National Foundation--March of Dimes, Division of Public Education, Box 2000, White Plains, N.Y. 10602.

# EXCEPTIONAL CHILD—VISUAL AND HEARING IMPAIRMENT

## BOOKS

### Reference

American Foundation for the Blind. DIRECTORY OF AGENCIES SERVING THE VISUALLY HANDICAPPED IN THE UNITED STATES. New York: 1974. 381 p. Index.

> Organized by state. Lists the type of service rendered by each agency. Includes a separate list of specialized agencies and organizations.

### Current Sources

Harris, Grace M. LANGUAGE FOR THE PRESCHOOL DEAF CHILD. 3d ed. New York: Grune & Stratton, 1971. 354 p. Appendix, biblio., illus., index.

> The third edition contains many activities to help the hearing-imparied child develop language ability. Specific lesson plans are included in the appendix.

Lowenfeld, Berthold. OUR BLIND CHILDREN: GROWING AND LEARNING WITH THEM. Rev. ed. Springfield, Ill.: Charles C. Thomas, Publisher, 1971. 244 p. Biblio., illus., index.

> Simple but helpful guide for parents that is considered a classic. Covers the primary aspects of a blind child's development from birth through adolescence with clues for parental assistance.

Semple, Jean E. HEARING-IMPAIRED PRESCHOOL CHILD. Springfield, Ill.: Charles C. Thomas, Publisher, 1970. 86 p.

> Helpful and practical suggestions for helping deaf children to acquire speech. Includes a series of home lesson plans.

# Visual and Hearing Impairment

Ulrich, Sharon, and Wolf, Anna W.M. ELIZABETH. Introduction and commentary by Selma H. Fraiberg and Edna Edelson. Ann Arbor: University of Michigan, 1972. 122 p. Illus.

    Two experts describe the rearing of a blind child. The child's development is compared with that of a sighted child.

## PERIODICALS

NEW OUTLOOK FOR THE BLIND. New York: American Foundation for the Blind, 1907-- . Monthly, except July/August.

    Research articles plus listings of current literature, books, directories, pamphlets, and materials of interest to the blind and those who work with them.

## PAMPHLETS AND/OR GOVERNMENT DOCUMENTS

Unless otherwise noted the materials are available free of charge. Prices quoted are subject to change. Payment should accompany order.

### Bibliographies

DIRECTORY OF PROGRAMS AND SERVICES FOR THE DEAF IN THE UNITED STATES. Edited by William N. Craig and Helen B. Craig. 1975. 320 p. $5.00. Available from: Conference of Executives of American Schools for the Deaf, 5034 Wisconsin Avenue, N.W., Washington, D.C. 20016.

    Annual publication which includes state-by-state listings of public and private schools and classes for the deaf, speech and hearing agencies in the United States, summer camps for deaf and hard-of-hearing children, and rehabilitation centers.

SERVICES FOR THE BLIND PERSON, THE PUBLIC AND THE PROFESSIONAL. 1971. 12 p. Available from: Publications Division, American Foundation for the Blind, 15 West Sixteenth Street, New York, N.Y. 10011.

    Lists the aid, appliances, materials, and services available from the foundation.

VOLUNTEERS WHO PRODUCE BOOKS: BRAILLE, LARGE TYPE, TAPE. 1973. 65 p. Available from: Library of Congress, Division for the Blind and Physically Handicapped, Washington, D.C. 20542.

    This directory names the volunteer groups and individuals who transcribe and record reading materials for blind and physically handicapped persons. Listing is alphabetical by state. Also available in Braille.

# Visual and Hearing Impairment

## Current Sources

HEARING LOSS. 1973. 34 p. Available from: Information Office, National Institute of Neurological and Communicative Diseases and Stroke, National Institutes of Health, Bethesda, Md. 20014.

> Discusses the importance of early detection of hearing loss. Topics include testing and guarding a child's hearing, speech reading, auditory training, manual communication, sources of help, and additional information on materials and programs available to persons with hearing problems.

HELPING THE CHILD WHO CANNOT HEAR. By Samuel Moffat. 1972. 28 p. 35 cents. Publication no. 479. Available from: Public Affairs Committee, 381 Park Avenue, S., New York, N.Y. 10016.

> This pamphlet describes the symptoms that indicate possible hearing impairment even in very young infants and emphasizes the importance of early diagnosis. Also discusses sources for medical help and counseling, as well as the aids and educational programs available to the hearing-handicapped child.

THE PRESCHOOL DEAF BLIND CHILD--SUGGESTIONS FOR PARENTS. 1965. 8 p. Publication no. 9-A. Available from: Publications Division, American Foundation for the Blind, 15 West Sixteenth Street, New York, N.Y. 10011.

## ORGANIZATIONS AND/OR SOURCES OF MATERIALS, FREE OR AT LOW COST

Alexander Graham Bell Association
  for the Deaf
3417 Volta Place, N.W.
Washington, D.C. 20007   Phone (202) 337-5220

> The purpose of this organization is to help hearing-impaired children and adults to live fuller lives at home and in the community. It provides information services to parents and professionals and publishes the VOLTA REVIEW (monthly), as well as other books and brochures. Free information on the warning signs of hearing loss and the help available to hearing-impaired children can be obtained from HEARING ALERT! Washington, D.C. 20007.

American Foundation for the Blind
15 West Sixteenth Street
New York, N.Y. 10011   Phone (212) 924-0420

> A national organization which acts as a consultant to local agencies serving both blind and partially-sighted persons.

# Visual and Hearing Impairment

Carries on an active education program for professionals and for the general public. Publishes pamphlets of interest to parents and children.

Association for Education of the
  Visually Handicapped
919 Walnut Street, Fourth Floor
Philadelphia, Pa. 19107      Phone (215) 732-0100

Organization devoted to the education, guidance, vocational rehabilitation, or occupational placement of the fully or partially visually impaired.

Association for the Advancement of Blind
  and Retarded Children
164-09 Hillside Avenue
Jamaica, N.Y. 11432      Phone (212) 523-2222

Organization comprised of community groups and individuals interested in multi-handicapped blind children. Operates a state-approved school which enrolls primarily those blind children rejected by other schools.

National Association of Hearing and
  Speech Action
814 Thayer Avenue
Silver Spring, Md. 20910      Phone (301) 588-5252

A private nonprofit organization whose purpose is to promote high standards of professional service in the areas of diagnosis and evaluation, treatment, education, counseling and guidance, and rehabilitation in the various areas of speech disorders. Brochures and pamphlets are available free of charge. Postcard requests are preferred.

National Association of the Deaf
814 Thayer Avenue
Silver Spring, Md. 20910      Phone (301) 587-1788

The principal function of this group is to serve as a clearinghouse for information and referral services relating to deafness and the problems of the deaf. A complete list of publications is available free of charge.

National Society for the Prevention of
  Blindness
79 Madison Avenue
New York, N.Y. 10016      Phone (212) 684-3505

This national organization is devoted to preventing blindness

# Visual and Hearing Impairment

and conserving vision through a program of community service, publications, public information, education of laypersons and professionals, and research. Provides pamphlets on eye health and safety; also free films for both professional and nonprofessional audiences. Both are listed in the CATALOGUE OF PUBLICATIONS AND FILMS.

Recording for the Blind
215 East Fifty-eighth Street
New York, N.Y. 10022    Phone (212) 751-0860

Records textbooks, free of charge, for visually handicapped grade school, high school, and college students and for adults who request it. Publishes a catalog for its library.

## AUDIOVISUAL MATERIALS

## Films

EVERYTHING BUT HEAR. 1971. 15 min., sound.

Features a deaf woman who has learned to communicate despite her handicap. Of special interest are flashbacks of a 1955 film showing her early training in the basics at age five.

Available from: The Clarke School for the Deaf, Northampton, Maine 01060.

THE EYES OF A CHILD. 1970. 30 min., sound.

Follows children on a typical day at a special school for the blind.

Available from: Time-Life Films, 43 West Sixteenth Street, New York, N.Y. 10011.

WORLD OF DEAF-BLIND CHILDREN--HOW THEY COMMUNICATE. 1974. 16mm, 29 min., sound, color.

Documentary of the activities at the Perkins School for the Blind. Emphasizes that blind children are not helpless, even though they have limitations that a sighted child doesn't. No loan charge.

Available from: Campbell Films, Film Library, Saxtons River, Vt. 05154.

# FOOD, CLOTHING, AND FURNITURE

## BOOKS

### Reference

Nutrition Foundation. NUTRITION EDUCATION MATERIALS. Washington, D.C.: 1974. 162 p.

> Describes more than a thousand booklists, pamphlets, and audio-visual aids that can be obtained from federal agencies, professional societies, and educational organizations. Includes names and addresses of sources

### Current Sources

Association for Childhood Education International. COOKING AND EATING WITH CHILDREN, A WAY TO LEARN. Washington, D.C.: 1974. 48 p.

> Stresses the importance of providing children with nutritious foods and calls attention to the need for eating in a pleasant environment. Offers guidelines for children's cooking projects.

Baker, Samm Sinclair, and Stillman, Irwin Maxwell, M.D. THE DOCTOR'S QUICK TEENAGE DIET. New York: David McKay Co., 1971. 272 p. Index.

> The famous diet doctor writes for teenagers. Includes a preliminary pep talk, a specific seven-day diet, plus quick and easy recipes. Parental supervision is advisable.

Castle, Sue. THE COMPLETE GUIDE TO PREPARING BABY FOODS AT HOME. Garden City, N.Y.: Doubleday & Co., 1973. 314 p.

> Practical guide to planning, shopping, preparing, and storing of nutritious food.

## Food, Clothing, Furniture

Davis, Adelle. LET'S HAVE HEALTHY CHILDREN. New and expanded ed. New York: Harcourt Brace Jovanovich, 1972. 486 p. Illus., index.

> Sound nutritional advice for husbands and wives considering families, for pregnant women, and for children from birth to adolescence. Includes "Table of Food Composition."

Eden, Alvin N., M.D., and Heilman, Joan Rattner. GROWING UP THIN. New York: David McKay Co., 1975. 240 p. Index.

> Advice and information on calorie counting, exercise, and sound eating habits. Discusses nutrition from prenatal status to adolescence.

Goodwin, M.D., and Pollen, G. CREATIVE FOOD EXPERIENCES FOR CHILDREN. Washington, D.C.: Center for Science in the Public Interest, 1974. Paperbound.

> Easy-to-read guide for planning cooking and food-related activities that teach children the principles of good nutrition.

Gunther, Mavis, M.D. INFANT FEEDING. Chicago: Henry Regnery Co., 1970. 114 p. Biblio., illus., index.

> Describes the benefits of breastfeeding. Discusses physical and psychological blocks to successful nursing with possible solutions.

Hatfield, Antoinette K., and Stanton, Peggy. HELP! MY CHILD WON'T EAT RIGHT: A GUIDE TO BETTER NUTRITION. Washington, D.C.: Acropolis Books, 1973. 168 p. Illus., index. Paperbound.

> Handy, practical child feeding guide for parents. Uses recipes, poems, cartoons, meal plans, growth charts, and food composition tables as innovative devices to whet children's appetites.

Kenda, Margaret E., and Williams, Phyllis S. THE NATURAL BABY FOOD COOKBOOK. Los Angeles: Nash Publishing Corp., 1972. 168 p. Biblio., index.

> Collection of menus and recipes that provide an alternative to commercial baby food.

Lane, Carolyn, and Zapata, Pamela. THE MOTHER'S COOK AND COPE BOOK. New York: Viking Press, 1972. 208 p. Illus., index.

> Directions for preparing nutritious foods for the whole family and advice on coping with the eating habits of the child.

# Food, Clothing, Furniture

Larter, Vera. SEWING CHILDREN'S CLOTHING MADE EASY. Garden City, N.Y.: Doubleday & Co., 1971. 230 p. Illus., index.

> Gives directions for making clothes that grow with the child, for designing variations from one basic pattern, and for sewing costumes, contour crib sheets, bibs, and diapers.

Levine, Milton I., M.D., and Seligman, Jean H. YOUR OVERWEIGHT CHILD. Cleveland, Ohio.: World Publications, 1971. 167 p.

> Written for parents of overweight children, this book defines obesity, identifies the obese child, and outlines the treatment of obesity. The authors prescribe a weight control program that includes activity and diet plans.

Morris, Melinda. THE FIRST BABYFOOD COOKBOOK. New York: Grosset & Dunlap, 1972. 128 p. Illus.

> Gives recipes for easy-to-prepare, nutritious meals for children aged one month to fifteen months. Also includes suggestions on using leftovers.

Olds, Sally W., and Eiger, Marvin S., M.D. THE COMPLETE BOOK OF BREASTFEEDING. New York: Workman Publishing Co., 1972. 208 p. illus.

> Information for women deciding whether to breastfeed.

Palmer, Bruce. MAKING CHILDREN'S FURNITURE AND PLAY STRUCTURES. New York: Workman Publishing Co., 1974. 144 p. Appendix, illus. Paperbound.

> Well-illustrated workbook with designs for low-cost, lightweight, durable furniture and play equipment that can be built by parent and child together.

Parents' Nursery School. KIDS ARE NATURAL COOKS: CHILD-TESTED RECIPES FOR HOME AND SCHOOL USING NATURAL FOODS. New York: Houghton Mifflin Co., 1974. 129 p. Illus., index.

> Developed from actual experiences at the Parents' Nursery School in Cambridge, Massachusetts, this book not only provides many hours of recreation for young children but also explains to them the fundamentals of good nutrition and simple cooking methods. Includes fun-to-follow recipes suitable for all ages as well as guidelines for parents and teachers.

Pearlman, Ruth. YOUR BABY: THE SAFE AND HEALTHY WAY. New York: Random House, 1971. 140 p. Illus., index.

> Advice on feeding coupled with a variety of recipes for the child from birth to eighteen months.

# Food, Clothing, Furniture

Pryor, Karen. NURSING YOUR BABY. Rev. ed. New York: Harper & Row Publishers, 1973. 289 p. Biblio., photos., index.

>The new research on breastfeeding and what to expect in the day-to-day experiences from delivery to weaning.

Raphael, Dana. THE TENDER GIFT: BREASTFEEDING. Foreword by Margaret Mead. Englewood Cliffs, N.J.: Prentice-Hall, 1973. 200 p. Illus., photos.

>An anthropologist discusses breastfeeding: the process itself, its history, and the attitudes in our society which have discouraged it. She offers interesting suggestions on adopting the contemporary life-style to support the new mother.

Rodway, Pamela. CHILDREN'S CLOTHES: EASY TO MAKE CLOTHES FOR 1-10 YEAR OLDS. New York: Arco Publishing Co., 1975. 96 p. Illus. some color, photos.

>Twenty-one simple patterns for sewing, knitting, and crocheting.

Saville, F. REAL FOOD FOR YOUR BABY. New York: Simon & Schuster, 1973. 179 p.

>A mother of four children shares her methods for preparing baby foods at home. Contains a variety of recipes, for infants and toddlers, which are easy to prepare and nutritious.

Thomas, Linda L. CARING AND COOKING FOR THE ALLERGIC CHILD. New York: Drake Publishers, 1974. 144 p. Appendix, biblio., glossary, tables, index.

>The mother of an allergic child discusses the nature of allergies and the problems and precautions presented by a child's diet. Includes specific food substitutions and therapeutic recipes. Useful to professionals and parents.

Turner, Mary Dustan, and Turner, James S. MAKING YOUR OWN BABY FOOD. New York: Workman Publishing Co., 1972. 128 p. Illus.

>The authors assert that commercially processed baby food is not only lacking in nutrition but possibly dangerous. Therefore, they give menus and recipes for organic baby foods.

## PERIODICALS

JOURNAL OF HOME ECONOMICS. Washington, D.C.: American Home Economics Association, 1909-- . Monthly.

>Articles and news related to the field of home economics, including child development.

# Food, Clothing, Furniture

JOURNAL OF NUTRITION EDUCATION. Berkeley, Calif.: Society for Nutrition Education, 1969-- . Quarterly.

> Contains research articles, general articles, current topics, plus reviews of books and educational materials.

## PAMPHLETS AND/OR GOVERNMENT DOCUMENTS

Unless otherwise noted the materials are available free of charge. Prices quoted are subject to change. Payment should accompany order.

### Bibliographies

PUBLICATIONS. 1974. 19 p. Available from: U.S. Department of Agriculture, Food and Nutrition Service, Washington, D.C. 20250.

> Describes publications on the different federal food assistance programs. Includes publications in Spanish and many free items.

### Current Sources

FEEDING LITTLE FOLKS. 1971. 21 p. Available from: National Dairy Council, Chicago, Ill. 60606.

> This booklet describes the food habits of preschool children by tying them in with the child's physical and emotional development and activity. Educates parents to avoid the common eating problems of children.

FEEDING THE CHILD WITH A HANDICAP. 1973. 19 p. Available from: Public Inquiries, Health Services Administration, 5600 Fishers Lane, Rockville, Md. 20852.

> This pamphlet makes suggestions for meeting the special nutritional needs of certain handicapped children.

FEEDING THE INFANT. 1971. 4 p. Publication no. L-936. Available from: Texas Agricultural Experiment Station, Texas A&M University, College Station, Tex. 77843.

> What to feed a baby in its first year of life.

FOOD RIGHTS HANDBOOK. 1974. 44 p. Appendix, illus. Available from: The Children's Foundation, 1028 Connecticut Avenue, N.W., Washington, D.C. 20036.

> Concise description of federal food assistance programs including the school lunch program, the school breakfast program, and the

## Food, Clothing, Furniture

supplemental food program for nursing mothers and preschool children. Includes information on application procedures and eligibility.

FOOD STAMPS FOR YOU. Available from: Food Stamp Division, Food and Nutrition Service, U.S. Department of Agriculture, Washington, D.C. 20250.

Booklet designed to explain the food stamp program to eligible persons.

GOOD NEWS FOR KIDS. 1974. 8 p. Publication no. 034C. Available from: Consumer Information, Public Documents Distribution Center, Pueblo, Colo. 81009.

Games to teach children about food.

HOW CHILDREN GROW. 1972. 56 p. Available from: Information Office, Division of Research Resources, National Institutes of Health, Bethesda, Md. 20014.

Explains a new technique to determine whether an unborn baby is growing normally. Aimed at cutting the infant death rate by focusing on the problems of low-birth-weight babies. Reviews the effects of nutrition, hormones, illness, and emotion on the childhood years and the role of obesity and early and late puberty in adolescent growth.

HOW TO SELECT INFANTS AND CHILDREN'S CLOTHING. 1971. 19 p. Publication no. 10-A. Available from: Consumer Information Services, Sears, Roebuck and Co., Department 703-Public Relations, 303 East Ohio Street, Chicago, Ill. 60611.

Includes a developmental chart.

MEAL TIME! HAPPY TIME! 1975. Available from: The American Dietetic Association, 430 North Michigan Avenue, Chicago, Ill. 60611.

To guide parents in encouraging good eating habits in their children, this booklet describes the role of nutrients and includes charts showing children's food needs at different ages.

NUTRITION AND FEEDING TECHNIQUES FOR HANDICAPPED CHILDREN, PAMPHLET SERIES. 4 p. each. Available from: Bureau of Mental Retardation and Disabilities Services, California Department of Public Health, 2151 Berkeley Way, Berkeley, Calif. 94704.

A series of twelve practical and easy-to-understand pamphlets on different aspects of nutrition and feeding practices.

## Food, Clothing, Furniture

NUTRITION SURVIVAL KIT. 1973. 10 p. 25 cents. Available from: Action for Children's Television, 46 Austin Street, Newtonville, Mass. 02160.

> Helps parents counteract their children's demands for the non-nutritious food advertised on television. Suggests more nutritious foods as well as games and puzzles that educate children about their nutritional needs.

PREVENTION OF IRON-DEFICIENCY ANEMIA IN INFANTS AND CHILDREN OF PRESCHOOL AGE. 1970. 19 p. Available from: Health Services Administration, 5600 Fishers Lane, Rockville, Md. 20852.

> To combat the most prevalent deficiency disorder among infants and children in the United States, this booklet stresses that the diet of children contain adequate levels of all essential nutrients--not only iron.

PUT MUNCH IN THEIR MENU. 1971. 28 p. 15 cents. Available from: Inter Harvest, P.O. Box 2115, Salinas, Calif. 93901.

> Building better eating habits in children from infants through teenagers by including more fresh vegetables in their diet.

SKIM MILK IN INFANT FEEDING. By Samuel J. Fomon, M.D. 1973. 6 p. Available from: Maternal and Child Health Services. 5600 Fishers Lane, Rockville, Md. 20852.

> A specialist in child health assesses nutritional problems related to the feeding of skim milk to infants.

## ORGANIZATIONS AND/OR SOURCES OF MATERIALS, FREE OR AT LOW COST

American Home Economics Association
2010 Massachusetts Avenue, N.W.
Washington, D.C. 20036

> Pamphlets and reprints on nutrition.

Cereal Institute
135 South LaSalle Street
Chicago, Ill. 60603

> Leaflets, source books, charts, and filmstrips.

The Children's Foundation
1028 Connecticut Avenue, N.W.
Suite 1112
Washington, D.C. 20036     Phone (202) 296-4451

## Food, Clothing, Furniture

A national, nonprofit, anti-hunger and food rights advocacy group which monitors federal food programs and offers assistance to parent groups and community groups interested in food and child nutrition programs. Publishes fact sheets and booklets on food assistance programs for women, infants, migrant and Indian children, and children of the working poor.

National Dairy Council
6300 River Road
Rosemont, Ill. 60018    Phone (312) 696-1020

Serves as a national resource agency in nutrition education and research. Publishes and distributes news releases for newspapers and magazines and produces films and other literature on the importance of milk and milk products. Interested parents can send for their catalog of health education materials.

Nutrition Foundation
489 Fifth Avenue
New York, N.Y. 10017    Phone (212) 687-4830

Interested in supporting research and education in the science of nutrition this group publishes booklets and pamphlets for professionals and lay persons.

Society for Nutrition Education
2140 Shattuck Avenue
Suite 1110
Berkeley, Calif. 94704

Through its National Nutrition Education Clearinghouse, this organization provides resource lists which describe recommended publications (for professionals and general public), many of which are inexpensive.

U.S. Department of Agriculture
Office of Information
Washington, D.C. 20250

Booklets on nutrition.

## AUDIOVISUAL MATERIALS

### Films

CHILDREN'S CLOTHES--HOW TO CHOOSE THEM. 16mm, 26 min., sound, color.

# Food, Clothing, Furniture

Discusses quality fabrics, laundry tests, stitches, hems, labels, and other important factors in selecting children's clothing.

Available from: Association-Sterling Films, Executive Offices 866 Third Avenue, New York, N.Y. 10022.

FEEDING THE INFANT--BUILDING THE MAN. 16mm, 26 min., sound, color.

Physicians and nutrition experts discuss infant nutrition and its long-range effects.

Available from: Wyeth Film Library, P.O. Box 8299, Philadelphia, Pa. 19101.

NUTRITION: TO BABY WITH LOVE. 1973. 10 min., sound, color.

Stresses importance of good prenatal and infant nutrition. Should appeal to potential, prospective, and new parents.

Available from: West Glen Films, 565 Fifth Avenue, New York, N.Y. 10017.

TALKING ABOUT BREASTFEEDING. 1971. 16mm, 17 min., sound, color.

Advantages of breastfeeding.

Available from: Polymorph Films, 331 Newberry Street, Boston, Mass. 02115.

## Filmstrips and Slides

FOOD AS CHILDREN SEE IT. 1974. Filmstrip with record. 72 frames, 15 min.

Appropriate for young mothers' groups, this filmstrip shows parents good nutrition for preschoolers.

Available from: Betty Crocker Teaching Aids, 9200 Film Center, Box 1113, Minneapolis, Minn. 55440.

# GENETIC DISEASES

## BOOKS

### Current Sources

Linde, Shirley Motter. SICKLE CELL: A COMPLETE GUIDE TO PREVENTION AND TREATMENT. New York: Pavilion Publishing Co., 1972. 187 p. Illus., index. Paperbound.
> This work is a sound, well-written, and useful handbook designed to give the public a clearer understanding of sickle cell anemia. Lists of genetic counseling services and screening clinics are also included.

## PAMPHLETS AND/OR GOVERNMENT DOCUMENTS

Unless otherwise noted the materials are available free of charge. Prices quoted are subject to change. Payment should accompany order.

COOLEY'S ANEMIA. n.d. Available from: New York State Department of Health, Albany, N.Y. 12210.
> Brochure covering such aspects as what Cooley's Anemia is, how it is inherited, can it be cured?

FIGHTING SICKLE CELL DISEASE: TWO ARTICLES. 1971. 10 p. Available from: Office of Child Development, P.O. Box 1182, Washington, D.C. 20013.
> Covers the early diagnosis of sickle cell anemia and the care of children with the disease.

SICKLE CELL ANEMIA AND SICKLE CELL TRAIT. 1973. 6 p. Available from: National Heart and Lung Institute, National Institutes of Health, Bethesda, Md. 20014.

# Genetic Diseases

Question/answer brochure; also available in Spanish.

WHAT ARE THE FACTS ABOUT GENETIC DISEASE. 1974. 32 p. Available from: Office of Research Reports, National Institute of General Medical Sciences, National Institutes of Health, Bethesda, Md. 20014.

A new booklet details the progress in detecting, diagnosing, preventing, and treating genetic diseases. It also describes the various genetic diseases and the effects that they produce.

## ORGANIZATIONS AND/OR SOURCES OF MATERIALS, FREE OR AT LOW COST

Cooley's Anemia Blood and Research
  Foundation for Children
647 Franklin Avenue
Garden City, N.Y. 11530

Involved in finding the cause and cure for Cooley's Anemia, this organization is working on a program which includes research, education, and patient services. It maintains a blood credit program, in cooperation with the American Red Cross and other blood bank groups, through which local chapters supply free blood to anyone with Cooley's Anemia. Publishes literature about this handicap.

National Genetics Foundation
250 West Fifty-seventh Street
New York, N.Y. 10019    Phone (212) 265-3166

This foundation offers counseling for families and makes referrals to genetic counseling and treatment centers throughout the country. Sponsors a program to educate physicians and the general public on the importance of genetic counseling.

National Hemophilia Foundation
25 West Thirty-ninth Street
New York, N.Y. 10018    Phone (212) 279-0397

Voluntary health organization consisting primarily of hemophiliacs and their families. Disseminates literature for the general public and for medical and paramedical personnel. Publishes a DIRECTORY OF HEMOPHILIA TREATMENT CENTERS and other books of interest to hemophiliacs and their families.

# Genetic Diseases

National Sickle Cell Disease Program
National Heart and Lung Institute
National Institutes of Health
Bethesda, Maryland 20014

>Distributes an informational packet of materials on sickle cell disease.

National Tay-Sachs and Allied
 Diseases Association
122 East Forty-second Street
New York, N.Y. 10017

>This organization is composed of parents, physicians, and others interested in children and infants who suffer from Tay Sachs disease or allied degenerative diseases of the nervous system. It is the chief referral agency for carrier detection and genetic counseling facilities. Publishes pamphlets and books.

Sickle Cell Disease Foundation of
 Greater New York
144 West 125th Street
New York, N.Y. 10027     Phone (212) 850-1920

>This voluntary health agency was formed to support and conduct research and educational programs aimed at the control and eradication of sickle cell anemia. Offers training for screening and counseling programs, distributes educational materials, and maintains files on both organizations working to overcome the disease and services to families and patients with the disease. Has an informational film on the disease.

## AUDIOVISUAL MATERIALS

### Films

ANOTHER TOMORROW FOR TERESA.

>Informational film on Cooley's Anemia.

>Available from: Cooley's Anemia Blood and Research Foundation for Children, 647 Franklin Avenue, Garden City, N.Y. 11530.

# Genetic Diseases

## Filmstrips

SICKLE CELL--AN INHERITED DISEASE. 1972. Filmstrip. 35mm, 108 frames, with phonodisc.

> Designed to instruct black children and parents on the nature and treatment of the sickle cell anemia.
>
> Available from: Glen Educational Films, 312 Saddle River Road, Monsey, N.Y. 10952.

# GIFTED CHILD

## BOOKS

### Dated but Still Relevant

American Association for Gifted Children. THE GIFTED CHILD. Edited by Paul Witty. Lexington, Mass.: D.C. Heath & Co., 1951. 338 p.

> Comprehensive overview of the literature on the education of gifted children. Stresses how to recognize gifted children and further their development. Guides parents and teachers in helping bright children make the best use of their superior talents.

Cutts, Norma E., and Moseley, Nicholas. BRIGHT CHILDREN: A GUIDE FOR PARENTS. New York: G.P. Putnam's Sons, 1953. 238 p.

> General, nontechnical, and easily understood guide covering such topics as early identification, the right start in school, problems that confront the superior child at home and in school, the pros and cons of public versus private schools, the arguments for vocational versus college education, and sources of advice.

Terman, Lewis M., and Oden, Melita H. THE GIFTED CHILD GROWS UP: TWENTY-FIVE YEARS' FOLLOW-UP OF A SUPERIOR GROUP. Vol. 4. Stanford, Calif.: Stanford University Press, 1947. 448 p. Appendix, biblio., index.

> This book is volume 4 of the major research work in the field, THE GENETIC STUDIES OF GENIUS. Presents an overall report and summary of the educational and vocational histories and the general adjustment into young adult life of 1500 gifted California residents covering the years 1921-46. The investigation provides answers regarding the later careers of superior children and stresses the need for better programs to nurture the academically talented.

# Gifted Child

Witty, Paul A. HELPING THE GIFTED CHILD. Chicago: Science Research Associates, 1952. 48 p. Illus.

> One of the first publications addressed specifically to parents. Helps both parents and teachers to identify youngsters with superior ability, deal with their special problems, and encourage the use of their talent.

## Reference

Axford, Lavonne B. A DIRECTORY OF EDUCATIONAL PROGRAMS FOR THE GIFTED. New York: Scarecrow Press, 1971. 282 p. Biblio.

> Lists by state the private and public schools that offer special educational programs for children of "unusual academic talent, creativity and high intelligence." Includes a section on schools offering summer-only programs.

## Current Sources

Gowan, John C., and Torrance, E. Paul, eds. EDUCATING THE ABLEST. Itasca, Ill.: F.E. Peacock Co., 1971. 304 p. Biblio., index.

> Collection of readings mostly from the GIFTED CHILD QUARTERLY to aid both lay and professional people in their efforts to identify and nurture gifted children. Articles include both theoretical concepts and practical suggestions on topics ranging from identification of talented youngsters to the role of parents.

Rice, Joseph P. THE GIFTED: DEVELOPING TOTAL TALENT. Foreword by Max Rafferty. Springfield, Ill.: Charles C. Thomas, Publisher, 1970. 339 p. Biblio., tables, index.

> Discusses early childhood stimulation and the home environment in the rearing of the academically or mentally gifted.

Sanderlin, Owenita. TEACHING GIFTED CHILDREN. Cranbury, N.J.: A.S. Barnes & Co., 1973. 190 p. Index.

> A teacher and mother of gifted children covers many aspects of education from the question of IQ, to special classes, to the role of parents and teachers in guiding gifted children. Designed more as a manual for parents than a curriculum resource for teachers.

## PERIODICALS

THE GIFTED CHILD QUARTERLY. Hot Springs, Ark.: National Association for Gifted Children, 1957--. Quarterly.

> Although scholarly and primarily geared to psychologists and teachers of education, this journal is the only one in its field and may be of use to parents.

# Gifted Child

## PAMPHLETS AND/OR GOVERNMENT DOCUMENTS

Unless otherwise noted the materials are available free of charge. Prices quoted are subject to change. Payment should accompany order.

MENTALLY GIFTED CHILDREN AND YOUTH. 1973. 20 p. Available from: Pennsylvania Department of Education, Box 911, Harrisburg, Pa. 17126.

A guide for recognizing, understanding, and helping the gifted child who has special needs. Includes questionnaires, "Is Your Child Gifted," "Are You a Gifted Parent?," and "Does Your School Provide for the Gifted?"

## ORGANIZATIONS AND/OR SOURCES OF MATERIALS, FREE OR AT LOW COST

American Association for Gifted Children
15 Gramercy Park
New York, N.Y. 10003      Phone (212) 472-4266

This association seeks to encourage understanding on the part of the public about the needs and problems of the gifted and talented through a unique program of cooperation with the community and professional groups.

Foundation for Gifted and Creative Children
395 Diamond Hill Road
Warwick, R.I. 02886      Phone (401) 737-7481

The foundation works for a proper education of gifted and creative children through counseling, testing, and workshops for children and parents.

National Association for Creative Children
  and Adults
8080 Springvalley Drive
Cincinnati, Ohio 45236

An association of teachers, guidance counselors, psychologists, other professionals, and parents interested in working with the gifted child. They publish monographs and bibliographies and provide consultation services.

See also Council for Exceptional Children, "Exceptional Child--General."

# HEALTH—GENERAL

(See also Chapters on Child Development; Genetic Diseases)

## BOOKS

### Dated but Still Relevant

Geist, Harold. A CHILD GOES TO THE HOSPITAL: THE PSYCHOLOGICAL ASPECTS OF A CHILD GOING TO THE HOSPITAL. Springfield, Ill.: Charles C. Thomas, Publisher, 1965. 112 p. Biblio., illus., index.

> Useful suggestions for dealing with a child who is going into the hospital.

Karelitz, Samuel, M.D. WHEN YOUR CHILD IS ILL: A GUIDE TO INFECTIOUS DISEASES IN CHILDHOOD. Rev. ed. New York: Random House, 1969. 568 p. Glossary.

> A clear and comprehensive handbook that covers the common and not-so-common diseases of childhood and their treatment from respiratory infections to skin diseases. It includes a useful question-and-answer section at the end of each chapter.

### Reference

The Boston Children's Medical Center, and Feinbloom, Richard I., M.D. CHILD HEALTH ENCYCLOPEDIA: THE COMPLETE GUIDE FOR PARENTS. New York: Delacorte Press, 1975. 561 p.

> This well-written book emphasizes the common illnesses. It covers diet, safety, and home care for the sick child. It also includes the societies and publications that can provide additional information on health topics.

Broadribb, Violet, and Lee, Henry F., M.D. THE MODERN PARENT'S GUIDE TO BABY AND CHILD CARE. Philadelphia: J.B. Lippincott Co., 1973. 458 p. Biblio., illus., index.

## Health—General

> Practical advice on child care from pregnancy through adolescence. Half the book is devoted to prevention, recognition, and treatment of common illnesses, with extra consideration given to problems of the working mother. Special sections on first aid treatment, a safety-check for each age level, and references for further reading are included.

Community Council of Greater New York. DIRECTORY OF SOCIAL AND HEALTH AGENCIES OF NEW YORK CITY, 1973-1974. New York: Columbia University Press, 1973. 718 p. Index.

> Comprehensive but brief information about 1,300 public and voluntary welfare and health agencies serving New York City. Includes a subject index.

Horkheimer, Foley A., comp. and ed. EDUCATORS GUIDE TO FREE HEALTH, PHYSICAL EDUCATION AND RECREATION MATERIALS. Randolph, Wis.: Educators Progress Service, 1975. 633 p.

> Organized by subject and title, this annual lists over 3,000 free items including pamphlets, films, filmstrips, slides, transparencies, audiotapes, videotapes, and other materials. Comprehensive title, subject, and source availability indexes aid the reader in locating items of interest.

## Current Sources

Baird, Henry W., M.D. THE CHILD WITH CONVULSIONS: A GUIDE FOR PARENTS, TEACHERS, COUNSELORS, AND MEDICAL PERSONNEL. New York: Grune & Stratton, 1972. 145 p. Illus.

> Diagnosis and treatment for children with convulsions.

Bleiberg, Aaron H., and Leubling, Harry E. PARENTS' GUIDE TO CLEFT PALATE HABILITATION: THE TEAM APPROACH. New York: Exposition Press, 1971. 163 p. Appendix, biblio., glossary, illus., index.

> Informative and authoritative presentation in nontechnical language of the problems and procedures in the team approach (parents and professionals) of cleft palate habilitation. Includes a directory of cleft palate teams by state and city.

Cody, D., and Thane, R., M.D. YOUR CHILD'S EARS, NOSE AND THROAT. New York: Macmillan, 1974. 222 p. Illus., index.

> Comprehensive and readable guide to recognizing and dealing with the most common childhood problems of the ears, nose, and throat.

# Health—General

Hardgrove, Carol B., and Dawson, Rosemary B. PARENTS AND CHILDREN IN THE HOSPITAL: THE FAMILY'S ROLE IN PEDIATRICS. Boston: Little, Brown and Co., 1972. 276 p.

> Study of innovative programs in hospitals in which the child's family participates in his care.

Hudson, Ian, M.D., and Gordon, Thomas. WHAT TO DO UNTIL THE DOCTOR COMES. Princeton, N.J.: Auerbach Publishers, 1970. 269 p. Illus., index.

> Easy-to-read guide for handling the sick or injured child until medical help, if needed, is obtained.

LENGTHENING SHADOWS: A REPORT OF THE COUNCIL ON PEDIATRIC PRACTICE OF THE AMERICAN ACADEMY OF PEDIATRICS ON THE DELIVERY OF HEALTH CARE TO CHILDREN, 1970. Evanston, Ill.: American Academy of Pediatrics, 1971. 262 p.

> A detailed report on the problem of inadequate health care for the increasing numbers of poverty-stricken children, namely, the children of nonwhites, rural dwellers, migrants, and Indians.

Oremland, Evelyn K., and Oremland, Jerome, eds. THE EFFECTS OF HOSPITALIZATION ON CHILDREN. Springfield, Ill.: Charles C. Thomas, Publisher, 1973. 341 p. Photos.

> Specialists in medicine, social work, anthropology, and psychology provide insights into the personal and group encounters and experiences involved in hospitalization. Utilizing theory, research, and clinical practice, they cover such topics as the preparation of children for hospitalization, the newborn and the adolescent in the hospital, emergency procedures, and the dying child and the family.

Shiller, Jack G., M.D. CHILDHOOD ILLNESS: A COMMON SENSE APPROACH. New York: Stein & Day, 1972. 320 p. Glossary, illus., index.

> Well-balanced, clear, authoritative handbook for recognizing and treating common childhood ailments. Indicates the situations that require a physician's attention. An appendix of over-the-counter medicines, a guide to immunizations, and a chart on normal growth are included.

## PERIODICALS

FAMILY HEALTH. New York: William H. White, 1969-- . Monthly.

> A general, easy-to-understand family health magazine covering such topics as nutrition, food, child care, medicine, and others.

# Health—General

TODAY'S HEALTH. Chicago: American Medical Association, 1923--
Monthly.

> Covers a wide variety of topics--diet and foods, diseases, mental health, first aid, and safety tips. Column on care of children from birth to adolescence ("Child Sense") is a special feature.

## PAMPHLETS AND/OR GOVERNMENT DOCUMENTS

Unless otherwise noted the materials are available free of charge. Prices quoted are subject to change. Payment should accompany order.

## Bibliographies and Directories

BOOKS THAT HELP CHILDREN DEAL WITH A HOSPITAL EXPERIENCE. 1975. 22 p. Available from: Bureau of Community Health Services, Health Services Administration, 5600 Fishers Lane, Rockville, Md. 20852.

> Guide to selecting books for preschoolers and elementary students. Includes an annotated bibliography of children's books on the subjects of illnesses and hospitals.

HEALTH EDUCATION MATERIALS AND THE ORGANIZATIONS WHICH OFFER THEM. n.d. 25 p. Available from: Health Insurance Institute, 277 Park Avenue, New York, N.Y. 10017.

> Lists sources of free and inexpensive materials.

NATIONAL INSTITUTES OF HEALTH PUBLICATIONS LIST. 1975. 48 p. Available from: National Institutes of Health, Division of Public Information, Bethesda, Md. 20014.

> A list of printed materials which contain information on: the programs and functions of the different divisions and institutes of the National Institutes of Health, the nature of various diseases, and the research efforts to combat these diseases. The list is free, as are single copies of any publication listed.

PUBLICATIONS OF HEALTH SERVICES ADMINISTRATION. 1974. 32 p. Available from: Health Services Administration, 5600 Fishers Lane, Rockville, Md. 20852.

> Lists publications which reflect the activities of the HSA, including pamphlets on child health and handicapped children. The list is free as are single copies of many of the listed publications.

## Health—General

SPANISH-LANGUAGE HEALTH COMMUNICATION TEACHING AIDS. 1973. 55 p. Publication no. (HSM) 73-19. Available from: Health Services and Mental Health Administration, Office of Communications and Public Affairs, 5600 Fishers Lane, Rockville, Md. 20852.

> Lists sources of printed materials for use in health communication activities among Spanish-speaking Americans.

### Current Sources

CHILD HEALTH ISSUES IN NEW YORK. 1971. 11 p. By Shirley Mayer. $2.75. Available from: City Almanac, Center for New York Affairs, 72 Fifth Avenue, New York, N.Y. 10011.

> In this special issue of the City Almanac a former assistant commissioner for Maternal and Child Health examines some of the child health problems and programs shared by large cities. She discusses the services developed in New York during the last fifty years, including child health stations which serve infants and preschoolers, school health programs, dental services, and programs for the handicapped.

HOW CHILDREN GROW: CLINICAL RESEARCH ADVANCES IN HUMAN GROWTH AND DEVELOPMENT. 1972. 56 p. Available from: Division of Research Resources, National Institutes of Health, 9000 Rockville Pike, Bethesda, Md. 20014.

> This booklet describes the effects of nutrition, hormones, illness, and emotion on a child's growth.

## ORGANIZATIONS AND/OR SOURCES OF MATERIALS, FREE OR AT LOW COST

American Association for Maternal
  and Child Health
P.O. Box 965
Los Altos, Calif. 94022        Phone (415) 964-4575

> Compiles, publishes, and distributes information for the general public and professional persons to further the goals of "promoting the health of welfare mothers and children."

Blue Cross and Blue Shield
222 North Dearborn Street
Chicago, Ill. 60601

> Offers information on health.

# Health—General

Center for Disease Control
1600 Clifton Road, N.E.
Atlanta, Ga. 30333

> Offers pamphlets on venereal disease, smoking and health, and disease in general.

The Children's Hospital Medical Center
Education Department
300 Longwood Avenue
Boston, Mass. 02115

> Offers such health pamphlets as WHAT TO DO ABOUT CHILDREN'S COLDS AND SORE THROATS.

Kimberly-Clark Corporation
Life Cycle Center
Neenah, Wis. 54956

> A source of materials to supplement health and family life education courses.

Medic Alert Foundation International
1000 North Palm
Turlock, Calif. 95380     Phone (209) 632-2371

> An international, nonprofit organization whose goals are to encourage individuals with hidden medical problems such as diabetes, epilepsy, or allergies to drugs to wear an identifying emblem which might save their lives in case of an accident. The emblem is inscribed with the words "Medic Alert" and the symbol of the medical profession. The reverse side discloses the medical problems of the wearer, his/her file number, and a twenty-four-hour phone number in Turlock, California where the emergency file for each member is kept. Membership fee is $7.00 and includes the emblem.

National Dairy Council
111 North Canal Street
Chicago, Ill. 60606

> Provides free catalog of health education materials.

## AUDIOVISUAL MATERIALS

### Films

INFANT AND CHILD CARE. 1965. 16mm, 14 min., sound, color.
> Teaches parents how to care for the medical and health needs

# Health—General

of infants and children when medical assistance is not available.

Available from: National Audiovisual Center, Washington, D.C. 20409.

PATTERNS FOR HEALTH. 1967. 16mm, 14 min., black and white. Producer: United States Office of Economic Opportunity, Title no. 002790.

Early training in good health habits develops patterns for adulthood. This film covers general as well as specific health needs of the child aged four to five.

Available from: National Audiovisual Center (GSA), Washington, D.C. 20409.

# HEALTH—ALLERGIES AND RESPIRATORY ILLNESSES

## BOOKS

### Current Sources

Aas, Kjell. THE ALLERGIC CHILD. Springfield, Ill.: Charles C. Thomas, Publisher, 1971. 287 p.

>Essential information to improve the understanding and treatment of children with serious allergic diseases. Includes case histories. Discusses such topics as hay fever, asthma, allergy diagnosis, side effects, the allergic child and the school, among others.

Frazier, Claude A., M.D. PARENTS' GUIDE TO ALLERGY IN CHILDREN. Garden City, N.Y.: Doubleday & Co., 1973. 338 p. Index.

>Information on the symptoms and care of a large variety of allergies. Should not be used as a substitute for good medical care.

Rapp, Doris J. ALLERGIES AND YOUR CHILD. New York: Holt, Rinehart and Winston, 1972. 305 p. Biblio.

>Covers the causes of allergies and points out the special problems of infants.

Somekh, Emile, M.D. ALLERGY AND YOUR CHILD. New York: Harper & Row, Publishers, 1974. 271 p. Glossary, index.

>An authority on the subject covers all types of allergies by age level; discusses medication, special diets, and camps for asthmatic children; and carefully explains allergy problems to parents. Offers a practical plan for handling allergies which does not rely on the excessive use of drugs.

# Allergies, Respiratory Illnesses

_____. A PARENT'S GUIDE TO CHILDREN'S ALLERGIES. Springfield, Ill.: Charles C. Thomas, Publisher, 1972. 189 p.

> Answers the most frequently asked questions about skin eruptions, respiratory diseases, and allergies to food and pollen. Discusses the purchase of special foods, emergency kits, and breathing devices. Gives specific instructions for injections.

## ORGANIZATIONS AND/OR SOURCES OF MATERIALS, FREE OR AT LOW COST

Allergy Foundation of America
801 Second Avenue
New York, N.Y. 10017     Phone (212) 684-7875

> This national organization supports programs of research into the causes, diagnosis, prevention, and treatment of allergic diseases. It subscribes to national and regional programs for educating the public and will answer inquiries. It also supplies lists of qualified practicing allergists in any part of the country, as well as names of institutions and camps that accept asthmatic children and adults. Numerous publications are available on request.

American Lung Association
1740 Broadway
New York, N.Y. 10019     Phone (212) 245-8000

> This organization is interested in research and education regarding the prevention and control of lung disease and will make referrals to affiliates. Source of pamphlets, audio-visuals, and Spanish language materials.

Children's Asthma Research Institute and
  Hospital at Denver
1999 Julian Street
Denver, Colo. 80204     Phone (303) 458-1999

> "Conducts research in asthma and other allergic diseases and provides free care, treatment, and rehabilitation of intractable asthmatic children of all races and creeds from all parts of the United States and Canada."

Cystic Fibrosis Foundation
3379 Peachtree Road, N.E.
Atlanta, Ga. 30326     Phone (404) 262-1100

> Sponsors programs for public and professional education about the symptoms and treatment of cystic fibrosis and children's lung diseases. Source of publications on lung disease.

# Allergies, Respiratory Illnesses

National Foundation for Asthmatic
  Children at Tucson
P.O. Box 50304
Tucson, Ariz.  85703    Phone (602) 624-7481

> Child care agency which provides medical and social rehabilitation for chronic asthmatic children ages six to fifteen. Operates free weekly allergy outpatient clinic for all age groups, maintains free summer camp, and provides funds for research.

National Institute of Allergy and Infectious
  Diseases
Office of Information
Bethesda, Md.  20014

> A source of pamphlets, reprints, and reports.

## AUDIOVISUAL MATERIALS

### Films

ASTHMA AND YOUR CHILD.  16mm, 28 min., sound.

> Describes the work of a specialist in thoracic physiotherapy including simple exercises developed to aid asthma patients.
>
> Available from:  New Zealand Embassy, 19 Observatory Circle, N.W., Washington, D.C. 20008.

# HEALTH—DIABETES

## BOOKS

### Current Sources

Asher, Alfred E., M.D., and Horstmann, Dorothea L. A HANDBOOK FOR THE YOUNG DIABETIC. New York: Intercontinental Medical Book Corp., 1972. 76 p. Biblio.

> Brief, nontechnical guide to planning meals for the diabetic teenager.

Court, John M., M.D. HELPING YOUR DIABETIC CHILD. New York: Taplinger Publishing Co., 1975. 223 p. Appendix, biblio., illus., index.

> Practical information on diabetes, its treatment including insulin injections and reactions, and the care and use of necessary equipment. Discusses parent-child communications and attitudes, and answers questions most frequently asked by children and their parents. Recipes and a list of summer camps are also included.

Vanderpool, Sally. THE CARE AND FEEDING OF YOUR DIABETIC CHILD. New York: Frederick Fell, Publishers, 1968. 116 p. Appendix, biblio., index.

> A trained nutritionist with many years experience in childhood diabetes has put together hints and ideas for parents who have just learned that their child has diabetes.

## PAMPHLETS AND/OR GOVERNMENT DOCUMENTS

Unless otherwise noted the materials are available free of charge. Prices quoted are subject to change. Payment should accompany order.

# Diabetes

DON'T GAMBLE WITH YOUR HEALTH: DIABETES. Available from: Office of Information, National Institute of Arthritis, Metabolism, and Digestive Diseases, National Institutes of Health, Bethesda, Md. 20014.

Current information on diabetes.

REPRINTS--CHILDHOOD DIABETES, PARENTS MAGAZINE, NOVEMBER 1973. Available from: Public Inquiries Office, National Institute of Arthritis, Metabolism, and Digestive Diseases, National Institutes of Health, Bethesda, Md. 20014.

Covers new developments in the fight against childhood diabetes.

## ORGANIZATIONS AND/OR SOURCES OF MATERIALS, FREE OR AT LOW COST

American Diabetes Association
One West Forty-eighth Street
New York, N.Y. 10020      Phone (212) 541-4310

A national organization primarily concerned with education and research with respect to diabetes mellitus. It will make referrals to affiliates and answer questions. Publishes professional literature and reprints of articles.

Juvenile Diabetes Foundation
23 East Twenty-sixth Street
New York, N.Y. 10010      Phone (212) 689-7869

Founded in 1970 by a group of parents with diabetic children, this organization is now a nationally accredited voluntary health agency whose primary objective is to raise money for research on juvenile diabetes. It provides informational and educational services and counsels juvenile diabetics and their families. Issues a bimonthly newsletter, DIMENSIONS, which reports new developments in diabetes research.

# HEALTH—EPILEPSY

## BOOKS

### Current Sources

Lagos, Jorge C., M.D. SEIZURES, EPILEPSY AND YOUR CHILD: A HANDBOOK FOR PARENTS, TEACHERS AND EPILEPTICS OF ALL AGES. New York: Harper & Row Publishers, 1974. 238 p. Appendix, index.

> A pediatric neurologist uses question-and-answer format to describe seizures, conditions resembling epilepsy, treatment and effects, physical limitations, and social and legal status of epileptics.

## PAMPHLETS AND/OR GOVERNMENT DOCUMENTS

Unless otherwise noted the materials are available free of charge. Prices quoted are subject to change. Payment should accompany order.

HOPE THROUGH RESEARCH: EPILEPSY. 1927. 26 p. Available from: National Institute of Neurological Diseases and Stroke, 9000 Rockville Pike, Bethesda, Md. 20014.

> Discusses what is known about the disease and what can be done for the epileptic.

## ORGANIZATIONS AND/OR SOURCES OF MATERIALS, FREE OR AT LOW COST

Epilepsy Foundation of America
1828 L Street, N.W.
Washington, D.C. 20036     Phone (202) 293-2930

> This is the only national voluntary health agency concerned with epilepsy. Together with its chapters, it conducts pro-

# Epilepsy

grams in research, employment, public information, and patient services. Offers free pamphlets and information on epilepsy, including: "You, Your Child and Epilepsy," "Don't Be Afreaid of the Child With Epilepsy," and "Recognition, Onset, Diagnosis and Therapy." Loans films without charge.

National Children's Rehabilitation Center
P.O. Box 1260
Leesburg, Va.   22075      Phone (703) 777-3485

Independent residential treatment center supported largely by the Epilepsy Foundation of America. Accepts any epileptic child of average intelligence who suffers from learning, social, or emotional problems. The child must be a resident of the United States and be between the ages of six and sixteen.

# HEALTH—EYE AND DENTAL CARE

## BOOKS

### Dated but Still Relevant

Kraskin, Robert A. YOU CAN IMPROVE YOUR VISION. Garden City, N.Y.: Doubleday & Co., 1968. 128 p. Illus.

> One of the few books designed for parents about the care of a child's eyes.

### Current Sources

McKeown, Joe, D.D.S. EVERYBODY'S TOOTH BOOK: AN ILLUSTRATED GUIDE TO THE CARE AND FEEDING OF YOUR TEETH. Santa Cruz, Calif.: Happy Valley Apple Press, 1973. 129 p. Glossary, index.

> A simple-to-understand, well-illustrated layman's manual to dental health. It describes the causes of most dental problems, shows the corrective measures, and offers practical advice on preventing major dental problems.

## PAMPHLETS AND/OR GOVERNMENT DOCUMENTS

Unless otherwise noted the materials are available free of charge. Prices quoted are subject to change. Payment should accompany order.

A GUIDE TO DENTAL CARE. Available from: Medical Services Administration, Social and Rehabilitation Service, 330 C Street, S.W., Washington, D.C. 20201.

> Methods of diagnosing and treating dental disease.

# Eye and Dental Care

HOME EYE TEST KIT. Available from: National Society for the Prevention of Blindness, 79 Madison Avenue, New York, N.Y. 10016.

> This kit enables parents to test the vision of their preschool children. The kit includes a scale version of the Standard Snellen Symbol E chart as well as directions for training a child to take the test, for administering the test, and for interpreting results.

MOTHERS WANT TO HELP. 1970. 10 p. Available from: American Dental Association, 211 East Chicago Avenue, Chicago, Ill. 60611.

> Easy-to-read guide for mothers on protecting the dental health of babies and young children.

ORTHODONTICS: A SPECIAL KIND OF DENTISTRY. 1974. Leaflet. Available from: American Association of Orthodontists, 7477 Delmar Boulevard, St. Louis, Mo. 63130.

> Of interest to parents who have been advised to seek orthodontic treatment for their children.

TOOTH CARE. 1973. 24 p. Available from: Office of Information, National Institute of Dental Research, National Institutes of Health, Bethesda, Md. 20014.

> Illustrated booklet on maintaining healthy teeth and gums. Describes proper brushing and flossing techniques to remove plaque--one of the most common causes of tooth decay. Emphasizes the importance of teaching children about dental health. Discusses filling, capping, and treating teeth.

YOU AND YOUR TEETH. 1973. 15 p. Available from: Channing L. Bete Co., 45 Federal Street, Greenfield, Mass. 03101.

> Basics of oral hygiene.

YOU CAN TEACH TOOTH BRUSHING. n.d. Publication no. S-11. Available from: American Dental Association, Bureau of Dental Health Education, 211 East Chicago Avenue, Chicago, Ill. 60611.

> A handy fold-out guide for parents and teachers.

YOUR CHILD'S TEETH. 1971. 13 p. Available from: American Dental Association, 211 East Chicago Avenue, Chicago, Ill. 60611.

> Discusses dental health through adolescence.

# Eye and Dental Care

Additional pamphlets on blindness and its prevention may be obtained from the American Foundation for the Blind (see p. 133) and the National Society for the Prevention of Blindness (see p. 134).

## ORGANIZATIONS AND/OR SOURCES OF MATERIALS, FREE OR AT LOW COST

American Dental Association
211 East Chicago Avenue
Chicago, Ill. 60611     Phone (312) 944-6730

> A professional service organization with informational and referral services for the public. Publishes a catalog listing pamphlets, charts, posters, and audiovisual materials on dental care.

American Optometric Association
Division of Public Affairs
7000 Chippewa Street
St. Louis, Mo. 63119

> Pamphlets, posters, films, transcriptions, and a catalog are available.

American Society of Dentistry for Children
211 East Chicago Avenue
Chicago, Ill. 60611     Phone (312) 943-1244

> An organization whose primary aim is to distribute information on dentistry for children to both the dental profession and the general public. Its publications include the JOURNAL OF DENTISTRY FOR CHILDREN.

Better Vision Institute
230 Park Avenue
New York, N.Y. 10017

> Offers a packet of materials on vision.

# HEALTH—HEART CONDITION

## PAMPHLETS AND/OR GOVERNMENT DOCUMENTS

Unless otherwise noted the materials are available free of charge. Prices quoted are subject to change. Payment should accompany order.

HOW TO SAVE YOUR CHILD FROM RHEUMATIC FEVER. 1974. Available from: Abbott Laboratories, Public Relations Department, Abbott Park, North Chicago, Ill. 60064.

> Explains the cause and prevention of rheumatic fever.

PROTECT YOUR CHILD'S HEART. 1974. 16 p. Available from: American Heart Association, 44 East Twenty-third Street, New York, N.Y. 10010.

> For parents whose children have a greater-than-average risk of developing rheumatic fever. Contains illustrations and is available in Spanish as well as English.

## ORGANIZATIONS AND/OR SOURCES OF MATERIALS, FREE OR AT LOW COST

American Heart Association
7320 Greenville Avenue
Dallas, Tex. 75231      Phone (214) 750-5300

> National voluntary health agency dedicated to fighting heart disease through research, education, and community service. Free pamphlets include 1) IF YOUR CHILD HAS A CONGENITAL HEART DEFECT, 2) INNOCENT HEART MURMURS IN CHILDREN, 3) PROTECT YOUR CHILD'S HEART, and 4) YOU, YOUR CHILD, AND RHEUMATIC FEVER.

# HEALTH—LEUKEMIA

## BOOKS

### Current Sources

Johnson, F. Leonard, M.D., and Miller, Marc. SHANNON: A BOOK FOR PARENTS OF CHILDREN WITH LEUKEMIA. New York: Hawthorn Books, 1975. 132 p. Illus., index.

> Moving story of a little girl's fight against leukemia. The child's physician describes the medical treatment, the drugs used, and the side effects with warnings against cancer frauds. Shannon's grandmother depicts the family's response and provides human interest details.

## PAMPHLETS AND/OR GOVERNMENT DOCUMENTS

Unless otherwise noted the materials are available free of charge. Prices quoted are subject to change. Payment should accompany order.

CHILDHOOD LEUKEMIA--A PAMPHLET FOR PARENTS. 1972. 13 p. Publication no. 72-212. Available from: Public Inquiries Office, National Cancer Institute, National Institutes of Health, Bethesda, Md. 20014.

> Also available in Spanish.

PROGRESS AGAINST LEUKEMIA. 1973. 14 p. Available from: Public Affairs Office, National Cancer Institute, Bethesda, Md. 20014.

> Discusses both the status of current research on the causes of leukemia and the advances in treating it.

# Leukemia

## ORGANIZATIONS AND/OR SOURCES OF MATERIALS, FREE OR AT LOW COST

Leukemia Society of America
211 East Forty-third Street
New York, N.Y. 10017      Phone (212) 986-3330

    This organization, dedicated to the conquest of leukemia through medical research, supports patient-aid as well as public and professional education programs. Distributes pamphlets and loans audiovisual materials on leukemia.

# HEALTH—SUDDEN INFANT DEATH SYNDROME

## BOOKS

Current Sources

Bergman, Abraham B., M.D., and Choate, Judith. WHY DID MY BABY DIE? New York: Third Press, 1975. 152 p. Appendix, biblio., index.

> Discusses sudden infant death syndrome (SIDS), as well as past and present research on its causes. An appendix presents statistics gleaned from parent interviews relating to such factors as racial distribution of the disease, the best sources of help, and so on.

## PAMPHLETS AND/OR GOVERNMENT DOCUMENTS

Unless otherwise noted the materials are available free of charge. Prices quoted are subject to change. Payment should accompany order.

FACTS ABOUT SUDDEN INFANT DEATH SYNDROME. 1972. 12 p. Publication no. (NIH) 75-225. Available from: Public Inquiries Office, National Institute of Child Health and Human Development, National Institutes of Health, Bethesda, Md. 20014.

> Offers some basic facts about sudden infant death syndrome (crib death), a disease which causes the death of five to ten thousand infants a year in the United States. Lists sources of help and information.

SUDDEN INFANT DEATH SYNDROME. 1971. 42 p. Publication no. (NICH) 75-224. Available from: National Institute of Child Health and Human Development, National Institutes of Health, Bethesda, Md. 20014.

> Summarizes the proceedings of the second international conference

# Sudden Infant Death Syndrome

on the causes of sudden infant death, 1969, and reviews the research in the field since 1963.

## ORGANIZATIONS AND/OR SOURCES OF MATERIALS, FREE OR AT LOW COST

International Council for Infant Survival
7501 Liberty Road
Baltimore, Md. 21207     Phone (301) 944-2502

> Nonprofit, charitable, and educational organization dedicated to solving the phenomenon of "crib-death" through personal assistance to stricken families, public information, and scientific research. Also publishes pamphlets.

National Sudden Infant Death Syndrome Foundation
310 South Michigan Avenue
Chicago, Ill. 60604     Phone (312) 663-0650

> Organization of parents who have lost a child to sudden infant death syndrome. It assists bereaved parents who lose a child, supports research, and seeks to make the public aware that SIDS is a public health problem. Publishes a brochure and reprints of SIDS literature.

# HEALTH—MISCELLANEOUS

## PAMPHLETS AND/OR GOVERNMENT DOCUMENTS

Unless otherwise noted the materials are available free of charge. Prices quoted are subject to change. Payment should accompany order.

MUSCULAR DYSTROPHY. 1971. 18 p. Publication no. 72-77. Available from: National Institute of Neurological and Communicative Disorders and Stroke, National Institutes of Health, Bethesda, Md. 20014.

> Briefly describes symptoms, causes, treatment; also available in Spanish.

RUBELLA. 1972. 12 p. Available from: Maternal & Child Health Service, Rockville, Md. 20852.

> Describes the diagnosis and symptoms of rubella, its effect on the fetus when the disease is contracted early in pregnancy, the use of rubella vaccine, and the care of affected infants.

## ORGANIZATIONS AND/OR SOURCES OF MATERIALS, FREE OR AT LOW COST

American Cancer Society
777 Third Avenue
New York, N.Y. 10017   Phone (212) 371-2900

> Its major purpose is to campaign against cancer and its effects through medical research, professional and public education, and service and rehabilitation programs. A source of publications for laypeople and professionals, including such pamphlets as: CANCER IN CHILDREN.

# Health—Miscellaneous

The Arthritis Foundation
475 Riverside Drive, Room 240
New York, N.Y. 10027    Phone (212) 678-6372

> The foundation offers grants to medical institutions to help support clinical research centers. Local chapters also provide information to the public regarding local treatment facilities. Publishes authoritative booklets for parents, such as ARTHRITIS IN CHILDREN and RHEUMATOID ARTHRITIS--A HANDBOOK FOR PARENTS.

Muscular Dystrophy Association
810 Seventh Avenue
New York, N.Y. 10019    Phone (212) 586-0808

> Voluntary health organization created to foster research on muscular dystrophy. Programs include patient services, public education, creation and distribution of literature, films, research conferences, community clinics, flu shots, and summer camp referral. Offers fact sheets on each of the following diseases: muscular dystrophy (various forms), infantile spinal muscular atrophy, benign congenital hypotonia, and juvenile spinal muscular atrophy.

National Kidney Foundation
116 East Twenty-seventh Street
New York, N.Y. 10010    Phone (212) 889-2210

> The only voluntary health organization in the country devoted to the problems of kidney disease. Programs include research, patient services, nationwide organ donor program, professional training and education, public information, and community services. Source of literature about the various aspects of kidney disease.

National Multiple Sclerosis Society
Publications Department
257 Park Avenue, South
New York, N.Y. 10010    (Contact local chapters)

> Source of pamphlets, medical papers, audiovisual materials, films, and posters.

# HYPERACTIVE CHILD

## BOOKS

### Reference

Winchell, Carol Ann. THE HYPERKINETIC CHILD: A BIBLIOGRAPHY OF MEDICAL, EDUCATIONAL AND BEHAVIORAL STUDIES. Westport, Conn.: Greenwood Press, 1975. 182 p. Index.

> Comprehensive coverage from the 1950s through mid-1974 of books, pamphlets, theses and dissertations, conference reports, and journal articles.

### Current Sources

Adler, Sidney J., M.D., and Terry, Keith C. YOUR OVERACTIVE CHILD: NORMAL OR NOT? New York: Medcom Press, 1972. 70 p. Appendix, biblio., photos.

> This nontechnical manual, coauthored by a neurologic pediatrician and a father of a hyperactive child, is designed to help parents and teachers understand the hyperactive child in the classroom and at home. Advice is given on how to recognize hyperactive traits and in obtaining medical and educational help. The authors recommend the use of stimulant drugs together with constructive home supervision. A brief list of organizations and an annotated bibliography is also included.

Feingold, Ben F., M.D. WHY YOUR CHILD IS HYPERACTIVE. New York: Random House, 1975. 211 p.

> An eminent allergist and clinician sees a relationship between the ever-increasing harmful presence of coloring agents in our foods and an increase in hyperkinetic learning disability. He indicates that a change in diet can bring about improvement.

Reistroffer, Mary, and McVey, Helen. PARENTAL SURVIVAL AND THE HYPERACTIVE CHILD. Madison: University of Wisconsin Press, 1972. 55 p.

> A slim volume containing much helpful and practical advice for parents and foster parents of hyperactive children.

Renshaw, Domeena C., M.D. THE HYPERACTIVE CHILD. Chicago: Nelson-Hall Co., 1974. 304 p. Biblio., charts, tables, index.

> A highly informative and perceptive examination of all aspects of the identification, management, and treatment of the hyperkinetic, hyperanxious, hyperaggressive, and hyperactive child. Useful guide for both professionals and parents.

Schrag, Peter, and Divoky, Diane. THE MYTH OF THE HYPERACTIVE CHILD AND OTHER MEANS OF CHILD CONTROL. New York: Pantheon Books, 1975. 285 p. Appendix.

> Well-researched probe into the widespread use of drugs, data banks, psychological testing, and behavior modification to control children's lives. The authors contend that most of the research on hyperactivity and minimal brain dysfunction has been sloppy, distorted, and irresponsibly used. This promises to be a most controversial book.

Stewart, Mark Armstrong, M.D., and Olds, Sally [W.]. RAISING A HYPERACTIVE CHILD. New York: Harper & Row Publishers, 1973. 299 p. Biblio., index.

> Handbook which includes causes and characteristics of hyperactivity, as well as the appropriate schools, sports, activities, and drugs for the afflicted child. Discusses the problems of the hyperactive child at various stages of development and offers ways to help the child at home.

Sugarman, Gerald I., M.D., and Stone, Margaret N. YOUR HYPERACTIVE CHILD. Chicago: Henry Regnery Co., 1974. 152 p. Appendices, biblio., index.

> Pediatric neurologist uses a question-and-answer format to provide information, guidelines, and suggestions for troubled parents of hyperactive children. Emphasizes that the disorder can be treated. Names of organizations from which parents can obtain additional help are also included.

Wender, Paul H., M.D. THE HYPERACTIVE CHILD. New York: Crown Publishers, 1973. 120 p. Index.

> Wender, a specialist in the field, covers the subject of the hyperactive child from causes to treatment including the use of drugs. He also provides practical advice on the problems of rearing hyperactive children and offers valuable information

on finding professional help.

## PAMPHLETS AND/OR GOVERNMENT DOCUMENTS

Unless otherwise noted the materials are available free of charge. Prices quoted are subject to change. Payment should accompany order.

### Bibliographies

HYPERACTIVE CHILD: A SELECTED BIBLIOGRAPHY FOR PARENTS AND EDUCATORS. By Alyce J. Archuleta and Michael J. Archuleta. 1974. 26 p. $2.00. Available from: Current Bibliographic Series, Box 2709, San Diego, Calif. 92112.

### Current Sources

PARENTAL SURVIVAL AND THE HYPERACTIVE CHILD. By Mary Reistroffer. 1972. 56 p. $2.00. Available from: University of Wisconsin, Extension Publications Business Office, 432 North Lake Street, Madison, Wis. 54706.

   Advice on how to cope.

## AUDIOVISUAL MATERIALS

### Films

THE HYPERACTIVE CHILD. 32 min., sound, color.
   Basic information for the layperson on hyperactivity, its diagnosis, and treatment. Includes presentations by a number of American and British physicians.
   Available from: CIBA, Summit, N.J.

# LEARNING AND CREATIVITY

(See also Child Development—Infancy to Five Years)

## BOOKS

### Dated but Still Relevant

Bland, Jane C. ART OF THE YOUNG CHILD: UNDERSTANDING AND ENCOURAGING CREATIVE GROWTH IN CHILDREN THREE TO FIVE. Rev. ed. New York: Museum of Modern Art, 1968. 57 p.

> Covers the creative growth of children and helps parents to understand how children from ages three to five feel about their art.

Engelmann, Siegfried, and Engelmann, Therese. GIVE YOUR CHILD A SUPERIOR MIND: A PROGRAM FOR THE PRE-SCHOOL CHILD. New York: Simon & Schuster, 1966. 317 p. Illus.

> Most important for parents interested in the intellectual development of children in the preschool years. Includes some very specific suggestions.

Ginsburg, Herbert, and Opper, Sylvia. PIAGET'S THEORY OF INTELLECTUAL DEVELOPMENT: AN INTRODUCTION. Englewood Cliffs, N.J.: Prentice-Hall, 1969. 237 p. Illus.

> Simple and accurate introduction to Piaget including a biography, a review of his work, and a clear explanation of his theories.

Sheehy, Emma D. CHILDREN DISCOVER MUSIC AND DANCE. New York: Teachers College Press, 1968. 207 p. Biblio.

> Imaginative experiences for involving children with music and dance in the classroom or at home. Lists of songbooks and children's records are included.

# Learning and Creativity

Strang, Ruth. HELPING YOUR CHILD DEVELOP HIS POTENTIALITIES. New York: E.P. Dutton & Co., 1965. 256 p. Illus.

> Practical guide to understanding the various aspects of a child's development and cognitive abilities and to releasing the learning power in children. The author stresses physical growth, intelligence, and creativity, as well as social and moral values.

## Reference

Arbuthnot, May Hill, and Sutherland, Zena. CHILDREN AND BOOKS. 4th ed. Glenview, Ill.: Scott, Foresmen and Co., 1972. 836 p. Appendices, biblio., illus., index.

> Reference for parents interested in guiding their children to good reading.

Child Study Press. CHILDREN'S BOOKS OF THE YEAR, 1974. New York: 1975. 49 p.

> A useful, annotated, annual guide for parents, teachers, and librarians to about 600 books for children and young adults.

Curtis, Jean. A PARENT'S GUIDE TO NURSERY SCHOOLS. New York: Random House, 1971. 210 p.

> The president of a cooperative nursery school in Massachusetts discusses the types of nursery schools available, offers standards for judging their quality, and outlines procedures for enrolling a child. Provides a section on starting a nursery school.

FREE AND INEXPENSIVE LEARNING MATERIALS. Nashville, Tenn.: George Peabody College for Teachers, 1974. 244 p. Index.

> A subject guide for teachers, but many of the materials would be of interest to parents.

THE HANDBOOK OF PRIVATE SCHOOLS. Boston: Porter Sargent, 1974. Annual. 1,563 p. Illus., index.

> Lists over 2,000 leading private elementary and secondary schools in the United States including name, address, director, admissions, enrollment, faculty, tuition and scholarship information, and school calendar. Also includes a selective directory of summer academic programs and summer camps.

Hemsing, Esther D., ed. GOOD AND INEXPENSIVE BOOKS FOR CHILDREN. Washington, D.C.: Association for Childhood Education International, 1972. 64 p.

# Learning and Creativity

Annotated guide to more than 500 inexpensive books including picture books, fiction, biography, fairy tales, science, hobbies, and social studies.

La Crosse, E. Robert, Jr., M.D., ed. EARLY CHILDHOOD EDUCATION DIRECTORY: A SELECTED GUIDE TO 2,000 PRESCHOOL EDUCATION CENTERS. New York: R.R. Bowker Co., 1972. 455 p. Index.

This directory, arranged alphabetically by state and city, provides data on each organization's staff, programs, stated philosophy, general environment, fees, and budget. Also lists state certification requirements.

Larrick, Nancy. A PARENT'S GUIDE TO CHILDREN'S READING. 4th ed. New York: Bantam Books, 1975. 374 p. Illus., index.

Still one of the best books on children's reading. The fourth edition covers the best children's literature for every reading level and interest. Includes a guide to children's records, filmstrips, and films. It is a must for parents of preschoolers and others interested in seeing that children learn to read.

Markun, Patricia M., and Lane, Joan T., eds. BIBLIOGRAPHY OF BOOKS FOR CHILDREN. Washington, D.C.: Association for Childhood Education, 1974. 112 p. Index.

Annotated listing of quality selections arranged by subject category and general age levels. Includes all-time favorites, winners of major children's literary awards, and current titles.

Sutherland, Zena, ed. THE BEST IN CHILDREN'S BOOKS. Chicago: University of Chicago, 1973. 484 p. Index.

Compilation of reviews for 1400 books recommended in the BULLETIN OF THE CENTER FOR CHILDREN'S BOOKS during 1966-72. Includes subject index and grade levels. Useful as a selection guide for parents, teachers, and librarians.

## Current Sources

Ames, Louise Bates, and Chase, Joan Ames. DON'T PUSH YOUR PRESCHOOLER. New York: Harper & Row Publishers, 1974. 212 p. Appendix, biblio., illus., index.

Discusses the behavior to be expected at each age. Urges parents to relax and enjoy their children rather than push them beyond their natural limitations. Also encourages the housebound parent to engage a babysitter, weekly if not daily, to provide a refreshing pause from the demands of energetic preschoolers. Removes

## Learning and Creativity

much of the guilt that parents may feel about not providing all the resources and attention that are extolled in current parenthood literature (e.g., see Beck, Joan, below).

Arnold, Arnold. TEACHING YOUR CHILD TO LEARN FROM BIRTH TO SCHOOL AGE. Englewood Cliffs, N.J.: Prentice-Hall, 1971. 228 p. Biblio.

> A handy resource for parents which outlines activities and offers guidelines that stress the importance of the preschool years in establishing a secure base for future learning experiences.

Beadle, Muriel. A CHILD'S MIND: HOW CHILDREN LEARN DURING THE CRITICAL YEARS FROM BIRTH TO AGE FIVE. Hertfordshire, England: Hart-Davis, 1971. 294 p. Biblio., illus.

> The psychological, physiological, and sociological factors in learning are skillfully presented. An extensive bibliography and an index are included.

Beck, Helen. DON'T PUSH ME I'M NO COMPUTER: HOW PRESSURES TO "ACHIEVE" HARM PRE-SCHOOL CHILDREN. New York: McGraw-Hill Book Co., 1973. 171 p. Biblio., illus.

> A social worker presents a good case for a relaxed and warm atmosphere in which children can explore and experiment as opposed to one of over-stimulation, mechanical learning devices, and constant pressure.

Beck, Joan. HOW TO RAISE A BRIGHTER CHILD: THE CASE FOR EARLY LEARNING. Rev. and updated. New York: Simon & Schuster, 1975. 320 p. Biblio. Paperbound.

> A guide for nurturing the intelligence of children under the age of six. Includes specific methods. The author is a former child care columnist for the CHICAGO TRIBUNE.

Blumenfeld, Samuel L. HOW TO TUTOR: FOR PARENTS AND TEACHERS-- A GUIDE THAT WORKS. New Rochelle, N.Y.: Arlington House, 1973. 298 p.

> Basic approaches to teaching reading, writing, and arithmetic are presented in a clear and logical manner. Blumenfeld recognizes that learning demands mental effort, proper pacing of instruction, and personal adaptation on the part of the tutor.

Braga, Joseph L., and Braga, Laurie D. CHILD DEVELOPMENT AND EARLY

## Learning and Creativity

CHILDHOOD EDUCATION: A GUIDE FOR PARENTS AND TEACHERS. Chicago: Model Cities/CCVO, 1973. 121 p.

> A useful guide to general principles of child development and learning (birth to age five) intended for parents, child care workers, and nursery school teachers. Activities and instructional materials for different age groups are recommended including toys, furniture, books, and movies. Annotated bibliography is also included.

BRIGHT CHILD--POOR GRADES. New York: Dell Publishing Co., 1971. 164 p. Paperbound.

> A guide to recognizing, understanding, and helping the underachiever.

Burgess, Carol, et al. UNDERSTANDING CHILDREN WRITING. New York: Penguin Educational, 1973. 189 p. Illus.

> The authors investigate how children learn to write, the difficulties they encounter, and how they share experiences through writing.

Cohen, Dorothy H. THE LEARNING CHILD: GUIDELINES FOR PARENTS AND TEACHERS. New York: Pantheon Books, 1972. 360 p.

> Written primarily for parents, but helpful to professionals in education, this volume offers a thorough analysis of the developmental aspects of children's learning and growth from kindergarten through preadolescence. Using case studies to present insights into children's behavior, Dr. Cohen also discusses such issues as parental responsibility, sex-role stereotypes, and television's effect on children.

DiLeo, Joseph H., M.D. YOUNG CHILDREN AND THEIR DRAWINGS. New York: Brunner/Mazel, 1970. 386 p. Biblio., illus.

> Children's drawings at various stages of development as reflections of the child's personality and intellectual growth.

Ginott, Haim G. TEACHER AND CHILD: A GUIDE FOR PARENTS AND TEACHERS. New York: Macmillan, 1972. 323 p. Biblio., index.

> Guide to humanizing the educational experience through dialogues in which the words fit the feelings. Ginott includes good and bad examples of teachers interacting with students. He offers the teacher a method of expressing feelings without damaging the child. Parents as well as teachers should find it valuable.

# Learning and Creativity

Hainstock, Elizabeth G. TEACHING MONTESSORI IN THE HOME: THE SCHOOL YEARS. New York: Random House, 1971. 176 p. Illus.

> A practical guide for helping school-age children to learn and enjoy it.

Holt, Michael, and Dienes, Zoltan. LET'S PLAY MATH. New York: Walker & Co., 1973. 184 p. Illus.

> Math educators present eighty games, for children ages four to seven, involving mathematical concepts. Each game has easy-to-understand directions that parents can teach to children to stimulate their potential for clear thinking.

Hughes, Felicity. READING AND WRITING BEFORE SCHOOL. Introduction by Glenn Doman. New York: St. Martin's Press, 1972. 172 p. Biblio.

> Account of how the author taught her daughters at ages two and three to read and write using a "look-say" method to introduce sight recognition of key words. Further reinforcement techniques are outlined, but their implementation requires some training in the teaching of reading.

Inglis, Ruth Langdon. A TIME TO LEARN: A GUIDE FOR PARENTS TO THE NEW THEORIES IN EARLY CHILDHOOD EDUCATION. New York: Dial Press, 1973. 288 p.

> Well-documented book about stimulation and cognitive growth including a superb treatment of the effects of television.

Johnson, Joseph C. II. SCHOLARS BEFORE SCHOOL: A COMPLETE PRE-SCHOOL READING PROGRAM AND TEXT FOR PARENTS AND TEACHERS TO USE WITH THE VERY YOUNG. Durham, N.C.: Moore Publishing Co., 1970. 342 p. Biblio., illus.

> Guide for parents to use in teaching their preschool children to read.

Koontz, Charles W. THE KOONTZ CHILD DEVELOPMENTAL PROGRAM. Los Angeles: Western Psychological Services, 1974. Unpaged, biblio. Paperbound.

> Training activities for the child's first four years of life. For parents as well as teachers.

Kujoth, Jean Spealman, comp. READING INTERESTS OF CHILDREN AND YOUNG ADULTS. Metuchen, N.J.: Scarecrow Press, 1970. 449 p. Biblio., illus., tables.

> Anthology of articles from various education journals on such

topics as the motivations for reading, the factors influencing reading, and the literature that children enjoy.

Landreth, Catherine. PRESCHOOL LEARNING AND TEACHING. New York: Harper & Row Publishers, 1972. 201 p. Biblio. Paperbound.

> Introductory handbook for student teachers, paraprofessionals, and interested parents which outlines the development of children and the function of nursery schools and kindergartens.

Liepmann, Lise. YOUR CHILD'S SENSORY WORLD. New York: Dial Press, 1973. 325 p. Illus., index.

> Common-sense approach for parents about sensory awareness in children. Presents methods for developing a child's skills in hearing, seeing, touching, speaking, smelling, tasting, and moving. Such skills increase the child's capacity to learn and enjoy life. Games for each age group are included.

McKeown, Pamela. READING: A BASIC GUIDE FOR PARENTS AND TEACHERS. Boston: Routledge & Kegan Paul, 1974. 160 p.

> Nontechnical and meaningful presentation of such topics as modern educational practices, types of play, visually stimulating environments, methods, materials, and motivation--all revolving about the processes of reading.

Painter, Genevieve, M.D. TEACH YOUR BABY. New York: Simon & Schuster, 1971. 223 p. Illus.

> Dr. Painter offers a program of simple daily activities designed to develop the learning abilities of infants and small children.

Pulaski, Mary Ann Spencer. UNDERSTANDING PIAGET: INTRODUCTION TO CHILDREN'S COGNITIVE DEVELOPMENT. New York: Harper & Row Publishers, 1971. 241 p. Biblio., illus., index.

> Primarily a nontechnical overview and interpretation of the fundamental concepts of the noted Swiss psychologist. Authoritative and easy to read.

Sparkman, Brandon, and Carmichael, Ann. BLUEPRINT FOR A BRIGHTER CHILD. New York: McGraw-Hill Book Co., 1973. 118 p. Illus.

> Plainly written guide that emphasizes the parents' role in the child's intellectual, psychological, and physical growth and development. Includes suggestions for activities with infants and preschoolers.

# Learning and Creativity

Tinker, Miles A. PREPARING YOUR CHILD FOR READING. New York: Holt, Rinehart and Winston, 1971. 182 p. Index.

> Preparing the preschooler for reading and for the school experience inself. Emphasizes the necessary physical, emotional, and social growth.

Winick, Mariann P. BEFORE THE 3 R'S. New York: David McKay Co., 1973. 146 p. Biblio., photos., index.

> Using the research findings of Piaget and Montessori, the author outlines child development and the home environment that strengthens a child's learning potential. Includes an extensive bibliography of records, stories, and so forth.

## PERIODICALS

CHILDREN'S HOUSE. Caldwell, N.J.: Children's House, 1966-- . Bimonthly.

> Primarily a forum for the Montessori educator, this magazine includes articles on new methods of educating children both in the classroom and at home.

EARLY YEARS. Darien, Conn.: Allen Raymond, 1871-- . Monthly, nine issues a year.

> Useful in helping parents understand the educational process--for normal and exceptional children.

HORN BOOK MAGAZINE: ABOUT CHILDREN'S BOOKS AND READING. Boston: Horn Book, 1924-- . Bimonthly.

> Contains articles as well as book reviews of children's books grouped by age interest (preschool through junior high school).

P.A.R.E. New York: People Against Racism in Education, 1973-- . Monthly.

> Four-page paper which emphasizes the New York scene but also includes relevant items such as guidelines for determining racist/sexist elements in school texts and a heavy assault on "tracking" as a child-destroying tactic.

PTA MAGAZINE. Chicago: Parent Teacher Association, 1906-- . Monthly, except July and August.

> This is the official magazine of the National Congress of Parents and Teachers featuring good articles on child development, parenthood, and school-related matters. Includes book, motion picture, and television reviews.

# Learning and Creativity

## PAMPHLETS AND/OR GOVERNMENT DOCUMENTS

Unless otherwise noted the materials are available free of charge. Prices quoted are subject to change. Payment should accompany order.

## Bibliographies

CHILDREN'S BOOKS 1974. Library of Congress, Children's Book Section. 1975. 15 p. 40 cents. Available from: Superintendent of Documents, Government Printing Office, Washington, D.C. 20402.

> Selected annotated list suitable for children ages preschool through junior high. Includes the recommended audience for each book. Issued annually.

GUIDE TO CHILDREN'S MAGAZINES, NEWSPAPERS, REFERENCE BOOKS. 1974. 12 p. 50 cents. Available from: Association for Childhood Education International, 3615 Wisconsin Avenue, N.W., Washington, D.C. 20016.

> Acquaints parents and teachers with quality reading materials for children.

READING WITH YOUR CHILD THROUGH AGE 5. 1970. 32 p. $1.35. Available from: Child Study Association of America, 9 East Eighty-ninth Street, New York, N.Y. 10028.

> A guide to selecting books for reading aloud to young children.

"THE WAY IT SPOZED TO B". 1974. 8 p. Available from: Gilbert M. Simmons Library, 711 Fifty-ninth Place, Kenosha, Wis. 53140.

> Annotated bibliography to aid parents and citizens in defining educational goals for their school systems. A self-addressed stamped envelope must be included with each request.

## ORGANIZATIONS AND/OR SOURCES OF MATERIALS, FREE OR AT LOW COST

Association for Childhood Education
  International
3615 Wisconsin Avenue, N.W.
Washington, D.C. 20016

> Organization of teachers, parents, community workers, and others concerned with the education and well-being of children aged two to twelve. Publishes numerous bulletins and pamphlets. A catalog of publications is available on request.

# Learning and Creativity

Bank Street College of Education
610 West 112th Street
New York, N.Y. 10025

    Publishes books, booklets, and articles for teachers and parents.

Child Development Associate Consortium
7315 Wisconsin Avenue
Washington, D.C. 20014    Phone (301) 652-7144

    This group of national associations seeks to improve the quality and effectiveness of the care and education of three- to five-year-olds. Has developed a system for assessing the competency of personnel working in early childhood settings. Publishes numerous brochures, pamphlets, and reprints.

International Board on Books for Young People
IBBY Secretariat
Leinhardsgr 38a
CH-4051 Basle, Switzerland

    An international organization of institutions, publishing houses, and groups interested in juvenile literature. Encourages promotion and distribution of good books for children.

National PTA
700 North Rush Street
Chicago, Ill. 60611    Phone (312) 787-0977

    An organization of parents and professionals interested in "uniting the forces of home, school and community in behalf of children and youth." Publishes PTA MAGAZINE and pamphlets on parent education, children of various ages, mental health, safety, and parent-teacher relationships.

Office of Child Development
Project Head Start
P.O. Box 1182
Washington, D.C. 20013

    Provides a list of films suitable for Head Start programs.

## AUDIOVISUAL MATERIALS

### Films

LEARNING TO LEARN IN INFANCY. 1970. 16mm, 30 min., sound, black and white. Producer: U.S. Department of Health, Education and Welfare. Title no. 00251.

    Ways in which parents can help infants to differentiate between objects and to develop the early communication skills.

# Learning and Creativity

Available from: Reference Branch, National Audiovisual Center (GSA), Washington, D.C. 20409.

PARENTS ARE TEACHERS TOO. 1967. 16mm, 18 min., sound, black and white. Producer: Office of Education, Department of Health, Education and Welfare. Title no. 584447.

Stresses that parents are the child's first teachers and that learning is easier when teachers and parents cooperate.

Available from: Reference Branch, National Audiovisual Center (GSA), Washington, D.C. 20409.

THE T.H. BELL SYSTEM OF HOME-BASED EARLY CHILDHOOD EDUCATION.

A package to instruct parents in establishing a learning environment for their preschoolers. The set consists of: 1) YOUR CHILD'S INTELLECT--a book of step-by-step instructions to be used at home, 2) "The Parent-Teacher Intro-Motivator"--16mm film designed to stimulate participation in the preschool program, 3) THE OLYMPUS TEACHING TOY LIBRARY--toys that aid skill development in children from birth to five years, 4) THE INSERVICE-TRAINING PACKAGE--four filmstrips which train educators to deal with parents, and 5) THE PARENT TRAINING PACKAGE--six filmstrips for parent training sessions.

Individual items are available from: Olympus Publishing Co., Five Olympus Plaza, 1670 East Thirteenth Street South, Salt Lake City, Ut. 84105. Phone (801) 583-3666.

## Filmstrips and Slides

BEFORE READING AND WRITING.

Sound-slide film which offers suggestions for preschool activities to help children develop pre-reading and writing skills.

Available from: Association of Childhood Education International, 3615 Wisconsin Avenue, N.W., Washington, D.C. 20016.

HELPING YOUNG CHILDREN DEVELOP COMMUNICATION SKILLS.

Sound-slide film which reviews the principles and techniques that can be used to help preschool children improve their ability to communicate.

Available from: Association for Childhood Education International, 3615 Wisconsin Avenue, N.W., Washington, D.C. 20016.

# Learning and Creativity

WHAT CAN YOU DO TO HELP YOUR CHILD SUCCEED? Filmstrip, color.

What parents can expect from school and how they can help solve some of the problems that children experience at school.

Available from: National Education Association, 1201 Sixteenth Street, N.W., Washington, D.C. 20036.

# LEARNING DISABILITIES

(See also Hyperactive Child)

## BOOKS

### Dated but Still Relevant

Cruickshank, William M. THE BRAIN-INJURED CHILD IN HOME, SCHOOL AND COMMUNITY. Syracuse, N.Y.: Syracuse University Press, 1967. 294 p. Biblio., illus.

> Specific classroom techniques to help brain-injured children develop to their fullest potential. Good material for parents as well.

### Reference

THE ACADEMIC UNDERACHIEVER 1970-1971. 2d ed. Boston: Porter Sargent, 1970. 343 p. Illus., index.

> Handbook of basic information about preparatory, tutorial, remedial, and diagnostic resources to be found in academic schools, specialized schools, alternative programs, and specialized clinics for the underachiever in the United States. Each entry includes data on fees, ages accepted, professional qualifications of staff, and other information.

Association for Children with Learning Disabilities. THE DIRECTORY OF EDUCATIONAL FACILITIES FOR THE LEARNING DISABLED. 5th ed. San Rafael, Calif.: Academic Therapy Publications, 1973. 48 p.

> Facilities are listed by state with such information as related professional service, type of care--residential or day, ages and gender accepted, dates open, and fees.

Ellingson, Careth, and Cass, James. DIRECTORY OF FACILITIES FOR THE LEARNING-DISABLED AND HANDICAPPED. New York: Harper & Row

# Learning Disabilities

Publishers, 1972. 624 p. Index.

> Describes and compares remedial, therapeutic, and developmental programs in the United States and Canada which serve children and adults.

## Current Sources

Ames, Louise Bates, et al. STOP SCHOOL FAILURE. New York: Harper & Row Publishers, 1972. 308 p. Biblio., illus., index.

> Experts from the Gesell Institute of Child Development, backed by years of clinical research, offer new insights to help parents cope with the learning disability of their child. Well-indexed.

Bierbauer, Elaine. IF YOUR CHILD HAS A LEARNING DISABILITY. Danville, Ill.: Interstate Printers & Publishers, 1974. 94 p.

> Helps parents understand minimal brain dysfunction. Offers tips for adjusting to the situation and helping the handicapped child.

Browning, Elizabeth. I CAN'T SEE WHAT YOU'RE SAYING. New York: Coward, McCann & Geoghegan, 1973. 198 p.

> A personal account of the medical and educational experiences of the author's son who was diagnosed as an aphasic at age three. The pains of adjustment on the part of the parents are well described.

Brutten, Milton, et al. SOMETHING'S WRONG WITH MY CHILD: A PARENTS' BOOK ABOUT CHILDREN WITH LEARNING DISABILITIES. New York: Harcourt Brace Jovanovich, 1973. 246 p. Appendices, biblio., index.

> Based on extensive clinical experience, this informative and practical book provides a means for recognizing learning disabilities, lists sources of help, and outlines a solution based upon a team approach. A useful appendix lists agencies and facilities to which the parent may turn for guidance.

Cameron, Constance Carpenter. A DIFFERENT DREAM. Englewood Cliffs, N.J.: Prentice-Hall, 1973. 241 p.

> Personal day-by-day account of the home training program that the author developed for her aphasic child. Describes the use of puzzles, flash cards, and cutouts to teach colors, basic concepts, simple numbers, and even reading.

Clarke, Louise [pseud.]. CAN'T READ, CAN'T WRITE, CAN'T TALK TOO GOOD EITHER: HOW TO RECOGNIZE AND OVERCOME DYSLEXIA IN

# Learning Disabilities

YOUR CHILD. New York: Walker & Co., 1973. 256 p. Biblio., illus., index.

> The author's personal experiences with a dyslexic son who overcame his handicap. Thorough coverage of dyslexia including its history, its symptoms, the educational problems it causes, and the resources available for treatment.

Ellingson, Careth. SPEAKING OF CHILDREN--THEIR LEARNING ABILITIES/DISABILITIES. New York: Harper & Row Publishers, 1975. 288 p. Biblio., charts, illus., index.

> Thorough description, based on the latest research, of the physiological processes involved in learning. Discusses the symptoms of learning difficulties, the sources for help, and the role of drugs in treating learning disabilities.

Freeman, Stephen W. DOES YOUR CHILD HAVE A LEARNING DISABILITY?: QUESTIONS ANSWERED FOR PARENTS. Springfield, Ill.: Charles C. Thomas, Publisher, 1974. 111 p. Biblio., index.

> Covers the causes of learning disabilities, characteristics of learning disabilities, characteristics of learning disabled children, discipline, home training, and educational development.

Gardner, Richard A., M.D. MBD: THE FAMILY BOOK ABOUT MINIMAL BRAIN DYSFUNCTION. New York: Jason Aronson, 1973. 185 p. Illus.

> A noted child psychiatrist defines minimal brain dysfunction, discusses the possible causes, and offers suggestions to parents for dealing with it. Includes a section specifically written for children to read alone or with a parent.

Kronick, Doreen. A WORD OR TWO ABOUT LEARNING DISABILITIES. San Rafael, Calif.: Academic Therapy Publications, 1973. 271 p.

> A sensitive treatment of the stresses that learning disabled children place on parents, siblings, teachers, and the community. Discusses approaches to help these children function more fully within the family and community. Includes sections on the development of social skills and recreation.

Levy, Harold, M.D. SQUARE PEGS, ROUND HOLES: THE LEARNING-DISABLED CHILD IN THE CLASSROOM AND AT HOME. Boston: Little, Brown and Co., 1973. 250 p.

> A pediatrician enables parents to understand and help solve the problems of intelligent children who have trouble learning because of biochemical imbalances.

# Learning Disabilities

Rosner, Jerome. HELPING CHILDREN OVERCOME LEARNING DISABILITIES: A STEP-BY-STEP GUIDE FOR PARENTS AND TEACHERS. New York: Walker & Co., 1975. 321 p. Appendix, illus., index.

> A practical course of action for parents when their child is failing in school due to learning problems. Discusses the use of test results as a basis for corrective action. Also covers methods of preventing this disability.

Siegel, Ernest. THE EXCEPTIONAL CHILD GROWS UP: GUIDELINES FOR UNDERSTANDING AND HELPING THE BRAIN-INJURED ADOLESCENT AND YOUNG ADULT. New York: E.P. Dutton & Co., 1974. 227 p. Appendix, biblio., index.

> See Siegel, p. 105.

Stott, Denis Herbert. THE PARENT AS TEACHER: A GUIDE FOR PARENTS OF CHILDREN WITH LEARNING DIFFICULTIES. Belmont, Calif.: Fearon Publishers, 1974. 138 p. Illus. Paperbound.

> Practical activities and methods to involve parents in the education of learning disabled children. The author treats the subject most sympathetically and includes an appendix of learning games available in kits.

Wagner, Rudolf E. DYSLEXIA AND YOUR CHILD: A GUIDE FOR PARENTS AND TEACHERS. New York: Harper & Row Publishers, 1971. 148 p. Illus., index.

> Compact guide to identifying reading problems and helping children overcome them in the absence of reading clinics or remedial teachers. Describes remedial techniques and lists sources of relevant materials.

Wunderlich, Ray C., M.D. KIDS, BRAINS, AND LEARNING: WHAT GOES WRONG--PREVENTION AND TREATMENT. St. Petersburg, Fla.: Johnny Reads, 1970. 534 p. Illus., index. Paperbound.

> Dr. Wunderlich discusses such topics as learning disorders, brain damage, home teaching methods, and therapeutic systems.

## PERIODICALS

ACADEMIC THERAPY. San Rafael, Calif: Academic Therapy Publications, 1965-- . Quarterly.

> Scholarly as well as practical ideas are included in this journal which focuses on understanding children who have problems with reading, learning, communication, and/or traditional educational methods.

# Learning Disabilities

JOURNAL OF LEARNING DISABILITIES. Chicago: Professional Press, 1967-- Monthly, except June/July and Aug./Sept. which are combined.

> Articles of interest to both professionals and parents on programs, materials, techniques, and research on children with learning (including reading disabled children) and behavior problems. Has book reviews.

## PAMPHLETS AND/OR GOVERNMENT DOCUMENTS

Unless otherwise noted the materials are available free of charge. Prices quoted are subject to change. Payment should accompany order.

HELPING YOUR LD CHILD AT HOME. 1973. 59 p. $2.50. Available from: Academic Therapy Publications, 1539 Fourth Street, San Rafael, Calif. 94901.

> Suggestions for parents of learning disabled children.

LEARNING DISABILITIES DUE TO MINIMAL BRAIN DYSFUNCTION. 1973. 20 p. Publication no. (NIH) 73-154. Available from: National Institute of Neurological and Communicative Disorders and Stroke, National Institutes of Health, Bethesda, Md. 20014.

> Aid to identifying and helping the child with learning problems due to minimal brain dysfunction.

MINIMAL BRAIN DYSFUNCTION IN CHILDREN. 1970. 81 p. $1.00. Public Health Service Publication no. 2015. Available from: Superintendent of Documents, Government Printing Office, Washington, D.C. 20402.

> Report of a task force on learning disabilities.

SOMETHING'S WRONG WITH MY CHILD. By Sylvia O. Richardson. 1975. 12 p. 65 cents. Available from: American Montessori Society, 175 Fifth Avenue, New York, N.Y. 10010.

> Outlines learning disabilities in children such as hyperkinesia and dyslexia. Suggests ways to help disabled children in school and at home.

SPEECH, LANGUAGE AND HEARING PROGRAMS--1973. Available from: Project Head Start, P.O. Box 1182, Washington, D.C. 20013.

> Offers suggestions for parents and teachers to stimulate normal language development, teach speech and language skills, and help children who have speech, language, and hearing handicaps.

# Learning Disabilities

YOUR CHILD HAS A LEARNING DISABILITY--WHAT IS IT? 1971. 18 p. Available from: National Easter Seal Society for Crippled Children and Adults, 2023 West Ogden Avenue, Chicago, Ill. 60012.

    For parents and teachers.

## ORGANIZATIONS AND/OR SOURCES OF MATERIALS, FREE OR AT LOW COST

Association for Children With
   Learning Disabilities
5225 Grace Street
Pittsburgh, Pa. 15236    Phone (412) 881-1191

    National organization of parents and interested professionals. Provides schools, camps, recreation programs, parent education, and information services. Informational material and a list of publications is available on request. Publishes a DIRECTORY OF ORGANIZATIONS CONCERNED WITH LEARNING DISABILITIES.

Institutes for the Achievement of Human
   Potential
8801 Stenton Avenue
Philadelphia, Pa. 19118    Phone (215) 248-2550

    Children's Institute conducts evaluation, reevaluation, programming, and parent orientation for patients ranging from the brain-injured child with severe disability, to the apparently well child who is not realizing his potential, to the school child unable to read.

Orton Society
8415 Bellona Lane
Towson, Md. 21204    Phone (301) 296-0232

    Nonprofit educational and scientific organization of professionals and parents interested in the study, prevention, and treatment of specific language difficulty, or simple dyslexia. Publishes an annual bulletin and a newsletter, as well as a bibliography, monographs, and reprints of papers.

## AUDIOVISUAL MATERIALS

## Films

BRIGHT BOY, BAD SCHOLAR. 1966. 28 min., sound, black and white. Producer: Robert Anderson, Associates.

    Explores the problems of schoolchildren with learning disabilities

# Learning Disabilities

and the effects of repeated failure. Physician who works with this problem suggests appropriate treatment.

Available from: McGraw-Hill Films, 330 West Forty-second Street, New York, N.Y. 10001.

EARLY RECOGNITION OF LEARNING DISABILITIES. 1969. 16mm, 30 min., sound, color.

Presents the early symptoms of learning disabilities and encourages parents to seek immediate help if they recognize such symptoms in their child. A most useful film. Available on loan from: The National Medical Audiovisual Center, Station K, Atlanta, Ga. 30324.

Available for purchase from: The National Audiovisual Center, National Archives and Records Services, Washington, D.C. 20409.

MEET LISA. 1971. 5 min., sound.

The world as seen through the eyes of a brain-injured child and her parents.

Available from: AIMS Instructional Media Services, P.O. Box 1010, Hollywood, Calif. 90210.

# MULTIPLE BIRTHS

## BOOKS

### Dated but Still Relevant

Gehman, Betsy Hollard. TWINS: TWICE THE TROUBLE, TWICE THE FUN. Philadelphia: J.B. Lippincott Co., 1965. 224 p. Biblio.

> A practical guidebook for parents of twins. Emphasizes that twins should be treated as individuals.

Scheinfeld, Amram. TWINS AND SUPERTWINS. Philadelphia: J.B. Lippincott Co., 1967. 292 p. Appendix, biblio., tables, index.

> A thorough, readable, and fact-filled inside view of the lives of the multiple-born from conception to maturity. Emphasizes the pleasures as well as the burdens of raising twins.

### Current Sources

Gaddis, Vincent H., and Gaddis, Margaret. THE CURIOUS WORLD OF TWINS. New York: Hawthorn Books, 1972. 209 p. Biblio., index.

> Well-researched book helps parents to understand the reasons for multiple birth and to recognize the differences in twins.

## PAMPHLETS AND/OR GOVERNMENT DOCUMENTS

Unless otherwise noted the materials are available free of charge. Prices quoted are subject to change. Payment should accompany order.

AND THEN THERE WERE TWO: A HANDBOOK FOR MOTHERS AND FATHERS

# Multiple Births

OF TWINS. Rev. ed. 1971. 32 p. Available from: Child Study Association of America, 50 Madison Avenue, New York, N.Y. 10028.

    Practical information about the care of twins and the special adjustments required from their parents.

## ORGANIZATIONS AND/OR SOURCES OF MATERIALS, FREE OR AT LOW COST

National Organization of Mothers of
    Twins Clubs
5402 Amberwood Lane
Rockville, Md. 20853    Phone (301) 460-9108

    This organization serves as an interchange of information between parents, educators, doctors, and others to broaden the understanding of those aspects of child development and rearing which relate especially to twins.

# PARENTHOOD

(See also Chapters on Child Development; Discipline; Working Mother)

## BOOKS

### Historical Perspective

Abbott, John Stevens Cabot. THE MOTHER AT HOME: OR THE PRINCIPLES OF MATERNAL DUTY. 1834. Reprint. New York: Arno Press, 1972. 184 p.

> Prescribes the social norms that parents are to follow in raising their children.

### Dated but Still Relevant

Bettelheim, Bruno. DIALOGUES WITH MOTHERS. New York: Free Press, 1962. 216 p.

> This book is based upon taperecorded sessions between Dr. Bettelheim and a group of mothers regarding the behavior of their children. Enlightening to parents.

Ginott, Haim G. BETWEEN PARENT AND CHILD. New York: Macmillan, 1969. 256 p. Biblio., index.

> Popular and easily understood collection of helpful ideas and direct advice on developing a mutual relationship of love and respect through new lines of communication. Now a bestseller.

Gruenberg, Sidonie [M.]. THE PARENTS' GUIDE TO EVERYDAY PROBLEMS OF BOYS AND GIRLS: HELPING YOUR CHILD FROM FIVE TO TWELVE. New York: Random House, 1958. 363 p. Biblio.

> Suggestions for improving daily life and family relationships with children in this often-overlooked age group.

# Parenthood

Ilg, Frances [L.], and Ames, Louise Bates. PARENTS ASK. New York: Harper & Row Publishers, 1962. 425 p. Biblio., index.

> Down-to-earth advice on a wide range of topics. Based upon questions that parents have submitted to the authors' daily newspaper column.

Le Shan, Eda J. HOW TO SURVIVE PARENTHOOD. New York: Random House, 1965. 242 p. Biblio.

> A specialist in the field of family counseling stresses the needs of parents rather than the demands of children in this thoughtful analysis of parent-child relationships.

Newton, Niles. THE FAMILY BOOK OF CHILD CARE. New York: Harper & Row Publishers, 1957. 477 p. Illus.

> Down-to-earth approach to practical problems of child raising-- from the fetal stage through grade school years.

Rule, Lareina. NAME YOUR BABY. New York: Bantam Books, 1963. 214 p.

> Lists over 6500 names (boys and girls) including origins, meanings, nicknames, and the personalities who made each name famous. Provides a chapter on astrology and the baby.

Salk, Lee, and Kramer, Rita. HOW TO RAISE A HUMAN BEING: A PARENTS' GUIDE TO EMOTIONAL HEALTH FROM INFANCY THROUGH ADOLESCENCE. New York: Random House, 1969. 205 p.

> Useful and clearly written advice on helping children to realize their full potential. Emphasizes the first three years. This book is unique in its emphasis on avoiding problems before they arise.

Simon, Anne W. STEPCHILD IN THE FAMILY: A VIEW OF CHILDREN IN REMARRIAGE. New York: Odyssey Press, 1964. 256 p. Biblio.

> The author, who is herself a stepchild and a stepmother, presents a well-documented examination of the problems of children in remarriage.

Spock, Benjamin. PROBLEMS OF PARENTS. New York: Houghton Mifflin Co., 1962. 308 p.

> Based upon articles that appeared in LADIES HOME JOURNAL, this book was written to enable parents to deal with their feelings. Contains warm and compassionate advice on such topics as quarreling, guilt over favoritism, and difficulties in telling children about sex and death.

# Parenthood

Thomson, Helen. THE SUCCESSFUL STEP-PARENT. New York: Harper & Row Publishers, 1966. 237 p. Biblio., index.

> Practical and informative suggestions on dealing with the problems of being a step-parent. Includes the positive aspects as well.

## Reference

Ames, Winthrop, ed. WHAT SHALL WE NAME THE BABY. New York: Pocket Books, 1975. 208 p. Paperbound.

> The first edition of this standard book of names was published in 1941. The current edition is an alphabetical listing of first names, their meanings, and origins. It includes a capsule history of names and a list of birthstones.

Browder, Sue. THE NEW AGE BABY NAME BOOK. New York: Workman Publishing Co., 1974. 270 p.

> Source of over 3,000 names for girls and boys. Gives pronunciation, origin, and meaning for each, including many ethnic names. Presents material on choosing an ethnic name and on creating a name. Also offers astrological guides.

International Association of Counseling Services. 1973 DIRECTORY OF COUNSELING SERVICES. Washington, D.C.: 1973. 273 p.

> Comprehensive state-by-state listing of counseling (personal, educational, vocational, psychological) agencies and services that meet the standards of the American Personnel and Guidance Association. Covers counseling for children with learning and behavioral disabilities, family counseling, juvenile delinquent counseling, and psychological testing.

Schlesinger, Benjamin. THE ONE-PARENT FAMILY. Buffalo, N.Y.: University of Toronto Press, 1970. 138 p. Appendix, index.

> Three essays on the one-parent family and widowhood. Includes a comprehensive annotated bibliography of books, pamphlets, and journal articles.

## Current Sources

Anthony, E. James, M.D., and Benedek, Therese, M.D., eds. PARENTHOOD: ITS PSYCHOLOGY AND PATHOLOGY. Boston: Little, Brown and Co., 1970. 617 p. Biblio., illus.

> Presents parenthood in the context of biological and environmental evaluation of human behavior.

# Parenthood

Arnold, Arnold. YOUR CHILD AND YOU. Chicago: Henry Regnery Co., 1970. 274 p.

> Based on the author's column, "Parents and Children," this volume provides a concise and coherent approach to child-rearing.

Benning, Lee Edwards. HOW TO BRING UP A CHILD WITHOUT SPENDING A FORTUNE. New York: David McKay Co., 1975. 326 p.

> Practical hints for saving on food, shelter, recreation, medical bills, and education. Includes dollar figures and "A Directory of Sources for You To Contact, Send for, or Read. . . . "

Berends, Polly Berrien. WHOLE CHILD, WHOLE PARENT. New York: Harper's Magazine Press, 1975. 301 p. Biblio., illus.

> Child-rearing approached from the religious and philosophical aspects in the format of the WHOLE-EARTH CATALOG. Consumer advice and unique suggestions for supervising and being involved with the child are included. This book emphasizes the good that the child can do for the parent.

Bernard, Jessie. THE FUTURE OF MOTHERHOOD. New York: Dial Press, 1974. 426 p. Paperbound.

> The author challenges the myth of the motherhood instinct, yet believes that "motherhood" in the best sense of the word may be salvaged in the future.

Bernhardt, Karl S., and Bernhardt, David K., eds. BEING A PARENT: UNCHANGING VALUES IN A CHANGING WORLD. Buffalo, N.Y.: University of Toronto Press, 1970. 187 p. Paperbound.

> Collection of articles by Karl S. Bernhardt on the theme that children still need parents to guide them.

Bird, Joseph, and Bird, Lois. POWER TO THE PARENTS!: A COMMONSENSE PSYCHOLOGY OF CHILD RAISING FOR THE 70'S. Garden City, N.Y.: Doubleday & Co., 1972. 215 p.

> Written from the viewpoint that parents must once again become authority figures who accept full responsibility for rearing their children. Offers sound, practical methods for dealing with drug abuse, sexual permissiveness, education, communication, and other areas.

Bricklin, Barry, and Bricklin, Patricia M. STRONG FAMILY, STRONG CHILD: THE ART OF WORKING TOGETHER TO DEVELOP A HEALTHY CHILD. New York: Delacorte Press, 1970. 229 p. Biblio., index.

# Parenthood

Two psychiatrists advise parents on effectively dealing with children's problems. They devise a strategy to deal with parent-child conflict by setting limits for behavior, encouraging independence, and recognizing and understanding a child's feelings.

Bronfenbrenner, Urie. TWO WORLDS OF CHILDHOOD: U.S. & U.S.S.R. New York: Russell Sage Foundation, 1970. 190 p. Illus.

> Concise comparative analysis of Soviet and American child-rearing methods. Concludes that improving the place of the child in American society requires more adult involvement.

Callahan, Sidney Cornelia. PARENTING: PRINCIPLES AND POLITICS OF PARENTHOOD. Garden City, N.Y.: Doubleday & Co., 1973. 208 p.

> A literature survey of attitudes and problems in child rearing. Encourages parents to develop a more sound future for each child.

Cheavens, Sam Frank. CREATIVE PARENTHOOD: ADVANTAGES YOU CAN GIVE YOUR CHILD. Waco, Tex.: Word Books, 1971. 183 p. Biblio.

> A psychologist offers practical suggestions on guiding children towards creative and mature adulthood.

Deakin, Michael. THE CHILDREN ON THE HILL: THE STORY OF AN EXTRAORDINARY FAMILY. New York: Bobbs-Merrill Co., 1973. 125 p.

> Narrative of a Welsh family of prodigies in which the children thrive on love, constant attention, and pacifism.

Dechter, Midge. LIBERAL PARENTS, RADICAL CHILDREN. New York: Coward, McCann & Geoghegan, 1975. 284 p.

> A controversial look into why the children of the 1960s did not meet the expectations of their liberal middle-class parents.

De Rosis, Helen, M.D. PARENT POWER/CHILD POWER: A NEW AND TESTED METHOD FOR PARENTING WITHOUT GUILT. Indianapolis: Bobbs-Merrill Co., 1974. 237 p. Index.

> A specialist in parent counseling explores reasons for the stresses and strains in parent-child relationships and offers ways of preventing conflict through parent education and the open door of communication.

Dodson, Fitzhugh. HOW TO FATHER. Freeport, N.Y.: Nash Publishing Corp., 1974. 535 p. Appendix, biblio., illus., index.

# Parenthood

> A father and psychologist delineates the father's role in child rearing from infancy to adolescence. It covers such topics as discipline, sibling rivalry, sex education, and drug awareness. Also includes a section on the problems of divorced and single fathers and appendices on selecting toys, books, and records for children.

\_\_\_\_\_. HOW TO PARENT. Freeport, N.Y.: Nash Publishing Co., 1970. 444 p. Appendix, illus.

> A practical approach to child raising based on a combination of love and discipline. Covers the ages from birth to five. Includes a suggested reading list for parents, as well as guides to childrens' toys and records.

Douglas, William. THE ONE-PARENT FAMILY. Nashville, Tenn.: Graded Press, 1971. 158 p.

> Methodist Church study focuses on particular problems faced by single parents.

Duberman, Lucille. THE RECONSTITUTED FAMILY: A STUDY OF REMARRIED COUPLES AND THEIR CHILDREN. Chicago: Nelson-Hall Co., 1975. 180 p. Biblio., illus., index.

> Highly relevant to contemporary life, this well-documented study reveals the complexities involved in remarriages where there are children.

Faber, Adele, and Mazlish, Elaine. LIBERATED PARENTS/LIBERATED CHILDREN. New York: Grossett & Dunlap, 1974. 238 p.

> The authors were members of a parent study group that worked for five years under the guidance of the late child psychologist and author, Dr. Haim G. Ginott. They recount their experiences in developing new methods of communicating and building better relationships with their children. Represents the application of the Ginott ideas expressed in BETWEEN PARENT AND CHILD (see p. 209).

Fletcher, Grace Nies. WHAT'S RIGHT WITH US PARENTS? New York: William Morrow & Co., 1972. 182 p. Index.

> Over 600 people including parents, children, doctors, psychiatrists, clergy, and teachers were interviewed regarding the attitudes and problems of the young and the need for parental understanding.

# Parenthood

Gordon, Thomas. PARENT EFFECTIVENESS TRAINING: THE "NO-LOSE" PROGRAM FOR RAISING RESPONSIBLE CHILDREN. New York: Peter H. Wyden/Publisher, 1970. 338 p. Biblio., illus.

>See Gordon, p. 80.

Group for the Advancement of Psychiatry. Committee on Public Education. THE JOYS AND SORROWS OF PARENTHOOD. New York: Charles Scribner's Sons, 1973. 159 p.

>The focus is on the parent as the authors explore the vital issues confronting parent-child relationships including values and discipline. The roles of step-parent, single parent, grandparent, and adoptive parents are well covered.

Hamilton, Russel, and Green, Stephanie, eds. WHAT BOTHERS US ABOUT GROWNUPS: A REPORT CARD ON ADULTS BY CHILDREN. Brattleboro, Vt.: Stephen Greene Press, 1971. 184 p. Illus.

>Results of a questionnaire submitted to 1200 children, ages eight to twelve, regarding what they dislike about grownups, how they will act with their own children including what they will say, and what they dislike about being children.

Hoover, Mary B. THE RESPONSIVE PARENT: MEETING THE REALITIES OF PARENTHOOD TODAY. New York: Parents' Magazine Press, 1972. 255 p. Biblio., illus., index.

>Helpful and reassuring guide that enables parents to examine their own attitudes and then apply their insights to the day-to-day experiences.

Kinkmeyer, Don C., and McKay, Gary D. RAISING A RESPONSIBLE CHILD: PRACTICAL STEPS TO SUCCESSFUL FAMILY RELATIONSHIPS. New York: Simon & Schuster, 1973. 256 p. Biblio., index.

>A guide for parents on successful child raising and problem handling based on the Adlerian school of psychology.

Klein, Carole. THE SINGLE PARENT EXPERIENCE. New York: Walker & Co., 1973. 241 p. Appendix, biblio.

>This study, based on interviews with single parents and professionals, reveals how single parents (divorced, widowed, or homosexual) manage their unique problems. A list of state sources for counseling on adoption, pregnancy, and related issues is included.

Lane, Mary B. EDUCATION FOR PARENTING. Washington, D.C.: National Association for the Education of Young Children, 1975. 84 p.

# Parenthood

> The director of the Cross-Cultural Family Center in San Francisco describes the needs of parents and young children with special emphasis on the problems of working mothers, single parents, and teenage parents. Useful and clear suggestions are provided for improved parent education programs.

Lemasters, E.E. PARENTS IN MODERN AMERICA. Homewood, Ill.: Dorsey Press, 1970. 232 p. Paperbound.

> Critical review of the literature on parent-child relations, based on the assumption that parenthood in America is difficult.

Le Shan, Eda J. NATURAL PARENTHOOD: RAISING YOUR CHILD WITHOUT A SCRIPT. New York: New American Library, 1970. 160 p. Paperbound.

> Help from a clear-sighted child psychologist in making common-sense decisions.

\_\_\_\_\_. ON "HOW DO YOUR CHILDREN GROW?": A DIALOGUE WITH PARENTS. Rev. ed. New York: David McKay Co., 1972. 306 p. Biblio.

> Selections from the author's television show. Parents speak freely on a wide range of topics from diapers to drugs.

Lowndes, Marion. A MANUAL FOR BABYSITTERS. 2d rev. ed. Boston: Little, Brown and Co., 1975. 184 p.

> See Lowndes, p. 45.

Moustakas, Clark E., and Perry, Cereta. LEARNING TO BE FREE. Englewood Cliffs, N.J.: Prentice-Hall, 1973. 184 p. Biblio. Paperbound.

> The authors recount their experiences as coleaders of a program on enhancing human potential in young children and their families. By means of sensitivity and play techniques, children were encouraged to become aware of and cope with their feelings. Parents and community leaders were also encouraged to vent their feelings toward each other.

Olshaker, Bennett, M.D. WHAT SHALL WE TELL THE KIDS? New York: Arbor House Publishing Co., 1971. 253 p. Index.

> Sensible advice to parents on a variety of subjects such as discipline, medical problems, divorce, remarriage, etc., with anecdotes preceding each section.

Radl, Shirley L. MOTHER'S DAY IS OVER. New York: Charterhouse Books, 1973. 234 p.

# Parenthood

The author examines the difficulties inherent in the motherhood role including a mother's real feelings, the social pressures, the inconveniences, and the joys.

Salk, Lee, M.D. PREPARING FOR PARENTHOOD. New York: David McKay Co., 1974. 206 p. Index.

Dr. Salk directs himself towards the psychological needs of both expectant and new parents.

_____. WHAT EVERY CHILD WOULD LIKE HIS PARENTS TO KNOW, TO HELP HIM WITH THE EMOTIONAL PROBLEMS OF HIS EVERYDAY LIFE. New York: David McKay Co., 1972. 239 p.

A readable guide, in question-and-answer format, to handling behavior problems, sex education, discipline, toilet training, death, and other areas of parent-child interaction.

Satir, Virginia. PEOPLEMAKING. Palo Alto, Calif.: Science & Behavior Books, 1972. 304 p. Illus.

A lively discussion of the influence of the family process on a child's development.

Shedd, Charlie. PROMISES TO PETER: BUILDING A BRIDGE FROM PARENT TO CHILD. Waco, Tex.: Word Books, 1970. 147 p.

A book about developing communication between parents and their children. Covers self-government, love, and the dignity of work.

Spock, Benjamin, M.D. RAISING CHILDREN IN A DIFFICULT TIME: A PHILOSOPHY OF PARENTAL LEADERSHIP AND HIGH IDEALS. New York: W.W. Norton & Co., 1974. 268 p.

An inquiry into the impact of today's cultural environment on parents and children. Spock covers special problems such as parents' rights and roles, drug use, divorce, day care, and family counseling. He underscores the importance of a strong family unit.

Stevens, Anita, and Freeman, Lucy. "I HATE MY PARENTS!": THE REAL AND UNREAL REASONS WHY YOUTH IS ANGRY. New York: Cowles Book Co., 1970. 183 p.

Ways for parents to offset relationships that create hatred. Includes an examination of the Charles Manson "family."

# Parenthood

Wesley, Frank. CHILDREARING PSYCHOLOGY. New York: Behavioral Publications, 1971. 243 p. Biblio.

>Two-part discussion of child rearing covering fifty years of research, including the theories of Watson, Freud, and Piaget. The author also examines such specific questions as toilet training, feeding, play, sleep, bedwetting, breast- or bottle-feeding

Wiener, Joan, and Glick, Joyce. A MOTHERHOOD BOOK: ADVENTURES IN PREGNANCY, BIRTH, AND BEING A MOTHER. New York: Macmillan, 1974. 131 p. Biblio., index.

>The authors write with joy and loving of their own experiences as young mothers. They include practical suggestions for those contemplating pregnancy, the already pregnant, and the new mother. Appendices list people and organizations who provide help or referrals in areas such as natural childbirth, breastfeeding, prenatal and postnatal care. Be wary: some views may not coincide with conventional medical opinion.

## PERIODICALS

FAMILY LIFE. Los Angeles: American Institute of Family Relations, 1941-- . Monthly.

>Monthly service bulletin with book reviews, articles on current trends, research notes, and new pamphlets.

FOCUS ON THE FAMILY. Eugene, Oreg.: E.C. Brown Center for Family Studies, 1970-- . Bimonthly.

>Articles and brief book reviews related to the family.

MOMMA: THE NEWSPAPER/MAGAZINE FOR SINGLE MOTHERS. Venice, Calif.: Momma/Organization for Single Parents, 1972-- . Monthly.

>Considers everything from child care centers to diet, welfare, and psychology. Of interest to all mothers not only the single ones.

THE SINGLE PARENT. Washington, D.C.: Parents Without Partners, 1959-- . Ten issues a year.

>Articles and news of interest to single parents.

## PAMPHLETS AND/OR GOVERNMENT DOCUMENTS

Unless otherwise noted the materials are available free of charge. Prices quoted are subject to change. Payment should accompany order.

# Parenthood

ONE-PARENT FAMILIES. 1974. 12 p. Publication no. (OHD) 74-44. Available from: Office of Human Development, Publications Distribution Unit, Department of Health, Education and Welfare, Washington, D.C. 20201.

> Case histories of one-parent families that have succeeded. Tells how to obtain help during the adjustment period.

SO YOU'RE GOING TO BE A NEW FATHER? 1973. 32 p. Publication no. (OCD) 73-28. Available from: Office of Human Development, Publications Distribution Unit, Department of Health, Education and Welfare, Washington, D.C. 20201.

> Educates husbands on all aspects of pregnancy and prepares them to give emotional support to their wives throughout this period.

## ORGANIZATIONS AND/OR SOURCES OF MATERIALS, FREE OR AT LOW COST

Family Service Association of America
44 East Twenty-third Street
New York, N.Y. 10010    Phone (212) 674-6100

> Organization of local agencies which "provide family counseling service . . . to help families with parent-child, marital, mental health and everyday problems of family living." Publishes manuals, pamphlets, and other informational materials. A publications list is sent on request.

Maternity Center Association
48 East Ninty-second Street
New York, N.Y. 10028    Phone (212) 369-7300

> Interested in the improvement of maternity care, maternal and infant health, and family life. Conducts classes on pregnancy, childbearing, and baby care for expectant mothers and fathers. Issues books, charts, pamphlets, filmstrips, and movies.

MOMMA
P.O. Box 567
Venice, Calif. 90291

> Organization to help "separated, divorced, widowed and never-been-married mothers with their common problems including child care, financial concerns and psychological adjustment."

Parents Without Partners
7910 Woodmont Avenue
Washington, D.C. 20014    Phone (301) 654-8850

# Parenthood

Founded in 1957 to promote the study of single parents (widowed, divorced, separated, or otherwise) with the aim of alleviating the problems they encounter in bringing up their children and in being accepted by society. Publishes SINGLE PARENT.

Single Parent Resource Center
3896 Twenty-fourth Street
San Francisco, Calif. 94114

Conducts workshops and rap sessions. Their central switchboard helps parents locate child care. Will soon be publishing THE SINGLE PARENT JOURNAL.

Sisterhood of Black Single Mothers
P.O. Box 155
Brooklyn, N.Y. 11203

This organization emphasizes positive thinking and action for black unmarried mothers. They conduct monthly meetings in Brooklyn and the Bronx and operate a clothing and equipment exchange. They also publish a newsletter which can be obtained by sending them a stamped self-addressed envelope along with twenty-five cents.

## AUDIOVISUAL MATERIALS

### Films

BRIDGING THE GAP. 1972. 16mm, 30 min., sound, color. Producer: Cinematic Concepts Corporation.

Exploration of the problems of communication between parents and children using the problemsolving technique of Gordon's Parent Effectiveness Training. (See Gordon, PARENT EFFECTIVENESS TRAINING, above.)

Available from: Effectiveness Training Associates, 110 South Euclid Avenue, Pasadena, Calif. 91101.

CHRIS AND BERNIE. n.d. 16mm, 25 min., sound, color.

Documentary of two young women, both single parents, living together in an alternative family style.

Available from: New Day Films, P.O. Box 315, Franklin Lakes, N.J. 07417.

GROWING UP TOGETHER: FOUR TEEN MOTHERS AND THEIR BABIES. 1974. 16mm, 56 min., sound, color.

# Parenthood

The meaning of unmarried parenthood as documented by the day-to-day lives of some young mothers and their children.

Available from: Children's Home Society of California, Public Relations Department, 3100 West Adams Boulevard, Los Angeles, Calif. 90018.

TO BE A PARENT. 1972. 16mm, 15 min., sound, color.

Combination of "cinema verite," animation, folk music, good photography, and spontaneous comments by teens and young adults on their perceptions of parenthood, parent-child and parent-teen relationships.

Available from: Billy Budd Films, 235 East Fifty-seventh Street, New York, N.Y. 10022.

## Filmstrips

PARENTING: FATHERS, MOTHERS AND OTHERS. 1975. 48 frames. Cassette, 10 min., sound.

Shows the relationships between parent and child and the role of communications skills in increasing effectiveness in parenting.

Available from: J.C. Penney Co. (Check with the manager of the nearest store.)

# PLAY

(See also Learning and Creativity)

## BOOKS

### Dated but Still Relevant

Arnold, Arnold. YOUR CHILD'S PLAY: HOW TO HELP YOUR CHILD REAP THE FULL BENEFITS OF CREATIVE PLAY. New York: Simon & Schuster, 1968. 120 p. Paperbound.

> Offers much sensitive advice on understanding and participating in children's play.

Hartley, Ruth E., and Goldenson, Robert M. THE COMPLETE BOOK OF CHILDREN'S PLAY. Rev. ed. New York: Thomas Y. Crowell Co., 1963. 484 p. Illus.

> A thoughtful evaluation of the activities and interests of children at various stages of growth from birth to adolescence. Suggestions for appropriate games, hobbies, pets, music, and art activities are included.

Matterson, Elizabeth M. PLAY AND PLAYTHINGS FOR THE PRESCHOOL CHILD. New York: Penguin Books, 1967. 180 p. Biblio., illus.

> The author stresses the importance of play for the emotional and intellectual development of preschool children.

Sharp, Evelyn. THINKING IS CHILD'S PLAY. New York: E.P. Dutton & Co., 1969. 157 p. Biblio., illus., index.

> The author first presents a theoretical overview of how young children learn to think based on the work of Piaget, Bruner, Karplus, and Suppes. She then offers forty games which teach the art of logical thinking to young children using very ordinary materials.

# Play

Staff of the Boston Children's Medical Center, and Gregg, Elizabeth M. WHAT TO DO WHEN "THERE'S NOTHING TO DO." New York: Delacorte Press, 1968. 158 p. Biblio., illus.

> Activities and games (601 in all) which make use of materials found at home, are inexpensive, and are based on sound child development principles.

Winn, Marie, and Porcher, Mary Ann. THE PLAYGROUP BOOK. New York: Macmillan, 1967. 210 p. Biblio., illus.

> Step-by-step instructions for setting up the equivalent of a nursery school in your own home.

## Reference

Arnold, Arnold. WORLD BOOK OF CHILDREN'S GAMES. New York: World Publications, 1972. 346 p. Biblio., illus., index.

> Well-organized encyclopedia of children's games, both indoor and outdoor, for children from preschool through elementary school ages.

## Current Sources

Alton, Walter George. TOYS THAT YOU CAN MAKE. New York: Taplinger Publishing Co., 1972. 95 p. Illus.

> Instructions for making wooden horses, furniture, houses, soldiers, and so on.

Bengtsson, Arvid, ed. ADVENTURE PLAYGROUNDS. New York: Praeger Publishers, 1973. 167 p.

> Describes facilities, programs, and history of adventure playgrounds. Personal experiences are also included.

Broad, Laura Peabody, and Butterworth, Nancy Tower. THE PLAYGROUND HANDBOOK. New York: St. Martin's Press, 1974. 306 p.

> For mothers planning play groups or dealing on an individual basis with their own children, this work outlines activities for children three years and older according to the months of the year. Could be considered a recipe book for children's play activities.

Caney, Steven. TOY BOOK. New York: Workman Publishing Co., 1972. 176 p. Illus.

# Play

> This well-illustrated book gives directions for making fifty-one toys using inexpensive objects such as straws, strings, cups, cardboard, and toothpicks. The toys are designed for children three years and up and are segregated by the appropriate age group. Most of the toys can be built by the children themselves using the easy-to-follow directions; however, children under six will generally require some supervision.

Caplan, Frank, and Caplan, Theresa. THE POWER OF PLAY. Garden City, N.Y.: Doubleday & Co., 1973. 334 p. Illus.

> The founders of Creative Playthings, the well-known maker of educational toys, present a comprehensive survey of research findings and theoretical views, backed by their own convictions on the importance of play as a means to promote physical and mental development, good family and social relations, as well as learning and creativity. New insights on play and creativity in other countries make this a valuable addition to the literature.

Cass, Joan E. HELPING CHILDREN GROW THROUGH PLAY. New York: Schocken Books, 1973. 176 p. Biblio., index.

> The why, how, and where of children's play as outlined by a British social worker and nursery school teacher.

Chapman, Arthur Harry, M.D. THE GAMES CHILDREN PLAY. New York: G.P. Putnam's Sons, 1972. 250 p. Index.

> Games psychology applied to children. Helps parents recognize unhealthy relationships at home and in school.

Gordon, Ira J. BABY LEARNING THROUGH BABY PLAY: A PARENT'S GUIDE FOR THE FIRST TWO YEARS. New York: St. Martin's Press, 1970. 121 p. Illus. Paperbound.

> Suggestions for playing with the very young. Explains the importance of playing with the child.

Gordon, Ira [J.], et al. CHILD LEARNING THROUGH CHILD PLAY. New York: St. Martin's Press, 1972. 116 p. Illus.

> Games to play with two- and three-year-olds to develop basic mental skills and physical coordination.

Hein, Lucille E. ENTERTAINING YOUR CHILD. New York: Harper & Row Publishers, 1971. 260 p.

> Suggests numerous constructive activities for the child from three to six years of age.

# Play

Ives, Suzy. CREATING CHILDREN'S COSTUMES FROM PAPER AND CARDBOARD. New York: Taplinger Publishing Co., 1973. 95 p. Illus.

> Relatively easy directions for making costumes and masks using sacks, cardboard, and boxes. Children making these items must be supervised to avoid suffocation tragedies.

Kaye, Marvin. A TOY IS BORN. New York: Stein & Day Publishers, 1973. 190 p.

> Kaye, a former editor of the trade magazine TOYS, has written a survey which ranges from the manufacture and marketing of the more popular creations like Monopoly and Scrabble to such issues as toy safety, television advertising, and new trends in toys.

Kraft, Arthur. ARE YOU LISTENING TO YOUR CHILD?: HOW TO BRIDGE THE COMMUNICATIONS GAP THROUGH CREATIVE PLAY SESSIONS. New York: Walker & Co., 1973. 239 p.

> A psychologist describes techniques of play therapy that parents can use to interact more effectively with their children.

Lobley, Priscilla. MAKING CHILDREN'S COSTUMES. New York: Taplinger Publishing Co., 1972. Photos., 26cm.

> Step-by-step instructions for making such costumes as crusader, medieval princess, butterflies, gypsies, cowboys, Indians, spacemen, and many others. Masks and makeup instructions are also included.

Lundell, Margaretta. MOTHERCRAFT. New York: Simon & Schuster, 1975. 155 p. Biblio., illus., index. Paperbound.

> Collection of games, nonsense songs, toys, and cooking recipes which have been culled from the past. Restores a mother's confidence in her ability to create sources of joy for her children and herself.

McLaren, Esme. MAKING GLOVE PUPPETS. Boston: Plays, 1973. 218 p. Illus.

> Necessary technical information and directions for making seven different puppets. For both adults and children.

Marzollo, Jean, and Lloyd, Janice. LEARNING THROUGH PLAY. New York: Harper & Row Publishers, 1972. 211 p. Illus., index.

> Clear and concise information on the educational value of play and games in the learning processes of preschoolers.

# Play

Matterson, Elizabeth [M.], comp. GAMES FOR THE VERY YOUNG: FINGER PLAYS AND NURSERY GAMES. New York: American Heritage Press, 1971. 206 p. Index.

> Over 200 finger plays, verses, rhymes, and games with easy-to-follow instructions. The collection covers a wide range of children's interests and can be adapted for use at home, on the road, or in school.

Maynard, Fredelle. GUIDING YOUR CHILD TO A MORE CREATIVE LIFE. Garden City, N.Y.: Doubleday & Co., 1973. 369 p. Index.

> Maynard, a teacher and mother, has combined child development theory and practical suggestions for creative play activities and experiences. Discusses the considerations in choosing the right musical instrument for a child to play. Useful resources list.

Scargall, Jeanne. 1,001 WAYS TO HAVE FUN WITH CHILDREN: A GUIDE TO GAMES, CRAFTS AND CREATIVE FUN. New York: Charles Scribner's Sons, 1973. 159 p. Illus.

> Includes projects with paper bags and shoe boxes, self-entertainment activities for children on long car rides, and ideas for encouraging good eating habits. For younger children.

Stein, Susan M., and Lottick, Sarah T. THREE, FOUR, OPEN THE DOOR: CREATIVE FUN FOR YOUNG CHILDREN. Chicago: Follett Publishing Co., 1971. 255 p. Biblio., illus., index.

> Compilation of enjoyable learning activities for parents and teachers to use with children from birth to six years.

Sutton-Smith, Brian, and Sutton-Smith, Shirley. HOW TO PLAY WITH YOUR CHILDREN (AND WHEN NOT TO). New York: Hawthorn Books, 1974. 274 p. Appendix, index.

> The authors stress play as a major influence in the social psychological, and intellectual development of children. They suggest ways that parents can encourage play situations at the various developmental stages from birth to thirteen.

Tyler, Mabs. THE BIG BOOK OF SOFT TOYS. New York: McGraw-Hill Book Co., 1973. 256 p. Illus., photos. (color).

> Guide to the construction of soft toys in order of difficulty including puppets, masks, knitted dolls, highly decorated toys, and the more traditional stuffed toys. Explanations are clear, and diagrams accompany each set of instructions.

Watts, Harriet. HOW TO START YOUR OWN PRESCHOOL PLAYGROUP.

# Play

New York: Universe Books, 1973. 153 p. Illus. Paperbound.

    Helpful advice for nonworking mothers who wish to expose their preschool children to a group experience.

Winnicott, D.W. PLAYING AND REALITY. New York: Basic Books, Publishers, 1971. 169 p. Biblio., index.

    This volume reflects the author's interest in and concern with play. He shows that play is important to an individual's emotional development.

## PERIODICALS

TOY REVIEW. Lincoln Center, Mass.: Toy Review Reader Service, 1972-- . Quarterly.

    New magazine devoted to the philosophy that there should be a positive and responsible approach to providing toys for children. Parents review individual toys with regard to educational value, fun value, and durability. A "Useful Information Department" tells parents about free items and provides directions for making toys from scrap metal.

## PAMPHLETS AND/OR GOVERNMENT DOCUMENTS

Unless otherwise noted the materials are available free of charge. Prices quoted are subject to change. Payment should accompany order.

BACKYARD PLAY EQUIPMENT. 1975. 4 p. Publication no. 320C. Available from: Consumer Information, Public Documents Distribution Center, Pueblo, Colo. 81009.

    Tips for safe assembly and use.

FUN IN THE MAKING. 1973. 29 p. Publication no. (OCD) 73-31. Available from: Office of Human Development, Publications Distribution Unit, Department of Health, Education and Welfare, Washington, D.C. 20201.

    Toys and games which can be made by children and adults from materials found in the home. Also available in Spanish.

THE PARENT/CHILD TOY-LENDING LIBRARY. 1972. 152 p. Publication no. 1780-0993. 60 cents. Available from: Superintendent of Documents, Government Printing Office, Washington, D.C. 20402

    A detailed guide issued by the Far West Laboratory for Educational

Research and Development, Berkeley, California. Gives instructions for securing funds to set up a toy library and for training the parents of three- to five-year-olds to become actively involved in the educational development of their children. Directions for making additional toys and games to supplement the eight basic ones are also included.

PLAY. 1971. 14 p. Available from: Social & Rehabilitation Service, Publications Distribution Center, Department of Health, Education and Welfare, Washington, D.C. 20201.

Stresses the importance of play in the mental, emotional, and social development of a child. Includes activities for preschoolers.

## ORGANIZATIONS AND/OR SOURCES OF MATERIALS, FREE OR AT LOW COST

Far West Laboratory
1855 Folsom Street
San Francisco, Calif. 94103

Offers advice and literature on setting up a toy lending library.

Play Schools Association
111 East Fifty-ninth Street
New York, N.Y. 10022    Phone (212) 759-2449

Provides training, workshops, and discussions for teachers, group leaders, parents, nurses, students, volunteers, and paraprofessionals on the constructive use of children's play in promoting the healthy development of children. Produces films and pamphlets.

## AUDIOVISUAL MATERIALS

### Slides

FUN IN THE MAKING.

This sound-slide film demonstrates how to make developmental toys from throw-a-way household items.

Available from: Association for Childhood Education International, 3615 Wisconsin Avenue, N.W., Washington, D.C. 20016.

# SAFETY

## BOOKS

### Current Sources

Abramson, Seth F., M.D., and Schultz, Dodi. HOME AND FAMILY EMERGENCIES: A GUIDE TO PREVENTION AND FIRST AID. Des Moines, Iowa: Meredith Corp., 1973. 321 p. Illus.

> Clear, readable handbook which identifies the danger areas in the home and the neighborhood, and provides specific information for safety proofing these areas. Includes tips for hiking and camping safety, courses of action in emergencies, and a guide for dealing with poisoning cases until help arrives.

American National Red Cross. STANDARD FIRST AID AND PERSONAL SAFETY. Washington, D.C.: 1973. 268 p. Illus., index.

> Provides basic information on personal safety and accident prevention. Describes the appropriate first aid for a variety of emergencies.

Benjamin, Bry, and Benjamin, Annette Francis. IN CASE OF EMERGENCY: WHAT TO DO UNTIL THE DOCTOR ARRIVES. Rev. ed. Garden City, N.Y.: Doubleday & Co., 1970. 224 p. Illus., index.

> Handy home medical guide that covers basic lifesaving procedures and the appropriate first aid for such emergencies as deep cuts, broken bones, head injuries, internal bleeding, burns, accidental poisoning, insect bites, and many others.

Fales, Edward D., Jr. BELTS ON BUTTONS DOWN: WHAT EVERY MOTHER SHOULD KNOW ABOUT CAR SAFETY. New York: Delacorte Press, 1972. 164 p. Illus., index.

> A handy guide, based on much research, which deals with car

# Safety

maintenance, safety devices, rules for the kids, instructions for emergencies, and activities to amuse youthful automobile passengers. A game and activity appendix is included.

Fontana, Vincent [James], M.D. A PARENTS' GUIDE TO CHILD SAFETY. New York: Thomas Y. Crowell Co., 1973. 260 p. Appendix, biblio., illus., index.

A noted authority in the field of child protection examines a gamut of accidents ranging from contact with poison plants to gunshot wounds. He discusses the causes of and treatment for such accidents, but really advocates prevention. Includes illustrative line drawings, as well as a list of poison control centers with phone numbers.

Kalt, Bruson R., and Bass, Ralph. THE MOTHER'S GUIDE TO CHILD SAFETY. New York: Grosset & Dunlap, 1971. 118 p. Illus., index.

Slim but informative guide to eliminating safety hazards from the environment of young children. Lists poison control centers across the country with telephone numbers.

Swartz, Edward M. TOYS THAT DON'T CARE. Boston: Gambit, 1971. 289 p. Biblio., illus., index.

A nationally known attorney indicts the American toy industry. He questions both the safety standards of its products and the integrity of its sales techniques. He advises parents on selecting new toys, provides the means for assessing the safety of toys already in the home, and offers suggestions for correcting the abuses in the manufacture and marketing of toys.

## PAMPHLETS AND/OR GOVERNMENT DOCUMENTS

Unless otherwise noted the materials are available free of charge. Prices quoted are subject to change. Payment should accompany order.

### Bibliographies and Directories

CONSUMER INFORMATION. Available from: Consumer Information, Public Documents Distribution Center, Pueblo, Colo. 81009.

A quarterly index which lists selected free and inexpensive federal publications of particular interest to consumers. Includes section on child care. Spanish language version is also available. Ask to be placed on their mailing list.

# Safety

NATIONAL CLEARINGHOUSE FOR POISON CONTROL CENTERS BULLETIN. May/June 1975. 20 p. Available from: Food and Drug Administration, Public Health Service, Rockville, Md. 20852.

>Directory of poison control centers.

## Current Sources

BANNED PRODUCTS LIST, 1973. Publication no. 037B. Available from: Consumer Information, Public Documents Distribution Center, Pueblo, Colo. 81009.

>List of toys banned by the federal government.

THE CARE AND SAFETY OF CHILDREN. Available from: Council on Family Health, Department C, Information Department, 633 Third Avenue, New York, N.Y. 10017.

>Basics of home safety and child care including tips on poison prevention.

CHILDHOOD LEAD POISONING: AN ERADICABLE DISEASE. Reprint. 1970. 7 p. Publication no. OM-2118. Available from: Health Services Administration, 5600 Fishers Lane, Rockville, Md. 20852.

>General information about methods of preventing lead poisoning.

CHILD SAFETY. 1974. 16 p. Publication no. 029C. Available from: Consumer Information, Public Documents Distribution Center, Pueblo, Colo. 81009.

>The purchase, safe use, and care of cribs, tricycles, and playground equipment.

CRIB SAFETY. 1973. 5 p. Publication no. 039B. Available from: Consumer Information, Public Documents Distribution Center, Pueblo, Colo. 81009.

>Checklists for purchasing a new crib and correcting unsafe features in older ones.

DENNIS THE MENACE TAKES A POKE AT POISON. 1973. 20 p. Available from: National Planning Council for National Poison Prevention Week, P.O. Box 1453, Washington, D.C. 20013.

>Comic book which illustrates safety rules for protecting the family against poisoning.

DOES YOUR CHILD PLAY WITH MATCHES? 1974. Brochure. Available from: International Association of Fire Chiefs, Suite 1112, 1725 K Street, N.W., Washington, D.C. 20006.

# Safety

Instructions for teaching children about the hazards of matches.

FIRST AID IN THE HOME. 1974. Wall chart. Available from: Council on Family Health, Information Department, 633 Third Avenue, New York, N.Y. 10017.

>Wall chart displaying first aid measures for poisoning, cuts, and other emergencies.

FOR KIDS' SAKES! THINK TOY SAFETY. 1975. Leaflet. Available from: U.S. Consumer Product Safety Commission, Washington, D.C. 20207.

>Highlights toy hazards.

MAKING THE HOME SAFER FOR CHILDREN. 1973. 12 p. Publication no. 73-7018. Available from: Food and Drug Administration, Consumer Affairs Staff, 5600 Fishers Lane, Rockville, Md. 20852.

>How to protect children from poisoning and other hazards.

NO MORE LEAD FOR LEROY. 1972. 16 p. Available from: Children's Hospital of Philadelphia, 1470 Bainbridge Street, Philadelphia, Pa. 19146.

>Booklet, in story form, that can be colored by children. It describes lead paint poisoning in terms of its occurrence and prevention.

PARENTS, BABY-SITTERS AND FIRE. 1972. Leaflet. Available from: International Association of Fire Chiefs, Suite 1112, 1725 K Street, N.W., Washington, D.C. 20006.

>Promotes a cooperative effort on the part of parents and baby-sitters to guard against fire in the home.

PREVENTING LEAD POISONING IN CHILDREN. By Jane S. Lin-Fu, M.D. Reprint of January/February 1973 issue of CHILDREN TODAY. 5 p. Available from: Bureau of Community Health Services, Technical Information Branch, Rockville, Md. 20852.

>Discusses both the sources of lead exposure and the relevant federal legislation. Offers suggestions for preventing lead poisoning.

SAFE TOYS FOR YOUR CHILD--HOW TO SELECT THEM, HOW TO USE THEM SAFELY. 1971. 8 p. Publication no. (OCD) 72-2. Available from: Office of Human Development, Publications Distribution Unit, Department of Health, Education and Welfare, Washington, D.C. 20201.

>Guide to selection and care of toys, and to the relevant safety legislation.

# Safety

SAFE TOY TIPS. 1974. 4 p. Publication no. 039C. Available from: Consumer Information, Public Documents Distribution Center, Pueblo, Colo. 81009.

> Checklist for selection, care, and safe use of toys.

SAVE YOUR CHILD FROM POISONING. 1973. Brochure. Available from: Aetna Life and Casualty, Public Relations and Advertising, 151 Farmington Avenue, Hartford, Conn. 06115.

> Names the poisonous substances, gives instructions for their safe storage, and describes the action to take if a child swallows them.

WATCH OUT FOR LEAD PAINT POISONING. 1971. 4 p. Available from: Maternal & Child Health Service, Rockville, Md. 20852.

> Tips for preventing lead paint poisoning of children. Also available in Spanish.

YOUNG CHILDREN AND ACCIDENTS IN THE HOME. 1974. 28 p. Publication no. (OHD) 74-34. Available from: Office of Human Development, Publications Distribution Unit, Department of Health, Education and Welfare, Washington, D.C. 20201.

> Informative pamphlet stressing accident prevention and action to take when an emergency occurs. Covers falls, cuts, suffocation, poisoning, drowning, fires, burns, and electric shock. Provides a useful tear-out first aid chart. Also available in Spanish.

## ORGANIZATIONS AND/OR SOURCES OF MATERIALS, FREE OR AT LOW COST

Action for Child Transportation Safety
400 Central Park West
New York, N.Y. 10025    Phone (212) 866-8208

> An organization of citizens dedicated to publicizing and reducing the dangers to child passengers in motor vehicles, including private automobiles and school buses.

Action for Prevention of Burn Injuries
  to Children
P.O. Box 347
Burlington, Mass. 01803

> Organization of teachers, parents, lawyers, and doctors devoted to educating the public regarding fire prevention programs and the consequences of fire. Emphasizes consumer demand for safer clothing and other products. Conducts school programs and slide and film presentations. Issues a newsletter.

# Safety

Aetna Life & Casualty
Public Relations and Advertising Department
151 Farmington Avenue
Hartford, Conn. 06115

>Offers the free loan of films on safety.

American Academy of Pediatrics
1801 Hinman Avenue
Evanston, Ill. 60204

>Publications on childhood accidents for the professionals and the general public.

American Insurance Association
Engineering and Safety Service
85 John Street
New York, N.Y. 10038

>Leaflets, pamphlets, film list on accident prevention.

American National Red Cross
Seventeenth & D Streets, N.W.
Washington, D.C. 20006

>Contact the local Red Cross chapters as well for pamphlets, films, and textbooks on safety.

Connecticut General Life Insurance Co.
Advertising & Public Relations--319
Hartford, Conn. 06115

>Pamphlets on accident prevention.

Consumer Product Safety Commission
Toll-free Hotline: Nationwide (800) 638-2666
Maryland residents only, (800) 492-2937

>The hotlines disseminate information on safe toys and cribs, flamable liquids, bicycle safety, and other areas of consumer product information. The caller will also be told about the safety literature that the commission publishes. The same information can be gained by writing the commission at Washington, D.C. 20207.

The Institute for Safer Living
American Mutual Liability Insurance Co.
Wakefield, Mass. 01880

>Pamphlets on safety.

# Safety

Liberty Mutual Insurance Co.
Public Relations Department
175 Berkeley Street
Boston, Mass  02117

>Pamphlets on accident prevention.

Metropolitan Life Insurance Co.
Health and Welfare Division
One Madison Avenue
New York, N.Y.  10010
   or
P.O. Box 7750
San Francisco, Calif.  94120

>Distributes educational materials on child health and safety including "A Medical Emergency Guide-Panic/or Plan?," "Your Child's Safety," and "Sitting Safely" (a guide for babysitters). Free catalog of their materials, HEALTH AND SAFETY EDUCATIONAL MATERIALS, is available on request.

National Association of Retail Druggists
One East Wacker Drive
Chicago, Ill.  60601

>Sponsors a poison prevention campaign. Distributes free pamphlets on first aid for household poisons. Offers information on the poisonous parts of common house and garden plants that children may ingest.

National Child Safety Council
4065 Page Avenue, P.O. Box 280
Jackson, Mich.  49203    Phone (517) 764-6070

>A national organization interested in furthering the safety education of children. Furnishes child safety manuals, posters, brochures, and films for children. Also assists the parents or guardians of children involved in accidents.

National Clearinghouse for Poison
   Control Centers
Poison Control Program
Bureau of Drugs
Food and Drug Administration
Department of Health, Education and Welfare
5401 Westbard Avenue
Bethesda, Md  20016

>Central source of information on poisons and potential poisons for local poison control centers. Periodically issues a "Direc-

## Safety

tory of Poison Control Centers" as part of its bulletin.

National Safety Council
425 North Michigan Avenue
Chicago, Ill. 60611

> National organization whose purpose is to reduce the number and severity of all kinds of accidents through preventive measures. Publishes posters, booklets, newsletters, and other safety literature, as well as films.

The Union Central Life Insurance Company
P.O. Box 179
Cincinnati, Ohio 45201

> Issues a booklet on accident prevention.

## AUDIOVISUAL MATERIALS

### Films

CHILD SAFETY IS NO ACCIDENT. 1974. 16mm, 13 min., sound, color.

> Illustrates the prevention and treatment of accidents involving children. Covers auto safety, burn hazards, poison prevention, and so on.
>
> Available from: Modern Talking Picture Service (consult your local phone book).

LEAD POISONING. 1973. 16mm, sound, color.

> Alerts parents to the hazards of older homes and apartments with respect to lead poisoning of children.
>
> Available from: West Glen Films, 565 Fifth Avenue, New York, N.Y. 10017.

LEAD POISONING: THE HIDDEN EPIDEMIC. 1972. 16mm, 10 min., sound, color.

> Illustrates the horrors of lead poisoning in young children through an actual case history. Discusses causes of lead poisoning, shows methods of identifying and treating the illness, and proposes programs for detection and prevention.
>
> Available from: Long Island Film Studios, P.O. Box P, Brightwaters, N.Y. 11718.

# Safety

PROTECTING YOUNG LIVES. n.d. 16mm, 15 min., sound, color.

> Lynda Johnson Robb and Dr. Jay Arena of the American Academy of Pediatrics educate viewers on the prevention of accidental poisonings and burns.
>
> Available from: Walter J. Klein Co., Distribution Director, Charlotte, N.C. 28211.

## Filmstrips and Slides

BABIES AND ACCIDENTS IN THE HOME. n.d.

> Sound/slide film presents an in-depth look at hazards in the home. Depicts preventive action to avert tragedy.
>
> Available from: Association for Childhood Education International, 3615 Wisconsin Avenue, N.W., Washington, D.C. 20016.

SAFE-TOY ENVIRONMENTS. 1975. Filmstrip. 53 frames, cassette, 5 min., color.

> Gives pointers on choosing safe toys and discusses the impact of consumer choice on the toy industry.
>
> Available from: J.C. Penney Co. (See the nearest store manager).

# SEX EDUCATION

(See also Adolescence)

## BOOKS

### Dated but Still Relevant

Arnstein, Helene S., in consultation with the Child Study Association of America. YOUR GROWING CHILD AND SEX: A PARENT'S GUIDE TO THE SEXUAL DEVELOPMENT, EDUCATION, ATTITUDES, AND BEHAVIOR OF THE CHILD--FROM INFANCY THROUGH ADOLESCENCE. New York: Bobbs-Merrill Co., 1967. 188 p.

> Within a Freudian framework, the author explores the sexual growth of boys and girls. Offers suggestions for helping children develop inner controls. Excellent aid--especially valuable for dealing with teenagers.

Demarest, Robert, and Sciarra, John J., M.D. CONCEPTION, BIRTH AND CONTRACEPTION: A VISUAL PRESENTATION. Introduction by Mary Calderone. New York: McGraw-Hill Book Co., 1969. 129 p.

> Valuable, scientific, and pictorial aid to answering the questions of young adolescents.

### Current Sources

Anderson, Wayne J. HOW TO EXPLAIN SEX TO CHILDREN. Minneapolis, Minn.: T.S. Denison & Co., 1971. 176 p. Illus., color.

> Ways to handle sex education at various age levels.

Bird, Lewis, and Weilly, Christopher T. LEARNING TO LOVE: A GUIDE TO SEX EDUCATION THROUGH THE CHURCH. Waco, Tex.: Word Books, 1971. 177 p. Biblio.

> The authors present a comprehensive guide to sex education using the church as a focal point.

# Sex Education

Block, William A. WHAT YOUR CHILD REALLY WANTS TO KNOW ABOUT SEX--AND WHY. Englewood Cliffs, N.J.: Prentice-Hall, 1972. 325 p. Illus., index.

> Based upon the simple thesis that no question is too simple or unimportant to answer. Respecting the feelings of both parents and children, Dr. Block offers wise and practical methods for handling a child's questions regarding sex. A much needed book. Certain chapters require a discerning reader.

Botwin, Carol. SEX AND THE TEENAGE GIRL. New York: Lancer Books, 1972. 176 p.

> Common sense information on the emotional and sexual needs of teenage girls and boys. Also discusses the boy-girl relationship.

Child Study Association of America. WHAT TO TELL YOUR CHILD ABOUT SEX. New York: Pocket Books, 1974. 141 p. Illus., index. Paperbound.

> A factual, objective, and plainly written manual for parents. A classic guide in question-and-answer format.

Colton, Helen. ADULTS NEED SEX EDUCATION TOO. Los Angeles, Calif.: Family Forum, 1970. 127 p. (o.p.)

> Gives parents a sound foundation in sex education in preparation for teaching their children.

Conference on Human Sexuality and the Mentally Retarded. HUMAN SEXUALITY AND THE MENTALLY RETARDED. New York: Brunner/Mazel, 1973. 374 p. Biblio., index.

> Report of a conference supported by the National Institute of Child Health and Human Development on the little discussed problem of sex and mental retardation. Psychosocial development, sex education, biological aspects, and research are clearly defined and documented.

Daniels, Ada, and Hoover, Mary [B.]. Rev. ed. WHEN CHILDREN ASK ABOUT SEX. New York: Child Study Press, 1974. 42 p.

> Practical guide written from the perspective that a "child's sexual development is part of his total growth and that his questions about sex should be answered honestly and in terms appropriate to his ages and needs."

de Schweinitz, Karl. GROWING UP, HOW WE BECOME ALIVE. 5th ed. New York: Macmillan, 1974. 54 p. Paperbound.

> For parents to read to small children or for children to read to themselves, this book enhances the young child's sex education.

# Sex Education

Suitable for teachers as well as parents.

Fleischhauer-Hardt, Helga. SHOW ME! A PICTURE BOOK OF SEX FOR CHILDREN AND PARENTS. New York: St. Martin's Press, 1975. 176 p. Illus., photos.

>Intended for parents and children to read together, this book utilizes a new approach to sex education. Explicit photographs and accompanying comments are intended to spark conversation between parent and child. Some parents may find the pictures somewhat disturbing. The photography, captions, and designs are by Will McBride.

Gordon, Sol, and Gordon, Judith. DID THE SUN SHINE BEFORE YOU WERE BORN? New York: Third Press, 1974. 41 p. Illus.

>A book for parents to read with their children that explains how families begin and grow.

_____. FACTS ABOUT VD FOR TODAY'S YOUTH. New York: John Day Co., 1973. 48 p. Paperbound.

>Concise, well written guide on recognizing, preventing, and curing venereal disease.

_____. LET'S MAKE SEX A HOUSEHOLD WORD, A GUIDE FOR PARENTS AND CHILDREN. New York: John Day Co., 1975. 256 p. Appendix, biblio., glossary.

>A clinical psychologist explores the area of childhood sexuality including parental worries, double standards, and the emotional and moral questions asked by parents and children alike. He stresses that parents are responsible for adequately informing children about their sexuality.

Grams, Armin. SEX EDUCATION: A GUIDE FOR TEACHERS AND PARENTS. 2d ed. Danville, Ill.: Interstate Printers & Publishers, 1970. 128 p.

>Practical and factual discussion of the role that teachers and parents should play in the sex education of the child.

Grant, Wilson W., M.D. FROM PARENT TO CHILD ABOUT SEX: INCLUDING QUESTIONS FOR DISCUSSION AND THOUGHT. Grand Rapids, Mich.: Zondervan Corp., 1973. 183 p. Index.

>"Designed for Christian parents," Dr. Grant takes a "sane view of the need for sex education in the home, church and school." His discussions of masturbation, homosexuality, contraception, and nudity are confusing. However, the subjects of pornography, abortion, and bad language are handled rather well.

# Sex Education

Grover, John W., M.D., and Dick, Grace. VD: THE ABC'S. Englewood Cliffs, N.J.: Prentice-Hall, 1971. 148 p.

> All the facts about the symptoms and treatment of venereal disease plus a consideration of the problem today. Well written.

Gruenberg, Sidonie [M.]. THE WONDERFUL STORY OF HOW YOU WERE BORN. Rev. ed. Garden City, N.Y.: Doubleday & Co., 1970. 48 p.

> The facts about conception, birth, and growth are explained by an expert. Written for preschoolers and older children. Includes a valuable guide for parents.

Jensen, Gordon D., M.D. YOUTH AND SEX: PLEASURE AND RESPONSIBILITY. Chicago, Ill.: Nelson-Hall Co., 1973. 156 p. Illus., index.

> Frank treatment for teenagers, of masturbation, VD, homosexuality, virginity, and the decision to have intercourse. Gives adults an insight into the thoughts of young people.

Learning Technology Incorporated. HOW TO TALK WITH CHILDREN ABOUT SEX. New York: John Wiley & Sons, 1973. 122 p. Paperbound.

> An open-dialogue approach to explaining basic sexual facts and myths in terms that children understand.

Lehman, Edna. TALKING TO CHILDREN ABOUT SEX. New York: Harper & Row Publishers, 1970. 235 p. Biblio.

> A step-by-step approach for talking to children about sex. Provides information geared to each age level from infancy to adolescence.

Lentz, Gloria. RAPING OUR CHILDREN: THE SEX EDUCATION SCANDAL. New Rochelle, N.Y.: Arlington House, 1972. 224 p.

> Diatribe against sex education programs in schools. Raises some good points regarding unnecessary invasion of privacy, incompetent teachers, and inefficient school boards. For the most part, however, a highly biased account by an ex-reporter.

Mayle, Peter. WHERE DID I COME FROM. Illustrated by Arthur Robins. Secaucus, N.J.: Lyle Stuart, 1973. 44 p.

> Humorous book about the facts of life with a little extra emphasis upon lovemaking. For parents to read with children.

Neumann, Hans H., M.D., and Simmons, Sylvia. THE STRAIGHT STORY ON VD: A DOCTOR ANSWERS 201 OF THE MOST COMMON QUESTIONS ABOUT VENEREAL DISEASES. New York: Warner Paperback Library, 1973.

## Sex Education

261 p. Index. Paperbound.

> Clear and honest presentation of the basic facts concerning VD. An appendix lists telephone numbers for treatment information on the state level, and provides the addresses of local clinics.

Pomeroy, Wardell B., M.D. YOUR CHILD AND SEX: A GUIDE FOR PARENTS. New York: Delacorte Press, 1974. 256 p. Biblio., index.

> Answers such questions as what to say when your son brings home a pornographic book, and should you advocate the use of birth control pills to a teenage girl. Dr. Pomeroy also delves into such areas as drugs, puberty, and infants.

Preston, Harry, and Margolin, Jeannette, M.D. HOW TO TEACH YOUR CHILDREN ABOUT SEX. Chatsworth, Calif.: Books for Better Living, 1974. 176 p. Paperbound.

> Helps parents give the facts in a clear, honest, and nonjudgmental fashion.

Selzer, Joae Graham, M.D. WHEN CHILDREN ASK ABOUT SEX. Boston: Beacon Press, 1974. 150 p. Biblio., illus., index.

> A child psychiatrist offers a clear and candid guide to a wide range of questions that children from preschool to adolescence ask about sex. The suggested answers are drawn from Dr. Selzer's extensive research.

Welsh, Mary M. PARENT, CHILD AND SEX. Dayton, Ohio: Pflaum/Standard, 1970. 120 p. Biblio., illus.

> Conservative but honest approach to help parents decide what to teach children and when.

## PERIODICALS

SIECUS REPORT. New York: Siecus Publications Office, 1965-- . Bi-monthly.

> Articles, news items, reviews of print and nonprint materials in areas of human sexuality and sex education.

## PAMPHLETS AND/OR GOVERNMENT DOCUMENTS

Unless otherwise noted the materials are available free of charge. Prices quoted are subject to change. Payment should accompany order.

# Sex Education

CONCERNS OF PARENTS ABOUT SEX EDUCATION. By Thomas E. Brown. 1971. 33 p. 50 cents. Available from: Sex Information and Education Council of the United States, 122 East Forty-second Street, Suite 922, New York, N.Y. 10017.

> This SIECUS study guide focuses on the anxiety that parents experience with regard to the sex education of their children.

FACTS AREN'T ENOUGH. 1962. 72 p. 30 cents. Available from: American Medical Association, 535 North Dearborn Street, Chicago, Ill. 60610.

> A very detailed guide to aid adults in helping children form sound ideas regarding reproduction and family living. Covers preschool through adolescent years.

HOMOSEXUALITY IN OUR SOCIETY. 1972. 28 p. 35 cents. Publication no. 484. Available from: Public Affairs Committee, 381 Park Avenue S., New York, N.Y. 10016.

> Considers possible causes of homosexuality and offers some thought for parents about their children and sexuality.

LOVE, SEX AND BIRTH CONTROL FOR MENTALLY RETARDED: A GUIDE FOR PARENTS. By Winifred Kempton et al. 1971. 35 p. Available from: Planned Parenthood Association of Southeastern Pennsylvania, 1402 Spruce Street, Philadelphia, Pa. 19102.

> Reassuring guide for parents who are concerned with giving a constructive sex education to their retarded children.

WHAT EVERYONE SHOULD KNOW ABOUT SYPHILIS AND GONORRHEA. 1974. 15 p. 25 cents. Available from: Channing L. Bete Co., 45 Federal Street, Greenfield, Mass. 01301.

> Explains symptoms, consequences, and spread of the named diseases. Emphasizes the importance of seeking immediate medical help.

## ORGANIZATIONS AND/OR SOURCES OF MATERIALS, FREE OR AT LOW COST

American Social Health Association
260 Sheridan Avenue
Palo Alto, Calif. 94306

> Primarily a resource agency that works with and through local health, social, welfare, and law enforcement agencies. Seeks to combat venereal disease, commercialized prostitution, and drug addiction through research, information dissemination, and education. Offers literature on venereal disease.

# Sex Education

National Center for Disease Control
1600 Clifton Road, N.E.
Atlanta, Ga. 30333

    Pamphlets and display material on venereal disease.

SIECUS (Sex Information and Education
   Council of the United States)
122 East 42d Street, Suite 922
New York, N.Y. 10017    Phone (212) 661-7010

    Acts as a clearinghouse for information on human sexuality for educators, physicians, and others interested in helping people to understand sex and use it meaningfully. Publishes reprints of major articles from professional and lay journals.

## AUDIOVISUAL MATERIALS

### Films

BIRDS, BEES AND STORKS. 8 min., sound, color.

    A cartoon film for parents who want to give sex education but feel inhibited. Humorous.

    Available from: Contemporary Films, McGraw-Hill, 1221 Avenue of Americas, New York, N.Y. 10020.

HOW TO TALK WITH YOUR TEENAGER ABOUT VD. 1974. 16mm, 20 min., sound, color.

    Designed especially for parent groups. Teenagers discuss the problems they have in communicating with parents. A health officer comments on venereal disease.

    Available from: Travelers Film Library, West Glen Films, 565 Fifth Avenue, New York, N.Y. 10017.

OLD ENOUGH TO KNOW. 1972. 16mm, 22 min., sound, color.

    Designed to help parents become more comfortable with childhood sexuality. Covers such topics as body exploration, masturbation, reproduction, menstruation, and the sexual vocabulary.

PARENTS AND SEX INSTRUCTION. 1966. 16mm, 15 min., sound, black and white.

    Helps parents answer the sex questions of children ages eight to adolescence.

# Sex Education

Available from: Know the Truth, St. Anthony Retreat Center, Marathon, Wis. 54448.

SEX MIS-EDUCATION. 11 min., sound.

Young peoples' candid observations on the follies of sex education by both parents and schools. They ask for more reliable information.

Available from: Dimension Films, 733 North La Brea Avenue, Los Angeles, Calif. 90038.

## Filmstrips

THE MIRACLE OF NATURE. 1966. Filmstrip, silent, color.

Gentle, sensitive presentation of the menstrual cycle. Should appeal to teachers, parents, and students.

Available from: Glenn Educational Films, P.O. Box 371, Monsey, N.Y. 10952.

## Records, Tapes, Cassettes

EXPLAINING SEX TO YOUR LITTLE BOY AND EXPLAINING SEX TO YOUR LITTLE GIRL. By W.W. Bauer and Florence M. Bauer. Records.

One side talks to parents. The other side is a conversation between the Bauers depicting how easy it can be for parents to discuss reproduction with their children.

Available from: Family Recordings Division, Western Springs, Ill.

HOW TO TEACH CHILDREN THE WONDER OF SEX. By J.D. Willke, M.D. and Barbara Willke. Records.

Gives advice on the how, when, where, and why of sex education.

Available from: Hiltz Publishing Co., 6304 Hamilton Avenue, Cincinnati, Oh. 45224. Phone (513) 681-7559.

WHAT SHALL I TELL MY CHILD ABOUT SEX? Tape. 15 min.

Available from: University of Minnesota, Audio-Visual Extension Service, 2037 University Avenue, S.E., Minneapolis, Minn. 55455.

# SPORTS AND RECREATION

## BOOKS

### Dated but Still Relevant

Newman, Virginia. TEACHING AN INFANT TO SWIM. New York: Harcourt Brace Jovanovich, 1967. 116 p. Photos.

> Excellent suggestions by a private swimming instructor with many years experience.

### Reference

THE GUIDE TO SUMMER CAMPS AND SUMMER SCHOOLS, 1973-1974. Boston: Porter Sargent, 1973. 480 p. Illus., index.

> Comprehensive reference to facilities, offerings, and costs of hundreds of private camps and specialized summer programs. Includes programs for the physically handicapped and the maladjusted.

NATIONAL DIRECTORY OF ACCREDITED CAMPS FOR BOYS AND GIRLS. Martinsville, Ind.: American Camping Association, 1973. 314 p.

> State-by-state listing of camps approved by the American Camping Association. Includes address, names of director and operators, capacity, sessions, fees, facilities, and programs.

### Current Sources

Cowle, Lucile. TEACHING YOUR TOT TO SWIM. New York: Vantage Press, 1970. 80 p. Illus.

> Illustrated parents' guide with ten successive steps.

# Sports and Recreation

Craig, Marjorie. MISS CRAIG'S GROWING-UP EXERCISES: TO HELP CHILDREN GROW UP TO BE HEALTHY ADULTS. New York: Random House, 1973. 96 p. Photos.

> Clearly defined exercises to promote good health among children ages five and up. Includes exercises for rehabilitating children with special problems and warns against harmful exercises.

Levy, Janine, M.D. THE BABY EXERCISE BOOK: FOR THE FIRST FIFTEEN MONTHS. New and exp. ed. Translated from the French by Eira Gleasure. New York: Pantheon Books, 1974. 113 p. Photos. Paperbound.

> Easy-to-follow instructions for exercises that utilize a baby's natural movements.

Prudden, Bonnie. YOUR BABY CAN SWIM. New York: Reader's Digest Press, 1974. 245 p. Illus., index.

> A practical step-by-step guide to time-tested teaching procedures complemented by numerous action photographs. Prudden also stresses the importance of the emotional development of the child.

Prudden, Suzy, and Sussman, Jeffrey. SUZY PRUDDEN'S CREATIVE FITNESS FOR BABY AND CHILD. New York: William Morrow & Co., 1972. 160 p. Photos., index.

> Filled with full-page photographs for easy how-to-do-it instruction. The exercise programs concentrate on emotional and physical fitness for the child from three months to four years of age.

Timmermans, Claire. HOW TO TEACH YOUR BABY TO SWIM. New York: Stein & Day Publishers, 1975. 160 p. Illus.

> Extensive program whose results seem quite impressive. Techniques and skills for parents are carefully explained and illustrated.

## PAMPHLETS AND/OR GOVERNMENT DOCUMENTS

Unless otherwise noted the materials are available free of charge. Prices quoted are subject to change. Payment should accompany order.

A CHILD'S GARDEN: A GUIDE FOR PARENTS AND TEACHERS. 48 p. Available from: Chevron Chemical Company, Public Relations, P.O. Box 3744, San Francisco, Calif. 94119.

> Many gardening ideas including experiments. Well illustrated.

# Sports and Recreation

## AUDIOVISUAL MATERIALS

### Films

TEACHING JOHNNY TO SWIM. 1972. 16mm, 14 1/2 min., sound, color.
   Provides the steps in teaching a child to swim.
   Available from: American National Red Cross (contact a local chapter).

# TELEVISION

(See also Child Development—Sex Roles; Learning and Creativity)

## BOOKS

### Current Sources

Kaye, Evelyn. THE FAMILY GUIDE TO CHILDREN'S TELEVISION: WHAT TO WATCH, WHAT TO MISS, WHAT TO CHANGE AND HOW TO DO IT. New York: Pantheon Books, 1974. 197 p. Illus.

> This comprehensive manual, written by the executive director of Action for Children's Television, examines the dangers and the delights of children's television. Discusses violence on television, children's cartoons, program evaluation, and the parent's role in guiding a child's TV watching. Includes a list of useful addresses for parents, teachers, and child developmental professionals. Perceptive handbook that parents can use to protect their children from the abuses of television.

Lesser, Gerald S. CHILDREN AND TELEVISION: LESSONS FROM SESAME STREET. Foreword by Joan Ganz Cooney. New York: Random House, 1974. 290 p. Biblio., illus.

> The educational director of Sesame Street has produced a readable and well-researched account of this popular children's television program. Includes a section on criticism and program results. An extensive bibliography is provided.

Liebert, Robert M., et al. THE EARLY WINDOW: EFFECTS OF TELEVISION ON CHILDREN AND YOUTH. Elmsford, N.Y.: Pergamon Press, 1973. 193 p. Appendix, illus., index.

> Evaluating the results of numerous studies, the authors clearly state that violence on television does affect children's behavior and their perceptions of reality. They offer concrete suggestions for change.

# Television

Melody, William H. CHILDREN'S TELEVISION: THE ECONOMICS OF EXPLOITATION. New Haven, Conn.: Yale University Press, 1973. 164 p. Paperbound.

> This study, commissioned by Action for Children's Television, focuses on commercial television programming that exploits the economic potential of child consumers. Professor Melody suggests alternate ways of financing children's television to avoid such exploitation.

Morris, Norman S. TELEVISION'S CHILD. Boston: Little, Brown and Co., 1971. 238 p.

> Advice on supervising children's TV viewing. Discusses both the advantages and disadvantages of the medium in this context. Highly readable.

## PAMPHLETS AND/OR GOVERNMENT DOCUMENTS

Unless otherwise noted the materials are available free of charge. Prices quoted are subject to change. Payment should accompany order.

CHILDREN ARE CENTERS FOR UNDERSTANDING MEDIA. $3.95. Available from: Association for Childhood Education International, 3651 Wisconsin Avenue, N.W., Washington, D.C.

> Booklet relating to children ages two to twelve and to the development of "a more selective and intelligent audience of young viewers" for various media. Ideas for involving children as photographers, filmmakers, and videotapers so that they become doers rather than spectators.

TELEVISION AND GROWING UP: THE IMPACT OF TELEVISED VIOLENCE. By the Surgeon General's Scientific Advisory Committee on Television and Social Behavior. 1972. 169 p. $2.25. Order no. HE 20.2403, T23. Available from: Superintendent of Documents, Government Printing Office, Washington, D.C. 20402.

> Summary of the effects of television violence on children. Not easy reading.

## ORGANIZATIONS AND/OR SOURCES OF MATERIALS, FREE OR AT LOW COST

Action for Children's Television
46 Austin
Newtonville, Mass. 02160     Phone (617) 527-7870.

> Begun in 1968, this national organization of parents and pro-

fessionals is dedicated to achieving child-oriented quality TV without commercialism. Offers free copies of two different resource lists for materials relating to children and television. They also publish a newsletter.

Several TV shows now provide printed materials to encourage parents and others to participate in children's viewing:

"Sesame Street" and "Electric Company" publish a newsletter and magazines. Available from: Children's Television Workshop, One Lincoln Plaza, New York, N.Y. 10023.

"Mister Rogers Neighborhood" publishes a newsletter and parents letter. Available from: Around the Neighborhood, Box 1623, Columbus, Ohio 43216.

"Captain Kangaroo" publishes a guide to activities related to the week's programs. Available from: Clinch-Powell Educational Cooperative, Harrogate, Tenn. 37552.

# WORKING MOTHER

(See also Parenthood)

## BOOKS

### Dated but Still Relevant

Albrecht, Margaret. THE COMPLETE GUIDE FOR THE WORKING MOTHER. Garden City, N.Y.: Doubleday & Co., 1967. 348 p.

> Reference book full of information for the working mother in her many roles--woman, wife, housekeeper, and parent.

Cotton, Dorothy W. THE CASE FOR THE WORKING MOTHER. New York: Stein & Day Publishers, 1965. 185 p.

> Practical suggestions to help the mother who works, including developing family routines and coping with troublesome feelings.

### Current Sources

Callahan, Sidney Cornelia. THE WORKING MOTHER. New York: Macmillan, 1971. 264 p. Biblio.

> Interviews with sixteen working mothers point out their common problems.

Levison, Teddi, and Silverstein, Mickie. HAVE YOU HAD IT IN THE KITCHEN? New York: Grosset & Dunlap, 1971. 149 p.

> Two mothers who returned to work when their children were still young offer some very practical suggestions.

McBride, Angela Barron. THE GROWTH AND DEVELOPMENT OF MOTHERS. New York: Harper & Row Publishers, 1973. 158 p.

> Describes the evolution in the author's thought and feelings from the time she anticipated motherhood until she went to work on a

# Working Mother

part-time basis and began making demands on her family.

Schwartz, Felice. HOW TO GO TO WORK WHEN YOUR HUSBAND IS AGAINST IT, YOUR CHILDREN AREN'T OLD ENOUGH AND THERE'S NOTHING YOU CAN DO ANYHOW. New York: Simon & Schuster, 1972. 348 p.

> Valuable guide for the wife and mother considering returning to work. Includes case studies, material on educational opportunities, and a description of fifty-three occupations and the training required for each.

Skelsey, Alice. THE WORKING MOTHER'S GUIDE TO HER HOME, HER FAMILY, AND HERSELF. New York: Random House, 1970. 246 p.

> Practical and understanding suggestions in areas such as scheduling time, training children to help, planning meals and fostering family relationships.

Smuts, Robert W. WOMEN AND WORK IN AMERICA. New York: Schocken Books, 1971. 176 p. Biblio. Paperbound.

> Analyzes the problems which face the woman who works and does her housekeeping as well.

## PAMPHLETS AND/OR GOVERNMENT DOCUMENTS

Unless otherwise noted the materials are available free of charge. Prices quoted are subject to change. Payment should accompany order.

MOTHERS AT WORK. 1973. 14 p. Available from: Health & Welfare Division, Metropolitan Life Insurance Co., One Madison Avenue, New York, N.Y. 10010 or P.O. Box 7750, San Francisco, Calif. 94120.

> Concise pamphlet offers practical suggestions for the working mother and her family.

A WORKING WOMAN'S GUIDE TO HER JOB RIGHTS. Revised. 1975. 34 p. Available from: Women's Bureau, Employment Standards Administration, U.S. Department of Labor, Washington, D.C. 20210.

> Highlights laws and executive orders that affect women when they look for a job, while they are on the job, and when they retire. Includes information on maternity leaves and tax deductions for child care and household help. Lists sources of assistance and addresses of state labor offices and human rights commissions.

# Working Mother

## ORGANIZATIONS AND/OR SOURCES OF MATERIALS, FREE OR AT LOW COST

Maternal Information Services
46 West Ninty-sixth Street
Suite 1E
New York, N.Y. 10025

>Publishes the newsletter, THE WORKING MOTHER.

## AUDIOVISUAL MATERIALS

Films

CHILDREN OF CHANGE. 1961. 31 min., sound, black and white.

>Depicts problems of working mothers and children left alone during the day.

>Available from: International Film Bureau, 332 South Michigan Avenue, Chicago, Ill. 60604.

## Appendix A
## INDEXES OF GENERAL INTEREST

EDUCATION INDEX. New York: H.W. Wilson, 1929-- . Monthly, except July and August.

> An author/subject index to educational material in the English language: periodicals, proceedings, yearbooks, bulletins, monographs, and publications from the U.S. Office of Education.

PUBLIC AFFAIRS INFORMATION SERVICE BULLETIN. New York: Public Affairs Information Service, 1915-- . Weekly.

> Selective subject list of books, pamphlets, government publications, reports of public and private agencies, and periodical articles relating to economic and social conditions, public administration, and international relations published in English throughout the world.

READER'S GUIDE TO PERIODICAL LITERATURE. New York: H.W. Wilson, 1900-- . Semimonthly, September to June.

> Indexes by author and subject the articles in more than one hundred of the most widely read general magazines.

VERTICAL FILE INDEX. New York: H.W. Wilson, 1932-- . Monthly.

> Subject and title index to selected pamphlets in many fields including infant care, child care, day-care, handicapped children, adoption, etc. Some free, most inexpensive.

## Appendix B
## CHILDREN'S MAGAZINES

Some magazines published for children which may broaden parents' understanding of the child's world.

AMERICAN GIRL. New York: Girl Scouts of the U.S.A., 1917-- . Monthly.

> Official organ of the Girl Scouts but wider in scope including fashion, movie and record reviews.

BOYS' LIFE. New Brunswick, N.J.: Boy Scouts of America, 1911-- . Monthly.

> For the adolescent male (ages nine to sixteen) including articles on hobbies, stamp and coin collecting, jokes, nature, autos, chess, and girls.

CHILD LIFE. Indianapolis: 1921-- . Monthly.

> For the elementary school child. Includes poems, jokes, riddles, letters to the editor, and activities.

CHILDREN'S DIGEST. New York: Parents' Magazine Enterprises, 1950-- . Monthly.

> Includes games, riddles, jokes, and play activities. Fiction articles comprise such authors as Kipling, Stevenson, and Milne. Picture book and book reviews for ages seven to twelve are also included.

CHILDREN'S PLAYMATE. Indianapolis: Children's Playmate Magazine, 1929-- . Ten issues a year.

> For ages three to eight--activities, articles, poems, and stories.

CRICKET. LaSalle, Ill.: Open Court Publishing Co., 1973-- . Monthly, except June/July.

# Children's Magazines

Puzzles, games, stories, folk tales, history, and science for the elementary school child.

EBONY, JR! Chicago: Johnson Publishing Co., 1973-- . Monthly, except June/July and August/September.

    For black children of elementary age--stories, games, puzzles, history, and biography. Much like JACK AND JILL, see below.

ELECTRIC COMPANY MAGAZINE. New York: Children's Television Workshop, 1974-- . Monthly.

    Companion to SESAME STREET MAGAZINE, intended for children aged five to eight. Contains puzzles, jokes, games, comics, and stories featuring the television personalities. Intended to teach reading, social studies, and math.

GOLDEN MAGAZINE. Indianapolis: Review Publishing Co., 1964-- . Monthly.

    Fiction, adventure, history, science, geography, games, and jokes for children nine to thirteen. Includes a "How-To" section.

HIGHLIGHTS FOR CHILDREN. Columbus, Ohio: 1946-- . Eleven issues a year.

    To help the preschool and elementary child to think logically and to be creative. Edited by specialists.

HUMPTY DUMPTY'S MAGAZINE: MAGAZINE FOR LITTLE CHILDREN. New York: Parents' Magazine Enterprises, 1952-- . Monthly except June and August.

    To entertain and educate three- to seven-year-olds, this magazine features stories and articles intended to develop reading and vocabulary. Also contains good book reviews.

JACK AND JILL MAGAZINE. Indianapolis: Jack and Jill Publishing Co., 1938-- . Monthly.

    A variety of articles and stories directed towards children five to twelve. Also includes contests, games, and puzzles. "Let's Discover America" describes interesting places to visit.

KIDS. New York: Valentine Smith Co., 1970-- . Ten issues a year.

    Contains original poetry, plays, fiction, and articles on things to make.

# Children's Magazines

PACK-O-FUN. Park Ridge, Ill.: Clapper Publishing Co., 1951-- . Ten issues a year, except July/August.

>   Good source for how-to-do-it stunts, games, and crafts for children of elementary school age.

SESAME STREET. New York: Children's Television Workshop, 1970-- . Ten issues a year.

>   Spin-off of the television program with the same educational goals. English and Spanish text.

STONE SOUP. Santa Cruz, Calif.: 1973-- . Three times a year.

>   Stories, art work, and book reviews written by children.

WEE WISDOM. Unity Village, Mo.: Unity School of Christianity, 1893-- . Monthly.

>   Aimed at third grade reading level for the purpose of building character, this magazine contains stories, poems, and things to do.

WORLD TRAVELER. Washington, D.C.: Alexander Graham Bell Association for the Deaf, 1969-- . Ten issues a year, September to June.

>   For the language-handicapped teenager who cannot read above third grade level. Each issue is devoted to single subjects.

YOUNG WORLD. Indianapolis: Curtis Publishing Co., 1964-- . Ten times a year.

>   For ages eight to twelve. Contains stories, poems, games, jokes, and riddles.

# Appendix C
# DIRECTORY OF POISON CONTROL CENTERS

Derived from the NATIONAL CLEARINGHOUSE FOR POISON CONTROL CENTERS, Food and Drug Administration, Department of Health, Education and Welfare, Bethesda, Md. 20014, May-June 1975.

## ALABAMA

STATE COORDINATOR
(205) 832-3194

State Department of
  Public Health
Montgomery  36104

Anniston
(205) 237-5421
Ext. 307

Poison Control Center
Anniston Memorial
  Hosp.
Pharmacy Department
400 E. 10th St.
36201

Auburn
(205) 826-4037
Night 887-6778, 3235

Poison Control Center
Auburn University
School of Pharmacy
36830

Birmingham
(205) 933-4050

Poison Control Center
Children's Hospital
1601 6th Ave., S.
35233

Dothan
(205) 794-3131
Ext. 521

Poison Control Center
Southeast Alabama
Gen. Hosp.  36301

Florence
(205) 764-8321
Ext. 206, 207

Poison Control Center
Eliza Coffee Memorial
  Hosp.
600 W. Alabama St.
35630

Gadsden
(205) 492-1240
Ext. 205

Poison Control Center
Baptist Memorial Hosp.
1007 Goodyear Ave.
35903

Mobile
(205) 473-3325

Poison Control Center
Mobile General Hosp.
2451 Fillingim St.
36617

## ALASKA

STATE COORDINATOR
(907) 586-6311

State Department of
  Health & Welfare
Juneau  99801

Anchorage
279-6661
Ext. 208, 209, 210, 211

Poison Control Center
Alaska Native Medical
  Center
Public Health Service
Box 7-741  95501

# Poison Control Centers

## ALASKA - Continued

**Anchorage**
277-6671

Poison Control Center
Providence Hospital
3200 Providence Dr.
99504

**Fairbanks**
456-6655
Ext. 35

Poison Control Ctr.
Fairbanks Memorial
  Hospital
1650 Cowles  99701

**Juneau**
586-2611

Poison Control Center
Greater Juneau
  Borough Hospital
419 6th St.  99801

**Ketchikan**
225-5171
Ext. 31

Poison Information
  Center
Ketchikan General
  Hospital
3100 Tongass Ave.
99901

**Mt. Edgecumbe**
966-8347

Poison Control Center
Alaska Native Hosp.
Public Health Service
99835

## ARIZONA

**STATE COORDINATOR**
602 884-1587

College of Pharma-
  cology
University of Arizona
Tucson  85721

**Douglas**
602 364-8473

Poison Control Center
Cochise County Hosp.
West of Douglas
85607

**Flagstaff**
602 744-5233
Ext. 255

Poison Control Center
Flagstaff Hospital
1215 N. Beaver St.
86001

**Ganado**
602 755-3411

**Kingman**
602 757-2101
Ext. 247

**Nogales**
602 287-2771
Ext. 94

**Phoenix**
602 252-6611
Ext. 111

602 267-5011

602 252-5911

602 277-6611
Ext. 2481

602 258-7373
Ext. 291

**Prescott**
602 445-2700
Ext. 25, 58

Poison Control Center
Project Hope
Sage Memorial Hosp.
Box 457  86505

Poison Control Center
Mohave General Hosp.
301 W. Beale  86441

Poison Control Center
St. Joseph's Hospital
Target Range Road
P.O. Box 1809
85621

Poison Control Center
Good Samaritan Hosp.
1033 E. McDowell Rd.
85006

Poison Control Center
Maricopa County
  General Hospital
2601 E. Roosevelt
85008

Poison Control Center
Memorial Hospital
1200 S. 5th Avenue
85003

Poison Control Center
St. Joseph's Hospital
350 W. Thomas Rd.
85013

Poison Control Center
St. Luke's Hospital
Medical Center
525 N. 18th St.
85006

Poison Control Center
Yavapai Community
  Hospital
1003 Willow Creek Rd.
86301

# Poison Control Centers

## ARIZONA - Continued

Tucson
602 624-2721
Ext. 220
    Poison Control Center
    Pima County General
    Hospital
    2900 S. 6th Avenue
    85713

602 882-6300
    Poison Information
    Center
    College of Pharmacy
    University of Arizona
    85721

602 622-5833
Ext. 724
    Poison Control Center
    St. Mary's Hospital
    1700 W. St. Mary's
    Road  85703

602 327-5461
Ext. 428
    Poison Control Center
    Tucson Medical Ctr.
    E. Grant Rd. at
    Beverly Blvd.
    85716

Winslow
602 289-4691
    Poison Control Center
    Winslow Mem. Hosp.
    116 E. Hillview St.
    86047

Yuma
602 344-2000
Ext. 221
    Poison Control Center
    Yuma Regional Med.
    Center
    Avenue A & 24th St.
    85364

## ARKANSAS

STATE
COORDINATOR
501 661-2136
    State Department of
    Health
    Little Rock  72201

El Dorado
501 863-2266
Ext. 221
    Poison Control Center
    Warner Brown Hosp.
    460 West Oak St.
    71730

Fort Smith
501 782-3071
Ext. 210

501 441-4381

Harrison
501 365-6141
Ext. 124

Helena
501 338-6411
Ext. 271

Little Rock
501 664-5000
Ext. 415

501 666-5532

Osceola
501 563-2611
Ext. 53

Pine Bluff
501 535-6800
Ext. 225

Poison Control Center
St. Edward's Mercy
Hospital
1411 Rogers Avenue
72901

Poison Control Center
Sparks Regional Med.
Center
1311 S. Eye St.
72901

Poison Control Center
Boone County Hosp.
620 N. Willow St.
72601

Poison Control Center
Helena Hospital
Hospital Dr.  72342

Poison Control Center
Univ. of Arkansas
Medical Center
4301 W. Markham St.
72201

Poison Control Drug
Information Center
Univ. of Arkansas
School of Pharmacy
4301 W. Markham St.
72201

Poison Control Center
Osceola Mem. Hosp.
611 Lee Ave. West
72370

Poison Control Center
Jefferson Hospital
1515 W. 42nd Ave.
71601

# Poison Control Centers

## CALIFORNIA

STATE COORDINATOR
916 322-2300

Department of Health
Sacramento   95814

Fresno
209 233-0911
 Ext. 2431
 Night 233-7547

Poison Control Center
Fresno Comm. Hosp.
Fresno & R Sts.
P.O. Box 1232
93715

Los Angeles
213 664-2121

Poison Control Center
Thos. J. Fleming
 Memorial Center
Children's Hosp. of
 Los Angeles
P.O. Box 54700
4650 Sunset Blvd.
90054

Oakland
415 652-8171

Poison Control Center
Alameda-Contra
 Costa Med. Assn.
6230 Claremont Ave.
94618

415 654-5600
 Ext. 343

Poison Control Center
Children's Hosp. of
 East Bay
51st & Grove Sts.
94609

Orange
714 633-9393
 Ext. 273

Poison Control Center
Orange County Med.
 Center
101 City Drive South
92668

San Diego
714 291-4900

Poison Information
 Center
University Hospital
225 W. Dickinson St.
92103

San Francisco
415 431-2800

Poison Control Center
Central Emergency
 Medical Service
135 Polk St.   94102

San Jose
408 293-0262
 Ext. 318 or
 319

Poison Control Center
Santa Clara Valley
 Medical Center
751 S. Bascom Ave.
95128

## CANAL ZONE

Balboa Heights
2-2600

Poison Information
 Center
Gorgas Hospital
Box 0

## COLORADO

STATE COORDINATOR
303 388-6111

State Department of
 Public Health
Denver   80220

Alamosa
303 589-2511
 Ext. 54

Poison Control Center
Alamosa Community
 Hospital
1st & Creston Sts.
81101

Aurora
303 366-1531

Poison Control Center
L.K. Professional
 Pharmacy
9240 E. Colfax Ave.
80010

Cortez
303 565-3448

Poison Control Center
Southwest Mem. Hosp.
925 S. Broadway
81321

# Poison Control Centers

## COLORADO - Continued

**Denver**
303 893-7771 — Rocky Mtn. Poison Control Center
Denver Gen. Hosp.
W. 8th Ave. & Cherokee St. 80204

303 825-9011 Ext. 2387 — Poison Control Center
St. Anthony's Hosp.
4231 W. 16th Ave.
80204

**Grand Junction**
303 242-1197 Ext. 715 — Poison Control Center
St. Mary's Hospital
7th & Patterson Rd.
81501

**Greely**
303 352-4121 Ext. 648 — Poison Control Center
Weld County General Hospital
16th St. at 17th Ave.
80631

**Longmont**
303 776-1422 Ext. 257 — Poison Control Center
Longmont Community Hospital
1950 W. Mt. View Avenue 80501

**Pueblo**
303 542-8680 Ext. 778 — Poison Control Center
Parkview Episcopal Hospital
400 W. 16th Ave.
81003

## CONNECTICUT

STATE COORDINATOR
203 566-3456 — State Department of Health
Hartford 06115

**Bridgeport**
203 334-3566 — Poison Control Center
Bridgeport Hospital
267 Grant St. 06602

203 334-1081 — Poison Control Center
St. Vincent's Hospital
2820 Main St.
06606

**Danbury**
203 744-2300 — Poison Control Center
Danbury Hospital
95 Locust Avenue
06810

**Hartford**
203 566-3456 — Poison Information Center
State Dept. of Health
State Office Bldg.
06115

**Middletown**
203 347-9471 — Poison Control Center
Middlesex Mem. Hosp.
28 Cresent St.
06457

**New Britain**
203 224-5672 — Poison Control Center
New Britain General Hospital
100 Grand St.
06050

**New Haven**
203 772-3900 — Poison Control Center
The Hospital of St. Raphael
1450 Chapel St.
06511

203 436-1960 — Poison Control Center
Yale-New Haven Hospital
789 Howard Avenue
06504

**Norwalk**
203 838-3611 — Poison Control Center
Norwalk Hospital
24 Stevens St.
06852

# Poison Control Centers

## CONNECTICUT - Continued

Waterbury
203 756-8351

Poison Control Center
St. Mary's Hospital
56 Franklin St.
06702

## DELAWARE

Wilmington
302 655-3389

Poison Information
  Service
501 W. 14th St.
19899

## DISTRICT OF COLUMBIA

Washington
202 835-4080
  or 4081

Poison Control Center
Children's Hospital
13th & W Sts., N.W.
20009

## FLORIDA

STATE
COORDINATOR
904 354-3961

Department of Health
and Rehabilitative
Services
Jacksonville   32201

Apalachicola
904 653-3311

Poison Control Center
George E. Weems
  Memorial Hospital
P.O. Box 610-
  Franklin Sq.   32320

Bartow
813 533-1111
  Ext. 237

Poison Control Center
Polk General Hospital
2010 E. Georgia St.
P.O. Box 81   33830

Bradenton
813 746-5111
  Ext. 466

Poison Control Center
Manatee Mem. Hosp.
206 2nd St.   33505

Daytona Beach
904 255-4411
  Ext. 256

Poison Control Center
Halifax District Hosp.
Clyde Morris Blvd.
32015

Fort Lauderdale
305 525-5411
  Ext. 513

Poison Control Center
Broward General Hosp.
1600 S. Andrews Ave.
33316

Fort Myers
813 334-5286

Poison Control Center
Lee Memorial Hosp.
2776 Cleveland Ave.
33902

Ft. Walton Beach
904 243-7611
  Ext. 223

Poison Control Center
Ft. Walton Beach
  Hospital
207 Hospital Dr., N.E.
32548

Gainesville
904 372-4321

Poison Control Center
Alachua General
  Hospital
912 S.W. 4th Ave.
32602

904 392-3389

Poison Information Ctr.
J. Hillis Miller Health
  Center
University of Florida
32601

Jacksonville
904 389-7751
  Ext. 315

Poison Control Center
St. Vincent's Hospital
Barrs St. & St. Johns
  Avenue   32204

Key West
305 294-5531

Poison Control Center
Florida Keys Mem.
  Hospital
P.O. Box 1359
33040

# Poison Control Centers

**FLORIDA** - Continued

Lakeland
813 686-1111
Ext. 2597

Leesburg
904 787-7222
Ext. 221

Melbourne
305 727-7000
Ext. 704

Miami
305 371-9611
Ext. 378

Miami Beach
305 674-2121
or 2200

Naples
813 649-3131
Ext. 221

Ocala
904 732-1111
Ext. 15

Poison Control Center
Lakeland General
  Hospital
Lakeland Hills Blvd.
88301

Poison Control Center
Leesburg General
  Hospital
600 E. Dixie  32748

Poison Control Center
Brevard Hospital
1350 S. Hickory St.
32901

Poison Control Center
Jackson Mem. Hosp.
1700 N.W. Tenth
  Avenue  33136

Poison Control Center
Mt. Sinai Hosp. of
  Greater Miami
4300 Alton Rd.
33140

Poison Control Center
Naples Community
  Hospital
350 7th St. N.
33940

Poison Control Center
Munroe Mem. Hosp.
1410 S.E. Orange St.
32670

Orlando
305 841-8411
Ext. 656

Panama City
904 769-1511

Pensacola
904 434-4011
Ext. 4811

Plant City
813 752-1188

Pompano
305 941-8300
Ext. 710

Punta Gorda
813 639-2191
Ext. 129

Rockledge
305 636-2211
Ext. 506

St. Petersburg
813 894-1161
Ext. 242

Poison Control Center
Orange Mem. Hosp.
1416 S. Orange Ave.
32806

Poison Control Center
Memorial Hospital of
  Bay County
600 N. MacArthur Ave.
32401

Poison Control Center
Baptist Hospital
1000 W. Moreno St.
32501

Poison Control Center
South Florida Baptist
  Hospital
Drawer H  33566

Poison Control Center
No. Broward Hospital
201 Sample Rd.
33064

Poison Control Center
Medical Center
809 E. Marion Ave.
33950

Poison Control Center
Wuesthoff Mem. Hosp.
110 Longwood Ave.
32955

Poison Control Center
Bayfront Medical
  Center, Inc.
701 6th St., S.
33701

# Poison Control Centers

## FLORIDA - Continued

**Sarasota**
813 955-1111
Ext. 1241
Poison Control Center
Memorial Hospital
1901 Arlington Ave.
33579

**Tallahassee**
904 599-5411
Poison Control Center
Tallahassee Memorial
  Hospital
Magnolia Dr. and
Miccosukee Road
32303

**Tampa**
813 251-6995
Poison Control Center
Tampa General Hosp.
Davis Islands 33606

**Titusville**
305 269-1100
Ext. 474
Poison Control Center
Jess Parrish Mem.
  Hospital
951 N. Washington
  Avenue 32780

**West Palm Beach**
306 655-5511
Ext. 341
Poison Control Center
Good Samaritan Hosp.
1300 N. Dixie Hwy.
33402

**Winter Haven**
813 293-1121
Ext. 222
Poison Control Center
Winter Haven Hosp.,
  Inc.
200 Ave. F, N.E.
33880

## GEORGIA

**STATE COORDINATOR**
404 656-4883
Department of Human
  Resources
Atlanta   30308

**Albany**
912 883-1800
Ext. 158
Poison Information Ctr.
Phoebe Putney Mem.
  Hospital
P.O. Box 115
31701

**Athens**
404 549-9977
Ext. 357
Poison Control Center
Athens General Hosp.
797 Cobb St.   30601

**Atlanta**
404 659-1212
Ext. 4893
Poison Control Center
Grady Mem. Hosp.
80 Butler St., S.E.
30303

**Augusta**
404 724-7171
Ext. 2176
Poison Information Ctr.
University Hospital
1350 Walton Way
30902

**Columbus**
404 324-4711
Ext. 431
Poison Information Ctr.
The Medical Center
19th St. & 18th Ave.
31902

**Macon**
912 742-1122
Ext. 3144
Poison Control Center
Medical Center of
  Central GA.
777 Hemlock St.
31201

**Rome**
404 232-1541
Ext. 223
Poison Control Center
Floyd Hospital
Turner & McCall Blvd.
30161

**Savannah**
912 355-3200
Ext. 455
Poison Control Center
Memorial Med. Cntr.
63rd & Waters Ave.
31405

# Poison Control Centers

## GEORGIA - Continued

Thomasville
912 226-4121
Ext. 169

Valdosta
912 242-3450
Ext. 717

Waycross
912 283-3030
Ext. 240

Poison Control Center
John D. Archbold
 Memorial Hospital
900 Gordon Ave.
31792

Poison Control Center
S. Georgia Med. Ctr.
Pendleton Park
31601

Poison Control Center
Memorial Hospital
410 Darling Avenue
31501

## GUAM

STATE
COORDINATOR
742-4158

Agana
746-9171

Department of Public
 Health & Social
 Services
Agana  96910

Poison Control Center
Guam Memorial Hosp.
96910

## HAWAII

STATE
COORDINATOR
808 531-7776

Honolulu
808 537-1831

Department of Health
Honolulu  96801

Poison Information
 Center
Kauikeolani Chil-
 dren's Hospital
226 N. Kuakini St.
96817

## IDAHO

STATE
COORDINATOR
208 384-2390

Boise
208 376-1211

State Department of
 Health
Boise  83701

Poison Control Center
St. Alphonsus Hosp.
Pharmacy Department
1055 N. Curtis Rd.
83703

## ILLINOIS

STATE
COORDINATOR
217 782-3300

Alton
618 462-8851
Ext. 352

Aurora
312 897-6021
Ext. 725 or
726

Belleville
618 233-7750
Ext. 250

Belvidere
815 547-5441

Berwyn
312 797-3000
or 3159

Department of Public
 Health
Springfield  62761

Poison Control Center
Alton Mem. Hospital
Memorial Dr.  62002

Poison Control Center
Copley Mem. Hosp.
Lincoln & Weston Aves.
60507

Poison Control Center
Memorial Hospital
4501 N. Park Dr.
62223

Poison Control Center
Highland Hospital
1625 S. State St.
61008

Poison Control Center
MacNeal Mem. Hosp.
3249 Oak Park Ave.
60402

# Poison Control Centers

## ILLINOIS - Continued

Bloomington
309 828-5241
  Ext. 312

309 662-3311
  Ext. 352

Poison Control Center
Mennonite Hospital
807 N. Main   61701

Poison Control Center
St. Joseph's Hospital
2200 E. Washington
61701

Cairo
618 734-2400
  Ext. 42

Poison Control Center
Padco Community
  Hospital
2020 Cedar St.
62914

Canton
309 647-5240
  Ext. 230
  or 248

Poison Control Center
Graham Hospital Assn.
210 W. Walnut St.
61520

Carbondale
618 549-0721
  Ext. 341

Poison Control Center
Doctors Mem. Hosp.
404 W. Main St.
62901

Carthage
217 357-3131
  Ext. 84

Poison Control Center
Memorial Hospital
End S. Adams St.
62321

Centralia
618 532-6731
  Ext. 716

Poison Control Center
St. Mary's Hospital
400 N. Pleasant Ave.
62801

Champaign
217 337-2533

Poison Control Center
Burnham City Hospital
407 S. 4th St.
61820

Chanute AFB
217 495-3133
  or 3134

Poison Control Center
USAF Hospital
Chanute Air Force
  Base   61868
(Limited for treatment
of military personnel
and families, except
for indicated civilian
emergencies)

Chester
618 826-4581
  Ext. 244

Poison Control Center
Memorial Hospital
1900 State St.
62233

Chicago
312 942-5969

Chicago Master Ctr.
Rush-Presbyterian-St.
  Luke's Med. Center
1753 W. Congress Pkwy.
60612

312 292-5319

Poison Control Center
St. Mary of Nazareth
  Hospital Center
1120 North Leavitt St.
60622

312 978-2000
  Ext. 264,
  265, 297

Poison Control Center
So. Chicago Commu-
  nity Hospital
2320 E. 93rd St.
60617

Danville
217 443-5221

Poison Control Center
Lake View Memorial
  Hospital
812 N. Logan Ave.
61832

217 442-6300

Poison Control Center
St. Elizabeth's Hosp.
600 Sager Avenue
61832

# Poison Control Centers

## ILLINOIS - Continued

**Decatur**
217 877-8121
Ext. 676

Poison Control Center
Decatur Mem. Hosp.
2300 N. Edward St.
62526

217 429-2966
Ext. 640

Poison Control Ctr.
St. Mary's Hospital
1800 E. Lakeshore Dr.
62525

**Des Plaines**
312 297-1800
Ext. 856

Poison Control Center
Holy Family Hospital
100 N. River Road
60016

**East St. Louis**
618 874-7076
Ext. 216
or 232

Poison Control Center
Christian Welfare
Hospital
1509 Martin Luther
King Drive   62201

618 274-1900
Ext. 204,
268, 283

Poison Control Center
St. Mary's Hospital
129 N. 8th St.
62201

**Effingham**
217 342-2121
Ext. 211
or 212

Poison Control Center
St. Anthony's Mem.
Hospital
503 N. Maple
62401

**Elgin**
312 695-3200
Ext. 348

Poison Control Center
St. Joseph's Hospital
77 Airlite St.
60120

312 742-9800
Ext. 681
or 682

Poison Control Center
Sherman Hospital
934 Center St.
60120

**Elmhurst**
312 833-1400
Ext. 550

Poison Control Center
Memorial Hospital of
 Du Page County
209 Avon Road
60127

**Evanston**
312 492-6460

Poison Control Center
Evanston Hospital
2650 Ridge Avenue
60201

312 492-2440

Poison Control Center
St. Francis Hospital
355 Ridge Avenue
60202

**Evergreen Park**
312 445-6000
Ext. 221

Poison Control Center
Little Company of
 Mary Hospital
2800 W. 95th St.
60642

**Fairbury**
815 692-2346

Poison Control Center
Fairbury Hospital
519 S. 5th St.
61739

**Freeport**
815 233-4131
Ext. 228

Poison Control Center
Freeport Memorial
Hospital
420 S. Harlem Ave.
61032

**Galesburg**
309 343-4121
Ext. 336

Poison Control Center
Galesburg Cottage
Hospital
695 N. Kellogg St.
61401

309 343-3161
Ext. 210

Poison Control Center
St. Mary's Hospital
239 S. Cherry St.
61401

# Poison Control Centers

## ILLINOIS - Continued

**Granite City**
618 876-2020
Ext. 421

Poison Control Center
St. Elizabeth Hosp.
2100 Madison Ave.
62040

**Harvey**
312 333-2300
Ext. 5296

Poison Control Center
Ingalls Mem. Hosp.
One Ingalls Dr.
60426

**Highland**
618 654-2171
Ext. 297

Poison Control Center
St. Joseph's Hospital
1515 Main St.
62249

**Highland Park**
312 432-8000

Poison Control Center
Highland Park Hosp.
Foundation
718 Glenview Ave.
60035

**Hinsdale**
312 887-2600

Poison Control Center
Hinsdale Sanit. &
Hospital
120 N. Oak St.
60521

**Hoopeston**
217 283-5531

Poison Control Center
Hoopeston Community
Memorial Hospital
701 E. Orange
60942

**Jacksonville**
217 245-9541

Poison Control Center
Passavant Memorial
Area Hospital
1600 W. Walnut St.
62650

**Joliet**
815 725-7133
Ext. 679,
680

815 729-7563

**Kankakee**
815 933-1671
Ext. 606

815 939-4111
Ext. 735

**Kewanee**
309 853-3361
Ext. 219

**Lake Forest**
312 234-5600
Ext. 608,
645 or 683

**La Salle**
815 223-0607
Ext. 14

**Lincoln**
217 732-2161
Ext. 346

Poison Control Center
St. Joseph's Hospital
333 N. Madison St.
60435

Poison Control Center
Silver Cross Hospital
1200 Maple Road
60432

Poison Control Center
Riverside Hospital
350 N. Wall St.
60901

Poison Control Center
St. Mary's Hospital
500 West Court
60901

Poison Control Center
Kewanee Public Hosp.
719 Elliott St.
61443

Poison Control Center
Lake Forest Hospital
660 N. Westmoreland
Road   60045

Poison Control Center
St. Mary's Hospital
1015 O'Conor Ave.
61301

Poison Control Center
Abraham Lincoln
Memorial Hospital
315 Eighth St.
62656

# Poison Control Centers

## ILLINOIS - Continued

**McHenry**
815 385-2200
Ext. 614

Poison Control Center
McHenry Hospital
3516 W. Waukegam Road 60050

**Macomb**
309 833-4101
Ext. 433

Poison Control Center
McDonough District Hospital
525 E. Grant St. 61455

**Mattoon**
217 234-8881
Ext. 43

Poison Control Center
Memorial Hospital District of Coles County
2101 Champaign Ave. 61938

**Maywood**
312 531-3886

Poison Control Center
Loyola Univ. Hosp.
2160 So. 1st Ave. 60153

**Melrose Park**
312 681-3000
Ext. 226
or 239

Poison Control Center
Westlake Hospital
1225 Superior St. 60160

**Mendota**
815 539-7461
Ext. 225

Poison Control Center
Mendota Community Hospital
Rt. 51 & Memorial Dr. 61342

**Moline**
309 762-3651
Ext. 232

Poison Control Center
Moline Public Hosp.
635 10th Ave. 61265

**Monmouth**
309 734-3141
Ext. 244

Poison Control Center
Community Memorial Hospital
1000 W. Harlem Ave. 61462

**Mt. Carmel**
618 262-4121
Ext. 231

Poison Control Center
Wabash General Hosp.
1418 College Dr. 62863

**Mt. Vernon**
618 242-4600
Ext. 521

Poison Control Center
Good Samaritan Hosp.
605 N. 12th St. 62864

**Naperville**
312 355-0450
Ext. 326

Poison Control Center
Edward Hospital
S. Washington St. 60540

**Normal**
309 829-7685
Ext. 274

Poison Control Center
Brokaw Hospital
Pharmacy Dept.
Franklin & Virginia Aves. 61761

**Oak Lawn**
312 425-8000
Ext. 382

Poison Control Center
Christ Community Hospital
4440 W. 95th St. 60453

**Oak Park**
312 383-6200

Poison Control Center
W. Suburban Hosp.
518 N. Austin Blvd. 60302

**Olney**
618 395-2131
Ext. 226

Poison Control Center
Richland Mem. Hosp.
800 E. Locust St. 62450

# Poison Control Centers

## ILLINOIS - Continued

Ottawa
815 433-3100
Ext. 227
or 228

Poison Control Center
Community Hospital
of Ottawa
1100 E. Norris Dr.
60506

Park Ridge
312 696-5151

Poison Control Center
Lutheran General
Hospital
1775 Dempster St.
60068

Pekin
309 347-1151
Ext. 241

Poison Control Center
Pekin Mem. Hospital
14th & Court Sts.
61554

Peoria
309 685-6511
Ext. 250
or 360

Poison Control Center
Methodist Hospital
of Central Illinois
221 N.E. Glen Oak
Ave. 61603

309 691-4702
Ext. 791

Poison Control Center
Proctor Community
Hospital
5409 N. Knoxville
61614

309 672-2109

Poison Control Center
St. Francis Hospital
530 N.E. Glen Oak
Ave. 61603

Peru
815 223-3300
Ext. 53

Poison Control Center
Peoples Hospital
925 West St. 61354

Pittsfield
217 285-2526
Ext. 238

Poison Control Center
Illini Community
Hospital
640 W. Washington
Street 62363

Princeton
815 875-2811

Quincy
217 223-5811
Ext. 255

217 223-1200
Ext. 275

Rockford
815 968-6861
Ext. 441

815 226-2041

815 968-6898
Ext. 635

Rock Island
309 793-1000
Ext. 2106

St. Charles
312 584-3300
Ext. 229

Scott Air Force Base
618 256-7363
Ext. 596,
597

Poison Control Center
Perry Memorial Hosp.
530 Park Ave. E
61356

Poison Control Center
Blessing Hospital
1005 Broadway
62301

Poison Control Center
St. Mary's Hospital
1415 Vermont St.
62301

Poison Control Center
Rockford Mem. Hosp.
2400 N. Rockton Ave.
61103

Poison Control Center
St. Anthony's Hosp.
5666 E. State St.
61108

Poison Control Center
Swedish-American
Hospital
1316 Charles St.
61108

Poison Control Center
Rock Island Franciscan
Hospital
2701 17th St. 61201

Poison Control Center
Delnor Hospital
975 N. 5th Ave.
60174

Poison Control Center
USAF Medical Center
62225

# Poison Control Centers

## ILLINOIS - Continued

**Springfield**
217 528-2041
Ext. 460

217 544-6464
Ext. 210

**Spring Valley**
815 663-2611
Ext. 464,
466

**Streator**
815 673-2311
Ext. 221
or 222

**Urbana**
217 337-3100

217 337-2233

**Waukegan**
312 688-6470

312 688-4181

Poison Control Center
Memorial Med. Ctr.
1st & Miller Sts.
62701

Poison Control Center
St. John's Hospital
800 East Carpenter
62701

Poison Control Center
St. Margaret's Hosp.
600 East 1st St.
61362

Poison Control Center
St. Mary's Hospital
111 E. Spring St.
61364

Poison Control Center
Carle Foundation
Hospital
611 W. Park Ave.
61801

Poison Control Center
Mercy Hospital
1400 W. Park Ave.
61801

Poison Control Center
St. Therese Hospital
2615 W. Washington
St.   60085

Poison Control Center
Victory Memorial
Hospital
1324 N. Sheridan Rd.
60085

**Winfield**
312 653-6900
Ext. 557

**Woodstock**
815 338-2500
Ext. 218

**Zion**
312 872-4561

## INDIANA

**STATE
COORDINATOR**
317 633-4830

**Anderson**
317 649-2511
Ext. 251

**Angola**
219 665-2141
Ext. 42 or
665-2166

**Crown Point**
219 738-2100

**East Chicago**
219 392-1700
or 7203

Poison Control Center
Central DuPage Hosp.
0 North, 025 Winfield Rd.   60190

Poison Control Center
Memorial Hosp.-
McHenry Cnty.
527 W. South St.
60098

Poison Control Center
Zion-Benton Hospital
Shiloh Blvd.   60099

State Board of Health
Indianapolis 46206

Poison Control Center
St. John's Hickey
Memorial Hospital
2015 Jackson St.
46014

Poison Control Center
Cameron Mem. Hosp.,
Inc.
416 East Maumee St.
46703

Poison Control Center
St. Anthony Medical
Center
Main at Franciscan Rd.
46307

Poison Control Center
St. Catherine Hospital
4321 Fir St.   46312

# Poison Control Centers

## INDIANA - Continued

**Elkhart**
219 294-2621

Poison Control Center
Elkhart General Hosp.
600 East Blvd.
46514

**Evansville**
812 426-3405

Poison Control Center
Deaconess Hospital
600 Mary St.    47710

812 477-6261

Poison Control Center
St. Mary's Hospital
3700 Washington Ave.
47715

812 426-8000

Poison Control Center
Welborn Mem. Baptist Hospital
401 S.E. 6th St.
47713

**Fort Wayne**
219 484-6836
Ext. 7800

Poison Control Center
Parkview Mem. Hosp.
220 Randalia Dr.
46805

219 423-2614

Poison Control Center
St. Joseph's Hospital
700 Broadway    46802

**Frankfort**
317 654-4451

Poison Control Center
Clinton County Hosp.
1300 S. Jackson St.
46041

**Gary**
219 886-4710

Poison Control Center
Methodist Hosp. of
   Gary, Inc.
600 Grant St.
46402

**Goshen**
219 533-2141
Ext. 462

**Hammond**
219 932-2300
Ext. 700

**Huntington**
219 356-3000

**Indianapolis**
317 639-6671

317 924-8355

**Kokomo**
217 453-0702
Ext. 444

**Lafayette**
317 742-0221
Ext. 428, 421

**LaGrange**
219 463-2144

Poison Control Center
Goshen General Hosp.
200 High Park Ave.
46526

Poison Control Center
St. Margaret Hospital
25 Douglas St.
46320

Poison Control Center
Huntington Mem. Hosp.
1215 Etna Ave.
46750

Poison Control Center
Marion County Gen.
   Hospital
960 Locke St.
46202

Poison Control Center
Methodist Hospital of
   Indiana, Inc.
1604 N. Capitol Ave.
46202

Poison Control Center
Howard Community
   Hospital
3500 S. LaFountain St.
46901

Poison Control Center
St. Elizabeth Hospital
1501 Hartfort St.
47904

Poison Control Center
LaGrange County
   Hospital
Route #1    46761

# Poison Control Centers

**INDIANA** - Continued

LaPorte
219 362-7541
Ext. 212

Poison Control Center
LaPorte Hospital, Inc.
205 E. St.
P.O. Box 670
46350

Lebanon
317 482-2700
Ext. 44

Poison Control Center
Witham Mem. Hosp.
1124 N. Lebanon St.
46052

Madison
812 265-5211
Ext. 14

Poison Control Center
King's Daughter's
 Hospital
112 Presbyterian
P.O. Box 447
47250

Marion
317 662-4694

Poison Control Center
Marion General Hosp.
Wabash & Euclid Ave.
46952

Mishawaka
219 259-2431

Poison Control Center
St. Joseph's Hospital
215 W. 4th St.
46544

Muncie
317 747-3241

Poison Control Center
Ball Memorial Hosp.
2401 University Ave.
47303

Portland
317 726-7131
Ext. 159

Poison Control Center
Jay County Hospital
505 W. Arch St.
47371

Richmond
317 692-7010
Ext. 622

Shelbyville
317 392-3211
Ext. 52

South Bend
219 284-7458

219 234-2151
Ext. 253,
264

Terre Haute
812 232-0361
Ext. 397,
398

Vincennes
812 885-3348

Poison Control Center
Reid Mem. Hospital
1401 Chester Blvd.
47374

Poison Control Center
Wm. S. Major Hosp.
150 W. Washington St.
46176

Poison Control Center
Memorial Hosp. of
 South Bend
615 Michigan St.
46601

Poison Control Center
St. Joseph's Hospital
811 E. Madison St.
46622

Poison Control Center
Union Hospital, Inc.
1606 N. 7th St.
47804

Poison Control Center
The Good Samaritan
 Hospital
410 S. 7th St.
47591

## IOWA

STATE
COORDINATOR
515 281-3826

Des Moines
515 283-6212

Department of Health
Des Moines  50319

Poison Information
 Center
Iowa Methodist Hosp.
1200 Pleasant St.
50308

# Poison Control Centers

## IOWA - Continued

**Fort Dodge**
515 573-3101

**Iowa City**
319 356-1616

Poison Center No. 1409
Dept. of Pharmacy
Trinity Regional Hosp.
Kenyon Rd.  50501

Poison Control Center
Pharmacy Dept.
University of Iowa
 Hospital and Clinics
52240

## KANSAS

**STATE COORDINATOR**
913 296-3708

**Atchison**
913 EM7-2131

**Dodge City**
316 227-8111

**Emporia**
316 DI2-7120
Ext. 330

**Fort Riley**
913 239-2323

**Fort Scott**
316 223-2200
Night:
223-5165

Department of Health
 & Environment
Topeka  66620

Poison Control Center
Atchison Hospital
1301 N. 2nd St.
66002

Poison Control Center
Trinity Hospital
1107 6th St.  67301

Poison Control Center
Newman Memorial
 Hospital
12th & Chestnut Sts.
66801

Poison Control Center
Irwin Army Hospital
66442

Poison Control Center
Mercy Hospital
821 Burke St.  66701

**Great Bend**
316 793-3523
Night:
792-2511

**Hays**
913 625-3441

**Kansas City**
913 831-6633

913 MA1-6600

**Lawrence**
913 VI3-3680

**Parsons**
316 421-4880

**Salina**
913 TA7-5591
Ext. 112

**Topeka**
913 CE4-9961
Ext. 150

Poison Control Center
Central Kans. Med.
 Center
3515 Broadway
67530

Poison Control Center
Hadley Regional Med.
 Center
201 E. 7th St.
67601

Poison Control Center
Univ. of Kansas Med.
 Center
39th & Rainbow Blvd.
66103

Poison Control Center
Bethany Med. Center
51 No. 12th St.
66102

Poison Control Center
Lawrence Memorial
 Hospital
325 Maine Street
66044

Poison Control Center
Labette County Med.
 Center
So. 21st Street
67357

Poison Control Center
St. John's Hospital
139 N. Penn St.
67401

Poison Control Center
Stormont-Vail Hosp.
10th & Washburn Sts.

# Poison Control Centers

## KANSAS - Continued

Wichita
316 685-2151
Ext. 7515

Poison Control Center
Wesley Med. Center
550 N. Hillside
Ave. 67214

## KENTUCKY

STATE
COORDINATOR
502 564-4935

Department For Human
Resources
Frankfort 40601

Ashland
606 325-7755
Ext. 444

Poison Control Center
King's Daughters
Hospital
2201 Lexington Ave.
41101

Berea
606 986-3061

Poison Control Center
Porter Moore Drug,
Inc.
124 Main St. 40403

Fort Thomas
606 292-3215

Poison Control Center
St. Lukes Hospital
85 No. Grand Ave.
41075

Lexington
606 278-3411

Poison Control Center
Central Baptist Hosp.
1740 So. Limestone
Street 40503

Louisville
502 589-8222

Poison Control Center
Norton-Children's
Hospital
Emergency Room
200 E. Chestnut St.
40202

Murray
502 753-5131
Ext. 302

Owensboro
502 683-3511
Ext. 275 or
232-night

Paducah
502 444-6361
Ext. 284 or
541-night

Pikesville
606 437-9621

Prestonsburg
606 886-8511

Whitesburg
606 633-2160

Poison Control Center
Murray-Calloway
County Hospital
803 Popular 42071

Poison Control Center
Owensboro-Daviess
County Hospital
811 Hospital Court
42301

Poison Control Center
Western Baptist Hosp.
2501 Kentucky Ave.
42001

Poison Control Center
Methodist Hospital
219 High St. &
Harolds Br.
41501

Poison Control Center
Highland Regional
Medical Center
Auxler Rd. & U.S.
23 N.
Box 351 41653

Poison Control Ctr.
Quillen Rexall
Drug Store 41858

## LOUISIANA

STATE
COORDINATOR
504 527-5822

Bogalusa
504 735-1322

State Department of
Health
New Orleans 70160

Poison Inform. Ctr.
Washington-St.
Tammany Charity
Hospital
400 Memphis St.
70427

# Poison Control Centers

## LOUISIANA -Continued

Monroe
318 325-6454
Night:
325-2611

New Orleans
504 899-3409
524-3617 or
3618

Shreveport
318 222-0709

Poison Control Center
St. Francis Hospital
309 Jackson St.
71201

Louisiana Poison
 Control Center at
 New Orleans
Charity Hosp.,
 Pharm. Dept.
1532 Tulane Ave.
70140

Poison Control Center
T.E. Schumpert Mem.
 Hospital
915 Margaret Pl.
71101

## MAINE

STATE
COORDINATOR
207 623-4511

Portland
207 871-0111

Dept. of Health and
 Welfare
Augusta   04330

Poison Control Center
Emergency Division
Maine Medical Ctr.
22 Bramhall St.
04102

## MARYLAND

STATE
COORDINATOR
301 383-2668

Annapolis
301 268-4444
 Ext. 277

State Department of
 Health
Baltimore   21201

Poison Control Center
Anne Arundel Gen.
 Hospital
Franklin & Cathedral
 Sts.   21401

Baltimore
301 955-5000

301 528-7701

Bethesda
301 530-3880

Cumberland
301 722-6677

Easton
301 822-5555

Hagerstown
301 797-2400

Poison Control Center
Johns Hopkins Hosp.
601 N. Broadway
21205

Poison Information
 Center
Univ. of Maryland,
 School of Pharmacy
636 W. Lombard St.
21201

Poison Control Center
Suburban Hosp.-
 Emergency Rm.
8600 Old Georgetown
 Rd.   20014

Tri-State Poison
 Contr. Center
Sacred Heart Hosp.
900 Seton Dr.
21502

Poison Control Center
Memorial Hospital
S. Washington St.
21601

Poison Control Center
Washington County
 Hospital
King & Antietam Sts.
21740

## MASSACHUSETTS

STATE
COORDINATOR
617 727-2670

Boston
617 232-2120

State Department of
 Public Health
Boston 02111

Poison Control Center
N.E. Medical Center
300 Longwood Ave.
02115

# Poison Control Centers

## MASSACHUSETTS - Continued

Fall River
617 679-3131

New Bedford
617 997-1515

Springfield
413 788-7321

413 787-3200

Worcester
617 756-1551

Poison Control Center
Union Hospital
So. Main St.   02721

Poison Control Center
St. Luke's Hospital
101 Page St.   02740

Poison Control Center
Mercy Hospital
Carew St.   01104

Poison Control Center
Springfield Hospital
759 Chestnut St.
01107

Poison Control Center
Worcester City Hosp.
26 Queen St.
01609

## MICHIGAN

STATE
COORDINATOR
517 373-1448

Adrian
313 263-2412

Ann Arbor
313 764-5102

Battle Creek
616 963-5521

Department of Public
Health
Lansing   48914

Poison Control Center
Emma L. Bixby Hosp.
818 Riverside Ave.
49221

Poison Control Center
University Hospital
1405 E. Ann St.
48104

Poison Control Center
Community Hospital
200 Tompkins St.
49016

Bay City
517 893-5511

Berrien Center
616 471-7761

Coldwater
517 278-7361

Detroit
313 494-5711

313 872-1540

313 864-5400
Ext. 417 or
5536

Eloise
313 722-4748 Day
274-3000 Night

Flint
313 232-1161
Ext. 220

Poison Control Center
Bay Medical Center
100 15th St.   48706

Poison Control Center
Berrien General Hosp.
Dean's Hill Rd.
49102

Poison Control Center
Community Health
Center of Branch
County
274 E. Chicago St.
49036

Poison Control Center
Children's Hospital of
Michigan
3901 Beaubien
48201

Poison Information
Center
City Health Dept.
1151 Taylor Ave.
48202

Poison Control Center
Mount Carmel Mercy
Hospital
6071 W. Outer Dr.
48235

Poison Control Center
Wayne County Gen.
Hospital
30712 Michigan Ave.
48132

Poison Control Center
Hurley Hospital
6th Ave. & Begole
48502

# Poison Control Centers

## MICHIGAN - Continued

**Grand Rapids**
616 774-7740
Poison Control Center
Blodgett Mem. Hosp.
1840 Wealthy, S.E.
49506

616 774-1774
Poison Control Center
Butterworth Hospital
100 Michigan, N.E.
49503

616 452-5151
Poison Control Center
Grand Rapids
Osteopathic Hosp.
1919 Boston St., S.E.
49506

616 774-6789
Poison Control Center
St. Mary's Hospital
201 Lafayette, S.E.
49503

**Hancock**
906 482-1122
Poison Control Center
St. Joseph's Hospital
200 Michigan Ave.
49503

**Holland**
616 396-4661
Poison Control Center
Holland City Hosp.
602 Michigan Ave.
49423

**Jackson**
517 783-2771
Poison Control Center
W.A. Foote Mem.
Hospital
205 N. East St.
49201

**Kalamazoo**
616 383-4815
Poison Control Center
Borgess Hospital
1521 Gull Road
49001

616 383-6338
or 6386

Poison Control Center
Bronson Methodist
Hospital
252 E. Lovell St.
49006

**Lansing**
517 372-3610
Ext. 305

Poison Control Center
St. Lawrence Hosp.
1210 W. Saginaw St.
48914

**Marquette**
906 228-9440
Ext. 416

Poison Control Center
Marquette General
Hospital, N.
420 W. Magnetic
49855

**Midland**
517 835-6771
Ext. 308 or
328

Poison Control Center
Midland Hospital
4005 Orchard Dr.
48640

**Monroe**
313 241-6509

Poison Control Center
Mercy-Memorial
Hospital, Corp.
700 Stewart Rd.
48161

**Petoskey**
616 347-7373
Ext. 251

Poison Control Center
Little Traverse Hosp.
416 Connable   49770

**Pontiac**
313 858-3000

Poison Control Center
St. Joseph Mercy
Hospital
900 Woodward Ave.
48053

**Port Huron**
313 982-8511

Poison Control Center
Port Huron Hospital
1001 Kearney St.
48060

# Poison Control Centers

## MICHIGAN - Continued

**Saginaw**
517 753-3411

Poison Control Center
Saginaw General
  Hospital
1447 N. Harrison Rd.
48602

**Traverse City**
616 947-6140
  Ext. 280

Poison Control Center
Munson Medical Ctr.
Sixth St.  49684

## MINNESOTA

**STATE COORDINATOR**
612 296-5276

State Department of
  Health
Minneapolis  55440

**Bemidji**
218 751-5430

Poison Information
  Center
Bemidji Hospital
56601

**Brainerd**
218 829-2861

Poison Information
  Center
St. Joseph's Hosp.
56401

**Crookston**
218 281-4682
  Ext. 202

Poison Information
  Center
Riverview Hospital
320 So. Hubbard
56716

**Duluth**
218 727-6636

Poison Information
  Center
St. Luke's Hospital
Emergency Dept.
915 East First St.
55805

218 727-4551
  Ext. 359

St. Mary's Hospital
407 E. 3rd St.
55805

**Fergus Falls**
218 736-5475

Poison Information
  Center
Lake Region Hosp.
56537

**Fridley**
612 786-2200

Unity Hospital
550 Osborne Rd.
55432

**Mankato**
507 387-4031

Immanuel-St. Joseph's
  Hospital
325 Garden Blvd.
56001

**Marshall**
507 532-9661

Poison Information
  Center
Louis Weiner Mem.
  Hospital
56258

56258

**Minneapolis**
612 332-0282

Poison Information
  Center
Outpatient Dept.
Fairview Hospital
2312 So. 6th St.
55406

612 348-7981

Hennipen County
  Poison Control Cntr.
Hennipen County
  Medical Center
5th & Portland So.
55415

612 296-5276

Minn. Poison Info.
  Center
Minnesota Dept. of
  Health
717 Delaware St.,
  S.E.  55440

# Poison Control Centers

MINNESOTA - Continued

Minneapolis
612 588-0616        North Mem. Hosp.
                    3220 Lowry North
                    55422

612 874-4233        Poison Information
                    Center
                    Northwestern Hosp.
                    810 E. 27th St.
                    55407

Morris
612 589-1313        Poison Information
                    Center
                    Stevens County Mem.
                    Hospital
                    56267

Rochester
507 285-5123        S.E. Minnesota
or 282-4461         Poison Control Ctr.
                    201 W. Center St.
                    55901

St. Cloud
612 251-2700        
Ext. 221            Poison Information
                    Center
                    St. Cloud Hospital
                    1406 6th Ave. N.
                    56301

St. Paul
612 224-9121        Bethesda Lutheran
                    Hospital
                    559 Capitol Blvd.
                    55103

612 227-6521        The Children's Hosp.,
                    Inc.
                    311 Pleasant Ave.
                    55102

612 228-3132        St. John's Hospital
                    403 Maria Ave.
                    55106

612 291-3348        St. Joseph's Hosp.
or 3139             69 W. Exchange
                    55102

612 298-8201

612 222-4260

Virginia
218 741-3340

Willmar
612 235-4543

Worthington
507 372-2941

MISSISSIPPI

STATE
COORDINATOR
601 354-6650

Brandon
601 825-2811
Ext. 287,
288

Columbia
601 736-6303
Ext. 217

United Hospitals Inc.
St. Luke's Division
300 Pleasant Ave.
55102

St. Paul-Ramsey Hosp.
640 Jackson St.
55101

Poison Information
Center
Virginia Municipal
Hospital
55792

Poison Information
Center
Rice Memorial Hosp.
402 W. 3rd St.
56201

Poison Information
Center
Worthington Regional
Hospital
1016 6th Ave.
56187

State Board of Health
Jackson 39205

Poison Control Center
Rankin General Hosp.
350 Crossgates Blvd.
39042

Poison Control Center
Marion County
  General Hospital
39429

# Poison Control Centers

## MISSISSIPPI - Continued

**Greenwood**
601 453-9751
Ext. 231

Poison Control Center
Greenwood-LeFlore
  Hospital
River Road  38930

**Hattiesburg**
601 544-7000
Ext. 565

Poison Control Info.
  Center
Forrest County Gen.
  Hospital
400 S. 28th Ave.
39401

**Jackson**
601 948-5211
Ext. 201,
202, 203

Poison Control Center
Baptist Hospital
1190 N. State St.
39201

601 982-0121
Ext. 345

Poison Control Center
St. Dominic-Jackson
  Memorial Hospital
969 Lakeland Dr.
39216

601 354-6650

Poison Information
  Center
State Board of Health
Bur. of Disease
  Control  39205

**Keesler AFB
Biloxi**
601 377-2516
or 6555
or 6556

Poison Control Center
USAF Hosp. Keesler
Air Force Base
39534

**Laurel**
601 649-4000
Ext. 207,
218, 220,
248

Poison Control Center
Jones County Com.
  Hospital
Jefferson St. at 13th
  Ave.  39440

**Meridian**
601 483-6211
Ext. 54, 71

**Pascagoula**
601 762-6121
Ext. 654

**University**
601 234-1522

**Vicksburg**
601 636-2131
Ext. 250,
276

Poison Control Center
St. Joseph's Hospital
Highway 39, N.
39301

Poison Control Center
Singing River Hosp.
Highway 90 E.
39567

Poison Control Center
School of Pharmacy
University of
  Mississippi  38677

Poison Control Center
Mercy Regional Med.
  Center
100 McAuley Dr.
39181

## MISSOURI

**STATE
COORDINATOR**
314 751-4667

**Cape Girardeau**
314 334-4461
Ext. 49

**Columbia**
314 882-8091

**Hannibal**
314 221-0414
Ext. 213

Missouri Division of
  Health
Jefferson City  65101

Poison Control Center
St. Francis Hospital
825 Good Hope St.
63701

Poison Control Center
University of Missouri
  Medical Center
807 Stadium Blvd.
65201

Poison Control Center
St. Elizabeth Hosp.
109 Virginia St.
63401

# Poison Control Centers

## MISSOURI - Continued

Joplin
417 781-2727
Ext. 276

Kansas City
816 471-0626
Ext. 220

816 421-8060
Ext. 257,
235

Kirksville
816 665-4611
Ext. 240

Poplar Bluff
314 785-7721
Ext. 33

Rolla
314 364-3100
Ext. 31

St. Joseph
816 232-8461
Ext. 277

Poison Control Center
St. John's Medical
 Center
2727 McClelland
 Blvd.    64801

Poison Control Center
Children's Mercy
 Hospital
24th & Gillham Rd.
64108

Poison Control Center
Kansas City Gen.
 Hosp. and Med.
 Center
23rd and Cherry St.
64108

Poison Control Center
Kirksville Osteo-
 pathic Hospital
800 W. Jefferson St.
63501

Poison Control Center
Lucy Lee Hospital
330 N. 2nd St.
63901

Poison Control Center
Phelps County Mem.
 Hospital
1000 W. 10th St.
65401

Poison Control Center
Methodist Hospital &
 Medical Center
8th & Faraon Sts.
64501

St. Louis
314 865-4000
Ext. 417

314 367-6880
Ext. 220

Springfield
417 836-3193

417 881-8811
Ext. 248,
241

West Plains
417 256-3141
Ext. 8

## MONTANA

STATE
COORDINATOR
406 449-3895

Bozeman
406 586-5431

Poison Control Center
Cardinal Glennon Mem.
 Hosp. for Children
1465 S. Grand Ave.
63104

Poison Control Center
St. Louis Children's
 Hospital
500 S. Kingshighway
63110

Poison Control Center
Lester E. Cox Med.
 Center
1423 N. Jefferson St.
65802

Poison Control Center
St. John's Hospital
1235 E. Cherokee
65804

Poison Control Center
West Plains Memorial
 Hospital
1103 Alaska Ave.
65775

Montana State Dept.
 of Health & Envi-
 ronmental Sciences
Helena   59601

Poison Control Center
Bozeman Deaconess
 Hospital
15 West Lamme
59715

# Poison Control Centers

## MONTANA - Continued

Great Falls
406 761-1200

Poison Control Center
Montana Deaconess
Hospital
1101 26th St. So.
59401

Helena
406 442-2480
Ext. 137

Poison Control Center
St. Peter's Hospital
59601

## NEBRASKA

STATE
COORDINATOR
402 471-2122

State Department of
Health
Lincoln  68508

Lincoln
402 473-3244

Poison Control Center
Bryan Mem. Hosp.
4848 Sumner St.
68506

Omaha
402 553-5400

Poison Control Center
Children's Memorial
Hospital
44th & Dewey Sts.
68105

## NEVADA

STATE
COORDINATOR
702 885-4750

Las Vegas
702 385-2000

Department of Human
Resources
Carson City  89701

Poison Control Center
Southern Nevada
Memorial Hospital
1800 W. Charleston
Blvd.  89102

Reno
702 785-4129
Night:
785-4140

Poison Control Center
Washoe Med. Center
77 Pringle Way
89502

## NEW HAMPSHIRE

Hanover
603 643-4000

Dartmouth-Hitchcock
Poison Control Center
Mary Hitchcock Hosp.
2 Maynard St.  03755

## NEW JERSEY

STATE
COORDINATOR
609 292-8103

Department of Health
Trenton  08625

Atlantic City
609 344-4081

Poison Control Center
Atlantic City Medical
Center
1925 Pacific Ave.
08401

Belleville
201 751-1000

Poison Control Center
Clara Maass Mem.
Hospital
1A Franklin Ave.
07109

Boonton
201 334-5000

Poison Control Center
Riverside Hospital
Powerville Rd.
07005

Bridgeton
609 451-6600

Poison Control Center
Bridgeton Hospital
Irving Ave.  08302

# Poison Control Centers

## NEW JERSEY - Continued

**Camden**
609 795-5554

Poison Control Center
West Jersey Hospital
Evesham Ave. and
  Voorhees Twp.
08104

**Denville**
201 627-3000

Poison Control Center
St. Clare's Hospital
Pocono Rd.  07834

**East Orange**
201 672-8400

Poison Control Center
East Orange Gen.
  Hospital
300 Central Ave.
07019

**Elizabeth**
201 527-5000

Poison Control Center
St. Elizabeth Hosp.
225 Williamson St.
07207

**Englewood**
201 568-3400

Poison Control Center
Englewood Hospital
350 Engle St.
07631

**Flemington**
201 782-2121

Poison Control Center
Hunterdon Med. Ctr.
Route #31  08822

**Livingston**
201 992-5500

Poison Control Center
St. Barnabas Med.
  Center
Old Short Hills Rd.
07039

**Long Branch**
201 222-2210

Poison Control Center
Monmouth Med. Ctr.
Dunbar & 2nd Ave.
07740

**Montclaire**
201 746-6000

**Morristown**
201 538-0900

**Mount Holly**
609 267-0700

**Neptune**
201 988-1818

**Newark**
201 923-6000
Ext. 214,
278, 288

**New Brunswick**
201 828-3000

201 545-8000

**Newton**
201 383-2121

Poison Control Center
Mountainside Hospital
Bay & Highland Ave.
07042

Poison Control Center
Community Health
  Center
95 Mount Kemble Ave.
07960

Poison Control Center
Burlington County
  Memorial Hospital
175 Madison Ave.
08060

Poison Control Center
Jersey Shore Medical
  Center Fitkin Hosp.
1945 Corlies Ave.
07753

Poison Control Center
Newark Beth Israel
  Medical Center
201 Lyons Ave.
07112

Poison Control Center
Middlesex Gen. Hosp.
180 Somerset St.
08901

Poison Control Center
St. Peter's Gen. Hosp.
254 Easton Ave.
08903

Poison Control Center
Newton Memorial
  Hospital
175 High St.  07860

# Poison Control Centers

## NEW JERSEY - Continued

**Orange**
201 678-1100

Poison Control Center
Hosp. Center at
  Orange
188 So. Essex Ave.
07051

**Passaic**
201 473-1000

Poison Control Center
St. Mary's Hospital
211 Pennington Ave.
07055

**Perth Amboy**
201 442-3700

Poison Control Center
Perth Amboy Gen.
  Hospital
530 New Brunswick
  Ave.   08861

**Phillipsburg**
201 859-1500

Poison Control Center
Warren Hospital
185 Roseberry St.
08865

**Point Pleasant**
201 892-1100

Poison Control Center
Point Pleasant Hosp.
Osborn Ave. &
  River Front   08743

**Princeton**
609 921-7700

Poison Control Center
Medical Center at
  Princeton
253 Witherspoon St.
08540

**Saddle Brook**
201 843-6700

Poison Control Center
Saddle Brook Gen.
  Hospital
300 Market St.
07662

**Somers Point**
609 927-3501

**Somerville**
201 725-4000

**Summit**
201 522-2232

**Teaneck**
201 837-3070

**Trenton**
609 396-1077

**Union**
201 687-1900

**Wayne**
201 684-6900

Poison Control Center
Shore Mem. Hospital
Shore & Sunny Aves.
08244

Poison Control Center
Somerset Hospital
Rehill Ave.   08876

Poison Control Center
Overlook Hospital
193 Morris Ave.
07901

Poison Control Center
Holy Name Hospital
718 Teaneck Rd.
07666

Poison Control Center
Helene Fuld Hospital
750 Brunswick Ave.
08638

Poison Control Center
Memorial Gen. Hosp.
1000 Galloping Hill
  Rd.   07083

Poison Control Center
Greater Paterson Gen.
  Hospital
224 Hamburg Twp.
07470

## NEW MEXICO

STATE
COORDINATOR
505 827-2693

Environmental
  Improvement Agency
Santa Fe   87501

# Poison Control Centers

## NEW MEXICO - Continued

**Alamogordo**
505 437-3770
Ext. 260

Poison Control Center
Gerald Champion
Mem. Hospital
1209 9th St.  88310

**Albuquerque**
505 265-4411
Ext. 2130

Poison Control Center
Bernalillo County
Medical Center
2211 Lomas Blvd.,
N.E.  87131

**Carlsbad**
505 887-3521
Ext. 266

Poison Control Center
Carlsbad Regional
Medical Center
Northgate Center
P.O. Box 1479
88220

**Clovis**
505 763-4493
Ext. 131

Poison Control Center
Clovis Mem. Hosp.
1210 Thornton St.
88101

**Las Cruces**
505 524-8641
Ext. 25, 61

Poison Control Center
Mem. Gen. Hospital
Alameda & Lohman
88001

**Roswell**
505 622-8170
Ext. 26

Poison Control Center
Eastern New Mexico
Medical Center
405 Country Club
Rd.  88201

## NEW YORK

STATE
COORDINATOR
518 474-3664

State Department of
Health
Albany  12210

**Albany**
518 445-3131
Emergency
Room

**Binghamton**
607 772-1100
Ext. 431

607 729-6521

**Buffalo**
716 878-7000

**Dunkirk**
716 366-1111
Ext. 414,
415

**East Meadow**
516 542-2323
or 2324, 2325

**Elmira**
607 734-5221
Ext. 237,
238, 331

607 733-6541
Ext. 535,
213, 271,
289

Poison Control Center
Albany Med. Center
Hospital
New Scotland Ave.
12208

Poison Control Center
Binghamton Gen. Hosp.
Mitchell & Park
13903

Poison Control Center
Our Lady of Lourdes
Memorial
169 Riverside Dr.
13905

Poison Control Center
Children's Hospital
219 Bryant St.
14222

Poison Control Center
Brooks Mem. Hosp.
529 Central Ave.
14048

Poison Control Center
Nassau County Med.
Center
2201 Hempstead Trnpk.
11554

Poison Control Center
Arnot Ogden Hospital
Roe Ave. & Grove
14901

Poison Control Center
St. Joseph's Hospital
555 E. Market St.
14902

# Poison Control Centers

## NEW YORK - Continued

Endicott
607 754-7171
Ext. 66

Glens Falls
518 792-3151

Ithaca
607 274-4011
or 4383
or 4411

Jamestown
716 487-0141

Johnson City
607 773-6611

Kingston
914 331-3131
Ext. 250

New York
212 340-4495

Poison Control Center
Ideal Hospital
600 High Ave.
13760

Poison Control Center
Glens Falls Hospital
100 Park St.   12801

Poison Information
 Center
Tompkins County
 Hospital
1285 Trumansburg Rd.
14850

Poison Control Center
W.C.A. Hospital
207 Foote Ave.
14707

Poison Control Center
Wilson Mem. Hosp.
33-57 Harrison St.
13790

Poison Control Center
Kingston Hospital
396 Broadway   12401

Poison Information
 Center
N.Y. City Dept. of
 Health
Bureau of Laboratories
455 First Ave.
10016

Niagara Falls
716 278-4511

Nyack
914 358-6200
Ext. 451 or
452

Oswego
315 343-1920

Rochester
716 275-5151

Syracuse
315 476-3166
or 473-5831

Watertown
315 788-8700

## NORTH CAROLINA

STATE
COORDINATOR
919 684-8111

Asheville
704 255-4660

Poison Control Center
Niagara Falls Mem.
 Medical Center
621 Tenth St.
14302

Poison Control Center
Nyack Hospital
North Midland Ave.
10960

Poison Control Center
Oswego Hospital
110 West Sixth St.
13126

Poison Control Center
Strong Mem. Hosp.
260 Crittenden Blvd.
14620

Poison Control Center
Upstate Medical Ctr.
750 E. Adams St.
13210

Poison Information
 Center
House of the Good
 Samaritan Hospital
Washington & Pratt
13602

Duke University
 Medical Center
Durham 27710

Poison Control Center
Memorial Mission Hosp.
509 Biltmore Ave.
28801

# Poison Control Centers

## NORTH CAROLINA - Continued

Charlotte
704 334-6831
Poison Control Center
Mercy Hospital
2000 E. 5th St.
26204

Durham
919 684-8111
Poison Control Center
Duke University
Medical Center
Box 3007, 27710

Greensboro
919 379-4109
Poison Control Center
Moses Cone Hospital
1200 N. Elm St.
27401

Hendersonville
704 693-6522
Poison Control Center
Margaret R. Pardee
Hosp.
Fleming St. 28739

Hickory
704 328-2191
Poison Control Center
Catawba Mem. Hosp.
Fairgrove-Church Rd.
28601

Jacksonville
919 347-2141
Poison Control Center
Onslow Mem. Hosp.
College St. 28540

Wilmington
919 763-9021
Ext. 311
Poison Control Center
New Hanover Mem.
Hospital
2431 S. 17th St.
28401

## NORTH DAKOTA

STATE
COORDINATOR
701 224-2348
State Department of
Health
Bismark 58501

Bismarck
701 223-1420
Poison Control Center
Quain & Ranstad
Clinic
Burleigh County
58501

Dickinson
701 225-6771
Ext. 329,
259
Poison Control Center
St. Joseph's Hospital
7th St., W. 58601

Fargo
701 237-8115
Poison Control Center
College of Pharmacy
North Dakota State
University 58102

Grand Forks
701 775-4241
Poison Control Center
Grand Forks Deaconess
Hospital
212 S. 4th St.
58201

Jamestown
701 252-1050
Poison Control Center
Jamestown Hospital
419-5th St., N.E.
58401

Minot
701 838-0341
Ext. 253
Poison Control Center
St. Joseph's Hospital
304 4th St. 58701

Williston
701 572-2188
Poison Control Center
Mercy Hospital
Washington Ave. &
Broadway 58801

## OHIO

STATE
COORDINATOR
614 466-2544
Department of Health
Columbus 43216

# Poison Control Centers

## OHIO - Continued

Akron
216 379-8562

Poison Control Center
Children's Hospital
Buchtel at Bowery
44308

Canton
216 452-9911

Poison Information
Center
Aultman Hospital
2600 6th St., S.W.
44710

Cincinnati
513 872-5111

Drug & Poison Info.
Center
Univ. of Cincinnati
College of Med.
234 Goodman St.
45229

Cleveland
216 231-4455

Poison Information
Center
Cleveland Academy
of Medicine
10525 Carnegie Ave.
44106

Columbus
614 228-1323

Poison Control Center
Children's Hospital
17th at Livingston
43205

Dayton
513 257-2969

Poison Control Center
USAF Medical Ctr.
Wright Patterson AFB
45433

Lorain
216 282-2220

Poison Control Center
Lorain Community
Hospital
3700 Kolbe Rd.
44052

Mansfield
419 522-3411
Ext. 545

Springfield
513 325-0531

Toledo
419 382-7971

Youngstown
216 745-7231

Zanesville
614 454-4000

Poison Control Center
Mansfield Gen. Hosp.
335 Glessner Ave.
44903

Poison Control Center
Community Hospital
2615 E. High St.
45505

Poison Information
Center
Medical College Hosp.
P.O. Box 6190
43614

Poison Control Center
St. Elizabeth Hosp.
1044 Belmont Ave.
44505

Poison Information
Center
Bethesda Hospital
2951 Maple Ave.
43701

## OKLAHOMA

STATE
COORDINATOR
405 271-5062
or 5454

Lawton
405 355-8620
Ext. 232,
234

Oklahoma City
405 231-1811
Night and
Weekends
271-5454

State Department of
Health
Oklahoma City
73105

Poison Control Center
Comanche County
Memorial Hospital
Gore Blvd. 73501

Poison Information
Center
St. Anthony's Hosp.
Emergency Room
601 9th St. 73102

# Poison Control Centers

## OKLAHOMA - Continued

Oklahoma City
405 271-5062
Weekends &
Night: 5454
Poison Information Center
State Dept. of Health 73105

Ponca City
405 765-3321
Ext. 372
Poison Control Center
Ponca City Hospital
14th & Hartford
74601

Tulsa
918 584-1351
Ext. 598
Poison Control Center
Hillcrest Med. Ctr.
Utica on the Park
74104

## OREGON

Portland
503 225-8500
Poison Control Registry, Pediatrics Dept.
University of Oregon Medical School
3181 S.W. Sam Jackson Park Rd.
97201

## PENNSYLVANIA

STATE COORDINATOR
717 787-2307
State Department of Health
Harrisburg  17120

Allentown
215 433-2311
Poison Control Center
Allentown Sacred Heart Hospital
1200 Cedarcrest Blvd.
18105

Chambersburg
717 264-5171
Poison Control Center
The Chambersburg Hospital
7th & King Sts.
17201

Chester
215 494-0721
Ext. 232

Danville
717 275-6211
or 6116

Easton
215 258-6221
Ext. 235, 210, 321

East Stroudsburg
717 421-4000
Ext. 666

Erie
814 864-4031
Ext. 27

814 455-6711
Ext. 521

814 459-4000
Ext. 300

Hanover
717 637-3711
Ext. 111

Poison Control Center
Sacred Heart General Hospital
9th & Wilson Sts.
19013

Poison Control Center
George F. Giesinger Memorial Hospital
Montour County
17821

Poison Control Center
Easton Hospital
21st & Lehigh Sts.
18042

Poison Control Center
General Hospital of Monroe County
206 E. Brown St.
18301

Poison Control Center
Erie Osteopathic Hosp.
5515 Peach St.
16509

Poison Control Center
Hamot Medical Ctr.
2nd & State Sts.
16512

Poison Control Center
St. Vincent Hospital
232 W. 25th St.
16512

Poison Control Center
Hanover General Hosp.
300 Highland Ave.
17331

# Poison Control Centers

## PENNSYLVANIA - Continued

Harrisburg
717 782-3639    Poison Control Center
Harrisburg Hospital
S. Front & Mulberry
Sts. 17101

717 782-4141
Ext. 4132    Poison Control Center
Polyclinic Hospital
3rd and Polyclinic
Ave. 17105

Johnstown
814 535-5353    Poison Control Center
Mercy Hospital
1020 Franklin St.
15905

Lancaster
717 299-4546    Poison Control Center
St. Joseph's Hosp.
250 College Ave.
17604

Lewistown
717 248-5411
Ext. 392    Poison Control Center
Lewistown Hospital
Highland Ave.
17044

Philadelphia
215 WA2-5523    Poison Information
Center
City of Philadelphia
Office of Medical
Examiner
321 University Ave.
19104

Pittsburgh
412 681-6669    Pittsburgh Poison Ctr.
Children's Hospital
125 Desoto St.
15213

412 766-8300    Poison Control Center
St. John's General
Hospital
3339 McClure Ave.
15212

Scranton
717 343-5566    Poison Control Center
Community Med. Ctr.
316 Colfax Ave.
18510

Sharon
412 981-1700
Ext. 281    Poison Control Center
Sharon General Hosp.
740 E. State St.
16146

Wilkes-Barre
717 823-1121
Ext. 222    Poison Control Center
Wilkes-Barre General
Hospital
North River & Auburn
Sts. 18702

York
717 843-8623
Ext. 274, 275    Poison Control Center
Mem. Osteopathic
Hospital
325 S. Belmont St.
17403

717 771-2311
Emergency
Room    Poison Control Center
York Hospital
George St. & Rathton
Rd. 17403

## PUERTO RICO

STATE COORDINATOR
809 765-4880
or 0615    University of Puerto
Rico
Rio Piedras

Arecibo
809 878-3535    Poison Control Center
District Hospital of
Arecibo 00613

Fajardo
809 863-0505    Poison Control Center
District Hospital of
Fajardo 00649

# Poison Control Centers

## PUERTO RICO - Continued

Mayaguez
809 832-8686
Poison Control Center
Mayaguez Med. Ctr.
Department of Health
P.O. Box 1868
00709

Ponce
809 842-8354
or 2080
Poison Control Center
District Hospital of
Ponce   00731

Rio Piedras
809 764-3515
Poison Control Center
Medical Center of
Puerto Rico

## RHODE ISLAND

STATE
COORDINATOR
401 277-2401
State Department of
Health
Providence   02908

Kingston
401 792-2775
or 2762
Poison Control Center
College of Pharmacy
University of Rhode
Island   02881

Pawtucket
401 724-1230
Poison Control Center
Memorial Hospital
Prospect St.   02860

Providence
401 277-4000
Poison Control Center
Rhode Island Hospital
593 Eddy St.   02902

## SOUTH CAROLINA

STATE
COORDINATOR
803 758-5407
State Department of
Health
Columbia   29201

Charleston
803 792-0211
Poison Control Center
Medical Univ. of
South Carolina
80 Barre St.   29401

Columbia
803 254-7382
Poison Control Center
Richland Mem. Hosp.
2020 Hampton St.
29204

## SOUTH DAKOTA

STATE
COORDINATOR
605 224-3361
State Department of
Health
Pierre   57501

Sioux Falls
605 336-3894
Poison Control Center
McKennan Hospital
800 East 21st St.
57101

## TENNESSEE

STATE
COORDINATOR
615 741-3644
State Department of
Public Health
Nashville   37219

Chattanooga
615 755-6100
Poison Control Center
T.C. Thompson
Children's Hospital
910 Blackford St.
37403

Columbia
615 388-2320
Ext. 49
Poison Control Center
Maury County Hosp.
Mt. Pleasant Pike
38401

Cookeville
615 528-2541
Poison Control Center
Cookeville Gen. Hosp.
142 W. 5th St.
38501

# Poison Control Centers

## TENNESSEE - Continued

Jackson
901 424-0424

Poison Control Center
Madison Gen. Hosp.
708 W. Forest
38301

Johnson City
615 928-3112

Poison Control Center
Memorial Hospital
Boone & Fairview
Ave. 37601

Knoxville
615 971-3261

Knoxville Poison
  Control Center
Memorial Research
  Center & Hospital
Univ. of Tennessee
Alcoa Highway
37920

Memphis
901 525-3005

Poison Control Center
LeBonheur Children's
  Hospital
Adams Ave. at
  Dunlap 38103

Nashville
615 322-3391

Poison Control Center
Vanderbilt University
  Hospital
21st & Garland
37232

## TEXAS

STATE
COORDINATOR
512 454-3781

State Department of
  Health
Austin 78756

Abilene
915 677-3551
Ext. 266,
267

Poison Control Center
Hendrick Hospital
19th & Hickory Sts.
79601

Amarillo
806 376-4431
Ext. 321,
322

Poison Control Center
Northwest Texas Hosp.
2203 W. 6th St.
79106

Austin
512 478-4490

Poison Control Center
Brackenridge Hospital
14th & Sabine Sts.
78701

Beaumont
713 833-7409

Poison Control Center
Baptist Hospital of
  Southeast Texas
College & 11th St.
Box 1591   77701

Corpus Christi
512 884-4511
Ext. 273

Poison Control Center
Mem. Medical Center
2606 Hospital Blvd.
Box 5280   78405

El Paso
915 544-1200

Poison Control Center
R.E. Thomason Gen.
  Hospital
4815 Alameda Ave.
79905

Fort Worth
817 336-5521
Ext. 17
Night:
336-5527

Poison Control Center
W.I. Cook Children's
  Hospital
1212 W. Lancaster Ave.
76102

Galveston
713 765-1420
or 2408

Poison Control Center
Univ. of Texas Med.
  Branch
8th & Mechanic Sts.
77550

Grand Prairie
214 264-1651

Poison Control Center
Mid-Cities Mem. Hosp.
2733 Sherman Rd.
75050

# Poison Control Centers

## TEXAS - Continued

**Harlingen**
512 423-1224
Ext. 23

Poison Control Center
Valley Baptist Hosp.
2101 S. Commerce
St. 78550

**Laredo**
512 722-2431
Ext. 29

Poison Control Center
Mercy Hospital
1515 Logan 78040

**Lubbock**
806 795-4321
Ext. 234

Poison Control Center
Methodist Hosp.
Pharmacy
3615 19th St.
79410

**Midland**
915 684-8257

Poison Control Center
Midland Mem. Hosp.
1908 W. Wall
79701

**Odessa**
915 337-7311
Ext. 250

Poison Control Center
Medical Center Hosp.
600 W. 4th St.
P.O. Box 633
79760

**Plainview**
806 296-9601

Poison Control Center
Plainview Hospital
2404 Yonkers St.
79072

**San Angelo**
915 653-6741
Ext. 210

Poison Control Center
Shannon West Texas
  Memorial Hospital
9 S. Magdalen St.
76901

**San Antonio**
512 223-1481

Poison Control Center
Bexar County Hosp.
  District
c/o Department of
  Pediatrics
Univ. of Texas Med.
  School
7703 Floyd Curl Dr.
78229

**Tyler**
214 594-9361
Ext. 255

East Texas Poison
  Control Center
Medical Center Hosp.
1100 S. Beckham St.
75701

**Waco**
817 753-1412
or 756-6111

McLennan County
  Poison Info. Center
Hillcrest Hospital
3000 Herring Ave.
76708

**Wharton**
713 532-2440
Night:
532-1440

Poison Control Center
Caney Valley Mem.
  Hospital
3007 N. Richmond Rd.
77488

**Wichita Falls**
817 322-6771

Poison Control Center
Wichita Gen. Hosp.
Emergency Room
1600 8th St.
76301

## UTAH

STATE
COORDINATOR
801 328-6191
or 6131

State Division of
  Health
Salt Lake City
84113

# Poison Control Centers

## UTAH - Continued

Salt Lake City
801 581-7503
Intermountain Region-
al Poison Control
Center
50 N. Medical Dr.
84112

## VIRGIN ISLANDS

STATE
COORDINATOR
809 774-1321
Ext. 275

Department of Health
St. Thomas   00801

St. Croix
809 773-1212
or 1311
Ext. 221

Poison Control Center
Charles Harwood Mem.
Hospital
Christiansted   00820

809 772-0260
or 0212

Poison Control Center
Ingeborg Nesbitt
Clinic
Fredericksted   00840

St. John
809 776-1469

Poison Control Center
Morris F. DeCastro
Clinic
Cruz Bay   00830

St. Thomas
809 774-1321
Ext. 266

Poison Control Center
Knud-Hansen Mem.
Hospital   00801

## VIRGINIA

STATE
COORDINATOR
804 770-4265

State Department of
Health
Richmond   23219

Alexandria
703 370-9000
Ext. 555

Poison Control Center
Alexandria Hospital
709 Duke St.   22314

Arlington
703 558-6161

Blacksburg
804 951-1111

Charlottesville
804 296-9888

Danville
804 799-2100
Ext. 3869

Falls Church
703 698-3600
or 3111

Hampton
804 722-1131

Harrisonburg
804 434-4421
Ext. 225

Lexington
804 463-9141

Poison Control Center
Arlington Hospital
5129 N. 16th St.
22205

Poison Control Center
Montgomery Cnty.
Commun. Hospital
Rt. 460, So.   24060

Poison Control Center
Univ. of Virginia
Hospital
Pediatric Clinic
22903

Poison Control Center
Danville Mem. Hosp.
142 S. Main St.
22201

Poison Control Center
Fairfax Hospital
3300 Gallows Rd.
22046

Poison Control Center
Hampton Gen. Hosp.
3120 Victoria Blvd.
23661

Poison Control Center
Rockingham Mem.
Hospital
738 S. Mason St.
22801

Poison Control Center
Stonewall Jackson
Hospital   22043

# Poison Control Centers

## VIRGINIA - Continued

Lynchburg
804 846-6511
Ext. 203

Poison Control Center
Lynchburg Gen.
  Marshall Lodge
  Hospital, Inc.
Tate Springs Rd.
24504

Nassawadox
804 442-8000

Poison Control Center
Northampton-Acco-
  mack Mem. Hosp.
23413

Norfolk
804 489-5111

Poison Control Center
DePaul Hospital
Granby St. at
  Kingsley La.
23505

Petersburg
804 732-7220
Ext. 327,
328

Poison Control Center
Petersburg Gen. Hosp.
Mt. Erin & Adams
  Sts.   23803

Portsmouth
804 397-6541
Ext. 418

Poison Control Center
U.S. Naval Hospital
23708

Richmond
804 770-5123

Poison Control Center
Medical College of
  Virginia Hospital
Pediatric OPD
Box 874, MCV Sta.
23298

Roanoke
703 981-7336

Poison Control Center
Roanoke Mem. Hosp.
Belleview & Lake
  Aves.   24014

Staunton
703 885-0361
Ext. 209,
247

Poison Control Center
King's Daughters' Hosp.
1410 N. Augusta St.
24401

Waynesboro
703 942-8355
Ext. 440,
500

Poison Control Center
Waynesboro Community
  Hospital
501 Oak Ave.
22980

Williamsburg
804 229-1120
Ext. 65

Poison Control Center
Williamsburg Commun.
  Hospital
Mt. Vernon Ave.,
Drawer H   23185

## WASHINGTON

STATE
COORDINATOR
206 743-3468

State Dept. of Social
  & Health Services
Olympia   98504

Aberdeen
206 533-0450
Ext. 277

Poison Control Center
St. Joseph's Hospital
1006 North H St.
98520

Bellingham
206 676-8400

Poison Control Center
St. Luke's Gen. Hosp.
809 E. Chestnut St.
98225

Longview
206 636-5252

Poison Control Center
St. John's Hospital
1614 E. Kessler
98632

Madigan
206 967-6972

Poison Control Center
Madigan Army Med.
  Center
Emergency Room
98431

# Poison Control Centers

## WASHINGTON - Continued

Olympia
206 491-0222

Poison Control Center
St. Peter's Hospital
413 No. Lilly Rd.
98501

Richland
206 943-1283

Poison Control Center
Kadlec Hospital
888 Swift Blvd.
99352

Seattle
206 634-5252

Poison Control Center
Children's Orthopedic
  Hosp. & Med. Ctr.
4800 Sandpoint Way,
  N.E.  98105

Spokane
509 747-1077

Poison Information
  Center
Deaconess Hospital
West 800 5th Ave.
99210

Tacoma
206 272-1281
Ext. 59

Poison Information
  Center
Mary Bridge Chil-
  dren's Hospital
311 So. L St.
98405

Vancouver
206 256-2064

Poison Control Center
St. Joseph Commun.
  Hospital
600 N.E. 92nd St.
98664

Yakima
206 248-4400

Poison Control Center
Yakima Valley Mem.
  Hospital
2811 Tieton Dr.
98902

## WEST VIRGINIA

STATE
COORDINATOR
304 348-2971

Beckley
304 252-6431
Ext. 10

Belle
304 949-4313
Ext. 261

Charleston
304 348-4211

Clarksburg
304 623-3444
Ext. 251

Huntington
304 696-6160

304 696-3760

Department of Health
Charleston  25305

Poison Control Center
Beckley Hospital
1007 S. Oakwood
  Ave.  25801

Poison Information
  Center
E.I. DuPont
  DeNemours & Co.
25015

Poison Control Center
Charleston Area Med.
  Center
Memorial Division
3200 Noyes Ave.
25304

Poison Control Center
United Hosp. Ctr.,
  Inc.
Downtown Division
Washington &
  Chestnut Sts.
26301

Poison Control Center
Cabell-Huntington
  Hospital
1340 16th St.  25701

Poison Control Center
St. Mary's Hospital
2900 1st Avenue
25701

# Poison Control Centers

## WEST VIRGINIA - Continued

Martinsburg
304 267-8981
Ext. 201,
216

Poison Control Center
Kings Dauthters Hosp.
25401

Morgantown
304 293-5341

Poison Control Center
West Virginia Univ.
Hospital  26505

Parkersburg
304 428-8011
Ext. 28,
130

Poison Control Center
Camden-Clark Hosp.
717 Ann St.  26101

304 422-8535
Ext. 251

Poison Control Center
St. Joseph's Hospital
19th St. & Murdoch
Ave.  26101

Pt. Pleasant
304 675-4340

Poison Control Center
Pleasant Valley Hosp.
Valley Drive  25550

Ronceverte
304 647-4411
4412, 4413
Ext. 33

Poison Control Center
Greenbrier Valley
    Hospital
608 Greenbrier Ave.
24970

Weirton
304 748-3232
Ext. 208

Poison Control Center
Weirton Gen. Hosp.
St. John's Rd.
26062

Weston
304 269-3000
Ext. 201,
228

Poison Control Center
Stonewall Jackson
    Hospital
507 Main Avenue
26452

Wheeling
304 233-4455
Ext. 224

Poison Control Center
Wheeling Hospital
109 Main St.  26003

## WISCONSIN

STATE
COORDINATOR
608 266-2611

Department of Health
    & Social Services
Madison  53701

Eau Claire
715 832-6611

Poison Control Center
Luther Hospital
310 Chestnut St.
54701

Green Bay
414 432-8621

Poison Information
    Center
St. Vincent Hospital
835 S. Van Buren St.
54305

Kenosha
414 656-2201

Poison Control Center
Kenosha Hospital
6308 8th Ave.
53140

Madison
608 262-3702

Poison Information
    Center
University Hospital
Dept. of Pharmacology
1300 University Ave.
53706

Milwaukee
414 344-7100

Poison Control Center
Milwaukee Children's
    Hospital
1700 W. Wisconsin
53233

# Poison Control Centers

## WYOMING

STATE
COORDINATOR
307 777-7511

Department of Public
  Health
Cheyenne 82001

Cheyenne
307 634-3341

Poison Control Center
Laramie County
  Memorial Hospital
23rd & House Sts.
82001

Casper
307 577-7201

Poison Control Center
Mem. Hosp. of
  Natrona Cnty.
1233 E. 2nd St.
82601

# Appendix D

# DIRECTORY OF BOOK PUBLISHERS

Abingdon Press
201 Eighth Avenue S.
Nashville, Tenn. 37202

Academic Therapy Publications
1539 Fourth Street
San Rafael, Calif. 94901

Ace Books
Division of Charter Communications
1120 Avenue of the Americas
New York, N.Y. 10036

Acropolis Books
2400 Seventeenth Street, N.W.
Washington, D.C. 20009

Aldine Publishing Co.
529 South Wabash Avenue
Chicago, Ill. 60605

Alfred Publishing Co.
75 Channel Drive
Pt. Washington, N.Y. 11050

Allyn & Bacon
470 Atlantic Avenue
Boston, Mass. 02210

American Academy of Pediatrics
1801 Hinmann Avenue
Evanston, Ill. 60204

American Bar Association
1155 East Sixtieth Street
Chicago, Ill. 60637

American Camping Association
Bradford Woods
Martinsville, Ind. 46151

American Foundation for the Blind
15 West Sixteenth Street
New York, N.Y. 10011

American Public Welfare Association
115 Sixteenth Street, N.W.
Washington, D.C. 20036

American Rehabilitation Foundation
123 East Grant Street
Minneapolis, Minn. 55403

Apollo Editions
666 Fifth Avenue
New York, N.Y. 10019

Appleton-Century-Crofts
    See: Prentice-Hall

Arbor House Publishing Co.
641 Lexington Avenue
New York, N.Y. 10021

# Publishers

Arco Publishing Co.
219 Park Avenue South
New York, N.Y. 10003

Arlington House
165 Huguenot Street
New Rochelle, N.Y. 10801

Arno Press
330 Madison Avenue
New York, N.Y. 10017

Jason Aronson
59 Fourth Avenue
New York, N.Y. 10003

Association for Childhood Education
 International
3615 Wisconsin Avenue, N.W.
Washington, D.C. 20016

Association Press
50 Rockefeller Plaza
New York, N.Y. 10020

Auerbach Publishers
 Orders to Mason and Lipscomb
 Publishers
384 Fifth Avenue
New York, N.Y. 10018

Avatar Press
P.O. Box 7727
Atlanta, Ga. 30309

Bantam Books
666 Fifth Avenue
New York, N.Y. 10019

A.S. Barnes & Co.
P.O. Box 421
Cranbury, N.J. 08512

Basic Books, Publishers
Ten East Fifty-third Street
New York, N.Y. 10022

Beacon Press
25 Beacon Street
Boston, Mass. 02108

Beck, Ernest W.
 Order through Simon & Schuster

Behavioral Publications
72 Fifth Avenue
New York, N.Y. 10011

Clark Boardman Co.
435 Hudson Street
New York, N.Y. 10014

Bobbs-Merrill Co.
4300 West Sixty-second Street
Indianapolis, Ind. 46206

Books for Better Living
Division of American Art Enterprises
21322 Lassen Street
Chatsworth, Calif. 91311

R.R. Bowker Co.
1180 Avenue of the Americas
New York, N.Y. 10036

Broadman Press
127 Nineth Avenue North
Nashville, Tenn. 37203

Brooks/Cole Publishing Co.
Subsidiary of Wadsworth Publishing Co.
540 Abrego Street
Monterey, Calif. 93940

Brunner/Mazel
64 University Place
New York, N.Y. 10003

R.E. Burdick
P.O. Box 52
Fair Lawn, N.J. 07410

Center for Science in the Public
 Interest
1779 Church Street, N.W.
Washington, D.C. 20036

Charterhouse Books
Affiliation of David McKay
750 Third Avenue
New York, N.Y. 10017

# Publishers

Children's Home Society of California
P.R. Department
3100 West Adams
Los Angeles, Calif. 90018

Child Study Press
50 Madison Avenue
New York, N.Y. 10010

Child Welfare League of America
67 Irving Place
New York, N.Y. 10003

Clarke School for the Deaf
Northampton, Me. 01060

Collier
    Order through Macmillan

Columbia University Press
562 West 113th Street
New York, N.Y. 10025

Colwell Press
500 South Seventh Street
Minneapolis, Minn. 55415

Committee for the Handicapped
1146 Sixteenth Street, N.W.
Washington, D.C. 20036

Cooley's Anemia Blood and
    Research Foundation for Children
3366 Hillside Avenue
New Hyde Park, N.Y. 11040

Cornell University Press
124 Roberts Place
Ithaca, N.Y. 14850

Council for Exceptional Children
1920 Association Drive
Reston, Va. 22091

Council on Family Health
Information Department
603 Third Avenue
New York, N.Y. 10017

Coward, McCann & Geoghegan
200 Madison Avenue
New York, N.Y. 10016

Cowles Book Co.
14 West Illinois Avenue
Chicago, Ill. 60610

CRM Books, Inc.
1104 Camino Del Mar
Del Mar, Calif. 92014

CRM Products
9263 Third Street
Beverly Hills, Calif. 90210

Betty Crocker Teaching Aids
9200 Film Center
Box 1113
Minneapolis, Minn. 55440

Croner Publications
211-03 Jamaica Avenue
Queens Village, N.Y. 11428

Thomas Y. Crowell Co.
666 Fifth Avenue
New York, N.Y. 10019

Crown Publishers
419 Park Avenue South
New York, N.Y. 10016

John Day Co.
666 Fifth Avenue
New York, N.Y. 10019

Delacorte Press
    Distributed by Dial Press
One Dag Hammarskjold Plaza
New York, N.Y. 10017

Dell Publishing Co.
One Dag Hammarskjold Plaza
New York, N.Y. 10017

T.S. Denison & Co.
5100 West Eighty-second Street
Minneapolis, Minn. 55437

# Publishers

Dial Press
One Dag Hammarskjold Plaza
245 East Forty-seventh Street
New York, N.Y. 10017

Dodd, Mead & Co.
79 Madison Avenue
New York, N.Y. 10016

Dorsey Press
Division of Richard D. Irwin
1818 Ridge Road
Homewood, Ill. 60430

Doubleday & Co.
501 Franklin Avenue
Garden City, N.Y. 11530

Drake Publishers
381 Park Avenue South
New York, N.Y. 10016

Duell, Sloan & Pearce
  Order through Meredith Corp.

E.P. Dutton & Co.
201 Park Avenue South
New York, N.Y. 10033

Educational Media Services
290 Herald R. Clark Building
Provo, Ut. 84601

Effectiveness Training Associates
110 South Euclid Avenue
Pasadena, Calif. 91101

M. Evans & Co.
216 East Forty-ninth Street
New York, N.Y. 10017

Eyre Methuen
11 Newfetter Lane
London, England

The Exchange
311 Cedar Avenue South
Minneapolis, Minn. 55404

Exposition Press
900 South Oyster Bay Road
Hicksville, N.Y. 11801

Family Forum
1539 North Courtney Avenue
Los Angeles, Calif. 90046

Fearon Publishers
c/o Lear Siegler
Six David Drive
Belmont, Calif. 94002

Frederick Fell, Publishers
386 Park Avenue, South
New York, N.Y. 10016

Free Press
  Distributed by Macmillan
866 Third Avenue
New York, N.Y. 10022

Funk & Wagnalls Publishing Co.
  Distributed by T.Y. Crowell
666 Fifth Avenue
New York, N.Y. 10019

Gambit
306 Dartmouth Street
Boston, Mass. 02107

General Learning Corp.
250 James Street
Morristown, N.J.

Gordon & Breach, Science Publishers
One Park Avenue
New York, N.Y. 10016

Graded Press
201 Eighth Avenue South
Nashville, Tenn. 37203

Stephen Greene Press
Box 1000
Brattleboro, Vt. 05301

Greenwood Press
51 Riverside Avenue
Westport, Conn. 06880

# Publishers

Grolier Educational Corp.
845 Third Avenue
New York, N.Y. 10022

Grosset & Dunlap
51 Madison Avenue
New York, N.Y. 10010

Grossman Publishers
625 Madison Avenue
New York, N.Y. 10022

Grune & Stratton
111 Fifth Avenue
New York, N.Y. 10003

Guidance Association
41 Washington Avenue
Pleasantville, N.Y. 10570

Harcourt Brace Jovanovich
757 Third Avenue
New York, N.Y. 10017

Harper & Row Publishers
Ten East Fifty-third Street
New York, N.Y. 10002

Harper's Magazine Press
Two Park Avenue
New York, N.Y. 10016

Hart-Davis, MacGibbon
Park Street, Frogmore
St. Albans, Hertfordshire
Al 2 2 NF   England

Harvard Educational Review
Longfellow Hall
13 Appian Way
Cambridge, Mass. 02138

Harvard University Press
79 Garden Street
Cambridge, Mass. 02138

Hawthorn Books
260 Madison Avenue
New York, N.Y. 10016

Health Sciences Publishing Corp.
451 Greenwich Street
New York, N.Y. 10013

D.C. Heath & Co.
125 Spring Street
Lexington, Mass. 02173

Herald Press
616 Walnut Avenue
Scottdale, Pa. 15683

Hiltz Publishing Co.
6304 Hamilton Avenue
Cincinnati, Oh. 45224

Holt, Rinehart and Winston
383 Madison Avenue
New York, N.Y. 10017

Houghton Mifflin Co.
One Beacon Street
Boston, Mass. 02107
     or
551 Fifth Avenue
New York, N.Y. 10017

Human Policy Press
P.O. Box 127
University Station
Syracuse, N.Y. 13210

Image Publishing Corp.
P.O. Box 14 North Station
White Plains, N.Y.

Intercontinental Medical Book Corp.
381 Park Avenue South
New York, N.Y. 10016

International Association of
   Counseling Services
1608 New Hampshire Avenue, N.W.
Washington, D.C. 20009

International Childbirth Education
   Association
P.O. Box 5852
Milwaukee, Wis. 53220

# Publishers

Interstate Printers & Publishers
19 North Jackson Street
Danville, Ill. 61832

Intext Educational Publishers
257 Park Avenue South
New York, N.Y. 10010

Johnny Reads
P.O. Box 12834
St. Petersburg, Fla. 33733

Johnson & Johnson Baby Products Co.
Consumer & Professional Services
New Brunswick, N.J. 08903

Jossey-Bass, Publishers
615 Montgomery Street
San Francisco, Calif. 94111

Judson Press
Valley Forge, Pa. 19481

Walter J. Klein Co.
Distribution Director
Charlotte, N.C. 28211

Alfred A. Knopf
    Order through Random House

Know The Truth
St. Anthony Retreat Center
Marathon, Wis. 54448

Lancer Books
1560 Broadway
New York, N.Y. 10036

J.B. Lippincott Co.
East Washington Square
Philadelphia, Pa. 19105

Little, Brown and Co.
34 Beacon Street
Boston, Mass. 02106

Liveright Publishing Corp.
500 Fifth Avenue
New York, N.Y. 10036

McGraw-Hill Book Co.
1221 Avenue of the Americas
New York, N.Y. 10036

David McKay Co.
750 Third Avenue
New York, N.Y. 10017

Macmillan
866 Third Avenue
New York, N.Y. 10022

Medcom Press
Two Hammerskjold Plaza
New York, N.Y. 10017

Media Medica, Inc.
555 Fifth Avenue
New York, N.Y. 10017

Meredith Corp.
Consumer Book Division
1716 Locust Street
Des Moines, Iowa 50336

Methuen and Co.
11 New Fetterlane
London, England
(Agent in U.S. is Harper)

Metropolitan Applied Research Center
60 East Eighty-sixth Street
New York, N.Y. 10028

Model Cities/CCVO
640 North La Salle
Chicago, Ill. 60610

Moore Publishing Co.
P.O. Box 3143
West Durham Station
Durham, N.C. 27705

William Morrow & Co.
105 Madison Avenue
New York, N.Y. 10016

Museum of Modern Art
    Distributed by New York
    Graphic Society

# Publishers

Nash Publishing Corp.
Distributed by E.P. Dutton Co.
201 Park Avenue
New York, N.Y. 10003

National Association of Coordinators of State Programs for the Mentally Retarded
2001 Jefferson Davis Highway
Arlington, Va. 22202

National Committee for Citizen Education
Wilde Lake Village Green
Columbia, Md. 21044

National Coordinating Council on Drug Abuse Education and Information
Suite 212, 1211 Connecticut Avenue, N.W.
Washington, D.C. 20036

National Council of Family Relations
1219 University Avenue, S.E.
Minneapolis, Minn. 55414

National Council of Jewish Women
One West Forty-seventh Street
New York, N.Y. 10036

National Council on Crime & Delinquency
411 Hackensack Avenue
Hackensack, N.J. 07601

National Easter Seal Society for Crippled Children & Adults
2023 West Ogden Avenue
Chicago, Ill. 60612

National Educational Consultants
5604 Rhode Island Avenue
Hyattsville, Md. 20781

National Education Association Publishing
1201 Sixteenth Street, N.W.
Washington, D.C. 20036

National Foundation-March of Dimes
Division of Public Education
Box 2000
White Plains, N.Y. 10602

National Society for the Prevention of Blindness
79 Madison Avenue
New York, N.Y. 10016

Nelson-Hall Co.
325 West Jackson Blvd.
Chicago, Ill. 60606

New American Library
1301 Avenue of the Americas
New York, N.Y. 10019

New York Graphic Society
11 Beacon Street
Boston, Mass. 02108

New York University School of Law
33 Washington Square West
New York, N.Y. 10011

New Zealand Embassy
19 Observatory Circle, N.W.
Washington, D.C. 20008

W.W. Norton
500 Fifth Avenue
New York, N.Y. 10036

Nutrition Foundation
888 Seventeenth Street, N.W.
Washington, D.C. 20006

Olympus Publishing Co.
Five Olympus Plaza
1670 East Thirteenth Street South
Salt Lake City, Ut. 84105

Pacific Books
Box 588
Palo Alto, Calif. 94302

Pantheon Books
Order through Random House

# Publishers

Parents' Magazine Press
52 Vanderbilt Avenue
New York, N.Y. 10017

Pavilion Publishing Co.
520 East 77th Street
New York, N.Y. 10021

George Peabody, College for Teachers
Nashville, Tenn. 37203

F.E. Peacock Co.
401 West Irving Park Road
Itasca, Ill. 60143

Penguin Books
7110 Ambassador Road
Baltimore, Md. 21207

Pergamon Press
Maxwell House
Fairview Park
Elmsford, N.Y. 10003

Pflaum/Standard
2285 Arbor Boulevard
Dayton, Oh. 45439

Pilgrim Book Press
c/o United Church Press
1505 Race Street
Philadelphia, Pa. 19102

Planned Parenthood Center of Seattle
202 Sixteenth Avenue, South
Seattle, Wash. 98144

Plays
Eight Arlington Street
Boston, Mass. 02116

Pocket Books
Division of Simon & Schuster
630 Fifth Avenue
New York, N.Y. 10020

Popular Science Publishing Co.,
355 Lexington Avenue
New York, N.Y. 10017

Praeger Publishers
111 Fourth Avenue
New York, N.Y. 10003

Prentice-Hall
Englewood Cliffs, N.J. 07632

Psychohistory Press
2315 Broadway
New York, N.Y. 10024

G.P. Putnam's Sons
200 Madison Avenue
New York, N.Y. 10016

Random House
201 East Fiftieth Street
New York, N.Y. 10022

Reader's Digest Press
201 Park Avenue
New York, N.Y. 10003

Readers Press
Box 131
Syracuse, N.Y.

Henry Regnery Co.
114 West Illinois Street
Chicago, Ill. 60610

Research Press
Box 3177
Country Fair Station
Champaign, Ill. 61820

Routledge & Kegan Paul
Nine Park Street
Boston, Mass. 02108

Russell Sage Foundation
230 Park Avenue
New York, N.Y. 10017

St. Martin's Press
175 Fifth Avenue
New York, N.Y. 10010

# Publishers

Porter Sargent
11 Beacon Street
Boston, Mass.  02108

W.B. Saunders Co.
218 West Washington Square
Philadelphia, Pa.  19105

Scarecrow Press
52 Liberty Street
Box 656
Metuchen, N.J.  08840

Schocken Books
200 Madison Avenue
New York, N.Y.  10016

Science & Behavior Books
P.O. Box 11457
Palo Alto, Calif.  94306

Science House
 See: Aronson, Jason

Science Research Associates
Subsidiary of I.B.M.
1540 Page Hill Road
Palo Alto, Calif.  94304

Scott, Foresman and Co.
1900 East Lake Avenue
Glenview, Ill.

Charles Scribner's Sons
597 Fifth Avenue
New York, N.Y.  10020

Sheed & Ward
475 Fifth Avenue
New York, N.Y.  10017

Simon & Schuster
630 Fifth Avenue
New York, N.Y.  10020

Singer/SVE
1345 Diversey Parkway
Chicago, Ill.  60614

Stein & Day Publishers
7 East Forty-eighth Street
New York, N.Y.  10017

Stratton Intercontinental Medical
 Book Corp.
381 Park Avenue South
New York, N.Y.  10016

Lyle Stuart
120 Enterprise Avenue
Secaucus, N.J.  07094

Stuart Finley
Falls Church, Va.  22041

Sutherland Learning Associates
8425 West Third Street
Los Angeles, Calif.  90048

Syracuse University Press
1011 East Water Street
Syracuse, N.Y.  13210

Taplinger Publishing Co.
200 Park Avenue South
New York, N.Y.  10003

Teachers College Press
Columbia University
1234 Amsterdam Avenue
New York, N.Y.  10027

Temple University Press
Philadelphia, Pa.  19122

Third Press
444 Central Park West
New York, N.Y.  10025

Charles C. Thomas, Publisher
301-27 East Lawrence Avenue
Springfield, Ill.  62717

Transaction Books
 Distributed by Dutton

Trident Press
 Division of Simon & Schuster

# Publishers

Tyndale House Publishers
336 Gundersen Drive
Wheaton, Ill. 60187

United Cerebral Palsy Association
66 East Thirty-fourth Street
New York, N.Y. 10016

U.S. News and World Report
 Distributed by Simon & Schuster

Universe Books
381 Park Avenue South
New York, N.Y. 10016

University of Chicago Press
5801 Ellis Avenue
Chicago, Ill. 60657

University of Michigan Press
615 East University
Ann Arbor, Mich. 48106

University of North Carolina Press
Chapel Hill, N.C. 27514

University of Pittsburgh Press
127 North Bellefield Avenue
Pittsburgh, Pa. 15213

University of Toronto Press
33 East Tupper Street
Buffalo, N.Y. 14208

University of Wisconsin Press
Extension Publications
432 North Lake Street
Madison, Wis. 53715

Vertex Books
1101 State Rd.
Princeton, N.J. 08540

Viking Press
625 Madison Avenue
New York, N.Y. 10022

Walker & Co.
720 Fifth Avenue
New York, N.Y. 10019

Warner Paperback Library
75 Rockefeller Plaza
New York, N.Y. 10019

Western Publishing Co.
850 Third Avenue
New York, N.Y. 10022

Western Psychological Services
12031 Wilshire
Los Angeles, Calif. 90025

John Wiley & Sons
605 Third Avenue
New York, N.Y. 10016

Women on Words & Images (Society)
P.O. Box 2163
Princeton, N.J. 08540

Word Books
4800 West Waco Drive
Waco, Tex. 76703

Workman Publishing Co.
231 East Fifty-first Street
New York, N.Y. 10022

World Publications
P.O. Box 366
Mountain View, Calif. 94040

Peter H. Wyden/Publisher
 Distributed by David McKay

Yale University Press
92A Yale Station
New Haven, Conn. 06520

Zondervan Corp.
1415 Lake Drive, S.E.
Grand Rapids, Mich. 49506

# AUTHOR INDEX

This index includes authors, editors, compilers, and those who have contributed introductions or forewords to works cited in the text. Alphabetization is letter by letter.

## A

Aas, Kjell  163
Abbott, John Stevens Cabot  209
Abrahamsen, David, M.D.  30
Abramson, Seth F., M.D.  231
Abt, Lawrence E.  76
Adler, Manfred  32
Adler, Sidney J., M.D.  183
Akmakjian, Haig  43
Albrecht, Margaret  2, 257
Allison, Junius L.  66
Alton, Walter George  224
Ambrosino, Lillian  2
American Association for Gifted Children  151
American Foundation for the Blind  131
American National Red Cross  231
Ames, Louise Bates  32, 51, 75, 189, 200, 210
Ames, Winthrop  211
Anderson, David C.  12
Anderson, Wayne J.  241
Andrews, Matthew  83
Ansfield, Joseph G., M.D.  12
Anthony, E. James, M.D.  211
Anthony, Sylvia  76
Apgar, Virginia, M.D.  102-3
Arbuthnot, May Hill  188
Archuleta, Alyce J.  185
Archuleta, Michael J.  185
Arnold, Arnold  190, 212, 223, 224
Arnstein, Helene S.  2, 75, 241
Asher, Alfred E., M.D.  167
Association for Childhood Education  83
Association for Childhood Education International  137
Association for Children with Learning Disabilities  199
Axford, Lavonne B.  152
Axline, Virginia M.  95
Ayrault, Evelyn West  101, 103, 109
Azrin, Nathan H., M.D.  43, 122

## B

Backer, Augusta  56
Baird, Henry W., M.D.  156
Bakan, David  23
Baker, Samm Sinclair  137
Baldwin, Victor L.  121
Bannatyne, Alexander  19
Bannatyne, Maryl  19
Barnes, Donald E.  84
Baruch, Dorothy  79
Bass, Ralph  232
Bauer, Florence M.  248
Bauer, W.W.  248
Bax, Martin  43

# Author Index

Beadle, Muriel 190
Beck, Helen 190
Beck, Joan 102, 190
Becker, Wesley C. 19
Beitler, Ken 2
Beltz, Stephen E. 19
Benedek, Therese, M.D. 211
Bengtsson, Arvid 224
Benjamin, Annette Francis 231
Benjamin, Bry 231
Benning, Lee Edwards 212
Berends, Polly Berrien 212
Bergman, Abraham B., M.D. 179
Berman, Claire 12
Bernal, Judy 43
Bernard, Jessie 212
Bernhardt, David K. 212
Bernhardt, Karl S. 212
Bettelheim, Bruno 113, 209
Bierbauer, Elaine 200
Biklen, Douglas 103
Biller, Henry B. 59
Bird, Joseph 212
Bird, Lewis 241
Bird, Lois 212
Blaine, Graham B. 2
Bland, Jane C. 187
Bleiberg, Aaron H. 156
Block, William A. 242
Blodgett, Harriet E. 121
Blum, Jeffrey D. 3
Blum, Richard H. 84
Blumenfield, Samuel L. 190
Bock, Richard 3
Boston Children's Medical Center 43, 155
Botwin, Carol 242
Braga, Joseph L. 190
Braga, Laurie D. 190
Brazelton, T. Berry, M.D. 42, 43
Breitbart, Vicki 69
Bremner, Robert H. 31
Brenner, Erma 44
Brenner, Joseph, M.D. 84
Bricklin, Barry 212
Bricklin, Patricia M. 212
Briggs, Dorothy Corkille 32
Broad, Laura Peabody 224
Broadribb, Violet 155
Bronfenbrenner, Urie 213

Browder, Sue 211
Brown, Daniel G. 21
Brown, Diana L. 103
Brown, Thomas E. 246
Browning, Elizabeth 200
Brutten, Milton 200
Buchanan, William 30
Bucker, Beatrice 122
Buhler, Charlotte M. 29
Burch, Claire 95
Burgess, Carol 191
Burnett, Dorothy 42
Butterworth, Nancy Tower 224

## C

Cable, Mary 33
Calderone, Mary 241
Callahan, Sidney Cornelia 213, 257
Cameron, Constance Carpenter 200
Caney, Steven 224
Caplan, Frank 45, 225
Caplan, Theresa 225
Carmichael, Ann 193
Carver, John N. 122
Carver, Nellie Enders 122
Cass, James 199
Cass, Joan E. 225
Castle, Sue 137
Cattell, Psyche 44
Cava, Esther Laden 33
Chapman, Arthur Harry, M.D. 225
Chase, Joan Ames 189
Chase, Naomi F. 23
Cheavens, Sam Frank 213
Chess, Stella, M.D. 42
Child, Lydia Maria 29
Child Study Association of America 84, 241, 242
Child Study Press 188
Child Welfare League of America 69
Chisholm, Shirley 70
Choate, Judith 179
Church, Joseph 31, 44
Clarke, Louise [pseud.] 200
Clarke-Stewart, Alison 70
Clinebell, Charlotte H. 96
Clinebell, Howard J. 96
Cody, D. 156

# Author Index

Cohen, Donald J., M.D. 72
Cohen, Dorothy H. 191
Cole, Larry 62
Colton, Helen 242
Comer, James P., M.D. 55
Community Council of Greater New York 156
Conference on Human Sexuality and the Mentally Retarded 242
Cooney, Joan Ganz 253
Corsini, Raymond J. 79
Cotton, Dorothy W. 257
Court, John M., M.D. 167
Cowle, Lucile 249
Craig, Helen B. 132
Craig, Marjorie 250
Craig, William N. 132
Croner, Helga B. 11
Cruickshank, William M. 199
Curtis, Jean 188
Cutts, Norma E. 151

# D

D'Ambrosio, Richard Anthony 23
Daniels, Ada 242
Davis, Adelle 138
Davis, Samuel M. 63
Dawson, Rosemary B. 157
Day, Beth 43, 96
Day Care and Child Development Council of America 69
Deakin, Michael 213
DeCamp, Catherine Crook 79
Dechter, Midge 213
De Courcy, Judith 23
De Courcy, Peter 23
Delacato, Carl H. 113
Della-Piana, Gabriel 33
Demarest, Robert 241
de Mause, Lloyd 33
Denzin, Norman K. 63
De Rosis, Helen, M.D. 213
de Schweinitz, Karl 242
Despert, J. Louise, M.D. 75, 96
Dewey, Evelyn 41
Dewey, Margaret A. 115
Dick, Grace 244
Dienes, Zoltan 192
DiLeo, Joseph H., M.D. 191

Divoky, Diane 184
Dobson, James C., Jr. 80
Dodson, Fitzhugh 213
Doman, Glenn 103, 192
Douglas, William 214
Dreikurs, Rudolf, M.D. 79, 80
Dryer, Bernard V., M.D. 94
Duberman, Lucille 214
Dwyasuk, Colette T. 12, 14

# E

Easson, William M., M.D. 76
Edelson, Edna 132
Eden, Alvin N., M.D. 138
Eiger, Marvin S., M.D. 139
Elbert, Edmund J. 3
Elkind, David 35, 51
Ellingson, Careth 199, 201
Engelmann, Siegfried 187
Engelmann, Therese 187
English, Abigail 3
Evans, E. Belle 69, 70

# F

Faber, Adele 214
Fahs, Sophia L. 30
Fales, Edward D., Jr. 231
Fanshel, David 12
Farson, Richard 63
Fein, Greta G. 70
Feinbloom, Richard I., M.D. 155
Feingold, Ben F., M.D. 183
Felker, Evelyn H. 13
Ferguson, Lucy Rau 33
Festinger, Trudy Bradley 13
Finch, Stuart McIntyre 3
Finnie, Nancie R. 117
Fleischhauer-Hardt, Helga 243
Fletcher, Grace Nies 214
Folks, Homer 11
Fomon, Samuel J., M.D. 143
Fontana, Vincent James, M.D. 23-24, 232
Foster, Henry H. 63
Foundation for Child Development 70
Foxx, Richard M., M.D. 43, 122
Fraiberg, Selma H. 42, 132

# Author Index

Frazier, Claude A., M.D.   163
Freeman, Lucy   217
Freeman, Stephen W.   201

## G

Gaddis, Margaret   207
Gaddis, Vincent H.   207
Gannon, Frank   84
Gardner, George E., M.D.   33
Gardner, Richard A., M.D.   51, 76, 201
Gehman, Betsy Hollard   207
Geist, Harold   155
Gersh, Marvin J., M.D.   3
Gersoni-Stavn, Diane   59
Gesell, Arnold   1, 29, 42, 44, 51
Gil, David G.   24
Gilbert, Sara D.   44
Ginott, Haim G.   2, 191, 209, 215
Ginsburg, Herbert   187
Gleasure, Eira   250
Glick, Joyce   218
Glover, Leland   42, 51
Gold, Don   3
Goldenson, Robert M.   223
Goldhill, Paul M.   84
Goldstein, Joseph   13
Goodwin, M.D.   138
Gordon, Ira J.   225
Gordon, Judith   243
Gordon, Michael Lewis   122
Gordon, Sol   243
Gordon, Thomas   80, 157, 215, 221
Gorham, Kathryn A.   125
Gottlieb, David   63
Gowan, John C.   152
Grams, Armin   243
Grant, Wilson W., M.D.   243
Green, Stephanie   215
Greenfield, Josh   113
Gregg, Elizabeth M.   224
Grey, Loren   80-81
Griffin, Al   70
Grollman, Earl A.   75, 76
Grossman, Frances Kaplan   114
Group for the Advancement of Psychiatry. Committee on Public Education   215
Grover, John W., M.D.   244

Grow, Lucille J.   13
Gruenberg, Sidonie M.   31, 209, 244
Gunther, Mavis, M.D.   138

## H

Hainstock, Elizabeth G.   192
Hall, Granville Stanley   1
Halporn, Roberta   76
Hamilton, Russel   215
Hardgrove, Carol B.   157
Harris, Grace M.   131
Harrison-Ross, Phyllis, M.D.   55
Hart, Hastings H.   61
Hart, Verna   103
Hartley, Ruth E.   223
Harvard Educational Review   64
Hatfield, Antoinette K.   138
Heilman, Joan Rattner   138
Hein, Lucille E.   225
Heisler, Verda   104
Helfer, Ray E.   24, 27
Hemsing, Esther D.   188
Hergenhahn, Baldwin Ross   19
Hesburgh, Rev. Theodore   85
Hewett, Sheila   117
Higgins, Jean C.   122
Hill, Margaret   5
Hogan, Louise E.   29
Hoggman, Ruth B.   104
Hogsett, Stanley G.   108
Holt, Emmett Luther   30
Holt, John Caldwell   64
Holt, Michael   192
Homan, Walter Joseph   79
Homan, William E., M.D.   33-34
Hoover, Mary B.   96, 215, 242
Hopper, Robert   34
Horkheimer, Foley A.   156
Horrobin, J. Margaret   119
Horstmann, Dorothea L.   167
Hudson, Ian, M.D.   157
Hughes, Felicity   192
Hundley, Joan M.   114
Hunter, Marvin H.   122
Hymes, James   43

# Author Index

## I

Ilg, Frances L. 51, 210
Inglis, Ruth Langdon 192
Institute of Judicial Administration 62
International Association of Counseling Services 211
Irwin, Theodore 25
Isaacs, Susan Sutherland 30, 34, 41
Ives, Suzy 226

## J

Jackson, Edgar N. 76
James, Howard 64
Jenkins, Shirley 13
Jensen, Gordon D., M.D. 244
Johnson, F. Leonard, M.D. 177
Johnson, Joseph C. II 192
Joint Commission on Mental Health of Children 96
Jones, Eve 30
Josselyn, Irene M., M.D. 4

## K

Kadushin, Alfred 13-14
Kalt, Bruson R. 232
Kamenetz, Herman L., M.D. 104
Kappelman, Murray 34
Karelitz, Samuel, M.D. 155
Karnes, Merle B. 104
Karraker, David 12
Katz, Sanford N. 61, 64
Kaye, Evelyn 253
Kaye, Marvin 226
Keister, Mary Elizabeth 73
Kempe, C. Henry 24, 27
Kempton, Winifred 246
Kenda, Margaret E. 138
Key, Ellen 61
Keyserling, Mary Dublin 70
Kinkmeyer, Don C. 215
Kirk, Samuel A. 121
Kirkland, Marjorie H. 126
Kiman, Brian H., M.D. 122
Kittman, Laura L. 125
Klein, Carole 215
Klibanoff, Elton 14
Klibanoff, Susan 14
Klinger, Judith L. 101
Knitzer, Jane 70
Koch, Kathryn J. 123
Koch, Richard, M.D. 123
Koontz, Charles W. 192
Kopp, Thusnelda 123
Kraft, Arthur 226
Kramer, Rita 210
Kraskin, Robert A. 171
Krogman, W.M. 34
Kronick, Doreen 201
Krumboltz, Helen B. 19
Krumboltz, John D. 19
Kujoth, Jean Spealman 192

## L

La Crosse, E. Robert, Jr., M.D. 72, 189
Lagos, Jorge C., M.D. 169
Land, Herman W. 83
Landreth, Catherine 193
Lane, Carolyn 138
Lane, Joan T. 189
Lane, Mary B. 215
Langer, John H. 87
Larrick, Nancy 189
Larter, Vera 139
Leach, Barry 87
Learning Technology Incorporated 244
Leavitt, Jerome E. 24
Lee, Henry F., M.D. 155
Lee, Ray S. 31
Lehman, Edna 244
Lemasters, E.E. 216
Lentz, Gloria 244
Lerrigo, Marion O. 101
Le Shan, Eda J. 210, 216
Lesowitz, Robert I. 34
Lesser, Gerald S. 253
Leubling, Harry E. 156
Levine, Milton I., M.D. 31, 60, 139
Levison, Teddi 257
Levy, Harold, M.D. 201
Levy, Janine, M.D. 250
Lieberman, Florence 84
Liebert, Robert M. 253

# Author Index

Liepmann, Lise 193
Liley, Helen Margaret Irwin, M.D. 43
Lind, Mariam Sieber 123
Linde, Shirley Motter 147
Linde, Thomas F. 123
Lin-Fu, Jane S., M.D. 234
Litt, Iris F., M.D. 3
Lloyd, Janice 226
Lobley, Priscilla 226
Lottick, Sarah T. 227
Lou, Herbert H. 61
Louria, Donald Bruce, M.D. 85
Love, Harold D. 85, 96, 104, 123
Lowenfeld, Berthold 131
Lowman, Edward, M.D. 101
Lowndes, Marion 45, 216
Lundell, Margaretta 226

## M

McBride, Angela Barron 257
McBride, Will 243
McIntire, Roger W. 20
McKay, Gary D. 215
McKeown, Joe, D.D.S. 171
McKeown, Pamela 193
McLaren, Esme 226
MacLeod, Anne 87
McNamara, Joan 14
McVey, Helen 184
Madsen, Charles H., Jr. 20, 81
Madsen, Clifford K. 20, 81
Mannoni, Maud 123
Margolin, Jeannette, M.D. 245
Marin, Peter 85
Markun, Patricia M. 189
Marshall, Justice Thurgood 55
Marzollo, Jean 226
Mather, June 125
Matterson, Elizabeth M. 223, 227
Mayer, Greta 96
Mayer, Shirley 159
Mayle, Peter 244
Maynard, Fredelle 227
Mazlish, Elaine 214
Mead, Margaret 101, 140
Melody, William H. 254
Melton, David 104
Meredith, Judith C. 14

Meyer, Roger E., M.D. 85
Michaels, Ruth 11
Miller, Marc 177
Minton, Lynn 4
Moak, Helen R. 95
Moffat, Samuel 133
Mogal, Doris P. 52
Moore, Dewey J. 20, 81
Morris, Melinda 139
Morris, Norman S. 254
Moseley, Nicholas 151
Moustakas, Clark E. 216
Murray, Anne-Marie 14

## N

Napear, Peggy 117
Naremore, Rita C. 34
National Association of Coordinators of State Programs for the Mentally Retarded 123
National Coordinating Council on Drug Abuse Education and Information 83
National Council on Crime and Delinquency 64
National Easter Seal Society for Crippled Children and Adults, The 102
National Society for Autistic Children 97
Needleman, Jacob 4
Neisser, Edith G. 45
Neumann, Hans H., M.D. 244
Newman, Virginia 249
Newton, Niles 210
Nichtern, Sol, M.D. 124
Noble, June 77
Noble, William 77
Nordoff, Paul 104
Norman, Elaine 13
Norman, Sherwood 64
Nutrition Foundation 137

## O

Oden, Melita H. 151
Olds, Sally W. 139, 184
Olshaker, Bennett, M.D. 216
Opper, Sylvia 187

# Author Index

Oremland, Evelyn K. 157
Oremland, Jerome 157

## P

Painter, Genevieve, M.D. 79, 193
Palmer, Bruce 139
Parents' Nursery School 139
Parker, Ronald K. 70
Peairs, Lillian 34
Peairs, Richard 34
Pearlman, Ruth 139
Perry, Cereta 216
Perske, Robert 124
Phillips, Lakin E. 20
Pilling, Doria 129
Polier, Justine Wise 61, 63
Pollen, G. 138
Pomeranz, Virginia E., M.D. 45
Pomeroy, Wardell B., M.D. 245
Porcher, Mary Ann 224
Porter, Judith D.R. 55
Post, Elizabeth 35
Poussaint, Alvin F., M.D. 55
Poznanski, Elva O. 3
Preston, Harry 245
Princeton Center for Infancy and Early Childhood 45
Prudden, Bonnie 250
Prudden, Suzy 250
Pryor, Karen 140
Pulaski, Mary Ann Spencer 193

## R

Radl, Shirley L. 216
Rafferty, Max 152
Ramah [pseud.] 117
Raphael, Dana 140
Rapp, Doris J. 163
Raymond, Louise 14
Redl, Fritz 52
Reed, Elizabeth L. 77
Reistroffer, Mary 184, 185
Renshaw, Domeena C., M.D. 184
Rice, Joseph P. 152
Richards, Louise G. 87
Richardson, Sylvia O. 203
Richmond, Peter Graham 35
Riis, Jacob A. 62

Rimland, Bernard 113
Rioux, J. William 65
Rivera, Geraldo 124
Robertson, Elizabeth Chant 45
Robins, Arthur 244
Robins, Clive 104
Robinson, Halbert B. 35
Roby, Pamela 70
Rodway, Pamela 140
Rondell, Florence 11, 14
Rosenthal, Mitchell S. 85
Roskies, Ethel 105
Rosner, Jerome 202
Rothstein, Jerome 124
Rowan, Robert L., M.D. 35
Rowland, Peter 77
Ruggieri, Bartholomew A., M.D. 81
Ruina, Edith 77
Rule, Lareina 210
Rutherford, Frederick W. 45
Rydell, Wendy 85
Rynders, John E. 119

## S

Saia, George E. 70
Salk, Lee, M.D. 31, 46, 210, 217
Sanderlin, Owenita 152
Sandow, Stuart A. 65
Satir, Virginia 217
Saville, F. 140
Scargall, Jeanne 227
Scheinfeld, Amram 207
Schepp, Steven 85
Schiff, Jacqui Lee 96
Schleichkorn, Jacob S. 109
Schlesinger, Benjamin 211
Schorr, Alvin L. 65
Schrag, Peter 184
Schultz, Dodi 45, 231
Schwartz, Felice 258
Schwarz, Berthold Eric, M.D. 81
Sciarra, John J., M.D. 241
Scott, Edward M. 85
Self, William L. 4
Seligmann, Jean H. 31, 60, 139
Selzer, Joae Graham, M.D. 245
Semple, Jean E. 131
Shapiro, Deborah 13
Sharp, Evelyn 223

# Author Index

Shaw, Charles, M.D.  96
Shedd, Charlie  217
Sheehy, Emma D.  187
Sheen, Fulton J.  81
Shiller, Jack G., M.D.  157
Siegel, Ernest  105, 202
Silverstein, Mickie  257
Sime, Mary  35
Simmons, Sylvia  244
Simon, Anne W.  210
Skelsey, Alice  258
Smith, A.M. Sheridan  123
Smith, Bert K.  97
Smith, David W.  119
Smith, Judith E.  3
Smith, Lendon H., M.D.  32
Smuts, Robert W.  258
Soltz, Vicki  79
Soman, Shirley Camper  65
Somekh, Emile, M.D.  163-64
Sorenson, Andrew A.  86
Sorenson, Robert C.  4
Sparkman, Brandon  193
Spock, Benjamin, M.D.  31, 101, 210, 217-18
Staff of the Boston Children's Medical Center  224
Stanton, Peggy  138
Stein, Sara Bonnett  105
Stein, Susan M.  227
Steinfels, Margaret O'Brien  71
Steinmetz, Suzanne K.  24
Stevens, Anita  217
Stewart, Mark Armstrong, M.D.  184
Stillman, Irwin Maxwell, M.D.  137
Stoenner, Herb  25
Stone, Lawrence Joseph  31
Stone, Margaret N.  184
Stott, Denis Herbert  202
Strang, Ruth  188
Straus, Murray A.  24
Strauss, Susan  114
Strouse, Jean  65
Stuart, Irving  76
Sugarman, Gerald I., M.D.  184
Surgeon General's Scientific Advisory Committee on Television and Social Behavior  254
Sussman, Jeffrey  250
Sutherland, Zena  188, 189

Sutton-Smith, Brian  227
Sutton-Smith, Shirley  227
Swartz, Edward M.  232
Swinyard, Chester A., M.D.  129

T

Terman, Lewis M.  151
Terry, Keith C.  183
Thane, R., M.D.  156
Thomas, Linda L.  140
Thomson, Helen  211
Thurston, Henry W.  11
Timmermans, Claire  250
Tinker, Miles A.  194
Torrance, E. Paul  152
Tough, Joan  52
Travers, Milton  86
Turner, James S.  140
Turner, Mary Dustan  140
Tustin, Frances  114
Tyler, Mabs  227

U

Ulrich, Sharon  132
U.S. News and World Report Books  79
U.S. President's Science Advisory Committee. Panel on Youth  4

V

Vanderpool, Sally  167

W

Wagner, Rudolf E.  202
Watson, John B.  41
Watson, Luke S., Jr.  20
Watts, Harriet  227
Weilly, Christopher T.  241
Weiner, Florence  102
Weiner, Irving B.  35
Weinstein, Grace W.  81
Weiss, Mark  32
Welsh, Mary M.  245
Wender, Paul H., M.D.  184
Wentworth, Elise H.  105
Wesley, Frank  218

# Author Index

White, Robin 124
White House Conference on Child Health and Protection 1, 30
White House Conference on Child Health and Protection. Section IV. The Handicapped Committee on Socially Handicapped 62
White House Conference on Children in a Democracy 62
Wiener, Daniel E. 20
Wiener, Joan 218
Wilkerson, Albert E. 65
Williams, Phyllis S. 138
Willie, Charles V. 55
Willke, J.D., M.D. 248
Wilson, Ann A. 119
Winchell, Carol Ann 183
Wing, Lorna, M.D. 114
Winick, Mariann P. 194
Winn, Marie 224

Winnicott, D.W. 228
Winship, Elizabeth C. 4
Witty, Paul 151, 152
Wolf, Anna W.M. 77, 132
Women on Words and Images 59
Wood, Abigail 4
Wood, Margaret I. 45
Wright, Beatrice A. 102
Wunderlich, Ray C., M.D. 202
Wyden, Barbara 55

## Y

Yamamoto, Kaoru 36

## Z

Zapata, Pamela 138
Zeligs, Rose 77
Zifferblatt, Steven Michael 20

# TITLE INDEX

In addition to books, this index also lists directories, pamphlets, government documents, and audiovisuals, including films, filmstrips, slides, records, tapes, and cassettes. In some cases, titles have been shortened. Alphabetization is letter by letter.

## A

Abnormality and Normality  105
About Handicaps  105
Academic Underachiever, The  199
Access Washington  108
Addiction: Why Drugs, Alcohol, Tobacco?  86
Adolescence  4
Adolescence: Psychology and Relations to Physiology, Anthropology, Sociology, Sex, Crime, Religion and Education  1
Adolescent Gap, The  85
Adolescent in the Family, The  1
Adolescent in Your Home, An  5
Adolescent Sexuality in Contemporary America  4
Adolescent Suicide  3
Adopted Child, The  12
Adopted Family, The  11
Adopting Older Children  13
Adoption--Is It for You?  12
Adoption: The Medical Aspects  15
Adoption Adviser, The  14
Adoption and After  14
Adults Look at Children's Values  37
Adults Need Sex Education Too  242
Adventure Playgrounds  224

Afraid of School  53
Aggressive Child  98
Aids to Independent Living  101
Airline Transportation for the Handicapped and Disabled  108
Allergic Child, The  163
Allergies and Your Child  163
Allergy and Your Child  163
All My Children  96
Almost Everyone Does  90
Alternatives in Quality Child Care  69
And Now We Are a Family  14
And Then There Were Two  207
Another Tomorrow for Teresa  150
Answers to the Most Frequently Asked Questions About Drug Abuse  87
Are Parents Bad for Children?  2
Are You Listening to Your Child?  226
Art of the Young Child  187
Ask Beth  4
Asthma and Your Child  165
As Your Child Grows  46
A to B  7
Autism and Childhood Psychosis  114
Autistic Children  114

# Title Index

## B

Babies and Accidents in the Home 239
Baby and Child Care 31
Baby Exercise Book, The 250
Baby Learning through Baby Play 225
Backward Child and His Mother, The 123
Backyard Play Equipment 228
Banned Products List, 1973 233
Baths and Babies 48
Battered Child: Selected Readings, The 24
Battered Child, The 24
Battered Child, The (film) 27
Becky 127
Bed-Wetting 35
Before Addiction 84
Before Reading and Writing 197
Before the 3 R's 194
Beginning with the Handicapped 103
Behavior Development in Infants 41
Behavior Modification in Child and School Mental Health 21
Being a Parent 212
Belts on Buttons Down 231
Be Not Afraid 124
Best in Children's Books, The 189
Best Records and Books for Exceptional Children 106
Better Homes and Gardens Baby Book 42
Between Parent and Child 209
Between Parent and Teenager 2
Beyond LSD 7
Beyond the Best Interests of the Child 13
Bibliography of Books for Children 189
Big Book of Soft Toys, The 227
"Bill of Rights" for Children, A 63
Biographies of Child Development 29
Birds, Bees and Storks 247
Birthrights: A Bill of Rights for Children 63
Black Child, The 55
Black Child Care 55
Black Children--White Parents 13
Black Child, White Child 55
Black Experience in Children's Books, The 56
Blueprint for a Brighter Child 193
Books That Help Children Deal with a Hospital Experience 158
Boys and Girls Book About Divorce, The 76
Brain Child 117
Brain-Injured Child in Home, School and Community, The 199
Brian at Seventeen 7
Bridging the Gap 221
Bridging the Generation Gap 4
Bright Boy, Bad Scholar 204
Bright Child--Poor Grades 191
Bright Children 151
Brothers and Sisters of Retarded Children 114
Bulletin of the Center for Children's Books 189

## C

Can't Read, Can't Write, Can't Talk Too Good Either 200
Care and Feeding of Your Diabetic Child, The 167
Care and Safety of Children, The 233
Care of Destitute, Neglected and Delinquent Children, The 11
Caring and Cooking for the Allergic Child 140
Caring for Your Disabled Child 101
Carriage of the Physically Handicapped on Domestic and International Airlines 109
Case for the Working Mother, The 257
Catalogue of Publications and Films 135
Century of the Child, The 61
Cerebral Palsy 118
Challenge of Child Training, The 80
Changing Children's Behavior 19
Changing Dimensions of Day Care, The 69
Channeling Children 59
Character in the Making 52
Child and His Family, The 29
Child and His Image, The 36

# Title Index

Child Behavior 51
Child Behavior--You 21
Child Behavior Modification 20
Child Called Noah, A 113
Child Care--Who Cares? 70
Child Care and Development 32
Child Care and Development (filmstrip) 39
Child Development: A Core Approach 35
Child Development and Early Childhood Education 190-91
Child Development in the Home 46
Child from Five to Ten, The 51
Child Goes to the Hospital, A 155
Child Growth 34
Child Health Encyclopedia 155
Child Health Issues in New York 159
Childhood: The Enchanted Years 38
Childhood and Adolescence 31
Childhood Illness 157
Childhood Lead Poisoning 233
Childhood Leukemia 177
Child Is Being Beaten, A 23
Child Learning through Child Play 225
Child Rearing Literature of Twentieth Century America, The 29
Childrearing Psychology 218
Children: The Challenge 79
Children and Books 188
Children and Decent People 65
Children and Drugs 83
Children and Dying 76
Children and Money 81
Children and Parents 81
Children and Quakerism 79
Children and Television 253
Children and Their Caretakers 63
Children and Youth in America 31
Children Apart 77
Children Are Centers for Understanding Media 254
Children Discover Music and Dance 187
Children Growing Up Series 38
Children in Trouble 64
Children of Change 259
Children of Divorce 75
Children of Separation and Divorce 76
Children of Special Value 12
Children of the Evening 97
Children of the Poor, The 62
Children on the Hill, The 213
Children, Parents and School Records 65
Children's Books 1974 195
Children's Books of the Year, 1974 188
Children's Bureau Publications for Parents 37
Children's Clothes 140
Children's Clothes--How to Choose Them 144
Children's Experience with Death 77
Children's Liberation 63
Children's Speech 34
Children's Television 254
Children Today 25
Child Safety 233
Child Safety Is No Accident 238
Child Sense 33
Child's Eye View, A 35
Child's Garden, A 250
Child's Mind, A 190
Child under Six, The 43
Child Welfare Services 14
Child with Convulsions, The 156
Child with Down's Syndrome (Mongolism), The 119
Child with Spina Bifida 129
Child with Spina Bifida, The 129
Chris and Bernie 220
Clinical Programs for Mentally Retarded Children 125
Complete Book of Breastfeeding, The 139
Complete Book of Children's Play, The 223
Complete Guide for the Working Mother, The 257
Complete Guide to Preparing Baby Foods at Home, The 137
Complete Question-and-Answer Book of Child Training, The 33
Conception, Birth and Contraception 241

# Title Index

Concerns of Parents about Sex Education 246
Confronting Drug Abuse 86
Consumer Information 232
Cooking and Eating with Children, a Way to Learn 137
Cooley's Anemia 147
Coping with Children's Misbehavior 80
Creating Children's Costumes from Paper and Cardboard 226
Creative Food Experiences for Children 138
Creative Parenthood 213
Crib Safety 233
Crisis and Growth 96
Crisis House 91
Crisis in Child Mental Health 96
Curious World of Twins, The 207
Custody Trap, The 77

## D

Dare to Discipline 80
Darkness, Darkness 91
Day Care 69
Day Care: Serving Infants 72
Day Care: Serving Preschool Children 72
Day Care: Serving School Age Children 72
Day Care and Preschool Services 70
Day Care Bibliography, A 71
Day Care Book, The 69
Day Care for America's Children 72
Day Care for Infants 70
Day Care for Your Children 72
Day Care in Context 70
Day Care Reference Sources 72
Dennis the Menace Takes a Poke at Poison 233
Dependent and Neglected Children 62
Dependent Child, The 11
Developing Basic Values 40
Development 38
Developmental Handicaps in Babies and Young Children 103
Development of Feelings in Children, The 39
Diagnosis Before Birth 111
Dialogues with Mothers 209
Dibs: In Search of Self 95
Did the Sun Shine before You Were Born? 243
Different Dream, A 200
Directories of Services and Facilities 107
Directory for Exceptional Children 102
Directory of Agencies Serving the Visually Handicapped in the United States 131
Directory of Educational Facilities for the Learning Disabled, The 199
Directory of Educational Programs for the Gifted, A 152
Directory of Facilities for the Learning-Disabled and Handicapped 199
Directory of Programs and Services for the Deaf in the United States 132
Directory of Social and Health Agencies of New York City 156
Directory of State and Local Resources for the Mentally Retarded 125
Discipline during Adolescence 7
Discipline without Fear 80
Discipline without Tyranny 81
Discovery of Death in Childhood and After, The 76
Doctor Answers Your Questions About Drugs, A 94
Doctor's Quick Teenage Diet, The 137
Does Your Child Have a Learning Disability? 201
Does Your Child Play with Matches? 233
Don't Gamble with Your Health: Diabetes 168
Don't Push Me I'm No Computer 190
Don't Push Your Preschooler 189
Drop Out, The 7
Drug Abuse and Your Child 87

# Title Index

Drug Age--What Do You Think of Your Father 91
Drug Education Directory 83
Drug Information Series--Narcotics 93
Drug Information Series--Psychedelics 93
Drug Information Series--Sedatives 93
Drug Information Series--Stimulants 93
Drugs: What They Are/How They Look/What They Do 84
Drugs and Youth 84
Drugs, Parents and Children 85
Drugs, Values and Personal Problems 93
Drug Taking in Youth 87
Dying Child, The 76
Dyslexia and Your Child 202

## E

Each Other's Victims 86
Early Child Care in the U.S.A. 35
Early Childhood Education Directory 189
Early Childhood Programs for Migrants 73
Early Recognition of Learning Disabilities 205
Early Window, The 253
Easter Seal Directory of Resident Camps for Persons with Special Health Needs, The 107
Educating the Ablest 152
Education for Parenting 215
Educators Guide to Free Health, Physical Education and Recreation Materials 156
Effects of Hospitalization on Children 157
Elizabeth 132
Emerging Personality, The 33
Emotional Care of Your Child, The 30
Emotional Care of Your Child, The 211
Emotionally Disturbed Child, The (Despert) 96
Emotionally Disturbed Child, The (Love) 96
Empty Fortress, The 113
Encyclopedia of Baby and Child Care, The 32
Entertaining Your Child 225
Escape from Childhood 64
Evan's Corner 39
Everybody's Tooth Book 171
Every Family Is Special 16
Everyone's Children, Nobody's Child 61
Everything but Hear 135
Exceptional Child, The 107
Exceptional Child Grows Up, The 105
Exceptional Child Grows Up, The 202
Exceptional Child Series, The 111
Explaining Death to Children 75
Explaining Divorce to Children 75
Explaining Sex to Your Little Boy and Explaining Sex to Your Little Girl 248
Eyes of a Child, The 135

## F

Facts about Autism 114
Facts About Mongolism for Women Over 35 119
Facts about Sudden Infant Death Syndrome 179
Facts About the Mental Health of Children 37
Facts about VD for Today's Youth 243
Facts Aren't Enough 246
Family and the Handicapped Child, The 117
Family Book of Child Care, The 210
Family Guide to Children's Television, The 253
Family of the Retarded Child, The 122
Family that Grew 11
Far from the Reservation 12
Father, Child, and Sex Roles 59
Federal Funds for Day Care Projects 73

# Title Index

Feeding Little Folks  141
Feeding the Child with a Handicap  141
Feeding the Infant  141
Feeding the Infant--Building the Man  145
Fighting Sickle Cell Disease  147
Filial Deprivation and Foster Care  13
Films Concerning Emotionally Handicapped Children  97
Final Report of the White House Conference on Children in a Democracy  62
First Aid in the Home  234
First Babyfood Cookbook, The  139
First Five Years, The  45
First Five Years of Life, The  42
First Twelve Months of Life, The  45
First Years Together, The  49
Flip City  91
Food As Children See It  145
Food Rights Handbook  141
Food Stamps for You  142
For Kids' Sakes  234
For Love of Children  20
Foster Parenting Young Children  13
Free and Inexpensive Learning Materials  188
Free for Baby and Mother  32
From Parent to Child about Sex  243
Fun in the Making  228
Fun in the Making (slides)  229
Future of Motherhood, The  212

## G

Games Children Play, The  225
Games for the Very Young  227
Genetic Studies of Genius, The  151
Getting Along With the Opposite Sex  9
Getting Along with Your Grown-Up Children  2
Gifted, The  152
Gifted Child, The  151
Gifted Child Grows Up, The  151

Give Your Child A Superior Mind  187
Glass Houses  91
Good and Inexpensive Books for Children  188
"The Good Life" for Infants and Toddlers  73
Good News for Kids  142
Got Me on the Run  3
Graduation Day  8
Greene Valley Grandparents  127
Grooving  92
Growing into Adolescence  4
Growing Pains  37
Growing Up, How We Become Alive  242
Growing Up in America  87
Growing Up Thin  138
Growing Up Together  220
Growth and Development of Mothers, The  257
Guidance--Big Sister  39
Guidance for the 70's  8
Guide for Planning Food Service in Child Care Centers, A  73
Guidelines for Adoption Service  15
Guides for Day Care Licensing  73
Guide to Children's Magazines, Newspapers, Reference Books  195
Guide to Dental Care, A  171
Guide to Drug Rehabilitation  85
Guide to Drug Abuse Education and Information Materials, A  86
Guide to Summer Camps and Summer Schools, 1974, The  249
Guiding Your Child to a More Creative Life  227

## H

Handbook for the Young Diabetic, A  167
Handbook of Adolescence, The  3
Handbook of Private Schools, The  188
Handicapped Child in the Family, A  104
Handicapped Child In Your Home, A  109
Handling the Young Cerebral Palsied

# Title Index

Child at Home  117
Have You Had It in the Kitchen?  257
Health Education Materials and the Organizations which Offer Them  158
Hearing-Impaired Preschool Child  131
Hearing Loss  133
Help! My Child Won't Eat Right  138
Help for Mark  21
Help for the Handicapped Child  102
Help for Your Troubled Child  97
Helping Boys and Girls Understand Sex Roles  60
Helping Children Grow through Play  225
Helping Children Overcome Learning Disabilities  202
Helping Children with the Mystery of Death  77
Helping the Battered Child and His Family  24
Helping the Child Who Cannot Hear  133
Helping the Gifted Child  152
Helping the Handicapped Teenager Mature  103, 109
Helping the Retarded Child  124
Helping the Trainable Mentally Retarded Child Develop Speech and Language  122
Helping Young Children Develop Communication Skills  197
Helping Young Children Develop Language Skills  104
Helping Your Child Develop His Potentialities  188
Helping Your Child to Understand Death  77
Helping Your Child to Understand Death (pamphlet)  78
Helping Your Diabetic Child  167
Helping Your LD Child at Home  203
History of Childhood, The  33
Home and Family Emergencies  231
Home Eye Test Kit  172

Homosexuality in Our Society  246
Hope through Research: Cerebral Palsy  118
Hope through Research: Epilepsy  169
Hope through Research: Spina Bifida  129
Horatio Alger's Children  84
How an Average Child Behaves  49
How Children Grow  142
How Children Grow: Clinical Research Advances in Human Growth and Development  159
How Parents Tell Their Children They Are Adopted  15
How to Bring Up a Child without Spending a Fortune  212
How to Build Furniture & Equipment for Handicapped Children  104
How to Explain Sex to Children  241
How to Father  213
How to Give Your Child a Good Start in Life  42
How to Go to Work When Your Husband Is Against It, Your Children Aren't Old Enough and There's Nothing You Can Do Anyhow  258
How to Guide Your School-Age Child  51
How to Make Johnny Want to Obey  19
How to Parent  214
How to Play with Your Children  227
How to Raise a Brighter Child  190
How to Raise a Human Being  210
How to Save Your Child from Rheumatic Fever  175
How to Select Infants and Children's Clothing  142
How to Start and Operate a Day Care Home  70
How to Start Your Own Preschool Playgroup  227
How to Survive Parenthood  210
How to Talk with Children (and Other People)  33
How to Talk with Children about

# Title Index

Sex 244
How to Talk with Your Teenager about VD 247
How to Teach Children the Wonder of Sex 248
How to Teach Your Baby to Swim 250
How to Teach Your Children about Sex 245
How to Tutor 190
How Your Children Can Learn to Live a Rewarding Life 19
Human Sexuality and the Mentally Retarded 242
Hyperactive Child, The (Renshaw) 184
Hyperactive Child, The (Wender) 184
Hyperactive Child, The (film) 185
Hyperactive Child: Selected Bibliography 185
Hyperkinetic Child, The 183

# I

I Can't See What You're Saying 200
If Your Child Has a Learning Disability 200
"I Hate My Parents!" 217
I Just Don't Dig Him 8
I'll Never Get Her Back 16
In Case of Emergency 231
Infancy 49
Infant and Child Care 160
Infant and Child in the Culture of Today 1-2, 44, 51
Infant Care 46
Infant Care and Development 49
Infant Feeding 138
Infantile Autism 113
Infants and Mothers 42
Intelligent Parents' Guide to Raising Children, The 30
Introduction to Piaget, An 35
Invisible Child, The 8
Is It Well with the Child? 114
Is My Baby All Right? 102
Isn't It Time He Outgrew This? 121
I Think 92

Ivan and His Father 99

# J

Jennifer Is a Lady 115
Johnny 99
Joys and Sorrows of Parenthood, The 215
Juvenile Court Comes of Age, The 66
Juvenile Courts in the U.S. 61
Juvenile Justice Confounded 64
Juvenile Justice Standards Project 62

# K

Kids Are Natural Cooks 139
Kids, Brains, and Learning 202
Kinships 8
Koontz Child Developmental Program, The 192

# L

Language for the Preschool Deaf Child 131
Lead Poisoning 238
Lead Poisoning: The Hidden Epidemic 238
Learning Child, The 191
Learning Disabilities Due to Minimal Brain Dysfunction 203
Learning through Play 226
Learning to Be Free 216
Learning to Learn in Infancy 196
Learning to Love 241
Leave the Light on for Kent 117
Legal Rights of Children, The 61
Lengthening Shadows 157
Let Our Children Go 103
Let's Have Healthy Children 138
Let's Make Sex a Household Word 243
Let's Play Math 192
Let's Stop Destroying Our Children 65
Let's Talk About Adoption 14
Letters to Tracy 3
Liberal Parents, Radical Children 213

# Title Index

Liberated Parents/Liberated Children 214
Lindy, My Retarded Child 122
Listen to Your Heart 105
Little Darlings, The 33
Little Miss Muffet Fights Back 60
Living with a Mentally Retarded Child 122
Love, Sex and Birth Control for Mentally Retarded 246

## M

Magic Years, The 42
Make the Most of Your Baby 125
Making Children's Costumes 226
Making Children's Furniture and Play Structures 139
Making Glove Puppets 226
Making the Home Safer for Children 234
Making Your Own Baby Food 140
Maltreated Child, The 23
Manual for Babysitters, A 216
Marijuana: What Can You Believe? 93
Marijuana, LSD, Narcotics, Sedatives, Stimulants--Five Leaflets 87
Maternal Physician, The 41
MBD: Family Book about Minimal Brain Dysfunction, The 201
Meal Time! Happy Time! 142
Meet Lisa 205
Mentally Gifted Children and Youth 153
Mentally Handicapped Child, The 122
Mentally Retarded Child and His Family, The 123
Mentally Retarded Child at Home, The 125
Mentally Retarded Children 121
Mental Retardation 124
Minimal Brain Dysfunction in Children 203
Miracle of Nature, The 248
Miss Craig's Growing-Up Exercises 250
Mr. Smith, Your Kid's Taking Drugs 92
Model for Quality Day Care, A 73
Modern Motherhood 43
Modern Parent's Guide to Baby and Child Care 155
Mom, Why Won't You Listen? 9
Mongolism (Down's Syndrome) 119
Mother at Home, The 209
Mothercraft 226
Motherhood Book, A 218
Mothers at Work 258
Mother's Book, The 29
Mother's Cook and Cope Book, The 138
Mother's Day Is Over 216
Mother's Guide to Child Safety, The 232
Mothers Want to Help 172
Moving: A Common-Sense Guide to Relocating Your Family 77
Muscular Dystrophy 181
Music Therapy in Special Education 105
My Son, Kevin 111
Myth of the Hyperactive Child and Other Means of Child Control, The 184

## N

Name Your Baby 210
National Clearinghouse for Poison Control Centers Bulletin 233
National Directory of Accredited Camps for Boys and Girls 249
National Directory of Hotlines, Switchboards, and Related Services 2
National Directory of Private Social Agencies 11
National Institutes of Health Publications List 158
National Park Guide for the Handicapped 107
Natural Baby Food Cookbook, The 138
Natural Child Rearing 30
Natural Parenthood 216
Natural Way to Raise Healthy Children, The 43

# Title Index

New Age Baby Name Book, The 211
New Alcoholics: Teenagers, The 87
New Baby! A 44
Newborn 49
New Dimensions in Adoption 14
New Directions for Parents of Persons Who Are Retarded 124
New Encyclopedia of Child Care and Guidance, The 31
New List of Books for Free Children, A 60
New Religions, The 4
New Ways in Discipline 79
1973 Directory of Counseling Services 211
1973 Public Welfare Directory 12
Ninety-Nine Bottles of Beer 92
No Crying He Makes 123
No Language But a Cry 23
No More Lead for Leroy 234
Nothing Left to Lose 3
Nursery Years, The 41
Nursing Your Baby 140
Nutrition: To Baby with Love 145
Nutrition and Feeding of Infants and Children under Three in Group Day Care 74
Nutrition and Feeding Techniques for Handicapped Children 143
Nutrition Education Materials 137
Nutrition Survival Kit 143

## O

Old Enough to Know 247
On Being the Parent of a Handicapped Child 109
One-Parent Families 219
One-Parent Family, The (Douglas) 214
One-Parent Family, The (Schlesinger) 211
1,001 Ways to Have Fun with Children 227
On "How Do Your Children Grow?" 216
Only Kid on the Block, The 112
Opening Doors for Physically Handicapped and Emotionally Disturbed Children 107
Orthodontics: A Special Kind of Dentistry 172
Our Blind Children 131
Our Children's Keepers 62
Overcoming Drugs 85

## P

Parental Attitudes toward Exceptional Children 104
Parental Survival and the Hyperactive Child 184, 185
Parent as Teacher, The 202
Parent, Child and Sex 245
Parent/Child Toy-Lending Library, The 228
Parent Effectiveness Training 215
Parenthood 211'
Parenting 213
Parenting: Fathers, Mothers and Others 221
Parent Power/Child Power 213
Parents and Children in the Hospital 157
Parents and Sex Instruction 247
Parents and Teen-Agers 2
Parents and Teenagers 5
Parents Are Teachers 19
Parents Are Teachers Too 196
Parents Ask 210
Parents, Baby-Sitters and Fire 234
Parents/Children/Discipline 81
Parents' Encyclopedia of Infancy, Childhood and Adolescence, The 31
Parents' Guide to Allergy in Children 163
Parent's Guide to Child Discipline, A 80
Parent's Guide to Children's Allergies, A 164
Parent's Guide to Children's Reading, A 189
Parents' Guide to Child Safety, A 232
Parents' Guide to Cleft Palate Habilitation 156
Parent's Guide to Drugs, The 83

# Title Index

Parents' Guide to Everyday Problems of Boys and Girls, The 209
Parent's Guide to Nursery Schools, A 188
Parent's Guide to the Prevention and Control of Drug Abuse, A 84
Parents in Modern America 216
Parents' Manual, A 32
Patterns for Health 161
Peoplemaking 217
Personality Development 33
Phenylketonuria 126
Physical Disability 102
Physician and Child-Rearing, The 30
Piaget's Theory of Intellectual Development 187
Plain Talk about Child Abuse 25
Play 229
Play and Playthings for the Preschool Child 223
Playground Handbook, The 224
Playgroup Book, The 224
Playing and Reality 228
Playmates 37
Play Therapy 95
Please Say Please 35
Pocket Guide to Babysitting, The 6
Pot, Pills and Powders 85
Power of Play, The 225
Power to the Parents! 212
Practical Parent, The 79
Pre-Adolescents 52
Preface to a Life 49
Pregnancy, Birth and the Newborn Baby 43
Premature Baby, The 47
Prenatal Care 47
Preparing for Parenthood 217
Preparing Your Child for Reading 194
Preschool Deaf Blind Child, The 133
Preschool Learning and Teaching 193
Preventing Drug Abuse 84
Preventing Lead Poisoning in Children 234
Preventing Misbehavior in Children 81
Prevention of Iron-Deficiency Anemia in Infants and Children of Preschool Age 143
Preventive Treatment of Neglected Children 61
Primer for Parents of a Mentally Retarded Child 126
Primer for Parents of Preschoolers 45
Problem Drinker at Home? 87
Problems of Parents 210
Progress against Leukemia 177
Promises to Peter 217
Protecting Young Lives 239
Protect Your Child's Heart 175
Psychological Care of Infant and Child 41
Publications (USDA) 141
Publications of Health Services Administration 158
Publications of the Office of Human Development 37
Put Munch in Their Menu 143

# R

Racism and Mental Health 55
Raising a Hyperactive Child 184
Raising a Responsible Child 215
Raising Children in a Difficult Time 217
Raising Children with Love and Limits 44
Raping Our Children 244
Reading: A Basic Guide for Parents and Teachers 193
Reading and Writing before School 192
Reading Interests of Children and Young Adults 192
Reading with Your Child through Age 5 195
Real Food for Your Baby 140
Reconstituted Family, The 214
Recreation for Autistic and Emotionally Disturbed Children 115
Registry of Private Schools for Children with Special Educational Needs 102
Reprints--Childhood Diabetes, Parents Magazine, November 1973 168

# Title Index

Responsive Parent, The 215
Retarded Child from Birth to Five, The 122
Retarded Children of the Poor 126
Rights of Children, The 64
Rights of Children: Emergent Concepts in Law and Society, The 65
Rights of Juveniles 63
Rights of the Mentally Handicapped, The 123
Rubella 181
Rules for Raising Kids 34
Runaways 2

## S

Safe-Toy Environments 239
Safe Toys for Your Child--How to Select Them, How to Use Them Safely 234
Safe Toy Tips 235
Sandcastles 39
Saturday Morning 9
Save Your Child from Poisoning 235
Scholars before School 192
Seizures, Epilepsy and Your Child 169
Selected Career Education Programs for the Handicapped 107
Selected Publications Concerning the Handicapped 108
Selected Reading Suggestions for Parents of Mentally Retarded Children 125
Selected References for Drug Information Centers 86
Selected References on the Abused and Battered Child 25
Self-Awareness Film Modules on Drug Abuse for Parents 92
Services for Crippled Children 108
Services for the Blind Person 132
Seventeen Book of Answers to What Your Parents Don't Talk About and Your Best Friends Can't Tell You, The 4-5
Sewing Children's Clothing Made Easy 139
Sex and the Teenage Girl 242

Sex Education 243
Sexism and Youth 59
Sex Mis-Education 248
Sex Role Development 60
Shannon 177
Shaping Your Child's Personality 19
Show Me! 243
Sickle Cell--An Inherited Disease 150
Sickle Cell: Guide to Prevention and Treatment 147
Sickle Cell Anemia and Sickle Cell Trait 147
Silent Tragedy, A 23
Single Parent Experience, The 215
Skim Milk in Infant Feeding 143
Slaughter of the Innocents 23
Small Outside, The 114
Social Development in Young Children 30
Something's Wrong with My Child 203
Something's Wrong with My Child: A Parents' Book about Children with Learning Disabilities 200
Somewhere a Child Is Crying 24
So You're Going to Be a New Father? 219
Spanish-Language Health Communication Teaching Aids 159
Speaking of Children--Their Learning Abilities/Disabilities 201
Speech, Language and Hearing Programs--1973 203
Spina Bifida--A Birth Defect 129
Square Pegs, Round Holes 201
Standard First Aid and Personal Safety 231
Statements Regarding Insurance Policies and Wills Directed to Adoptive Parents 15
Stepchild in the Family 210
Stop School Failure 200
Straight Story on VD, The 244
Stranger in the Family 95
Strong Family, Strong Child 212
Study of a Child, A 29
Successful Step-Parent, The 211
Sudden Infant Death Syndrome 179
Suzy Prudden's Creative Fitness for

# Title Index

Baby and Child  250
Sympathetic Understanding of the Child Six to Sixteen, A  51

## T

Talking About Breastfeeding  145
Talking About Death  76
Talking, Thinking, Growing  52
Talking to Children about Sex  244
Tax Deductions for Child Care  74
Teacher and Child  191
Teaching Gifted Children  152
Teaching Johnny to Swim  251
Teaching Montessori in the Home  192
Teaching Your Child to Learn from Birth to School Age  190
Teaching Your Tot to Swim  249
Teach Your Baby  193
Teach Your Child to Manage Money  80
Teenage Rebellion  9
Television and Growing Up  254
Television's Child  254
Telling a Child About Death  76
Tender Gift, The  140
T.H. Bell System of Home-Based Early Childhood Education, The  197
Thinking Is Child's Play  223
This Child Is Rated "X"  67
This List Is Not for Girls Only!  60
Three, Four, Open the Door  227
Three Years to Grow  44
Time to Learn, A  192
Tips on Drug Abuse Prevention  88
To Be a Parent  221
To Combat Child Abuse and Neglect  25
Today's Child  45
Today's Children and Yesterday's Heritage  30
Toddlers and Parents  43
To Give an Edge  119
Toilet Training in Less Than a Day  43
Toilet Training the Retarded  122
To Love a Child  17

Tomorrow Is Today  118
Tooth Care  172
Toy Book  224
Toy Is Born, A  226
Toys for the Handicapped  108
Toys That Don't Care  232
Toys That You Can Make  224
Training Children in Self-Discipline and Self-Control  20
Training Retarded Babies and Pre-schoolers  123
Transracial Adoption Today  13
Troubled Child, The  95
Troubles of Children and Parents  34
Truth About Drugs, The  94
Tuned-Out Generation, The  9
Twins: Twice the Trouble, Twice the Fun  207
Twins and Supertwins  207
Two World of Childhood  213

## U

Ultimate Stranger, The  113
Understanding Children  51
Understanding Children Writing  191
Understanding Drug Abuse  85
Understanding Early Childhood  50
Understanding Piaget  193
Understanding the Mentally Retarded Child  123
Understanding Your Child from Birth to Three  44
U.S. Facilities and Programs for Children with Severe Mental Illnesses  97
Up Against the Law  65

## V

VD: The ABC's  244
Violence against Children  24
Violence in the Family  24
Volunteers Who Produce Books  132

## W

Walk in Their Shoes  9
Walls and Windows  9

343

# Title Index

Watch Out for Lead Paint Poisoning 235
"The Way It Spozed to B" 195
Way Out, A 17
We Take This Child 12
What Are the Facts About Genetic Disease 148
What Bothers Us about Grownups 215
What Can You Do to Help Your Child Succeed? 197
What Do You Know About PKU? 126
What Every Child Needs 34
What Every Child Would Like His Parents to Know, to Help Him with the Emotional Problems of His Everyday Life 217
What Everyone Should Know about Syphilis and Gonorrhea 246
What Every Parent Should Know About Drugs and Drug Abuse 88
What Is Mongolism? 120
What Shall I Tell My Child about Sex? 248
What Shall We Name the Baby 211
What Shall We Tell the Kids? 216
What's Right with Us Parents? 214
What To Do About Your Brain-Injured Child 103
What To Do until the Doctor Comes 157
What to Do When "There's Nothing to Do" 224
What to Tell Your Child About Birth, Death, Illness, Divorce, and Other Family Crises 75
What to Tell Your Child about Sex 242
What You Can Do About Drugs and Your Child 83
What Your Child Is All About 34
What Your Child Really Wants to Know about Sex--and Why 242
Wheelchair Book, The 104
Wheelchair Interiors 109
Wheelchair Traveler, The 109
When Children Ask about Sex (Daniels and Hoover) 242
When Children Ask About Sex (Selzer) 245
When Children Move from School to School 78
When Children Need Help 104
When Children Need Special Help with Emotional Problems 96
When Parents Fail 64
When Your Child First Goes Off to School 47
When Your Child Is Ill 155
When Your Child Needs Help 96
Where Did I Come From 244
White House Conference on Children 66
Whole Child, Whole Parent 212
Whole-Earth Catalog 212
Who's Minding the Children 71
Who Will Love My Child? 130
Why and How of Discipline, The 82
Why Did My Baby Die? 179
Why Do They Beat Their Child 25
Why Some Choose Not to Adopt through Agencies 13
Why Your Child Is Hyperactive 183
Willowbrook 124
Windows on Day Care 70
Women and Work in America 258
Wonderful Story of How You Were Born, The 244
Word or Two about Learning Disabilities, A 201
Working Mother, The 257
Working Mother's Guide to Her Home, Her Family, and Herself, The 258
Working Woman's Guide to Her Job Rights, A 258
World Book of Children's Games 224
World of Deaf-Blind Children 135

## Y

You and the Other Generation 10
You and Your Baby 45
You and Your Child 11
You and Your Retarded Child 121
You and Your Teeth 172
You Can Help Your Child Improve Study and Homework Behavior 20
You Can Improve Your Vision 171

# Title Index

You Can Raise Decent Children  81
You Can Raise Your Handicapped Child  101
You Can Teach Tooth Brushing  172
Young Child in the Home, The  30
Young Children and Accidents in the Home  235
Young Children and Their Drawings  191
Youngest Minority, The  64
Your Baby  139
Your Baby Can Swim  250
Your Baby's First Year  47
Your Child  201
Your Child and Drugs  84
Your Child and Drugs (pamphlet)  88
Your Child and Sex  245
Your Child and You  212
Your Child from 1 to 6  47
Your Child from One to Twelve  46
Your Child from 6 to 12  52
Your Child Growing and Religion  31
Your Child Has a Learning Disability--What Is It?  204
Your Child Is a Person  42
Your Child's Ears, Nose and Throat  156
Your Child's First Five Years  43
Your Child's Play  223
Your Child's Self-Esteem  32
Your Child's Sensory World  193
Your Child's Teeth  172
Your Down's Syndrome Child  120
Your First Five Months with Your First Baby  47
Your Growing Child and Sex  241
Your Head Is Your Own Thing But . . . Don't Blow Your Kid's Mind  88
Your Hyperactive Child  184
Your Overactive Child  183
Your Overweight Child  139
Your Preschool Child  42
Youth:  Hope of the Harvest  3
Youth:  Its Education, Regimen, and Hygiene  1
Youth:  Transition to Adulthood  4
Youth:  Years from Ten to Sixteen  1
Youth and Sex  244
Youth and the Drug Problem  85
Youth Service Bureau, The  64

# INDEX OF ORGANIZATIONS AND SOURCES OF INFORMATION

This index lists alphabetically organizations, associations, and sources of materials which are either free or at low cost. Alphabetization is letter by letter.

## A

Action for Children's Television 254
Action for Child Transportation Safety 235
Action for Prevention of Burn Injuries to Children 235
Adoption Resource Exchange of North America 15
Aetna Life & Casualty 236
Aid to Adoption of Special Kids 15
Alcohol and Drug Abuse Education 88
Alexander Graham Bell Association for the Deaf 133
Allergy Foundation of America 164
American Academy of Pediatrics 236
American Association for Gifted Children 153
American Association for Maternal and Child Health 159
American Cancer Society 181
American Dental Association 173
American Diabetes Association 168
American Foundation for the Blind 133
American Heart Association 175
American Home Economics Association 143
American Humane Association 26
American Insurance Association 236
American Lung Association 164
American Medical Association 88
American National Red Cross 236
American Optometric Association 173
American Pharmaceutical Association 89
American Social Health Association 246
American Society of Dentistry for Children 173
Arthritis Foundation, The 182
Association for Childhood Education International 195
Association for Children with Learning Disabilities 204
Association for Children with Retarded Mental Development 126
Association for Education of the Visually Handicapped 134
Association for the Advancement of Blind and Retarded Children 134

## B

Bank Street College of Education 196
Beech-Nut 48
Better Vision Institute 173
Black Child Development Institute 56
Blue Cross and Blue Shield 159
Bureau of Education for the Handi-

# Organizations and Sources of Information

capped 110
Bureau of Narcotics & Dangerous Drugs 89

## C

Center for Disease Control 160
Cereal Institute 144
Change for Children 60
Child Development Associate Consortium 196
Children's Asthma Research Institute and Hospital at Denver 164
Children's Defense Fund 66
Children's Foundation, The 144
Children's Hospital Medical Center, The 160
Children's Rights 67
Child Study Association of America 38
Child Welfare League of America 16
Citizen's Committee for Children of New York City 67
Clearinghouse for Mental Health Information 98
Closer Look 110
Community Services Administration 110
Connecticut General Life Insurance Co. 236
Consumer Product Safety Commission 236
Cooley's Anemia Blood and Research Foundation for Children 148
Council for Exceptional Children 110
Council on Adoptable Children 16
Council on Interracial Books for Children 57
Cystic Fibrosis Foundation 164

## D

Day Care and Child Development Council of America, The 74

## E

Education Development Center 74
End Violence Against the Next Generation 26
Epilepsy Foundation of America 169

## F

Family Service Association of America 219
Far West Laboratory 229
Foreign Adoption Center 16
Foundation for Child Development 110

## H

Hogg Foundation for Mental Health 98

## I

Institute for Safer Living, The 236
Institutes for the Achievement of Human Potential 204
International Board on Books for Young People 196
International Council for Infant Survival 180

## J

John Hancock Mutual Life Insurance Co. 48
Johnson & Johnson 48
Juvenile Diabetes Foundation 168

## K

Kimberly-Clark Corporation 160

## L

Leukemia Society of America 178
Liberty Mutual Insurance Co. 237

## M

Maternal Information Services 259
Maternity Center Association 219
Mead Johnson & Co. 48
Medic Alert Foundation International 160
Medical Marketing Department 48
Metropolitan Life Insurance Co. 237
MOMMA 219

## Organizations and Sources of Information

Mothers of Children with Down's Syndrome 120
Muscular Dystrophy Association 182

### N

Narcotic Educational Foundation of America 89
National Association for Creative Children and Adults 153
National Association for Down's Syndrome 120
National Association for Mental Health 98
National Association for Retarded Citizens 127
National Association for the Education of Young Children 67
National Association of Hearing and Speech Action 134
National Association of Retail Druggists 237
National Association of the Deaf 134
National Center for Disease Control 247
National Center for the Prevention and Treatment of Child Abuse and Neglect 26
National Center on Child Abuse and Neglect 26
National Children's Rehabilitation Center 170
National Child Safety Council 237
National Clearinghouse for Alcohol Information 89
National Clearinghouse for Drug Abuse Information 89
National Clearinghouse for Poison Control Centers 237
National Clearinghouse on Child Neglect and Abuse 26
National Commission on Resources for Youth 6
National Committee for Prevention of Child Abuse 27
National Coordinating Council on Drug Education 90
National Council of Adoptive Parents Organizations 16
National Council on Crime and Delinquency 67
National Dairy Council 144, 160
National Easter Seal Society for Crippled Children and Adults 111, 130
National Foundation for Asthmatic Children at Tucson 165
National Genetics Foundation 148
National Hemophilia Foundation 148
National Institute of Allergy and Infectious Diseases 165
National Institute of Drug Abuse 90
National Kidney Foundation 182
National Multiple Sclerosis Society 182
National Organization of Mothers of Twins 208
National PTA 196
National Runaway Switchboard 6
National Safety Council 238
National Sickle Cell Disease Program 149
National Society for Autistic Children (New York) 115
National Society for Autistic Children (West Virginia) 115
National Society for the Prevention of Blindness 134
National Sudden Infant Death Syndrome Foundation 180
National Tay-Sachs and Allied Diseases Association 149
National Youth Alternatives Project 6
New Dimensions Publishing Co. 90
New York State Child Abuse and Maltreatment Register 27
Nutrition Foundation 144

### O

Office of Child Development 196
Operation Peace of Mind 6-7
Orton Society 204

### P

Parents Anonymous 27
Parents Without Partners 219
Play Schools Association 229

# Organizations and Sources of Information

Public Affairs Committee   38

## R

Recording for the Blind   135
Retarded Infants Services   127

## S

Sickle Cell Disease Foundation of Greater New York   149
SIECUS (Sex Information and Education Council of the United States)   247
Single Parent Resource Center   220
Sisterhood of Black Single Mothers   220
Smith, Kline and French Laboratories   90
Society for Nutrition Education   144
Special Action Officer for Drug Abuse Prevention   90
Spina Bifida Association of America   130
Student Association for the Study of Hallucinogens   90

## U

Union Central Life Insurance Company, The   238
United Cerebral Palsy Associations   118
U.S. Department of Agriculture   144

## W

Women's Action Alliance   74

## Y

Young Adult Institute and Workshop

# SUBJECT INDEX

This subject index also directs the reader to informational sources of pamphlets and audiovisuals on subjects covered in the text. Underlined numbers refer to areas of emphasis in the text. Alphabetization is letter by letter.

## A

Abortion 243
Accident prevention. See Safety education
Adler, Alfred 79, 80, 81, 214
Adolescence 1-5, 29, 31, 81, 245
   audiovisual materials about 7-10
   the handicapped during 103, 105, 109
   mental illness in 97
   organizations serving 6-7
   pamphlets about 5-6
   periodicals about 5
   See also Drug abuse; Marriage, teenage; Sex education; Teenage parents
Adoption 11-14, 32, 77, 215, 216
   audiovisual materials about 16-17
   organizations serving 15-16, 56
   pamphlets about 14-15
   See also Child placement; Foster grandparents program; Foster home care
Adoption, interracial 12, 13, 14, 17
   organizations serving 15, 16
Adoption agencies
   directories of 14
   failures of 13
Aggressiveness in children
   as an emotional problem 98

   from infancy to five years 44
Alcohol abuse 84, 86, 93
   adolescents and 3
   organizations concerned with 88, 89
   by parents 87-88
   psychological aspects of 92, 95
   See also Drug abuse
Alienation
   of adolescents 3
   drug abuse and 87
Allergies 32, 163-64
   audiovisual materials about 165
   diet and 140
   organizations concerned with 164-65
   See also Asthma; Hay fever
American Indians. See Indians
Anemia 143. See also Cooley's anemia; Sickle cell anemia
Anger 33, 35, 218
   drug abuse and 92
   See also Temper
Anthropology, adolescence and 1
Anxiety 39
Aphasia 200
Art 223
   preschool children and 187
   as a reflection of child development 191

# Subject Index

Arthritis, organizations concerned with  182
Arts and crafts  227
Asthma  163
   audiovisual materials about  165
   organizations concerned with  164, 165
Attitudes. See Values, social
Audiovisual materials
   about and for adolescents  7-10
   on adoption  16-17
   on asthma  165
   on autistic children  115
   on behavior modification  21
   on child abuse  27
   on child development  38-40
      infancy to five years  48-50
      six to twelve years  53
   on children's rights  67
   on clothing and dress  145
   for and about deaf-blind children  110, 135
   on drug and alcohol abuse  90-94
   on the emotionally disturbed  98-99
   on the exceptional child  111-12
   on genetic diseases  150
   on health and hygiene  160-61
   on hyperactivity  185
   on learning and creativity  196-97
   on learning disabilities  204-5
   on the mentally retarded  127
   on nutrition  145
   on parenthood  221
   on play  229
   on safety education  238-39
   on sex education  247-48
   on sex roles  60
   on spina bifida  130
   on sports and recreation  251
   on working mothers  259
Authority, family conflicts over  2
Autistic children  97, 102, 113-15

# B

Babies. See Child care and development (infancy to five years); Infants, premature; Names for babies; Sudden infant death syndrome
Babysitting and babysitters  6, 44-45, 189, 216
Barbiturates. See Drug abuse
Bathing of children  42, 48
Battered child syndrome. See Child abuse
Bed-wetting  35, 80, 218. See also Toilet training
Behavioral development of children  31, 32, 33, 34, 80, 81, 209, 217
   in adolescence  5-6
   counseling services in  211
   in Down's syndrome  120
   from infancy to five years  41, 44, 49
   from six to twelve years  51, 53
   See also Emotionally disturbed children
Behavior modification  19-21, 121, 184. See also Discipline of children
Bicycle safety. See Traffic safety
Big Brothers Clubs  61
Biology, human. See Physical development of children
Birth control. See Sex education
Birth defects  103
   audiovisual materials about  111, 112
   See also specific types of birth defects
Black children
   adoption of  13, 56
   development of  55-57
   See also Mothers, black; Sickle cell anemia
Blind. See Braille system; Eye care; Vision impairment
Books. See Children's literature; Textbooks for the visually handicapped
Braille system  132
Brain-damaged children. See Birth defects; Exceptional children; Mentally retarded children; Learning disabilities
Breastfeeding  32, 49, 138, 139, 140, 218
   audiovisual materials about  145

352

# Subject Index

Bruner 223
Burns and scalds 235

## C

Camps, directories of 249. See also School camps
Camps for the handicapped
　for asthmatics 163, 164, 165
　for autistic children 115
　for children with muscular dystrophy 182
　for diabetic children 167
　directories of 102, 107
　for the hearing impaired 132
　for the learning disabled 204
　See also School camps
Cancer, organizations concerned with 181
Cerebral palsied children 104-5, 117-18
Child abuse and neglect 11, 23-24, 61, 62, 63, 64, 65
　audiovisual materials about 27
　organizations concerned with 26-27
　pamphlets about 25-26
　See also Children's rights; Dependent children
Childbirth 75
　organizations concerned with 220
　See also Multiple births; Sex education
Childbirth, natural 218
Child care and development 29-36
　audiovisual materials about 38-40
　failure of programs for 65
　indexes to 261
　organizations concerned with 38
　pamphlets about 37-38
　parents role in ix-x
　periodicals about 36
　publishers of literature about 311-20
　in Russia 213
　See also Black children; Child welfare; Education of Children; Emotional development and needs in childhood; Health and hygiene in childhood; Intellectual development of children; Parenthood; Physical development of children; Psychological development and needs in childhood; Social development and needs in childhood
Child care and development (infancy to five years) 32, 41-46
　audiovisual materials about 48-50
　organizations concerned with 48
　pamphlets about 46-47
　periodicals about 46
　See also Bathing of children; Breastfeeding; Day care; Kindergartens; Nursery schools
Child care and development (six to twelve years) 51-52
　audiovisual materials about 53
　pamphlets about 52-53
　periodicals about 52, 157-58
Child custody 64, 77
　of the mentally ill 123
　See also Divorce
Child health stations 159. See also Health and hygiene in childhood
Childhood diseases. See Genetic diseases; Glandular diseases; Health and hygiene of children; names of specific diseases
Child management. See Behavioral modification; Discipline
Child placement 11. See also Adoption; Foster home care
Child psychology. See Emotional development and needs in childhood; Psychological development and needs in childhood
Child rearing. See Child care and development
Children, black. See Black children
Children, preschool. See Child care and development (infancy to five years)
Children's literature 194, 195, 214
　for the handicapped 107
　on illness and hospitalization 158
　magazines 263-65

# Subject Index

poetry 227
for the preschooler 44, 188, 189, 191
publishers of 311-20
racism and sexism in 56, 59, 60, 194
Children's rights 61-67
for the handicapped 103
for the mentally retarded 123, 124
See also Child abuse and neglect; Girl's liberation
Child welfare 62, 66
failure of programs for 3, 65
institutions serving 11, 14
organizations serving 67
periodicals about 66, 219
social policies in 3
See also Child abuse and neglect; Children's rights; School lunch programs; Social welfare
Cleft palate 103, 156
Clinics. See Child health stations; Mental health clinics; Rehabilitation centers and services
Clothing and dress for children 33, 39, 65
in adolescence 5-6, 7
from infancy to five years 42, 44
selection of 142, 145
sewing of 139, 140
for those with Down's syndrome 119
See also Grooming
Club foot 103
Cold (disease) 160
Communication with children 33, 75, 209, 213, 214, 217, 226
in adolescence 7, 8, 9
audiovisual materials about 221
drug abuse and 91
emotional problems and lack of 99
See also Parenthood
Communication skills 203
in infancy 196
See also Reading; Speech development; Writing, teaching of
Comprehensive Child Development Act (1971) 71
Conscience, development of 42

Contraception. See Sex education
Convulsions 156. See also Epileptic children
Cookery for children 226
Cooley's anemia 147
audiovisual materials about 150
organizations concerned with 148
Costumes, making of 226, 227
Counseling services 38, 211, 216, 218, 219-20
for the gifted child 153
in mental retardation 124, 126, 127
for runaways 3
Crafts. See Arts and crafts
Creativity. See Art; Dancing;, Intellectual development in childhood; Music
Cribs 233, 236. See also Sudden infant death syndrome
Crime. See Juvenile delinquency; Juvenile delinquents
Crippled children. See Exceptional children
Crisis intervention centers, directories of 2
Cruelty to children. See Child abuse and neglect
Culture
adolescents and 4, 5
child abuse and 23
See also Social development and needs of children
Cystic fibrosis, organizations concerned with 164-65

# D

Dancing 187
Dating 4, 5, 9. See also Love
Day care 14, 32, 35, 65, 69-71, 142, 218, 219
for autistic children 114
evils of 63
lack of 63
organizations serving 74
pamphlets about 32, 71-74
periodicals about 71
See also Nursery schools
Deafness. See Hearing impairment

354

# Subject Index

Death and children 33, 75, 76, 77, 78, 157, 210, 217
Dental care 171
   organizations concerned with 173
   pamphlets about 171-73
Dependent children 11
   organizations serving 16
   protection of 62
   See also Children's rights
Diabetes 167-68
Diets and dieting 137, 139
   for allergic children 163, 164
   for the diabetic 167
   hyperactivity and 183
   See also Nutrition in childhood
Discipline of children 32, 33, 34, 39, 79-82, 214, 215, 216, 217
   in adolescence 7, 29
   of the cerebral palsied 117
   from infancy to five years 42, 44, 47, 81
   of the learning disabled 201
   See also Behavior modification; Spanking
Discrimination in employment. See Labor laws
Diseases. See Genetic diseases; Glandular diseases; Health and hygiene of children; names of specific diseases
Divorce, children and 34, 75, 76, 217, 218. See also Child custody; Family, single parent; Marriage, teenage
Doctors. See Physicians
Dolls and puppets, making of 226, 227
Down's syndrome 119-20
Drawings. See Art
Dreikus, Rudolf 80
Dropouts 8, 66
Drowning. See Swimming
Drug abuse 2, 3, 4, 52, 81, 83-86, 213, 214, 216, 218, 245
   audiovisual materials about 90-94
   organizations concerned with 88-89, 246
   pamphlets about 86-88
   psychological aspects of 95

See also Alcohol abuse; LSD; Marijuana
Drugs
   in treating hyperactivity 183, 184
   in treating learning disabilities 201
   See also Medicines, over the counter
Dyslexia 200-201, 202, 203
   organizations concerned with 204

## E

Eating habits. See Breastfeeding; Diets and dieting; Feeding of children; Nutrition in childhood
Educational records, parent's right to 65
Education of children 34, 36, 63, 66, 67, 213
   in adolescence 1, 5
   of the autistic 114, 115
   of blacks 56
   divorce and 76
   of the exceptional 101, 104-5, 106, 129, 194
   of the gifted 151, 152
   from infancy to five years 194, 197, 226
   of the hearing impaired 133
   of the mentally retarded 122, 124, 125, 126
   monetary aspects 212
   play and 226
   sexism and 59
   from six to twelve years 53
   See also Dropouts; Head Start program; Intellectual development in childhood; Kindergarten; Montessori method of education; Textbooks for the visually handicapped; Underachievers; Vocational guidance and training
Electric shock 235
Emergency medical care. See First aid
Emotional development and needs in childhood 30, 32, 34, 39, 64, 142, 210, 211-12

# Subject Index

    in adolescence 5
    adoption and 13, 14, 17
    of blacks 55
    drug abuse and 91
    epilepsy and 170
    from infancy to five years 44, 45, 46, 50, 223
    learning and 194
    physical growth and 142, 159
    play and 223, 228, 229
    school changes and 78
    from six to twelve years 52
    of those with spina bifida 129
    See also Aggressiveness in children; Anger; Anxiety; Behavioral development of children; Fear; Psychological development and needs in childhood; Temper
Emotionally disturbed children 95-97, 102, 107-8
    audiovisual materials about 98-99
    behavior modification and 20
    organizations serving 67, 98
    pamphlets about 97-98
    See also Autistic children; Exceptional children; Music therapy; Play therapy; Psychotherapy; Schizophrenia
Emotions, of parents 45
Employment, child development and parental 44. See also Mothers, working; Vocational guidance and training; Work, dignity of
Environment
    child development and 29, 63, 212, 218
    the gifted child and 152
    learning potential and 194, 197
    the physically handicapped and 102
    suicide and 3
Epileptic children 124, 169-70
    education and training for 102
    See also Convulsions
Exceptional children ix, x, 34, 101-5
    adoption of 12, 14, 15, 16, 17
    audiovisual materials about 111-12
    organizations serving 110-11

    pamphlets about 106-10, 158
    periodicals about 106
    See also Birth defects; Camps for the handicapped; Emotionally disturbed children; Gifted children; Mentally retarded children; specific diseases and conditions
Exercise. See Physical education and fitness
Eye care 171
    organizations concerned with 173
    pamphlets about 172
    See also Vision impairment

# F

Family 50, 209
    adolescents and the 29
    child abuse and the 23, 24
    in drug abuse prevention 84, 90-91
    the dying child and the 157
    exceptional children and the 34, 101, 104, 105, 109, 117, 122, 123, 124, 125-26, 201
    gifted children and the 152
    periodicals about 218
    personality development and the 1
    See also Counseling; Parenthood
Family, single parent 44, 211, 214, 215, 216, 219
    adoption and the 14
    audiovisual materials about 221
    organizations concerned with 220
    periodicals about 218-19
    See also Divorce
Family courts, organizations serving 67. Juvenile courts and justice; New York City. Family Court
Family life education, organizations serving 38
Fathers 214, 219
    relationships with daughters 3
    relationships with sons 7, 8
Fear 44
    control through behavior modification 20

# Subject Index

drug abuse and 92
See also Phobias
Feeding of children 32, 33, 79, 80, 141, 218
   in day care centers 73, 74
   with Down's syndrome 119
   of the handicapped 143
   from infancy to five years 42, 44, 45, 47, 49
   See also Breastfeeding; Diets and dieting; Nutrition in childhood
Feelings. See Emotions, of parents
Fevers 32
Films for children 194
   infancy to five years 191, 196
   See also Audiovisual materials
Fire prevention 233-34, 235
   audiovisual materials about 238, 239
   See also Burns and scalds
First aid 46, 47, 156, 157, 158, 160-61, 231, 234, 235
   See also Burns and scalds; Electric shock; Poisoning; Safety education
Folks, Homer 62
Food, federal assistance programs 141-42, 144
Food coloring, learning disabilities and 183
Food stamps 142
Foster grandparents program 126
Foster home care 11, 13, 64, 65
   for abused children 25
   for emotionally disturbed children 96
   organizations serving 14, 16
   See also Adoption; Child placement
Freud, Sigmund 218, 241
Friendship among children 37-38
   in adolescence 5, 7
   from six to twelve years 52
Furniture
   construction of 139
   for handicapped children 104
   for the preschooler 191

# G

Games 223, 224, 225, 226, 227, 232

sexism and 59
See also Toys
Gardening 250
Generation gap 3, 7, 8, 10. See also Communication with children; Parenthood
Genetic counseling 31
   organizations concerned with 148, 149
   See also Heredity
Genetic diseases
   audiovisual materials about 150
   organizations concerned with 148-50
   pamphlets about 147-48
Genius. See Gifted children
Gesell Institute of Child Development 200
Gifted children 111, <u>151-53</u>, 213.
   See also Exceptional children
Ginott, Haim 215
Girl's liberation 33
Glandular diseases 3
Gonorrhea. See Venereal disease
Gordon, Thomas 221
Government documents. See Pamphlets, free and inexpensive
Grandparents 215. See also Foster grandparents program
Grooming, adolescents and 7. See also Clothing and dress
Guardianship. See Child custody
Guilt
   in child rearing 190, 210
   as a consequence of racism 56

# H

Halfway houses
   directories of 2
   for emotionally disturbed children 95, 98
   See also Settlement houses
Hallucinogenic drugs. See Drug abuse; LSD
Handicapped children. See Emotionally disturbed children; Exceptional children; Mentally retarded children
Hay fever 163

# Subject Index

Head Start program, films suitable for 196
Health agencies, directory of New York City 156. See also Child health stations; Mental health clinics
Health and hygiene in childhood 31, 32, 35, 36, 142, 155-57, 217
  of adolescents 1, 3, 4
  audiovisual materials about 160-61
  as a concern in adoption 15
  of the exceptional child 101
  inadequacies of 63
  from infancy to five years 42, 45, 47
  of the mentally retarded 123
  monetary aspects of 212
  nutrition and 142
  organizations serving 67, 159-60, 181-82
  pamphlets about 158-59, 181
  periodicals about 157-58
  programs and services for 65, 66
  from six to twelve years 52, 53
  for those with Down's syndrome 119
  See also Child health stations; Drugs; First aid; Genetic diseases; Glandular diseases; Hospitalization of children; Immunization; Medicines; Physicians; Poisoning; specific diseases and conditions
Hearing impairment 102, 103, 107, 131-32, 203
  audiovisual materials about 135
  organizations serving 110, 133-35
  pamphlets about 132-33
Heart disease 175
Hemophilia, organizations concerned with 149
Heredity 3. See also Genetic counseling; Genetic diseases
Hobbies 223
Homosexuality 2, 243, 244, 246
  in parents 216
Hormones, effect on physical growth 142, 159
Hospitalization of children 77, 157, 158

  psychological aspects of 155
  See also Mental health clinics; Rehabilitation centers and services
Household duties of children 79, 80
Hydrocephalus 103, 130
Hyperactive children 44, 64, 183-85
Hyperkinesia 203

# I

Identity, in adolescence 5, 7. See also Personality development in childhood; Self-image of children
Illegitimacy. See Mothers, unmarried
Illness. See First aid; Health and hygiene in childhood; specific diseases and conditions
Immunization 31, 157
Incentive system, in child rearing 19
Indians
  adoption of 12
  food assistance programs for 144
  health care of 157
Individuality 35. See also Personality development in childhood
Industrialization, effect on child development 63
Infants. See Child care and development (infancy to five years); Names for babies; Sudden infant death syndrome
Infants, premature 47
Institute for the Achievement of Human Potential 117
Intellectual development in childhood 32, 35, 39
  audiovisual materials about 196-97
  changes in during adolescence 5
  from infancy to five years ix, 41, 44, 45, 49, 50, 187-94
  organizations concerned with 195-96
  pamphlets about 195
  periodicals about 194
  from six to twelve years 51, 52
  See also Education of children;

# Subject Index

Gifted children; Learning disabilities; Underachievers
Intelligence quotient, of gifted children 152
Interpersonal relations. See Friendship among children; Personality development in childhood
Insurance, adopted children and 15

## J

Jealousy 35
Joint Commission on the Mental Health of Children 4
Juvenile courts and justice 61, 63, 65, 66
  organizations serving 67
Juvenile delinquency 1, 8
  prevention and control of 67
Juvenile delinquents
  care and treatment of 11, 62, 64, 67
  counseling of 211

## K

Karplus 223
Kidney disease, organizations concerned with 182
Kindergarten, function of 193

## L

Labor laws, women and 258
Language skills. See Communication with children; Communication skills; Speech defects; Speech development
Law
  adolescents and 5
  adoption and 14-15
  the autistic child and 115
  child abuse and 23, 24
  drug abuse and 85, 86
  epileptics and 169
  mentally retarded children and 123, 124
  See also Children's rights; Family courts; Juvenile courts and justice; Labor laws
Lead poisoning. See Poisoning
Learning. See Education of children; Intellectual development in childhood
Learning disabilities 199-202
  audiovisual materials about 204-5
  counseling services for 211
  epileptics and 170
  hyperactive children and 183
  organizations concerned with 110, 170, 204
  pamphlets about 203-4
  periodicals about 202-3
  See also Education of children; Intellectual development in childhood; Underachievers
Leisure 52
Leukemia 177-78
Literature for children. See Children's literature
Love
  in adolescence 5
  between parent and child 217
  in early child development 49
  See also Dating
LSD 7, 87. See also Drug abuse
Lung disease, organizations concerned with 164, 165
Lysergic acid diethylamide. See LSD

## M

Magazines. See Children's literature, magazines; Periodicals
Manners. See Social development and needs in childhood
Manson, Charles 218
Marijuana 87, 93
  treatment of users of 86
  See also Drug abuse
Marriage, teenage 2, 9. See also Divorce; Step-parents; Teenage parents
Masks. See Costumes
Mass media, mistreatment of children by 65. See also Television and children
Masturbation 243, 244
  audiovisual materials about 247
Mathematics, teaching of 192

# Subject Index

Maturity 3
Measles. See Rubella
Medical care. See Health and hygiene in childhood
"Medic Alert" program 160
Medical practices, drug abuse and 84, 88
Medicines, over-the-counter 157. See also Drugs
Menstruation, audiovisual materials about 247, 248
Mental development. See Intellectual development in childhood
Mental health
    organizations concerned with 196
    periodicals about 158
    See also Emotionally disturbed children
Mental health clinics 32. See also Rehabilitation centers and services
Mentally ill children. See Emotionally disturbed children
Mentally retarded children 95, 121-24
    audiovisual materials about 127
    behavior modification of 20, 21, 121
    organizations serving 126-27
    pamphlets about 125-26
    public institutions for 64
    sex education and 242, 246
Migrant laborers
    day care programs for 73
    food assistance programs for 144
    health care of 157
Milk and milk products
    in nutrition 143
    organizations concerned with 144
Minorities, health services for 157. See also Black children; Indians; Migrant laborers
Money management 2, 80, 81, 212, 220
Mongolism. See Down's syndrome
Montessori method of education 192, 194
Mothers
    black 220
    food assistance programs for 142, 144
    unmarried 220, 221
    working 44, 156, 216, 257-59
Motion pictures. See Films for children
Motivation, in child rearing 19
Motor skills. See Physical development of children
Movies. See Films for children
Multiple births 207-8
Multiple sclerosis, organizations concerned with 182
Muscular dystrophy 181
    organizations concerned with 182
Music 187, 223, 226, 227
    of adolescents 7
    See also Phonograph records
Music therapy 105

# N

Names for babies 210, 211
Narcotics. See Drug abuse; Drugs
National Children's Media Foundation (proposed) 66
National parks, provisions for the handicapped 107
Natural childbirth. See Childbirth, natural
Negroes. See Black children; Mothers, black
Nervous system, diseases of the 149
New York City. Family Court 64
Nursery schools
    directories of 188, 189
    function of 193
Nutrition in childhood 32, 35, 39, 137-40
    of adolescents 137
    audiovisual materials about 145
    for the handicapped 141, 143
    from infancy to five years 47, 74, 137, 138, 139, 140, 141, 142, 143, 145
    for the mentally retarded 123
    monetary aspects of 212
    organizations concerned with 143-44
    pamphlets about 141-43
    periodicals about 140-41, 157-58, 219

# Subject Index

physical growth and 159
See also Breastfeeding; Diets and dieting; Feeding of children; School lunch programs

## O

Obedience training 34
Oral hygiene. See Dental care
Organizations concerned with
  adolescents 6-7
  adoptive children 15-16
  allergies 164-65
  autistic children 115
  cerebral palsy 118
  child abuse 26-27
  child development 38
    from infancy to five years 48
  children's rights 62, 66-67
  day care 74
  deaf-blind children 133-35
  development of black children 56-57
  diabetes 168
  Down's syndrome 119
  drug and alcohol abuse 88-89
  the emotionally disturbed 98
  epilepsy 169-70
  exceptional children 110-11
  eye and dental care 173
  genetic diseases 148-50
  gifted children 153
  health and hygiene 67, 159-60, 181-82
  heart disease 175
  learning and creativity 195-96
  learning disabilities 110, 170, 204
  leukemia 178
  the mentally retarded 126-27
  nutrition 143-44
  parenthood 219-21
  play 229
  safety education 235-38
  sex education 246-47
  sexism 60
  spina bifida 130
  television programming 254-55
  working mothers 259
Orphans and orphanages 64

Orthodontics. See Dental care
Orthopedic handicaps 103

## P

Pamphlets, free and inexpensive
  on adolescence 5-6
  on adoption 14-15
  on autistic children 114-15
  on behavior modification 21
  on cerebral palsied children 118
  on child abuse 25-26
  on child development 37-38
    from infancy to five years 46-47
    from six to twelve years 52-53
  on children's literature for blacks 56
  on children's rights 66
  on clothing and dress 142
  on day care 71-74
  on the deaf-blind 132-33
  on death 78
  on diabetes 167-68
  on discipline 81-82
  on Down's syndrome 119-20
  on drug and alcohol abuse 86-89
  on the emotionally disturbed child 97-98
  on epilepsy 169
  on exceptional children 106-10
  on eye and dental care 171-73
  on genetic diseases 147-48
  on gifted children 153
  on health and hygiene 158-59
  on heart disease 175
  on hyperactivity 185
  on learning and creativity 195
  on learning disabilities 203-4
  on leukemia 177
  on the mentally retarded 125-26
  on multiple births 207-8
  on nutrition 141-43
  on parenthood 219
  on play 228-29
  on safety education 232-35
  on sex education 245-46
  on sex roles 59-60
  on spina bifida 129-30
  on sports and recreation 250

361

# Subject Index

on sudden infant death syndrome 179-80
on television programming 254
on working mothers 258
Parenthood 2, 3, 4, 5, 8, 10, 35, 209-18
  audiovisual materials about 221
  organizations concerned with 219-21
  pamphlets about 219
  periodicals about 218-19
  See also Child abuse; Child care and development; Communication with children; Discipline; Family; Fathers; Generation gap; Mothers; Teenage parents
Parents, emotions of 45
Parent-teacher relationships, organizations concerned with 196
Parks. See National parks
Pediatrics. See Health and hygiene of children; Hospitalization of children; Physicians; specific diseases and conditions
Peer groups, drug abuse and 91
Periodicals
  on adolescence 5
  on blindness 132
  on child development 36
    from infancy to five years 46
    from six to twelve years 52
  on children's rights 66
  on day care 71
  on exceptional children 106
  on gifted children 153
  on health and hygiene 157-58
  on learning and creativity 194
  on learning disabilities 202-3
  on nutrition 140-41
  on parenthood 218-19
  on play 228
  on racism and sexism in children's literature 56
  on sex education 245
  See also Children's literature, magazines
Perkin's School for the Blind 135

Personality development in childhood 33, 35, 36
  of adolescents 1, 9
  behavior modification and 19
  drawings and 191
  from infancy to five years 42
  suicide and 3
  See also Identity, in adolescence
Pets 223
Phenylketonuria 126
Phobias 34
Phonograph records 187, 188, 194, 214
  for the exceptional child 107
  for the visually handicapped child 135
  See also Music
Physical development of children 32, 34, 142, 212
  in adolescence 1, 3, 4, 5
  child abuse and 23, 24
  eating habits and 141
  from infancy to five years 43, 45, 46, 47, 49, 194
  learning and 190, 194, 201
  parent's role in 193
  play and 225
  from six to twelve years 52
  See also Maturity; Weight control (physiology)
Physical education and fitness 250
  free materials about 156
Physicians
  advice on child rearing 30
  involvement in child abuse cases 25
Piaget 35, 187, 193, 194, 218, 223
Playgrounds and equipment 224
  construction of 139, 228
  inadequacies of 63
  safe use of 233
Play of children 35, 218, 223-28
  audiovisual materials about 229
  from infancy to five years 45, 223, 225
  the mentally retarded and 125, 126
  organizations concerned with 229
  pamphlets about 228-29

# Subject Index

periodicals about 228
See also Arts and crafts; Games; Hobbies; Sports and recreation; Toys
Play therapy 95, 217, 226
Poetry for children. See Children's literature, poetry
Poison control centers 31-32, 232, 233, 237-38, 267-309
Poisoning 32, 231, 232, 233, 234, 235
    audiovisual materials about 238, 239
    organizations concerned with 237
Politics, implications of youth culture in 5
Pollution. See Environment
Poor 62
    health care of 157
    mental illness among 96
    mental retardation among 126
    See also Blacks; Child welfare; Food, federal assistance programs; Indians; Migrant laborers; Minorities; Social welfare
Pornography 243, 245
Poverty. See Poor
Pregnancy
    counseling services during 216
    rubella and 181
    See also Childbirth; Childbirth, natural; Prenatal care
Premature babies. See Infants, premature
Prenatal care 32, 43, 45, 218
    audiovisual materials about 49, 145
    nutrition in 138
    organizations concerned about 220
    pamphlets about 32, 47, 48
Preschool children. See Child care and development (infancy to five years)
Prisons, children in 66. See also Reformatories
Privacy
    need for 39
    right of 66, 244
Private schools, directory of 188

Promises 35, 39
Prostitution, organizations concerned with 246
Psychiatric hospitals. See Mental health clinics; Rehabilitation centers and services
Psychological development and needs in childhood 32, 35, 37, 38, 214, 219
    of adolescents 1, 5
    adoption and 13
    child abuse and 23, 24, 27
    death and 77
    drug and alcohol abuse and 92
    of the exceptional child 102, 105
    from infancy to five years 41, 42, 43, 44, 45, 47
    learning and 190
    of minorities 56
    parent's role in 193
    play and 227
    from six to twelve years 52
    See also Emotional development and needs in childhood; Fear; Phobias
Psychological testing 211
Psychotherapy 95. See also Music therapy; Play therapy
Puberty. See Adolescence
Public institutions 65
    environment of 64
    See also Orphans and Orphanages; Reformatories
Public welfare. See Child welfare; Social welfare
Public welfare agencies. See Social agencies; Social agencies (private)
Publishers. See Child care and development, publishers of literature about
Punishment. See Discipline
Puppets. See Dolls and puppets

# Q

Quakers, child discipline and the 79

# Subject Index

## R

Race problems and attitudes  55-56
  in children's literature  56, 194
  mental illness and  96
  organizations concerned with  57
Reading  194
  teaching of  192, 193, 197
Reasoning. See Intellectual development in childhood
Records (music). See Phonograph records
Recreation. See Play; Sports and recreation
Reformatories  61, 63. See also Halfway houses; Prisons
Rehabilitation centers and services  102, 103, 110
  for the emotionally disturbed  95, 96, 97, 98
  for the epileptic  170
  for the hearing impaired  132
  for the mentally retarded  122, 124, 125, 126
  See also Mental health clinics
Religion
  and adolescents  1, 3
  in child development  30, 31, 212
  death and  77
  divorce and  76
  drug abuse and  84
  sex education and  241
  See also Quakers
Remarriage. See Step-parents
Reproduction. See Sex education
Retarded children. See Mentally handicapped children
Rheumatic fever  175
Rheumatoid arthritis. See Arthritis
Rogers, Carl  95
Rubella  181
Runaways  3, 16
  organizations serving  2, 6, 7
Rural children, health services for  157

## S

Safety education  44, 155, 156, 196, 226, 231-32
  audiovisual materials about  238-39
  organizations concerned with  235-38
  pamphlets about  232-35
  periodicals about  158
  See also Fire prevention; First aid; Poisoning; Traffic safety
Schizophrenia  96
  organizations concerned with  97
School camps  188
School lunch programs  141-42
Schools
  for autistic children  115
  for the exceptional child  102
  for the gifted child  152
  for the hyperactive child  184
  for the hearing impaired  132
  for the learning disabled  199-200, 204
  problems in change of  78
  See also Education of children; Nursery schools; Private schools; School camps; Vocational guidance and training
Self-confidence  55
Self-image of children  x, 32, 36
  blacks  56
  drug abuse and  91
  from six to twelve years  52
  See also Identity
Sensitivity training  217
Separation (matrimonial). See Divorce
Settlement houses  61. See also Halfway houses
Sewing. See Clothing and dress; Costumes
Sex and children  81, 213, 217
  in adolescence  1, 2, 3, 4, 5, 9
  from infancy to five years  44
Sex education  33, 34, 210, 214, 241-45
  audiovisual materials about  247-48
  organizations concerned with  246-47
  pamphlets about  245-46
  periodicals about  245

# Subject Index

from six to twelve years 52
See also Childbirth; Masturbation; Menstruation; Pornography; Venereal disease
Sex roles 42, <u>59-60</u>
   children's literature and 56, 57, 194
   stereotyping of 191
   See also Girl's liberation; Women's liberation
Shoplifting. See Stealing
Shyness 34
Sibling rivalry 20, 33, 34, 42, 44, 49, 79, 80, 210, 214
   audiovisual materials about 39
   in learning disabled children 201
   mentally retarded children and 114, 123
Sickle cell anemia 147
   audiovisual materials about 150
   organizations concerned with 148, 149, 150
Single parent. See Family, single parent
Skin problems 3
Sleeping 33, 35, 79, 218
   from infancy to five years 44, 45
Smoking 3, 86, 160
Social agencies
   directories of 12, 156
   inadequacies of 23, 64
   mistreatment of children by 65
   See also Public institutions; Youth Service Bureau; Youth workers
Social agencies (private), directory of 11-12
Social class, drug abuse and 84
Social development and needs in childhood 30, 34, 35, 81
   of adolescents 1, 4, 5
   behavior modification and 20
   of the cerebral palsied 117
   in child abuse 24
   divorce and 76
   of epileptics 169, 170
   of the exceptional child 105
   from infancy to five years 194
   learning and 190, 194
   of the learning disabled 201, 202
   of the mentally retarded 121
   play and 227, 229

school changes and 78
sexism and 59
from six to twelve years 51
in those with spina bifida 129
See also Culture
Social roles
   of adolescents 6
   of parents 218
Social values. See Values, social
Social welfare 35. See also Child welfare
Songs for children. See Music; Phonograph records
Spanish language
   health aids in the 159, 164, 175, 177
   safety education information in the 232, 235
Spanking 81. See also Discipline of children
Speech defects 103, 104, 203
   bibliography 107
   organizations concerned with 134
Speech development 34, 44, 45, 52
   of autistic children 115
   of the deaf 131
   of the mentally retarded 121, 122, 126
Spina bifida 103, <u>129-30</u>
Sports and recreation <u>156</u>, <u>249-51</u>
   for autistic children 115
   for exceptional children 101
   for the hyperactive child 184
   for the learning disabled 201, 204
   for the mentally retarded 122, 126
   monetary aspects of 212
Stealing 81
Step-parents 210, 211, 214, 215, 217
Study habits, behavior modification and 20-21
Sudden infant death syndrome 179-80. See also Cribs
Suicide 3
Suppes 223
Swimming 235, 249, 250
   audiovisual materials about 251
Syphilis. See Venereal disease

# Subject Index

## T

Tax deductions, for child care 74
Tay Sachs disease, organizations concerned with 149
Teachers, interaction with children 191. See also Parent-teacher relationships
Teenage parents 216. See also Marriage, teenage
Teenagers. See Adolescence
Teeth, care of. See Dental care
Television and children 191, 192, 194, 226, 253-55
 drug advertising and 91
 sexism in 59
 from six to twelve years 52
Temper 33, 34, 79, 80
 control of through behavior modification 20
 See also Anger
Textbooks for the visually handicapped 135
Thalidomide 105, 112
Theft. See Stealing
Therapeutics. See Music therapy; Play therapy; Psychotherapy
Thought and thinking. See Intellectual development in childhood
Throat, diseases of the 160
Tobacco. See Smoking
Toilet training 33, 35, 42, 43, 44, 217, 218
 behavior modification in 19, 20
 in Down's syndrome 119
 of the mentally retarded 122
 See also Bedwetting
Toys 65, 214
 for the exceptional child 108
 lending libraries of 228, 229
 making of 224, 225, 227, 229
 periodicals about 228
 for the preschooler 44, 191, 197
 safety of 226, 232, 233, 234, 235, 236, 237
 sexism and 59
Traffic safety 231-32
 audiovisual materials about 238
 organizations concerned with 235, 236

Travel
 the exceptional child and 108, 109-10, 111
 the preschool child and 45
Traveler's Aid Societies, directory of 2
Trust, between parent and child 35
Twins. See Multiple births

## U

Underachievers 191, 199
U.S. Department of Defense, summer programs for ghetto youth 63
University of North Carolina at Greensboro, day care project 73
Unwed mothers. See Mothers, unmarried
Urbanization, child development and 63

## V

Values, social 37, 40, 188, 209, 212, 215
 adolescents and 9
 drug abuse and 84
Venereal disease 2, 160, 243, 244, 245, 246
 audiovisual materials about 247
 organizations concerned with 246, 247
Violence. See Television and children
Vision impairment 102, 103, 107, 131-32
 audiovisual materials about 135
 pamphlets about 132-33
 periodicals about 132
 organizations serving 133-35
 See also Braille system; Eye care; Textbooks for the visually handicapped
Vocational guidance and training
 for the handicapped 101, 105, 108
 for the learning disabled 202
 for the mentally retarded 122, 123
 for the visually impaired 134

# Subject Index

for working mothers 258

## W

Watson 218
Weight control (physiology) 142
    in adolescence 3
    programs of 139
Wheelchairs 104, 109-10
Widowhood. See Family, single parent
Willowbrook (state school for the mentally retarded) 124
Wills, adopted children and 15
Women. See Mothers

Women's liberation 61
    parenthood and 43
    See also Girl's liberation
Work, dignity of 217. See also Employment; Labor laws; Mothers, working
Writing, teaching of 191, 192, 197

## Y

Youth. See Adolescence
Youth Service Bureau 65
Youth workers, organizations serving 6